LIVING MOMENTS

LIVING MOMENTS

On the Work of Michael Eigen

edited by

Stephen Bloch and Loray Daws

KARNAC

First published in 2015 by
Karnac Books Ltd
118 Finchley Road, London NW3 5HT

British Library Cataloguing in Publication Data

A C.I.P. for this book is available from the British Library

ISBN 978 1 78049 184 4

Edited, designed and produced by The Studio Publishing Services Ltd
www.publishingservicesuk.co.uk
e-mail: studio@publishingservicesuk.co.uk

Printed in Great Britain

www.karnacbooks.com

CONTENTS

ACKNOWLEDGMENTS

My (Stephen Bloch's) gratitude to:

Michael Eigen, for his openness and encouragement, and for trusting us with this project. Previously, he had generously agreed for me to interview him on the subject of music and the psyche. I know him only through emails and his writing—songs of experience, raids on the unbearable.

Loray Daws, for his "spontaneous gesture" in Afrikaans via Michael Eigen's Yahoo! group, which led to our friendship and collaboration. Loray's academic acumen and feeling-based clinical approach greatly added to the project.

Paul Ashton, who allowed me to imagine that I could enter the world of writing and publishing; his influence as an editor permeates my contribution to this project.

Dr Yvonne Blake, for an eduring experience of the real nature of psychoanalysis.

Lois, Leila, Nina, Rafi, and Joni, as before, for support and their presence in my life.

Peter Anderson, Rod Anderson, Professor Astrid Berg, Penny Busetto, Sheila Cowburn, Ian Donald, Nuala Flynn, Jeffrey Rink, Alan Levy, Silvia Autiero, Paul Whelan, Sharon Hughes, Pete Hodson, and Patrick Tummon: friends and colleagues.

Debbie Aarons, Sharon Cort, Jan Duvenage, Tony Fluxman, Russell Caplan, Cliffy Matthews, Lynn Shakinovsky, Diane Wulfsohn: university friends from long ago.

My (Loray Daws') gratitude to:

To Michael Eigen. Your willingness, radical openness, and support of my grasping and faltering, ever present as background through your work, our correspondence, and those moments we met in person. This is but a small gesture of my appreciation and love for you and the work you have created for us.

To Stephen Bloch. I am deeply appreciative of your enthusiastic taking up of our shared dream of writing a *festschrift* for Eigen. Your keen editorial eye, feel for both Eigen's work and that of the various contributors has made this a learning experience. I hope our collaboration continues in the future.

My family, Tanja, Jemma, and Marcel, for remaining interested in this volume, listening to its contents with interest and even hovering support. Your background presence is as much part of this work as mine.

Ms. Annelies Cramer for a critical reading of my chapter and the various suggestions that made it read closer to its original intent. Your intuitive grasp of my work carries it further.

Last, but by no means least, the various contributors to this volume. I have been deeply touched by your enthusiastic support and your creative reading and holding of Eigen's work. It has been a rare privilege to both read and learn from your work.

Shared acknowledgments

We would also like to acknowledge the deeply felt encouragement of Karnac, especially Rod Tweedy, Oliver Rathbone, Cecily Blench, and Anita Mason and the team at The Studio. Your professional assistance and guidance made writing and editing this work a true pleasure.

And to our contributors, our gratitude for your enthusiastic response to our call for papers, for trusting us, meeting deadlines, and enduring the process of editing in good spirit.

We would also like to thank Anekke van Bell and Sophy Kohler, our copy editors in Cape Town.

Copyright permissions

Special appreciation and gratitude to the various publication houses and journals that graciously allowed the reproduction of various printed articles and materials. *The Psychoanalytic Review* for their permission to include the case illustration from Ofra Eshel's published paper "A beam of 'chimeric' darkness: Presence, interconnectedness, and transformation in the psychoanalytic treatment of a patient convicted of sex offenses", as well as both the Wesleyan Press and Taylor and Francis for various Eigen and Grotstein quotes in the paper of Daws; Shambhala Publications for the Sat Chuen Hon in the Bloch paper; the New Directions Publishing Corporation and Bloodaxe Books for the various images in the text of Campbell, and Coleman Barks' generous permission for Rumi's "The Guest House" in the work of Eaton. All attempts were made throughout by all the contributors and the editors to ensure copyright permission. Despite our best efforts, we were unable to obtain permission for the Moloise poem as it appeared in 1985 in the *Weekly Mail* in South Africa, as well as the Leonard Cohen lyrics as they appeared in the work of Anthony Molino.

ABOUT THE EDITORS AND CONTRIBUTORS

Peter Anderson is an award-winning South African writer. He holds a doctorate from Boston University, and is an associate professor of English at Austin College in North Texas. He is the author of a collection of poems, *Vanishing Ground;* in addition, his work in fiction and poetry has appeared in numerous literary magazines, and has been anthologized in both the United States and South Africa. Most recently, his novel, *The Unspeakable,* won the 2013 Alex la Guma Award for International Fiction. His research interests are in the connections between psychoanalysis, gnosis, and imaginative literature.

Rachel Berghash has been a psychotherapist in private practice in New York City and a teacher of interdisciplinary seminars grounded in spirituality. She was born and raised in Israel. She has published a memoir, *Half the House, My Life In and Out of Jerusalem,* Sunstone Press. Her poetry and poetry translations have appeared in numerous literary magazines. In 2009 her poetry was nominated for the Pushcart Prize in poetry. Her essays, with co-author Katherine Jillson, have appeared in *Journal of Religion & Health,* Tikkun, and elsewhere. In the 1980s, Berghash produced a series for WBAI radio in New York City that featured interviews with poets and writers.

Stephen Bloch is a clinical psychologist and Jungian analyst in Cape Town , South Africa. He is a founding member of the Southern African Association of Jungian Analysts and has served on its Executive Committee, Assessment and Review, Ethics and Library Committees. He has given training seminars on transference and countertransference, dream interpretation, Klein, Winnicott, Bion and Eigen, the psychoanalytic frame, music and psychoanalysis, embodiment, psychotherapy with the meditating patient. He has published papers and reviews and co-edited with Paul Ashton *Music and Psyche* (Spring, 2010).

Marian Campbell is a clinical psychologist and Jungian analyst living in Cape Town, South Africa. After working many years as a senior clinical psychologist and lecturer at Red Cross War Memorial Children's Hospital/ University of Cape Town, she is currently in full-time private practice. She is a member of the Southern African Association of Jungian Analysts and serves on their Curriculum Committee.

Loray Daws is a registered clinical psychologist and psychoanalytic psychotherapist currently in private practice in British Columbia, Canada. He is founding member of the South African and British Columbia Masterson Institutes as well as a faculty member of the International Masterson Institute in New York, where he completed a post-graduate treatment program in the psychoanalytic treatment of disorders of the self. He has published articles on dreaming, psychosomatic disorders (burning mouth syndrome and eating disorders), and the disorders of the self in journals such as the *International Journal of Psychotherapy*, *Issues in Psychoanalytic Psychology*, *South African Rorschach Journal*, *Clinical Counselling*, and *Contemporary Psychotherapy*. He has supervised and taught in South Africa, Canada, the USA, Australia, and Turkey, and currently serves as assistant editor for the *Global Journal of Health Sciences* and as a member of the *International Journal of Psychotherapy*'s International Advisory Board.

Jeffrey L. Eaton is a graduate and faculty member of the Northwestern Psychoanalytic Society and a Fellow of the International Psychoanalytic Association. He provides psychoanalysis and psychotherapy to children and adults in his private practice in Seattle, WA. He has a particular interest in the psychoanalytic treatment of autism and is a member of INSPIRA, the International Symposium on Psychoanalytic Intervention and Research into Autism. In 2006, he received the Francis Tustin Memorial Lecture Prize and later became a Trustee of the Francis Tustin Trust. He is actively engaged in studying, teaching, consulting, and writing about psychoanalysis and related subjects. His first book, *A Fruitful Harvest: Essays after Bion* was published in 2011 by Alliance Press.

Mark Epstein is a psychiatrist in private practice in New York City and the author of a number of books about the interface of Buddhism and psychotherapy, including *Thoughts without a Thinker*; *Going to Pieces without Falling Apart*; *Going on Being*; *Open to Desire*; and *Psychotherapy without the Self*. His newest work, *The Trauma of Everyday Life* (Penguin Press), uses the Buddha's biography as a means of exploring the hidden psychodynamics, and contemporary relevance, of Buddhist thought. He received his undergraduate and medical degrees from Harvard University and is currently Clinical Assistant Professor in the Postdoctoral Program in Psychotherapy and Psychoanalysis at New York University.

Ofra Eshel is a clinical psychologist and faculty member, training and supervising analyst of the Israel Psychoanalytic Society and Institute (IPA); co-founder, former coordinator and faculty member of the Program of Psychoanalytic Psychotherapy for Advanced Psychotherapists at the Israel Psychoanalytic Institute; co-founder, coordinator, and faculty member of the Israel Winnicott Center; and on the Advisory Board of the International Winnicott Association (IWA); lecturer at the Program of Psychotherapy, Sackler Faculty of Medicine, Tel-Aviv University. She is the Book Review Editor of *Sihot-Dialogue, Israel Journal of Psychotherapy*. Her papers have been published in psychoanalytic journals and presented at national and international conferences. Dr Eshel was the recipient of the Leonard J. Comess Fund grant at the New Center for Psychoanalysis (NCP), Los Angeles in 2011, visiting scholar at the Psychoanalytic Institute of North California (PINC) in 2013, and was awarded the Frances Tustin Memorial Prize for 2013. She practices in Tel-Aviv, Israel. Dr Eshel was featured in 2012 in *Globes* (Israel's financial newspaper and magazine) as one of the fifty most influential women in Israel.

Margaret Fetting has an MSW and a PhD from the University of Pennsylvania. She was first introduced to, studied, and practiced psychoanalysis when a member of an organizational consultant team at The Wharton School. Her private study began when she started reading Mike Eigen's work, starting with *The Psychotic Core*. She has been on the School of Social Work/USC's faculty since 1989. She also is a Visiting Faculty Member at the Los Angeles Institute and Society for Psychoanalytic Studies (LAISPS) in Los Angeles and the American College of Greece in Athens, Greece. Fetting, as a psychotherapist, teacher, and writer, has been dedicated to joining a psychoanalytic attitude with the treatment of substance use disorders (SUDs). She has written articles on the subject and recently published a text with Sage, *Perspectives on Addiction*. Fetting is currently writing a second edition. She has a private practice in Santa Monica, California.

Marlene Goldsmith is a clinical psychologist in private practice as well as a poet whose work has appeared both in the USA and abroad. She is a published writer, researcher, and lecturer in the area of women and creativity. Her writings and presentations have focused on the artists Frida Kahlo, Georgia O'Keefe, and Martha Graham; the psychoanalyst Sabina Spielrein, and the film *Black Swan*.

Aner Govrin, PhD, is a clinical psychologist and the director of academic doctoral program "Psychoanalysis and Hermeneutics" for mental health workers at The Department of Hermeneutics and Culture at Bar Ilan University. Dr. Govrin is in the private practice of psychotherapy and psychoanalysis in Tel Aviv. He is a member of the Tel Aviv Institute for Contemporary Psychoanalysis. His book *Between Abstinence and Seduction: The Analysis of American Psychoanalysis* (Dvir) was published in 2004 in Hebrew. His book *Conversations with Michael Eigen* was published by Karnac in 2007.

James S. Grotstein was Clinical Professor of Psychiatry at the David Geffen School of Medicine, UCLA, and training and supervising analyst at the New Center for Psychoanalysis and the Psychoanalytic Center of California, Los Angeles. He was a member of the Editorial Board of the *International Journal of Psychoanalysis* and past North American Vice-President of the International Psychoanalytic Association. He published over 250 papers including, "The seventh servant: the implication of the truth drive in Bion's theory of 'O'" (*International Journal of Psychoanalysis*), "Projective transidentification: an extension of the concept of projective identification" (*International Journal of Psycho-*

analysis), and, most recently "Dreaming as a 'curtain of illusion': revisiting the 'Royal Road' with Bion as our guide" (*International Journal of Psychoanalysis*). He authored many books, including, *Who Is the Dreamer Who Dreams the Dream? A Study of Psychic Presences* (2000) and *A Beam of Intense Darkness: Wilfred Bion's Legacy to Psychoanalysis* (Karnac, 2007), his most recent books being a two-volume work on psychoanalytic technique entitled *". . . But at the Same Time and on Another Level . . ." Psychoanalytic Technique in the Kleinian/Bionian Mode,* Volumes I and II (Karnac, 2009). In 2011, the IPA 47th Annual Congress in Mexico City featured a presentation and panel honoring his life's work. Dr. Grotstein also maintained a private practice in West Los Angeles.

Evan Malater is a psychoanalyst in private practice in New York City. He is a member of the National Psychological Association for Psychoanalysis. He is on the Editorial Board and chair of the Book Review Committee of the *Psychoanalytic Review.*

Anthony Molino is a practicing psychoanalyst and translator of Italian literature into English. Based in Italy, he is best known for the books *The Couch and the Tree: Dialogues in Psychoanalysis and Buddhism* and *Freely Associated: Encounters in Psychoanalysis with C. Bollas, N. Coltart, M. Eigen, J. McDougall and A. Phillips.* Other works include: *Where Id Was* (edited with C. Ware); *Culture, Subject, Psyche;* and *In Freud's Tracks* (edited with S. Benvenuto). A two-time recipient of a Gradiva Award from the National Association for the Advancement of Psychoanalysis, his most recent edited collection is *Crossroads in Psychoanalysis, Buddhism and Mindfulness* (Aronson, 2012).

Merle Molofsky is a poet and a psychoanalyst in private practice. She serves on the faculty of the Training Institute of NPAP, on the faculty and Advisory Board of Harlem Family Institute, on the Board of Directors of the International Forum for Psychoanalytic Education (IFPE), and on the Editorial Boards of the *Psychoanalytic Review* and *The Journal of Psychohistory*. She is former Dean of Training, NPAP, and former Editor of *Other/Wise,* the on-line psychoanalytic and creative arts journal of IFPE. Her articles and reviews have appeared in psychoanalytic journals. She contributed a chapter to *Defining Moments for Therapists* (2013), and a chapter to *Psychotherapy and Religion: Many Paths, One Journey* (2005). Her play *Koolaid* was performed at Lincoln Center, and her poetry and short fiction has been published in literary journals.

Her two volumes of poetry, *Ladder of Words* and *Mad Crazy Love: Love Poems and Mad Songs*, were published in 2011. In 2012, she received the Gradiva Award in Poetry from the National Association for the Advancement of Psychoanalysis.

Brent Potter is a psychotherapist with twenty years of direct clinical service. He is the Director for the Society for Laingian Studies. Brent is the author of numerous articles whose topics include: innovative and effective mental healthcare models; analytical psychology; humanistic psychology; existential phenomenology; psychoanalysis; the psychotic register of the mind; character and personality disorders; chemical dependency; child–adolescent mental health concerns. His first book, *Elements of Self-Destruction* is published by Karnac (2013), as well as *Elements of Reparation: Truth, Faith, and Transformation in the Works of Heidgger, Bion, and Beyond* (Karnac, 2015).

Louis Rothschild is a clinical psychologist in Providence, Rhode Island. He maintains a private practice in psychoanalytic psychotherapy in addition to providing supervision, writing articles and book reviews, and occasionally reviewing manuscripts. He is a past-president of the Rhode Island local chapter of the Division of Psychoanalysis (39) of the American Psychological Association.

Norma Tracey is a member of the Australian Association of Social Workers (AASW) and has been a member of the New South Wales Institute of Psychoanalytic Psychotherapy (NSWIPP) for many years. Apart from her private practice of thirty-five years, she has worked especially with Aboriginal mothers and infants in the past ten years. She is the author of two books, several booklets, and some twenty internationally published papers. She is founder of Gunawirra Limited, a group of twenty professionals who care for Aboriginal mothers and infants from pregnancy through to five years of age. They work in forty-three centers throughout NSW.

Lawrence Wetzler is a clinical psychologist and psychoanalyst in full-time private practice in Manhattan and Long Island. He is on the faculties of the Adelphi Postgraduate Program in Psychotherapy and Psychoanalysis, the Institute for Expressive Analysis, and the Object Relations Institute. An aspiring concert pianist, he gives yearly piano recitals in the area and writes on the relationship between music and psychoanalysis.

INTRODUCTORY NOTE

Michael Eigen

Many thanks to Stephen Bloch and Loray Daws for conceiving and carrying through this project. It is more than an honor—I felt touched by their love of the work. Special thanks to James Grotstein for writing a searching Foreword, sharing his vision of who I am and what I do. I remember the first talk of his I went to, possibly in the 1970s, and the thrill I felt hearing him speak of how the unconscious needs protection from the conscious, the id from the ego.

For me, this book is a blessing. What a wonderful group of papers, exploring and celebrating not only my work, but our shared human condition. The voice of the psyche is alive in each and every contribution. As Marion Milner might say, warts and all, but much more than warts. The authors face a full range of what we are up against, emotional toxins, strangled states, hells, crippled hopes, yet illumine areas of resilience, rhythms of faith, modes of coming through. Many dimensions of living are spanned, including creativity, spirituality, and everyday life. The chapters are colorful, broad, and deep, touching many patient populations and areas of experience. One gets a sense of how one is changed by the work, how it reverberates, permeates our beings.

Work with aboriginal mothers in Australia, autism, addiction, psychosis, art, music, to name a few. Depiction of work in South Africa, Israel, Canada, coast to coast in the USA. Buddhism, Bion, Winnicott, Lacan, Heidegger, Kali, William Blake, Kabbalah, love, violence, time experience, a spirit of welcoming presence—vast tapestries of life, voices mutually enriching. There is a chapter on my seminar, ongoing for forty years, another on supervision with me. What we do to and with each other, deep resources of self and more than self.

As you read, you will not miss how these works are related to mine. Signposts are there. But you will find new sparks coming into existence, writing itself an incessant birth process. The authors in their own ways, independently of one another, open veils, add to life, the feel of life.

You will be challenged, stimulated, inspired, led to wonder and care. You will find something that makes a difference. Soul, heart, nerves, mind all have their moments. You will find sentences, phrases, pages you will not want to leave. Appreciation for who we are and resources we draw on will heighten. And I suspect you will find yourself unexpectedly on friendlier, fuller, more intimate terms with yourself.

FOREWORD

Michael Eigen: psychoanalyst, philosopher, mystic

James S. Grotstein

Who—and what—is Michael Eigen? I begin to try to answer this question by calling him unique, multi-talented, complex, and gifted (and extraordinarily generous with his gifts to his audiences). A cross between minstrel, sage, and analyst laureate of our time.

That he is an unusually good psychoanalyst I can attest to from reading his case reports and by chance encounters with a few of his patients. I can attest to his generosity by having been the fortunate reader of the Bion Collective Website where, from its beginning, he has been a diligent, voluminous, and highly knowledgeable contributor. What he writes is ahead of the curve, at the creative edge of our understanding, and always enriches discussion. Although Michael is a private self, he is, paradoxically, phenomenally open and loves seminars (audience participation) as a way of teaching, learning, and sharing. This is only one of the traits in which he resembles Socrates and Bion. Other similarities are his love of paradox, his validation of the question over the answer, and his penchant for mysticism.

My purpose in beginning with this prelude, as you can now imagine, is to help locate on what existential, mystical, poetic latitude/longitude Michael Eigen lives and where he purchases the ingredients of his wondrous, enchanting prose, to say nothing of his presence as a person. When one speaks with him or listens to him at a lecture, one may find a friendly, outgoing, and involved speaker or conversationalist who easily engages about everyday matters. As one listens further, some other Michael Eigen may emerge: he will throw in meaningful but sometimes esoteric, exotic, mystical, and religious references and metaphors, for example, "Shekhinah". Mike is the only analyst I know who is comfortable discussing the "soul" and one of the few who is supportive of religious faith. I have reason to believe that Mike's religious faith is Jewish. The joy, ecstasy, passion, faith, and discipline we hear in his voice and read in his writings suggest that he is a Chasid, a spiritual descendant of the Baal Shem Tov. I am not a theological scholar, but it is my understanding that the latter was a courageous and daring innovator who tried to re-link emotional passion and mystical spirituality in a more natural form of worship, in contrast to the more strictly orthodox rabbinical form of worship that emphasized following the Mosaic Laws, that is, the Kashrus, etc. A similar conflict was to emerge in psychoanalysis between orthodox and liberal schools of thought and practice.

If one listens to, and reads and rereads, Michael over time, one may get a view of Michael as "acting in repertory" as a psychoanalyst, mystic, and philosopher—and many other roles, but these three seem to define him. A reviewer of one of one of his works called attention to his ontological bent: ". . . [H]e passionately asks that we make room for the deeper processes of our psyche, and take its movement seriously . . . Eigen brings attention to our self-disappearing nature. When we make ourselves disappear, we enter a state of madness", and "Eigen is direct about our love relationships. If we are to be in them, it's best to be prepared for violent and non-violent exchanges. We psychically kill each other as we try to survive in them", and "Eigen suggests that we all need to dream the resurfacing of the psychic scream within us, the scream that we are always not experiencing , as our infant's last scream just before hope was lost" (Fetting, 2013, Bion Collective, 4.26.13).

Earlier, I hypothesized that Michael, who is very reverent about the spiritual domain and who has a passionate belief in Faith, was a Chasidic Jew. I do not know how true that is, but I believe that, to his credit, his "psychoanalytic synagogue, temple, or church" would be harder to pick out. To me, he seems to be at home with the works of Winnicott (and the Independent School), Bion, Freud, Klein, Jung, and others, all interlaced with mysticism and ontology.

Earlier, I proffered the notion that Michael was a philosopher. I now should like to expand on that idea. Today, philosophy (and being a philosopher) is something quite different than it was in ancient times. Currently, it conjures recondite academic interests about human values. In ancient times, philosophy and philosophic ideas were commonly practiced, often in commune-like living arrangements. It was taken seriously and often literally. We get a hint of this from Plato and his Olive Garden and from what we have learned from the findings from the Dead Sea communities that authored the Dead Sea Scrolls. To me, Michael straddles both worlds. He presents profound philosophical ideas, often mystical or existential, but then offers quotidian mental hygiene advice. Put succinctly, he is near-messianic in his zeal to give of himself in order to help people, has a wide horizon for his ideas, and is unprejudiced religiously as well as psychoanalytically. Bion, we recall, associated "messiah" with "mystic" and/or "genius." In psychoanalysis, not too many individuals qualify. Michael *and* I would certainly nominate Freud, Bion, and Winnicott. I would also nominate Michael. I would nominate him as an (inter)-national treasure.

I close with a quotation from Michael's book (my favorite of his) *Kabbalah and Psychoanalysis*: "Kabbalah reaches us through broken forms touching a needy core. It is about a deep intimacy we sense and express, lose, re-find, re-create, in longing, suffering, and rejoicing" (Eigen, 2012, p. 5).

References

Eigen, M. (2012). *Kabbalah and Psychoanalysis.* London: Karnac.

Fetting, M. (2012). Review of *Michael Eigen in Seoul* (vol. 1): *Madness and Murder.* In: *bioncollective*, Friday, April 26, 2012.

Editors' introduction

A well-known adage, variously attributed, suggests that we write the book we would like to read. For many who have tracked Michael Eigen's prolific output over the years, there has always been a curiosity as to how his contributions would be grasped, worked with, and recreated. However, a book on Michael Eigen's work itself seemed beyond our reach at this stage, and it was, therefore, more realistic for us to collect a set of papers in honor of his contribution.

As editors, our collaboration began on Eigen's original Internet list server. Our emails quickly evolved into the idea of the two of us working on a *festschrift*. Besides our shared South African roots, we have both been avid and longstanding readers of Eigen. Early in his career, Loray Daws contacted Eigen while conducting research on alexithymia (1999). Stephen Bloch had previously carried out an email interview on Eigen's views on psychoanalysis and music (Ashton & Bloch, 2010). Perhaps Eigen's concerns also spoke to our shared experience in South Africa—the psychotic edges of trauma, rage, and murder, and the aliveness present in spite of, or even because of, these. As with so many other readers, we have always been struck by the originality and the unique vision he articulates. In reading two of his key early papers, "The area of faith in Winnicott, Lacan and Bion"

(1981) and "Towards Bion's starting point: from catastrophe to faith" (1985), we realized that a unique and astonishing voice was emerging. His papers and books reflect the range of his heartfelt concerns and a style that is uncompromising, vivid, and musical. The papers presented in this volume, we hope, will reveal the nodal and generative potential opened by Eigen's writings, yielding, in turn, creative responses, extensions, and improvisations.

Eigen's psychoanalytic concerns are vast and include "the facticity of damaged bonds, the infinite implications of entropy and psychic deadness, our psychotic core, as well as our inherent vitality and sensitive self potentiality" (Daws, this volume, p. 109). These areas were evident from the start and have occupied Eigen's clinical and theoretical work for decades, as he has continuously explored and expanded on the work of Freud, Milner, Elkin, Winnicott, Bion, Jung, and Lacan. Summarizing the various vertices explored by Michael Eigen since 1973, as seen in countless professional articles and more than twenty-three books, would entail many volumes in itself. For an overview of the first period of Eigen's writings, we refer the interested reader to consult the first collection of Eigen's papers by Adam Phillips (Eigen, 1993) and his introductory chapter, and, especially, Eigen's own introductory notes. It is a succinct and erudite summary of the major areas of his own unfolding psychoanalytic vision from the period 1973 to 1989, introducing core clinical and creative probes. It will be clear to the reader that Eigen's language allows for the possibility of a conceptual, theoretical, and clinical transcendence, ever expanding the contact potential between patient and analyst. Themes included the positive aspects of pathological tendencies, working with unwanted patients, ideal images, the "I not yet I", the sense of creativeness, dual union and differentiation, primary process work, permeability, "O", alpha function, demonized aspects of the self and other, living between catastrophe and faith, omnipotence–omniscience, doubleness and mystery, reparative tendencies, mindlessness–selflessness, and an area of faith. These concerns all served as foundational notations which were artistically furthered in later volumes such as *The Psychotic Core* (1986), *Psychic Deadness* (1996), *Damaged Bonds* (2001b), *Rage* (2002), *Lust* (2006), *Ecstasy* (2001a), *The Sensitive Self* (2004), *Feeling Matters* (2007), *Faith* (2014b), *A Felt Sense* (2014a), and many other works. By reading Eigen "one develops [a] sensitivity to the relative opening–closing that characterizes micro-moments and to an overall sense of fluidity–rigidity that tones personality" (2005, p. 155). Such a "sensitivity" is built on a rhythm of both recovery and faith, of new beginnings. For Eigen,

> [P]sychoanalysts and prophets have faith in new beginnings. You can start over again, in one way or another. . . . Outer layers of the soul fall away like dead skin . . . Personality is uneven and, like a tree, can be partly alive and partly dead at the same time, some aspects ready to bloom, some already vanishing. Since soul space is spaceless, a single 'area' can be simultaneously alive and dead—maximally–minimally and infinitely graded. (2004, p. 45)

Through continuous cultivation of this "soul space", Eigen's writing introduces a post-Bionian psychoanalysis with a "third kind of 'alpha work'" (2011, p. 67), which we believe will support many contemporary thinkers to contemplate deeper structures of moment-to-moment awareness. That is, Eigen's cultivation and languaging of a psychoanalytic experiential capacity is made possible through the use of this third alpha function (i.e., Eigen's "on–off alpha"), enabling the analytic couple to remain open to various experiences of self–no-self, God–no-God, mind–no-mind, being–non-being, full–empty, distinction–union, samsara–nirvana, attention–no-attention, words–wordless, and much more.

Many analysts have also praised Eigen's prolific output and clinical work over the years. A review of the work published on Bion and Winnicott show Eigen to be a significant interpreter of these major figures (Karnac, 2007, 2008). Both Claire Winnicott and Hans Loewald responded favorably to *The Area of Faith* in particular. A relationship of mutual support developed between Eigen and Marion Milner, who has praised his writing for constantly opening new vistas, returning again and again to her enjoyment of Eigen's fresh, jargon-free language (Eigen, 2014c). Adam Phillips edited the first collection of Eigen's papers, *The Electrified Tightrope* (1993), and Heinz Kohut acknowledged the value of his clinical work. James Grotstein has consistently embraced Eigen's work over the years, as well as in the Foreword to this volume.

More recently, Eigen's writings have been affirmed by many significant contemporary psychoanalysts. Thomas Ogden has described Eigen as one of the most original voices in contemporary psychoanalysis and his work as "extraordinary" (Eigen, 2014c). Jessica

Benjamin has described his rare ability to capture the intense emotional encounter of psychotherapy, both within the therapist and between patient and therapist. In her review of his 2001 book, *Damaged Bonds*, Benjamin affirms Eigen's ability to lead us into "the I–Thou of recognition, where self and other suffer and learn together"; in her endorsement of *Flames from the Unconscious* (2009), she takes note of his astonishing and gripping use of language, which leads us to confront shockingly raw and untheorizable dimensions of experience; in a note accompanying *Conversations with Michael Eigen* (Eigen & Govrin, 2007), she highlights "life-in-truth versus deadness" as an essential theme in Eigen. Similarly, Christopher Bollas has praised many of Eigen's volumes, most notably *The Psychoanalytic Mystic*, describing them as clinically acute and his vision as spontaneous and singular (Eigen, 1998, backcover, and Eigen, 2014c).

For many analysts, Eigen has been a significant explorer of Bion's many perspectives and, in personal correspondence, Francesca Bion herself has commented on Eigen as being a stimulating writer on Bionian themes such as psychic aliveness and psychic deadness (Eigen, 2014c). Many other key figures have praised his work; the list includes Harold Boris, Mark Epstein, Antonino Ferro, Ignacio Matte-Blanco, Nancy McWilliams, Steven Mitchell, Marie Coleman Nelson, Clifford Scott, Donnel Stern, and Meg Harris Williams. Additionally, Harry Karnac (1920–2014) warmly responded to, and has supported many of, Eigen's writings, and his publishing house has since brought out sixteen of Eigen's books.

Recently, in a response to Eigen's *The Birth of Experience*, Giuseppe Civatarese, author of *The Violence of Emotions—Bion and Post-Bionian Psychoanalysis* (2012), articulated the essence of what many of Eigen's readers have felt, emphasizing that it is not only Eigen's alive language and ability to be theoretically sound without being academic that is significant, but also the way in which his texts allow the reader "*to experience in the reading what psychic growth means* . . . what he says about Kabbalah, mysticism, Bion, mental suffering has been deeply assimilated and re-dreamed" (Eigen, 2014c, our emphasis). In referring to Eigen's elaboration on Bion's notion of the beauty of psychoanalysis, Civatarese further says,

> Psychoanalysis aims at expanding our capacity to give a full meaning to experience, to live in a more intense and sensitive way. This is so

> true—that beauty is at the heart of psychic growth—that the new emerging paradigm in psychoanalysis can be defined "aesthetic". What changes us is something very close to the aesthetic experience as encountered at birth in the experience of being at unison with the mother. In fact at the heart of both aesthetic experience and psychic growth is the capacity to create/receive a form to contain our anxiety, that is, the capacity to tolerate the transience of all things. So the acceptance of transience is intrinsic to beauty. (In Eigen, 2014c)

We have quoted Civatarese at length here because his reflections highlight the two wings of Eigen's contribution; namely, his thorough clinical and theoretical understanding, and his characteristically evocative style. As Civatarese suggests, the content itself is not the only significant aspect of Eigen's body of work. Many readers and contributors to this volume have been struck by the poetic style of his texts; his visceral hermeneutic reading of Bion; and his intense, moving case histories. Eigen has found a voice to express the most profound psychic realities and experiences. It is a language of experience that itself contains and reveals experience. James Hillman laments the scientism of much of psychology's language and writes of "words [drained] of their blood . . . [which] made us in psychology lose faith in the power of words so that therapy must turn to cries and gestures". He continues: "after all this I am passionately urging a model of recuperating language by returning to speech that matters. I am also harkening back to Confucius who insisted that the therapy of culture begins with the rectification of language" (Hillman, 2009, p. 19). Cries, gestures, and, indeed, silence all have their place in psychotherapy. But we are involved in the "talking cure" and therefore we search not only for the words to say it, but words that evoke, quicken, and enliven. *Tikkun* is the Kabbalistic notion of the need for restitution and reparation of the broken sparks of our world. Eigen's texts are themselves this *tikkun*, this rectification of language. They are a poesis, a speech that matters.

The range of papers, though spontaneous, as no contributor actually knew what the others were writing, display the full panorama of Eigen's concerns, thus complementing one other. We have arranged the papers in three Parts:

Part I, Reflections: Papers that link his writings to broader concerns and other psychoanalysts, philosophical traditions, and thinkers (Bloch, Epstein, Goldsmith, Malater, and Potter).

Part II, Refractions: The papers in this section deal with the clinical implications of Eigen's work (Govrin, Eaton, Eshel, Campbell, Daws, Fetting, Tracey, and Wetzler).

Part III, Reveries: Eigen's intensely personal writing evokes equivalent responses and reveries in his readers. The papers in this section deal with the impact, often extremely personal, of Eigen's work (Anderson, Molino, Molofsky, Berghash, and Rothschild).

Reflections

In Chapter One, Stephen Bloch uses archetypal imagery and mythological musings to weave together a series of Kali themes in the work of both Eigen and Bion. According to Bloch, Kali as an archetypal image personifies not only trauma and terror, but also awe, fascination, and vitality: "Her image evokes a ferocious aliveness, a terrible vitality, and, in every representation, a pulsing combination of annihilatory and life-giving properties—nullity and plenitude" (p. 3). For Bloch, reflecting on Kali mythology, and, in particular, the symbol of her garland of skulls, may allow for a deeper psychoanalytic understanding of Eigen's destructive and undreamable objects, Klein's persecutory object, Bion's boundless object, and Eaton's obstructive object, as she represents unprocessed catastrophic realities which have to be contained and reworked before any transcendent and/or meditative states of consciousness can be tolerated, thereby opening creative space "for" and "in" O. Turning to Bion's experiences in the First World War, Bloch argues that Bion's lifelong emotional metabolization of his traumatization serves as a window on to his own encounter with Kali: that is, how affective thinking happens "at the edge of turbulence and catastrophe—Kali in her disruptive, dissolving aspects" (p. 6). In a fantasy, Bloch dreams into Bion's shattering war experiences (quoting excerpts from Bion's autobiographical accounts) a vision of Kali that Bion may have had in a crucial battle experience on 8 August 1917, which he endlessly relived and reworked throughout his life. Throughout his career, Bion faithfully traced the various destructive processes in the psyche, the central elements that may violently or subtly subvert thought and emotional growth. For Bionian psychoanalysis, this may entail Kali as catastrophe, but also the catastrophe that is in search of alpha dreaming. Bloch thickens Bion's Kali through an exploration of Eigen's work in four main areas: (a) catastrophe and faith; (b) the unbearable; (c) psychic deadness; and (d) destruction, creation, and aliveness.

In mapping these core areas, Bloch articulates the intimate relationship between catastrophe and faith, the radically open attitude that awaits the various impacts of Kali experiences, the suspension and bracketing of memory, desire, and understanding; the relinquishment of knowing (K) so as to allow a previously unborn image to emerge, faith (F) as the core psychoanalytic attitude; and the cultivation of an alive openness in relationship to its Kali aspects, even if it seems unbearable. He writes: "The movement from catastrophe to faith is the Kali explosion that struggles to find its way into form; the experience is redeemed because it has found the grace of containment and representation. The psychological gesture that allows this redemption is captured in Bion's Faith. With her stark imagery, Kali opens and develops the experiential capacity that this surrender demands" (p. 8). The need to remain open in the face of catastrophic impacts, Faith in O, is a trope that Eigen repeatedly mines for its implications for therapy and life. Eigen's work also explores the reality that the grace of containment and representation remains continuously fraught with undreamable states, damaged dreamwork, and the anti-dream object which can subvert psychological growth, exposing the psyche to Kali's wrath and destruction. How to hold, survive, and transform Kali's disruptive turbulence remains a central *leitmotif* in Bion and Eigen's psychoanalytic vision. Bloch links moments of Kali in several passages from the work of Eigen, especially in relationship to the risks inherent in too much aliveness. He concludes that, although not necessarily his conscious intention, Eigen's body of work stands as a testament to a deepening exposure to states of body–mind that are carried by the image of Kali.

The intersection of psychoanalysis and Buddhism is a growing area of exploration. A key and influential figure in this domain is Mark Epstein, who draws on the psychoanalytic contributions of Bion and Winnicott (Epstein, 1996, 2001). In his most recent publication, *The Trauma of Everyday Life* (2013), he references selected passages from Eigen concerning the nature of interrupted dreamwork. In his contribution to this volume (Chapter Two), Epstein brings our attention to the notion of a distinction–union movement and dynamic to explore the interpenetration of self and surround. Through Epstein, we see how there is continual tension between isolation and connection in human experience and how the "self" in the work of Eigen and Buddhism remains relational and contextual. Eigen describes an aloneness at the heart of individual existence which is, at the same time, supported by an unknown, boundless support. Psychodynamically, this support is found in the original mother–infant relationship, the containment by the good enough mother, in Winnicott's term. It is necessary to hold both a sense of self and non-duality in awareness, thereby rejecting an emphasis on one side or the other. As Epstein notes, "The implication is that the awakened state found by the Buddha does not exist apart from our everyday world, that the compressed knot of emotional pain described by Michael Eigen is also the ecstatic bliss of orgasm and enlightenment" (p. 25). This contiguity is called "the Great Seal" or "the Great Embrace" in the *Mahamudra.* In a chance encounter with an eighteenth century Mongolian poem, Epstein found expression of this interplay. Bloch notes a similar combination of opposites in his chapter on "Kali in Eigen and Bion". Eigen's writing traverses the spectrum from the most primitive and destructive states of mind to ecstatic and mystical experience. He writes of "the ever necessary confrontation of a mystical core with suffering, degradation, annihilation, and an endless play of destructive forces that exert deforming pressure" (Eigen, 2001, p. viii). Eigen's own writings on Distinction–union can be found in Chapter Fourteen of *The Electrified Tightrope* (1993) and Chapter One, "Distinction–union structure", in *Contact with the Depths* (2011), as well as in sections of *Coming through the Whirlwind* (1992) and *Reshaping the Self* (1995).

For Goldsmith (Chapter Three), Eigen's work actively brings us into the living pulse of his psychoanalytic vision and praxis. In Eigen's writing we are privileged to experience the vicissitudes of "patient and analyst in all their anguished, despairing, sacred, and ecstatic dimensions" (p. 33). Goldsmith's reading of Eigen reveals multiple prismatic facets of the inner world of both patient and analyst, where nothing can be univocal. Person-to-person deep affective engagement, as an evolving struggle, erases categorical thinking and facilitates a "raw aliveness of experience". Heart, as used by Goldsmith, refers "both to the core matter of psychoanalysis (the heart of the matter), and to the passion, lifeblood, and humanity enlivening this subject matter (a heart of flesh)" (pp. 33–34). Eigen's love of primary process remains evident in his evocative and poetic writings, for Goldsmith, endowing and re-envisioning psychoanalysis with "a heart", in both senses of the word. Through the exploration of four core or nodal "concepts", Goldsmith gracefully brings forth Eigen's central psychoanalytic "heartbeat"; the infinite boundless unknown as a source and background support of existence; feeling as a foundational psychic phenomenon; the primacy of Faith and emotional transformation. Goldsmith notes that the latter informs a heartfelt mode of existence, supporting and articulating "ineffable feelings, unspeakable wounds, wordless communications, living moments" (p. 49). As Goldsmith creatively writes on passion, lifeblood, and humanity, she also inevitably evokes primary process discourse. Daws reminds us in his paper that Eigen remains a true lover of primary process and its vicissitudes; "I must confess I am a primary process lover. In an important way, loving the flow of primary process meanings has made my life worthwhile" (1996, p. 142). Eigen remains true to primary process, in its shock, aliveness, and redemption, as well as its relationship with the infinite boundless unknown and Bion's conception of O. Goldsmith emphasises that the latter relationship allows us to become partners to the unfolding of O which is our very being, the origin of our creativity, and is the unseen mystery within which wordless transformations may occur. Given the latter, it may even be possible for therapists to serve as a Sabbath "point of the soul" (Eigen, 2011, p. 24), developing an affective register with the patient able to articulate and experience a fuller range of emotions. This affective interaction requires an "evocative language". Finally, Goldsmith also notes Eigen's creative writing style, his ability to meld content and form (language of rhythm) and his continual search for a language or therapeutic couple tongue that does not "castigate", "reduce", or "freeze" (Eigen, 2007). This allows for a fully evocative vivid and sensuous imagery that, by definition, involves a psychoanalytic "touch" that endows the encounter with much aliveness. As Goldsmith puts it, Eigen's words reverberate with wordless reality. In all of this, she concludes that the dimensions described by her require the development of the psychic organ of Faith as explored by Bion and Eigen, and discussed further in many chapters in this volume.

In Chapter Four, "Eigentime", Evan Malater explores a less apparent aspect of Eigen's writing: our experience of, and relationship to, time. The intersection of time and desire is a thread that winds its way through Eigen's texts in a non-linear way and is, therefore, not easy to grasp. Malater grapples with the complexity of this theme through a series of interconnected explorations. As he states, it is an essential and personal dimension of Eigen's own biography, as movingly described in his interviews with Govrin in *Conversations with Michael Eigen* (Eigen & Govrin, 2007). Malater begins by highlighting our desire for a quick fix in an age of "newness." Time and desire involve all of Eigen's major concerns: psychosis, trauma, and faith. In *The Psychotic Core*, Eigen asserts the centrality of psychosis to psychoanalysis. According to Malater, this involves three insights—that there is no continuity of time in early splitting, that desire measures and shatters time, and that absence and the hallucinated breast are sensuous feeling experiences, perhaps particularly with regard to the experience of deadness. The screaming baby, too, is in timelessness, the inverse of a mystical atemporality—a timeless hell that is the opposite of a timeless heaven. As Malater notes, the timeless scream at the origins of the personality permeates the whole of a lifetime: "the patient whose every word is a scream, whose every silence is a stifled cry". This endless scream has its origins in Winnicott's dimension "Z". The trauma of catastrophic impacts disrupts the continuity of time and the example of Eigen's patient demonstrates how old paradigms, linear and repetitive, defend against the "event" as an "unpredictable rupture" which allows the new to emerge. The paradox of this is that traumatic impacts themselves require time to be processed in order to be rendered historical. The earliest sense of self may be disembodied and only later become connected to sense of bodies in relationship to one another. Malater, through a quote from Beckett, describes how being "in time" includes all dimensions of experience as well as our need to hold the paradox of time and timelessness. The rhythms of breakdown and recovery are also rhythms within a sense of time, and the therapist must try hold the understanding of this. While Winnicott explores presence and absence through the lens of time, Bion's concern was with murder. By identifying with annihilatory forces, it is possible to "destroy" time. And once more it is Faith that sustains the analyst in this encounter, this recurrent murderous confrontation". Malater's paper reminds us how significant aspects of this Faith are the qualities of patience and the openness to what needs to emerge in an analytic session.

Brent Potter is the author of *Elements of Self Destruction* (2013). His chapter in this volume (Chapter Five) offers the reader a creative link between the work of Eigen and the phenomenologist Martin Heidegger. More specifically, Potter explores the tropism of creative faith and destructiveness in their work, and how these forces interact both within the individual and in the outer world. In reviewing Eigen's int(e)r(a)personal *pharmakon*, or poison-cure, of self-and-others, he shines a light on the development of psychic reality, its nurturing qualities but also its destructive elements. Potter observes how Eigen conducts micro-analyses of our internal evolution, in a similar vein to Bion, determining how this evolution goes awry as well as what we might need to survive our wounded natures. According to Potter, Heidegger, too, explores in detail the strategies people use to compensate for the wounding of/to their Being, and the meditative thinking needed to experience wholeness. In his view, modern man is engaged in a destructive attack upon meditative thinking through calculative thinking characterized by excessive cogitation, memorizing, structuring, ordering, and engineering all aspects of Being (Eigen's "winning lie"). Calculative thinking is addictive and destructive, an active modern day hallucinosis in service of evading reflective space as well as psychological and spiritual growth. Int(e)r(a)personal alexithymia permeates relatedness, both endopsychically and interpersonally. In Potter's words, "[i]ndividual and collective anti-reality strategies leading to existential–psychic alexithymia necessitate an ever increasing amount of distance from emotional awareness, social attachment, and interpersonal relating. The more int(e)r(a)personal difficulty in distinguishing and appreciating emotional life, the more alexithymic the condition. It is a vicious, never-ending cycle of increasing deadness and decreasing aliveness" (pp. 72–73). Here we find Potter amplifying the work of Eigen, Bion, Klein, and Freud, as well as the radical openness (F in O) needed to re-engage Being with itself and the world in meditative thinking. The fundamental interconnected "circulatory system" means that Being, that is, Being-in-the-world and the world of *Dasein*, is a *with-world*. It is always *Being-in* and *Being-with* others. By opening ourselves to the latter, we may restore this interconnectedness and the ways to nurture an "intimate distance that calls for respect as well as caring. To see and sense as a form of giving" (Eigen, 2011b, p. 4).

Refractions

Marian Campbell, in Chapter Six, presents a moving clinical exploration of Bion and Eigen's notion of being "murdered into life". The case of a single, divorced, professional woman in her late thirties, with a history of early emotional neglect as well as sexual trauma, is presented to articulate the psychological experience of deadness. In a manner similar to Eigen, Campbell poignantly illustrates how patients characterized by feelings of deadness do not lack emotion or meaning *per se*, but are rather "untouched by their experiences" (Eigen, 1996, p. xiii). With careful analytic holding, and a reliance on her patient's own use of Christian iconography, the patient's frozen child-self is awakened, serving as a signifier of psychic rebirth following her trauma, and taking the form of being "murdered into life" (Eigen, 2004, p. 31). The basic *iconographic rhythm* is explored in depth by the analytic pair, beginning with the Virgin and Child, and the Annunciation as a prerequisite for, and a kind of heralding of, the birth; moving to the *dead* Christ *before* reaching the crucified Christ, that is, returning to Annunciation and Birth. According to Campbell, it was as if the patient needed to become aware of her own psychic deadness, to *live* it with the help of another, "before she could experience the murderous pain behind the deadness" (p. 87). Within this iconographic rhythm of faith, the analytic relationship came to hold many facets of the patient's transformation. Fragments of intense feeling of pain, rage, and loneliness were lived by both Campbell and her analytic co-participant, ever enduring them "if only a little, or a little at a time" (Eigen, 2004, p. 26)—a living moment in search for another to experience it, supporting the *resurrection* of the vital self.

In Loray Daws' contribution (Chapter Seven), special emphasis is given to Eigen's concepts of wounded nourishment and primary process work, his unique rhythm of faith, and the importance of becoming a welcoming other to primary process impacts (see Eaton, this volume). Daws looks specifically at how Eigen's rhythm of faith, an Elkin–Winnicott–Bion songline, protects and enlivens the self from the various trauma-globs evident in relating to a wounding–obstructive–obdurate object. As psychological midwife, Eigen's rhythm of faith serves as an open invitation to the sense of self left behind, remaining hopeful in transforming states of mind characterized by stagnation, radioactive waste, and deadness. As welcoming other, the analyst is envisioned as serving as a primary process guardian, enabling emotional digestion even when it entails deep contact with primary process debris that is difficult to metabolize. Given its impact, the therapist may experience anxiety and resistance about dreaming the patient, that is, making the patient real, taking the patient into one's psychic bloodstream, thereby postponing the necessary primary process work to be done. Despite such a reaction, Eigen remains hopeful of our ability within the rhythm of faith. It is with these concepts in mind that Daws introduces his work with a homeless bipolar man. Throughout the case, Daws tries to convey to the reader the difficulties in dreaming a patient saturated with radicalized states of mind and how relying on Eigen's rhythm of faith enabled a togetherness able to restore a "Memory of justice", as described by James Grotstein.

Jeff Eaton's chapter, "The welcoming object" (Chapter Eight), needs to be read as continuation of the term he introduced in an earlier paper "The obstructive object" (2011). The obstructive object refers to a catastrophic disruption of containment in the mother–infant dyad where there is a failure of maternal reverie and impairment or absence of alpha function. Eaton cites Bion (1959), "The establishment of a projective-rejecting object means that instead of an understanding object the infant has a wilfully misunderstanding object with which it is identified" (Bion, 1959, p. 117). By contrast, Eaton invites us to consider the welcoming object that absorbs and suffers projective identification in the service of the infant and the infant in the patient. He focuses on Bion's and Eigen's writing on the necessity of finding ways to be, face, tolerate, and communicate with and about these undreamt and undreamable objects. In Eaton's words, if we can *reverse* the habit of rejection, we may become more experienced as a *welcoming* object and can cultivate and sustain a compassionate attention to truth (p. 132). He found a living example of this attitude in Eigen's papers where the layers and textures of this perspective are explored. This is particularly so in "The sensitive self" (2004), which also functions as an encouragement to therapists to maintain this openness. In parallel to the notion of catastrophe and faith, there is also the rhythm of breakdown and repair, a process that is repeated over and over in infancy and throughout a lifetime. This process is inextricably interpersonal and intrapsychic and Eaton touches on how this awareness includes the body and breathing: the welcoming object is in exquisite relationship with the sensitive self. Eaton's case description concerns a seven-year-old boy who was diagnosed with autism at age three. He describes a noise-making, cartoon-drawing process over time. Gradually, the patient allowed Eaton to talk about the emotional impacts these encounters were having on him, in contrast to the deeply private "secret movie" that was playing inside him. The secret movie was externalized and played out in different interactions and stage sets. An experience of significant development occurred in relation to a particularly frightening image of a dog. At this point, the sharing of his secret movie allowed the scream inside the boy to become a dream, and, therefore, more workable in the interaction with Eaton. Previously, it had to be kept inside the patient for fear of it ruining everything. In subsequent sessions, the image of the dog, which was resistant to change, allowed itself to be expressed through the medium of love, as expressed in the Beatles' song "All you Need is Love". Although the evil badness could not be totally eradicated, it could be locked up, quarantined, so to speak. Eaton describes the core process in the work with his patient as that of providing a space of welcoming the unwanted, providing a receptive context for the dreaming of previously split-off toxic elements. An essential aspect of this is for the therapist to be welcoming of his own unwelcome parts and experience, including, and especially, violent and destructive parts. He sees in Eigen's work an example of this receptivity and expresses how much the texts have helped him maintain this perspective. He concludes, "The silent scream can eventually be heard, and the scream that never stops screaming can become part of a larger rhythm of breakdown, repair, discovery, and gratitude" (p. 147).

Winnicott's 1945 notion of patient and analyst needing to live an experience together is an important pillar of Eshel's contribution (Chapter Nine). For Eshel, it is imperative for the analyst to give himself over to become fully part of the analysand's ongoing emotional reality and ontological experience; "Patient and analyst, thereby, forge an emergent new experiential–emotional entity that goes beyond the confines of their separate subjectivities and the simple summation of the two—an entity (unit or being) of interconnectedness, 'withness,' or 't(w)ogetherness.' *Two-in-oneness.* Treatment, thus, *creates* psychic reality, and a different kind of knowledge, experience, and powerful affects that come into being when the analyst interconnects psychically with the patient in living through the process" (p. 151). This is a key aspect of Eigen's clinical approach, as seen in many other chapters in this volume, for example, Molofsky's description of Candy, Daws' treatment of Pete, Eshel's holding of Reuben, and Eaton's contact with Steven. Eshel uses the terms "withness" and "presencing" to characterize the nature of such encounters. Eigen conceptualises "withness" as follows: "This collapse *into being with another*, the deepest states of the other—isn't this something of the kind of sensitivity that gives our annihilated states a home?" (Eigen, 2006, p. 38, our italics; also cited in Eshel, 2013b).

This is an act of radical courage on the part of the therapist embodying what Bion means when he talks of F in O. A further dimension of this concern with at-one-ment is that it may reach the scream that died out "before hope was abandoned" , a place of "dissociated breakdown". Given Eigen's sensibility, the notion of the dying scream is a theme he returns to often in both his writing and seminars, principally in *Rage* (2002). Eshel's concerns are similar and are illustrated in her striking case description of an extremely disturbed, acting out individual who was *met* by her in the actuality of the unthinkable realities of his symptoms and his developmental history. Remaining present and available to such an encounter is a true illustration of F in O. Eshel provides rich descriptions of concepts such as boundless patience and the importance of a willingness to "wait in silence", despite the emergence of dissociative breakdown: "At the next session, he said that he told me too many thoughts, fantasies, that he had reached his limit. And then silence reigned for over four months" (p. 164). The waiting finally supported the breaking through of the wall of silence, fully exposing the patient to a vulnerability born out of immense rejection and abandonment, leading to the return of the dissociated. Eshel's work serves as an important reminder that progress and the establishment of a true faith, as opposed to a simple trust, is based on "*this collapse into being-with* the patient's unbearable states of breakdown and madness, catastrophe and the failing last scream before, and even more so after, hope was abandoned" (p. 169).

Margaret Fetting's chapter addresses the issue of psychoanalytic "faith" as it relates to addiction treatment (Chapter Ten). She begins by emphasizing the value that Eigen's texts have had for her both professionally and personally, paying particular attention to the trauma of the self in addictive processes. In the contemporary psychotherapy of the addicted individual, one often encounters the medicalization and control of the individual, rather, as argued by Fetting, than the absorption of the "impacts" that resulted in trauma clots. Control and medicalization may result in the premature foreclosure of the psychological complexity the addictive self has to face. Fetting's approach is courageous and would not meet with universal approval in addiction treatment protocols; however, she makes the crucial point of meeting the experience of the other with "Faith" and "Openness" no matter how extreme or risky the life situation is. As she herself states, Eigen's theoretical soundings, especially his concept of registering impacts, allows the clinician to be guided by the addict's felt presence, not the clinician's sense of what is right for the patient. This is a radical shift in the treatment of addiction. Her essential point is that transformational processes may not happen without this risking, the waiting in O. In the case of Lindsay, she demonstrates Eigen's "tapestry of ideas" and the various processes underlying self-medication, the importance when treating addiction to play for time so as to allow catastrophic beta buzz to be re-worked by alpha function, allowing links to be made (Eigen, 2011b, pp. 8, 18), and the turning of nameless dread into thinking or dreaming. In quoting Eigen, Fetting points to the grim (yet hopeful) paradox of being addicted: "The grim paradox is that insofar as [the addict] lacks the capacity to tolerate the sense of catastrophe that saturates [his] psychic reality, [the addict] may heighten external catastrophe [addiction] as a way of objectifying himself. He may finally 'know' himself through this dramatization [addiction]" (Eigen, 1999, p. 138).

In *Conversations with Michael Eigen* (2007), Aner Govrin provided a rich transcript of a supervision session with Eigen. This led to further interest and curiosity in many readers into the nature of supervision with Eigen. One aspect of Govrin's experience of interest was Eigen's encouragement of Govrin to let go "into the experience," and to be less concerned with clarity of rational discourse and understanding. Eigen also taught this by example, and less by simply pointing to the typical tendency to follow a scientific, theoretical approach. At the same time, despite this emphasis on "unknowing," Eigen's approach remains practical, focused, and purposeful. Eigen's voice was "searching ... responsive ... senstive" (this volume, p. 219). Eigen also constantly refrained from imposing an external concept of how the therapy should be, rather that vitality, true participation, and realness be appreciated throughout. The articulation of Eigen's approach is understood in terms of depressive position functioning, a forgoing of the need for a binary completeness. This "incompleteness" is unique to Eigen's paradoxical holding of presence and absence, where less is more and "true" emotional contact is possible.

Norma Tracey's theoretical and clinical work accentuates Eigen's seminal formulation of the movement between catastrophe and faith and its presence in the mother–child dyad. The catastrophe–faith trajectory was Eigen's summation of a crucial aspect of Bion's explorations and it is a theme he returns to repeatedly, suggesting recently that the catastrophe–faith link is a double arrowed movement (Eigen, 2012). Early in Chapter Twelve, Tracey introduces the complexity of this relationship when she states that when a sanity is prematurely superimposed in chaos, it may deaden psychic growth, whereas new psychic birth implies mother and infant growing together through chaos, catastrophe, incoherence, and nameless dread (p. 225–226). She takes this further by suggesting that there is no sense of self without a sense of catastrophe, the implication being that the presence of faith is an essential aspect of selfhood. She quotes Eigen, "Without a sense of catastrophe there would be no self and without self no sense of catastrophe" (1993, p. 218). Paradoxically, Bion also regards a sense of catastrophe as a binding agent in the psyche. This understanding serves as a basis for Tracey's work with Aboriginal mothers and babies in Australia. She movingly describes the case of a mother unable to hold her baby and how various "misadventures" open the possibility of a containing reflective space between her and the mother and, by extension, the baby. As part of the chapter she includes, with gratitude, vignettes of her own supervisory relationship over long distance with Eigen and his reflections on aspects of Christianity, in particular, "suffering the suffering".

In his authentic and emotionally based description of his long participation in Michael Eigen's weekly seminars on Bion, Winnicott, and Lacan, Wetzler (Chapter Thirteen) describes both his personal and professional development in this forum. He places emphasis on the evolving capacity of the psyche and the need for the embryonic nature of our psyches to develop through experience and to struggle against destructive forces. His chapter conveys a sense of the way in which Eigen deepens our understanding of Bion, often by what Wetzler describes as a meditative reading and rereading of passages, sentences, or phrases. In all of this, the emotionally resonant nature of Eigen's approach is emphasized. This is especially significant, as

Wetzler stresses that we can only access a small portion of Bion's emotional range and intensity. There might not be sufficient capacity to deal with emotional experience. Wetzler also notes the indeterminacy of emotional and psychic existence. Within this chapter are numerous reflections on the unknown, madness, and creativity. Schreber is a case that Eigen often references in his seminars as, in other chapters, the notion of therapeutic togetherness, the "partner", is also focused upon—the contributions of Eshel and Daws in particular. Of interest is that Wetzler also forms an intersection with Brent Potter's writing on the Heideggerian notion of "being with another".

Reveries

Many chapters in this volume have involved psychologists commenting on Eigen's writing style as unique within psychoanalysis. In Peter Anderson's contribution (Chapter Fourteen) we have a creative writer meeting Eigen as a creative writer, poet to poet. He affirms Eigen's literary merit and the poetic nature of his psychoanalytic writing. The essence lies early in his paper, in his citation of Gruber emphasising words as linguistic experience: "where words are less data of information than containers of transformative energy that facilitate a concentration and expansion of consciousness to the point of an awakening of the sacred" (Gruber, cited in Anderson, p. 254). Anderson particularly focuses on Eigen's monograph *Ecstasy* (2001) and also the psychotic kernel in every person as explored in *The Psychotic Core* (Eigen, 1986). With this as background, he explores the intersection of Eigen and Blake in terms of the divine–daemonic and the daemonic–divine. Of particular interest is the way in which Anderson has taught Eigen's *Ecstasy* to his literature students, and he gives some of their responses. Anderson further provides a non-clinician's vivid interaction with people, where he brings to bear an engaged poetic dialogue in the spirit of Eigen. In all of this, the autobiographical nature of his writing is similar to what Eigen does in his texts. There are evocative descriptions of Anderson's early life in South Africa, characterized by a direct, gritty style. Anderson casts his net wide, weaving references to Milton, Heidegger, Bob Dylan, Buddhism, and Kant, and he concludes with a rhetorical Nietzschean question to Eigen, inviting further opening and dialogue: "Why is it that 'light' should rhyme with 'night' . . .? Night is also a sun?" (p. 275).

In Chapter Fifteen, Rachel Berghash's two published poems reveal the creative workings of a sensitive reader of Eigen's work. According to her, Eigen's "teachings consists among other things, of openness to more and more reality, including unsolvable reality. There is no closure. The potential of being disappointed and frustrated described in Heaven Moment is freeing. It opens to seeing life as a continuous adventure, good/bad, bad/good" (Berghash, 2014). In response to the poem "Heaven Moment", Eigen himself commented on its delicacy and how disappointment can be "freed by the music of a poem" (Eigen, 2013, private communication to Rachel Berghash). Berghash's second poem, about the leper, is based on her conviction that Eigen remains sensitive and open to the leper in us all: "the appearance of the leper doesn't turn him away" (Berghash, 2014). Finally, she states, "Eigen invites us, in his teachings as well as in his writings, to surrender to whatever experience we are going through, to be open in a state of faith to being surprised and astonished. Not to refuse the darkness that pervades. Vital sparks will eventually be seen and lifted, our garden will grow, and even flourish" (Berghash, 2014).

Chapter Sixteen, Anthony Molino's contribution, is an improvisatory, freewheeling response to Michael Eigen. Among his other works, Molino has edited two books on psychoanalysis and Buddhism, *The Couch and the Tree* (1999), and, more recently, *Crossroads in Psychoanalysis, Buddhism, and Mindfulness* (Molino et al., 2013). Molino has as also previously interviewed Eigen (Molino, 1997) and began that interview with Eigen's insight that psychoanalysis has not wounded the Western ego as much as that psychoanalysis grew out of a wounded ego. The essential metaphor at the root of Eigen's thought is from a guide in the Nevada desert, who explained to Eigen that the branches of a cactus grow out of the place of woundedness and damage. The human personality, similarly, develops from points of injury and trauma. Molino emphasises the essential musicality of Eigen and the aesthetic nature of the psychoanalytic endeavour as a whole. The sense of being "tangled up in Mike" is derived from Molino's and many readers' sense of Eigen being in the mind of the reader in a creative dissolution of self–other distinctions, and through Eigen's capacity to articulate subtle states of mind. Besides Eigen and Molino being personal friends, they have a psychoanalytic ancestor in

Marie Coleman Nelson, who used the metaphor of harp strings to capture our disparate senses of self with the implicit sense of lack (Lacan), the crack, and opening. That opening becomes the Opening of the "Nothing (that) was all", from which the Branches of Light emerged. The inevitable deformities of being human lead Molino to reflections on Francis Bacon's painting and his feeling of their similarity to Eigen's descriptions of his patients—their beautiful, holy, yet ungodly, bodies. Molino further explores a song by the pop group Muse and evokes the image of a dying star, devoured by a black hole in an indifferent universe. By probing this image further, via the de-infinitization of the infant, Molino becomes aware of the gap though which light emerges. Molino concludes with a creative psychoanalytic deepening of Bacon's relationship to mouths and the imagery of orality. He references Eigen stating that not only is the face a source of light, but a matrix of faith.

In Chapter Seventeen, Molofsky engages with Eigen in the full ecstatic range of his writing. Herself a published poet and psychoanalytic writer, she opens by commenting on the vast and unboundaried range of Eigen's concerns. She writes in a highly personal and engaged manner, weaving Eigen's works on *Rage, Ecstasy,* and *Lust* with her own autobiographical and clinical material. By emphasising Eigen's title, "Feeling matters", she privileges an affective focus and directly takes as her starting point the experience of "craziness" as Eigen introduced in his first book, *The Psychotic Core.* The ego, Eigen contends, is both a hallucinatory organ and an adaptive agent with anti-hallucinatory properties. This allows for a language and psychological space in every person that has communicative value, and is not relegated to traditional medical model notions. As Daws reminds us in his chapter, Freud regarded the ego as a precarious clown attached to truth as much as delusion. Molofsky further conveys the sense of relief of having these psychotic elements of the psyche articulated—a language for primitive experience which is redemptive. For Molofsky, and Eigen as well, our original self is based in some form of madness, and a language that may express this makes for a creative acceptance of psychic life and its vicissitudes. Molofsky also artistically explores aspects of Eigen's affective trilogy, that is, *Ecstasy*, *Rage*, and *Lust* (Eigen, 2001, 2002, 2006), and its importance to affective, intrapsychic, and interpersonal growth. Through the key image of the Snake and the Snake Bite, Molofsky binds these themes together highlighting the intensity involved in "feeling" these feelings. For Molofsky, reading Eigen is a way in which she develops the capacity to reach these feelings on their own terms. In her case description of Candy, Molofsky describes an encounter with fragmentation and the potential for organization within primary process functioning, weaving together her own holding of "madness" and Eigen's affective trilogy.

Louis Rothschild, in Chapter Eighteen, explores Winnicott's "Z" dimension as it emerged in his personal life experience as well as Eigen's articulation of it. Winnicott's "Z" describes the absence beyond a period of time which then becomes unbearable for the infant. By taking this further and invoking the quality of mindfulness and mindful holding, Rothschild discusses the witnessing capacity that is needed to contain mother–infant interaction. This witnessing allows for a spacious containment of recurrent tragedies which, in Eigen's language, is the rhythm of catastrophe and faith, breakdown and recovery. As with other writers in this volume, Rothschild highlights mysticism, art, and joy as essential aspects of Eigen's perspective, emphasizing his poetic language, which has enlivened Rothschild as a person. Further, Rothschild foregrounds the importance of "decency" as an important attribute of the therapist. Following the Tibetan Buddhist teacher Chögyam Trungpa and adding another thread to the Buddhist–psychoanalysis dialogue, he writes, "Encounters with decency . . . are encounters with grace" (p. 312). By making reference to the popular cultural images of Mary Poppins and Harry Potter, he shows how these figures may not be characterised simply as sentimental or as part of denial, but may, in fact, through joy, be a way of being creatively present and, thereby, access O and the Real. The inevitable suffering of separation leads to the yearning for union, and this can be ameliorated by joy and the warmth of the therapeutic encounter. Rothschild's concerns become palpably real as he goes through a "scream cry" trauma with his son's hospitalization. This unbearable traumatic experience opens an opportunity for Rothschild to creatively work with the Kabbalah, containment, "Z", inevitable warping in experience, and the raw nakedness that this involves. He emphasizes the need for a "recovery space" where the scream can be met. In his moving description of his son's illness, Rothschild reaches the conclusion that it is bearing witness to "Z" that makes faith possible—"we find faith while listening to loss" (p. 321).

Eigen's oeuvre has been an extraordinary moment in the psychoanalytic canon—psychoanalysis in a new key, to paraphrase Suzanne Langer. Our call for papers was met with an enthusiastic and excited response from our contributors as well as from Karnac, suggesting that the idea was long overdue. Others regretted not being part of this project due to health and practical reasons. We were struck by the warm tone of the contributors in emails and papers, especially by those who have had direct contact with him, a mark of the respect and affection in which he is held. We are profoundly grateful for Michael Eigen's own encouragement and endorsement of this project and for suggesting the title of the book. It is our hope, as editors, that the reader may experience Eigen's vision and "soul" space in the various contributions of this volume.

We trust that this volume will be part of further extensions and evolutions of his contribution to psychoanalysis.

References

Civatarese, G. (2012). *The Violence of Emotions: Bion and Post-Bionian Psychoanalysis*. London: Routledge.

Civatarese G. (2014). Quoted by Eigen, M. MEigenworkshop@yahoogroups.com Sun 2014/03/09 12:57 a.m.

Daws, L. (1999). A psychodynamic study of differentiation impairment and symbiotic need in Burning Mouth Syndrome patients. Unpublished Masters Dissertation. University of Pretoria, South Africa.

Eaton, J. (2011). The obstructive object. In: J. L. Eaton (Ed.), *A Fruitful Harvest: Essays after Bion* (pp. 17–33). Seattle, WA: Alliance Press.

Eigen, M. (1981). The area of faith in Winnicott, Lacan and Bion. *International Journal of Psychoanalysis*, *62*: 413–433.

Eigen, M. (1985). Towards Bion's starting point: From Catastrophe to Faith. *International Journal of Psychoanalysis*, 66: 321–330

Eigen, M. (1986). *The Psychotic Core*. New York: Jason Aronson.

Eigen, M. (1992). *Coming though the Whirlwind*. Wilmette, IL: Chiron.

Eigen, M. (1993). *The Electrified Tightrope*, A. Phillips (Ed.). London: Karnac, 2004.

Eigen, M. (1995). *Reshaping the Self: Reflections on Renewal Through Therapy*. Madison, CT: Psychosocial Press (International Universities Press).

Eigen, M. (1996). *Psychic Deadness*. Northvale, NJ: Jason Aronson.

Eigen, M. (1998). *The Psychoanalytic Mystic*. London: Free Association Books.
Eigen, M. (2001a). *Ecstasy*. Middletown, CT: Wesleyan University Press.
Eigen, M. (2001b). *Damaged Bonds*. London: Karnac.
Eigen, M. (2002). *Rage*. Middletown, CT: Wesleyan University Press.
Eigen, M. (2004). *The Sensitive Self*. Middletown, CT: Wesleyan University Press
Eigen, M. (2005). *Emotional Storm*. Middletown, CT: Wesleyan University Press
Eigen, M. (2006). *Lust*. Middletown, CT: Wesleyan University Press.
Eigen, M. (2007). *Feeling Matters*. London: Karnac.
Eigen, M. (2009). *Flames from the Unconscious*. London: Karnac.
Eigen, M. (2011). *Contact with the Depths*. London: Karnac.
Eigen, M. (2012). *Kabbalah and Psychoanalysis*. London: Karnac.
Eigen, M. (2014a). *A Felt Sense*. London: Karnac.
Eigen, M. (2014b). *Faith*. London: Karnac.
Eigen, M. (2014c). Personal correspondence with Stephen Bloch and Loray Daws.
Eigen, M., & Govrin, A. (2007). *Conversations with Michael Eigen*. London: Karnac.
Epstein, M. (1996). *Thoughts without a Thinker*. London: Duckworth.
Epstein, M. (2001). *Going on Being*. New York: Broadway Books.
Epstein, M. (2013). *The Trauma of Everyday Life*. New York: Penguin.
Hillman, J. (2009). *Alchemical Psychology*. Putmann: CT: Spring.
Karnac, H. (2007). *After Winnicott: Compilation of Works based on the Life, Works and Ideas of D.W. Winnicott*. London: Karnac.
Karnac, H. (2008). *Bion's Legacy: Bibliography of Primary and Secondary Sources of the Life, Work and Ideas of Wilfred Ruprecht Bion*. London: Karnac.
Molino, A. (Ed.) (1998). *Freely Associated: Encounters in Psychoanalysis with Christopher Bollas, Joyce McDougall, Michael Eigen, Adam Phillips, Nina Coltart*. London: Free Association Books.
Molino, A. (1999). *The Couch and the Tree: Dialogues in Psychoanalysis and Buddhism*. New York: North Point Press.
Molino, A., Carnevali, R., Giannandrea, A., & Yang, D. (2013). *Crossroads in Psychoanalysis, Buddhism, and Mindfulness: The Word and the Breath*. New York: Jason Aronson.
Potter, B. (2012). *Elements of Self-destruction*. London: Karnac
Winnicott, D. W. (1945). Primitive emotional development. In: *Through Paediatrics to Psycho-Analysis*. London: Karnac, 1992.

PART I

REFLECTIONS

CHAPTER ONE

Bion, Eigen, and the dreaming of Kali

Stephen Bloch

Seeking out an old hermit
I climb the snowy peak to find his thatched hut empty.
As I descend empty hearted,
Suddenly, a wild singing, like murmurs of a dragon,
Echoes from the cloud-shrouded peak

(Sat Chuen Hon, 2003)

There are many images of the terrible mother, the dark goddess (Morrigan, the Black Madonna, Lilith, Medusa), but none strikes us as deeply as Kali. Kali is a personified archetypal image of terror and trauma and, at the same time, one of awe, fascination, and vitality. Her image evokes a ferocious aliveness, a terrible vitality, and, in every representation, a pulsing combination of annihilatory and life-giving properties—nullity and plenitude. Learning about Kali's symbolism and exploring her mysteries is experienced as an act of recognition, the rediscovery of something that has always been there. We know her name.

Jung (1959) speaks of Kali's paradoxical nature as being that of the loving and the terrible mother and, similarly, Zimmer (1972) writes of her creative and destructive principles as being one and the same. A more radical interpretation is suggested by Spielrein. In a paper entitled "Destruction as a cause of coming into being" (1912), she declares an originating primacy to the destructive dimension.

Kali's necklace of skulls, her long fangs, and her sword all point to the nature of existential suffering in what Rhode has called "an agony at the core" (2008, p. 147), as though she personifies the first noble truth of Buddhism, the actuality of suffering. In classical Indian symbolism, most of Kali's aspects refer to the sacrifice and necessary destruction of the ego in order to reveal non-dual awareness. We can, however, imagine her symbolism refracted though the prism of psychoanalysis. Here, her garland of skulls represents the unrepresentable: experiences that are unthinkable, destroy thinking, and that we cannot get our minds around. These are the primitive places where damage has occurred before thinking and image-forming capacities have developed. The skull garland comprises psychoanalytic understandings of the destructive object (Eigen, 1996), the persecutory object (Klein, 1946), the boundless object (Eigen, 1986), the obstructive object (Eaton, 2011), and the undreamable object (Eigen, 2000). Kali represents unprocessed catastrophic realities that have to be experienced before transcendent or meditative states of consciousness can be reached or, indeed, tolerated. Grotstein (1996) emphasises that whether the experience of O is ecstatic or one of horror is contingent on psychodynamic maturity, specifically, transcendence of the anxieties of the depressive position and the associated resolution of the mourning of object loss.

In this chapter, I intend to explore the imagery of Kali as it presents itself in the writings of Bion and Eigen. Although not mentioned directly by either writer, one can sense her presence as a backdrop to the work of both. In tracing a theme of Kali through aspects of Bion and Eigen, I hope to avoid a reductive "nothing but" approach. Rather, I intend to hold Kali up as an imaginal resonance and overtone to their work, to let her impact play off against their writings and enhance its significance, and to lift awareness to an implicit theme. And it is Bion and Eigen *in* Kali, for it is a contemporary hubris to view the deities as within, as part of us. As Christou writes, the psyche is not in us, but "it is we who are inside psyche" (1963, p. 75).

Kali in Bion

Bion's traumatisation in the First World War functions as a crucial bedrock of experience for, and root of, his writings. Its influence can be felt in both his clinical and autobiographical works, and there is now a significant body of papers that deal with this formative experience and its emergence in his theoretical concepts such as containment, beta and alpha functioning, and thinking under impact (see Brown, 2012; Souter, 2009; Szykierski, 2010). His emotional working through of this period continued throughout his life, as he attempted to digest an experience that was essentially unbearable; for example, in three different texts he works and reworks his abandonment of the dying Corporal Sweeting, on August 8 1917.

Bion's autobiographical works provide a major channel for narrative metabolisation. Yet, it may also be true that the grotesque experience of the war provided him with the content and form with which to dream even earlier experiences that were beneath and before representation, for which there was no name: annihilatory states for which there were no words, images or sounds—the "nameless dread".

* * *

A fantasy

Bion in no-man's land, in no-thing. He dies on August 8 1918 at Amiens. And never ceases dying, never ceasing to recover from his survival.

Never have I known such a bombardment like this

Never, never

Mother, Mother, Mother—

And then came the sound which came in gusts against the skin of face and hands as well as ears.[1]

Different silences. Tanks as containers—collapsing and exploding. Annihilatory flowering.

Hard, bright flames, as if cut from tinfoil, flickered and died, extinguished by the bright sun.[2]

Bion felt sick. He wanted to think ... He wanted to think ... He tried to think.[3]

Across the blasted landscape, at the edges Indian stretcher bearers, and through the fog Bion is calling to his ayah. A rising Black Sun. Gloss black against matt black. And a glimpse, the flash of an image from his childhood: Kali.

Urga-Kali, "the fierce Kali".

Something very beautiful—and very deadly.[4] She who dwells in the cremation grounds and battlefields.

An inverse flame opening into vastness.

He goes under, sinks down, beneath the capacity to think. And an old chant, a mantra, drifts through him. And the voice of his ayah: "*om hrim shreem klim adya kalika param eshwari swaha.*" The sound swells and disappears, carrying him, losing him, finding him. An ancient chant offering the possibility of coherence.

Bion is remembering a crude understanding of the chant, though the meaning is less consoling than the cadences of its sound: "Honour to She who is the originating one, her essence is an elemental blackness, the primordial feminine, who pierces illusion to the uncorrupted truth of existence."

* * *

It is not known if Bion knew of Kali from his *ayah*, or experienced an image of her at Amiens. We do know, however, that his Indian childhood remained with him throughout his life and that his *ayah* had recounted Indian mythological tales to him (Bleandonu, 1994). One can, however, sense the broad sweep of the mantra's meaning in his descriptions of O as the unknowable and unsymbolizable "ultimate reality"; "it is dark and formless" and "absolute truth" (Bion, 1970, p. 26). The experience of O is in some aspects one of dread, written in the key of terror, as Eigen has added.

Although not named as such, Kali can, in my understanding, also be seen as a background image to other of Bion's core themes. Bion is concerned with how thought happens at the edge of turbulence and catastrophe—Kali in her disruptive, dissolving aspects. His tracking of destructive processes in the psyche, elements which subvert thought and emotional growth, are essential aspects of his work. At the same time, Kali may be the catastrophic that needs to find a way to alpha dreaming. And when Kali reveals the Void, she is an expression of aspects of O, the beam of intense darkness, the awe of the dark and formless infinite. Bion asks us to tolerate both doubt and infinity.

Bion's arc passes from his *ayah* through Amiens and onwards; culminating in a vision of acute vulnerability and exquisite rapture:

> You would not know that the direction in which I was robbing you would lead from nothing to unconsciousness to sleep to dream to waking thoughts to dream thoughts to nothingness to O = zero, from O = zero to O which is Oh! = O which is a picture which is a picture of a hole or greedy mouth or vagina which offers perfect freedom which is death which is perfect freedom which is perfect pitch or absolute colour or Eternal Life or Eternal Death or Perpetual Motion or Perpetual Inertia or Absolute Space or space like mental space in which there are objects so compact they are like white dwarfs or so sparse and rare they can only be grasped by finite means . . . or so absolute a space that your mental life is itself destroyed . . . (1991, p. 38)

Kali in Eigen

Echoing Bion, Eigen writes, "Darkness becomes a mixture of menace and ecstasy . . . An electrified blackness and self-other awareness pass into one another" (1986, p. 167).

To become aware of Kali as an underlying image in Eigen's writings is to sense her traces everywhere. I suggest that she is an imaginal backdrop to his oeuvre, appearing in many of his books and papers, including *Rage* (2002), *Psychic Deadness* (1996), "Killers in dreams" (in Eigen, 2005), "Wordlessness" (in Eigen, 2011b), and *Ecstasy* (2001). Indeed, the titles of his two Seoul Seminars (2010, 2011a), "Madness and murder" and "Faith and transformation", would have been immediately recognisable to the great poet of the dark goddess, the eighteenth century Bengali poet, Ramprasad Sen.

I will trace the theme of Kali in four areas of Eigen's work:

1. Catastrophe and faith.
2. The unbearable.
3. Psychic deadness.
4. Destruction, creation, and aliveness.

Catastrophe and faith

In his seminal paper, "Toward Bion's starting points: between catastrophe and faith" (1985), Eigen traces a core trajectory in Bion's writing. Commenting that Bion's conclusions are difficult to hear, bear, or believe, Eigen explores further the clinical implications of the catastrophic origins of personality. Bion holds that our earliest experience can be likened to a Big Bang in which "primitive" and "incoherent" beta elements explode outward towards infinity with increasing velocity. The struggle of the infant and maternal container is to transform this disintegration into manageable experience. This involves the role of the containing mother in her reverie and the rudimentary alpha functioning of the infant. The crisis at the point of origination remains as an invariant and may be mapped into many other places of catastrophe, such as in failure, disease, castration, and falling. Just as the sound of the Big Bang can be discerned across great lengths of time, so, too, do the effects of psychological birth remain. According to Eigen, it is "an explosion that seems to go on forever, an ongoing catastrophic process expressed in the butcher's meat, wastelands and bleeding flowers of schizophrenic dreams" (2005, p. 38).

The faith that Bion is referring to is that radically open attitude that waits upon the impacts of experience. It involves the suspension and bracketing of memory, desire, and understanding. This surrender and relinquishment of knowing (K) allows a previously unborn image to emerge. Faith (F) is the psychoanalytic attitude that allows the selected fact, the selected image, to reveal itself. Eigen also states that it has a great deal to do with aliveness, a living of one's reality no matter the circumstances (Eigen, 2011a). The Pali word *sadha* carries with it meanings of faith, trust, and confidence: the gesture of placing your heart upon; of offering or giving over your heart (Salzburg, 2003). Similarly, Eigen evokes the biblical injunction of loving God with all your heart and mind in articulating the essential qualities involved in a lived relationship with the rawness of reality. In the context of this chapter, this requires an openness in relationship to its Kali aspects.

The movement from catastrophe to faith is the Kali explosion that struggles to find its way into form; the experience is redeemed because it has found the grace of containment and representation. The psychological gesture that allows this redemption is captured in Bion's Faith. With her stark imagery, Kali opens and develops the experiential capacity that this surrender demands.

T in O, F in O. T in Kali, F in Kali.

Kali connotes the primal catastrophe, its undreamable, unthinkable nature. At the same time, she is a portal to the great unknowing, the unforeclosed O, creative emptiness, and the transformations that occur here. These transformations in O are, in Eigen's elaborations, mysteries that are "wordless, imageless, and ineffable" (Eigen, 2011b, p. 4), in contrast to K transformations, which involve words, numbers, beliefs, and concepts. In this way, approaching the unknowable, ultimate reality involves an encounter with a destruction of knowledge, akin to the traditional symbolism of Kali's swords, which leads to the stripping away of mental constructs. O is involved in the "unobservable" and "inconceivable" domains captured by Eigen's citing of Buddhalands, a boundless silence as background support. There are transformations that occur in these wordless dimensions, beneath and unknown to our usual modes (see Eigen, 2011b, pp. 57–72). O is inexhaustible, "unknown and beckoning" (Eigen, 2012a, p. 45).

The unbearable

The need to endure unbearable experience is a *leitmotif* that runs through all of Eigen's work, and is perhaps *the* selected fact that emerges from the creative turbulence of his concerns. In *Damaged Bonds* (2000) he probes the difficulties of dreaming, which is, in Bion's use of the word, the way in which raw, beta elements are processed and digested by alpha functioning. Eigen's exploration reveals the full implications involved in this process: undreamable experience, damaged dreamwork, and an anti-dream object that subverts dreaming capacity. Where the impacts of experience and trauma are too overwhelming, the individual is unable to reach the necessary alpha dreaming capacity to digest and metabolise this experience. Dreamwork alpha cannot perform the psychological work necessary to recall, store, and process the material. The issue is that dismantled or corrupted dreamwork then results and therapy needs to support the development of dream-work alpha capacity.

According to Eigen,

> [t]he patient is terrified to assemble a dream in which the dreaded object or object beyond dread may appear . . . yet it is precisely the depths of death and shards of madness and the mad/maddening object that dream-work must endure or, at least, express. (2000, p. 38).

Here, Eigen highlights the place where broken dreams characterise the individual's experience and broken aspects of our sense of self (Eigen, 2010). Dreams depict interrupted, fragmented experience—processes which are in tatters and incomplete. Undreamable objects. Absence and no-thing. Broken dreams.

> Kali is the problematic in the dream—
> fragile alpha meeting
> the undigested beta impacts of O
> brave alpha wrestling
> the anti-dream object

Bion is concerned with the intersection of the infinite O and the lived emotional reality of every session—indeed, every moment and every dream. The impacts of O reach for the metabolisation and digestion through alpha dreamwork. Grotstein (2007) points out that these raw inchoate beta-elements are produced by the evolving O and its interaction with the emotional processing capacity of the subject. Like the Hadron particle accelerator, which creates ultra-high velocity collisions that result in the production of sub-atomic particles, we are tasked with digesting raw pre-thought particles spun off by the impacts of the infinite O with finite experience. An essential dimension of this is the processing of absence. The crisis is whether or not no-thing can be tolerated long enough for a thought, and finally a symbol, to emerge. The alternative is evacuation and the dismantling of mind. Mellick (1996) reflects that there is a place of absence, a void, in many dreams, perhaps in all. She notes how we encounter this in images of voiceless bodies, faceless figures, missing links between two dream scenes, and illogical endings. To this list we can add the e(E)mptiness of fading images, the help that cannot be contacted, broken cell phones, the lost passport, and the stolen credit card.

In his paper "Two kinds of no-thing" Eigen (1996b) extends Bion's assertion that we can only creatively grasp what *is* by awareness of what is *not*. The places an object does not occupy, its absence and nothingness function as a guardian of psychic life. Following on these insights, Becker and Shalgi expand on it clinical implications in their paper "On being, disappearing and becoming: a journey of surrender". They articulate the significance of non-being, vanishing, disappearing intrapsychically and interpersonally. The self creates and "becomes" through surrendering to this absence. An essential rhythm of appearing–disappearing is essential to vitality and protects against overpresencing, literalization, and concretization. The container–contained intersubjective field must itself yield to no-thing and live a creative oscillation between presence–absence; form–formlessness; being–not-being. This movement of becoming occurs in a dyadic surrender to "the infinite form of I–Thou" (Becker & Shalgi, 2013, p. 430).

In his paper "Killers in dreams", Eigen further explores facets of destruction and the murderous superego that destroys dreamwork, but which can be imaged as "various killers, invaders, kidnappers, rapists, shadow figures, predators threatening annihilation" (Eigen, 2005, p. 143). He also describes a radical, uncompromising, annihilatory force in the psyche, a force that shreds "and keeps on shredding until nothing is left . . . a relentless ethic, a nakedness [where] everything is stripped so that faith shines more brightly" (Eigen, 2005, p. 120). In these passages, Eigen draws on Bion's suggestion of a relentlessly destructive force that continues until time and space are themselves annihilated.

Eigen places the encounter between the catastrophic and the attitude of F within the context of Job and Yahweh, often referring to the core statement of Job, "Yea though you slay me, yet will I trust you," an imperative to embrace and stay open to redemptive possibility within unyieldingly painful and impinging experiences. This dialogue can also be imagined as taking place in the earliest relationship to the archaic feminine and the psychoanalytic garland of skulls described earlier. Job's words can be translated as expressing the faith and redoubled openness required in the face of destruction that Kali demands: the naked surrender in F needed to reach a sense of vitality. Eigen's explorations lead him to a double arrow between faith and catastrophe. It is not only from catastrophe to faith, but both dimensions have no meaning unless held in relationship to each other:

> faith is deeper than destruction and destruction deeper than faith. I want them as one thing . . . And maybe there are lots of different relations to each other . . . antagonistic relations, oppositional, maybe sometimes synchronous, fused, sometimes oscillating, sometimes all together at once. (Eigen, 2012a, p. 45)

Kali's disruptive turbulence has to be lived through before the creative emptiness is experienced. The no-thing void is Kali's home, but there is no access to this fertile void save through an initial confrontation with her frightening aspects. Eigen, in a passage in *Feeling Matters*, writes: "It is important for a baby to stare into the immensity of breathing and relax into the vast darkness surrounding light" (2007, p. 41). Without this capacity there is a frightening, paranoid, eye-filled landscape. Here, Eigen is exploring, among other things, persecutory monster eyes, and fields of impact and no-impact in the mother–infant and analytic fields. Kali breathes here, in being and non-being, presence and absence, nullity and aliveness. If the monstrous can be tolerated for long enough, the infant and the infant-in-us open up to the vast darkness surrounding light. Eigen's writings traverse both poles—early destroyed, murderous, and murdered states, and the fertile wordlessness of the creative void. Eigen has always held that vitality emerges out of the opening and exploration of dark places and catastrophic psychic realities, the greatest traction being rooted in work with extreme states of mind.

> In the sombre symbol of her eyeless muse
> The abysm of the unbodied infinite
> A fathomless zero occupied the world.
> As if a childlike finger laid on a cheek . . .
> An infant longing clutched the sombre Vast
>
> (from *Savitri*, Sri Aurobindo, 1954)

Deadness

Psychic deadness, a major concern of Eigen's, is the theme of his collection of essays of the same title (1996). Throughout his work, he traces the ubiquitous feeling of deadness in clinical cases and through theory, referring to Freud and Klein, but mainly to Winnicott and Bion.

In his case description of Lucy, in "The psychoanalytic mystic", Eigen explores protracted shutting down and the confluence of suffering and intensity. It is but one published example of how he works with deadness, deadliness, and nullity—Eigen at play in the fields of Kali. Eigen emphasises that for many years he did not try to take away Lucy's misery and agony. He felt that his task was to hold therapeutic "openness" as opposed to neutrality, and to live, indeed to be overcome by, these deathly states. For him, this involved experiencing feelings of vanishing and dying out into oblivion. He would feel the nulling, the going under, with her, and the sense of being annihilated by lethal forces. He describes how crucial it was for the "no-place chronic vanishing" to be allowed, for it to breathe: "Therapy provided the only no-where for Lucy's non-existence, a place/no-place where pain could reach vanishing points, and vanishing points could reach pain" (Eigen, 1996, p. 10). She hovered over zero, and was zero. Although not directly named, one can sense the pulse of Kali as Eigen and Lucy together lived through this destruction: "the formless poisonous obliteration ... [an] anti-O, a null-O, an O of poisonous blankness" (Eigen, 1998, p. 176). But Kali is not only these dark aspects. By staying close and honoring it, the malignant O began to shift and evolve, although never disappearing completely. A redemptive O began to emerge "smiling" at them both, becoming a place of rest rather than torment. A background unknown revealed itself as containing rather than tormenting and persecutory.

Destruction, creation, and aliveness

Another important theme in Eigen's texts is the roots of creation and aliveness in destruction. In a recent paper, Eigen returns to Winnicott to emphasise the destructiveness that is part of being alive and is more primary than models that focus on frustration—hate and guilt—reparation. Eigen writes of a "primordial destruction that is part of the rhythm of life" (2012a, p. 93); he notes how the world, life, and objects all partake of this basic pulse that is described in images, myths, psychotic experience, and trauma. I suggest that one such image is that of Kali. Winnicott himself described early experiences of breathing as fiery, and fire as having constructive and destructive meanings. Kali not only represents Thanatos but, perhaps even more, the terrors of aliveness inextricably tied into destructiveness. We hope that our Kali moments will be survived and not stifled into patterns of submission and false self. This survival allows for a sense of the other, the real, and, for Eigen, a sense of relief and joy. A great deal rests on the capacity to survive one another and for the self to survive its own destructive tendencies.

Themes of destruction and aliveness lead Eigen to a conjunction of Winnicott and Bion through the link of murder. While Winnicott explores the anxieties and fantasies of murdering, Bion describes states of *being* murdered (Eigen, 2004, pp. 27–36) and internal murderous forces. In all of this is a plea from Eigen for ways to bring the saving grace of awareness to murderous interaction, the double arrow of mutual killing as an unconscious conduit in psychotherapy and relationships. Here again, Kali is part of the interpersonal third in the emotional storm of two personalities meeting.

The paths surrounding Kali run in both directions; it is not only that aliveness originates in a sense of destruction. Eigen goes further, to describe how aliveness, specifically our emotional aliveness, may itself be destructive. In this way, vitalising emotions take the form of, and act as, killers in dreams, as though a raw energy builds up flooding the capacity to contain and represent it; there is "a feared overwhelming rise in energy, aliveness as destructive" (Eigen, 2005, p. 139). This represents a further nuance in the Kaliesque contiguity of aliveness and destructiveness. Eigen writes that Winnicott "[does] not emphasize a death drive . . . because the life drive wreaks enough havoc . . . Aliveness destroys—aliveness is dangerous" (Eigen, 2012b, pp. 1449–1450). Kali's symbolism invites a visceral encounter with this felt sense, and Eigen captures this destructive vitality when he writes, "A crucial part of what makes us feel alive threatens to murder us in our dreams . . . our sense of aliveness transforms into fear of annihilation" (2005, p. 140). Within Eigen's essays are insights regarding the difficulties in tolerating aliveness and beauty and, indeed, the potentially deadly aspects of being too alive. His insights constitute a significant lead into a theory of psychosomatics.

In several places, but principally in his Epilogue to *Psychic Deadness*, Eigen refers to a patient that Susan Deri presented to Bion. Deri maintained and contained a patient who would have then been described as chronic schizophrenic in a long-term therapy. The therapy allowed the patient to reach an acceptable level of functioning in terms of work and existence in general; he kept developing as an individual. Deri became anxious when her patient fell in love and feared that he might be overreaching himself—indeed, the patient died of a heart attack on his honeymoon. Deri, and later Eigen, questioned whether the patient's love and subsequent marriage were a bridge too far, a "burst of aliveness" which was too much for his psychophysical capacity. The narrative becomes a psychoanalytic cautionary tale as Eigen asks the crucial question: "How much aliveness can one take?" (Eigen, 1996, p. 225)

Eigen explores this theme further in a subsection to his paper, "The area of freedom" (1996, pp. 69–87), entitled "More than the heart can bear"; he writes of Winnicott's life experience, his psychophysical capacity, and his bodily sensitivity. He traces Winnicott's heart problems from soon after his father's death to the heart attack following his bruising presentation of his classic "Use of the object" paper to a group of New York analysts in 1968. What Eigen is concerned with is our capacity and equipment to deal with vitality and emotional aliveness. Eigen concludes, "Apparently Winnicott's psyche soma was unable to hold and process the affective impact at hand without explosive collapse" (1996, p. 84).

In his case description of Alice (1999, p. 80), Eigen again articulates the problems faced when therapy stimulates an aliveness that the body and psyche cannot sustain. Alice grew up in an environment of hate and loathing where her urge to be more was seen as menacing and "bug-like"; it had to be squashed. In her therapy, emergent aliveness fell flat because it could not be supported and bolstered by her system. She developed an autoimmune illness, a physical representation of her incapacity to handle too much of herself; aliveness itself was dangerous. There was only one way through for Eigen and Lucy: "To outflank the damage caused by becoming alive, we had to build a psyche to support the growing aliveness as we went, never without mishaps and ghastly setbacks" (Eigen, 1999, p. 81). These explorations have direct clinical implications—a patient may become too well for themselves.

Eigen also cautions against too much aliveness in the therapist, in the face of deadened and damaged states in a patient. Intensity overwhelms capacity, as in the Lurianic Kabbalistic image of the shattering of the vessels. In the end, these are alive or dead experiences in psychophysical capacity, in the body-mind, and are not merely emotional. Kali is one image with which to represent these surges, both in aliveness and destructiveness, and allow them to become creatively workable; she is a vessel, however grotesque, to hold experience.

Testament

Kali, in her radical O-therness, abjection, and alterity, hovers on the border of that which can be represented and that which remains undreamt, experiences which defeat mind and thought and also attack and destroy these processes. She initiates change and the catastrophic transformations that Bion addresses. At the same time, she opens into pregnant Emptiness and is life-giving. As Ramprasad sang, there is "grace and mercy in her wild hair" (1999).

A Kabbalistic injunction suggests that we each need to write our own Kabbalah, forged within, and filtered through, our own experience. The same may be true of Bion's texts. We each write our own Bion, our formulations wrought from our experience of him. Bion's theoretical and clinical writings are initially often obtuse and difficult to approach, requiring that the reader learn from the experience of metabolizing his unsaturated texts. Eigen's evocative, poetic style of writing is one such interpretation of Bion; it is a voice and a hermeneutic from within the emotional storm of experience, a howl from within the whirlwind. His dreaming and reading of Bion is a singular and evocative oeuvre—providing the emotional resonance, the affective heart to Bion's texts. Eigen dreams Bion and asks us to dream Bion with him. At the same time, we are being dreamed by Eigen in unique passages in which he explores his own psyche and draws us into our own, holding us as he probes deeper into the most searing, primal dimensions of psyche. To quote Eigen, quoting Bion, "I am his other self and it is a dream" (Eigen, 2009, p. 139).

Both Bion and Eigen have opened themselves up to a naked and flaying Kali, in both her destructive and transcendent forms. Both have emphasised the importance of psychoanalytical writing that evokes experience. As Bion notes,

> the criteria for a psychoanalytic paper are that it should stimulate in the reader the emotional experience that the writer intends, that its power to stimulate should be durable, and that the emotional experience thus stimulated should be an accurate representation of the psychoanalytic experience that stimulated the writer in the first place. (Bion, 1965, p. 65)

An important aspect of Kali's iconography is her tongue, which drinks up the blood of the *arusas*—the demons. The tongue is associated with tasting, the beginnings of digestion and absorption, but also with speech. There is much in Eigen on the importance of psychic taste buds in the savouring and deepening of experience. Many of his readers have felt the effects of his coruscating and courageous passages as deepening, containing, and opening experience. He has allowed himself to be immersed in, and acted upon, by intensely primitive parts of the psyche and found a voice to give them form, to convey a sense of their lived experience and evoke it in his reader. He has also, paradoxically, liberated an aliveness in his embrace of psychotic and destructive domains. It is not only that there may be valid parallels that can be traced between Eigen's work and the imagery of Kali but, more importantly, it is that his work represents a vivid description of Kali-like impacts moving in, around, and through him. It is a phenomenology of these states of mind. As such, Eigen's opus can be understood as a testament to an initiation.

Notes

1. "Never have I known . . . as well as ears" (Bion, 1997, p. 252).
2. "Hard bright flames . . . bright sun" (Bion, 1982, p. 254).
3. "Bion felt sick . . . tried to think" (Bion, 1997). I am indebted to L. J. Brown (2012, p. 1) for abstracting this crucial sequence in Bion's autobiographical writing.
4. "very beautiful [. . .] deadly" (Bion, 1997, p. 47).

References

Becker, M., & Shalgi, B. (2013). On being, disappearing, and becoming: a journey of surrender. *Psychoanalytic Dialogues: International Journal of Relational Perspectives*, *23*(4): 426–438.

Bion, W. R. (1965). *Transformations*. London: William Heinemann [reprinted London: Karnac, 1984].

Bion, W. R. (1970). *Attention and Interpretation*. London: Heinemann.

Bion, W. R. (1982). *The Long Week-End, 1897–1919: Part of a Life*. Abingdon: Fleetwood Press.

Bion W. R. (1991). *A Memoir of the Future*. London: Karnac

Bion, W. R. (1997). *War Memoirs: 1917–1919*. London: Karnac.

Bleandonu, G. (1994). *Wilfred Bion: His Life and Works*. London: Free Association Books.

Brown, L. J. (2012). Bion's discovery of alpha function: thinking under fire on the battlefield and in the consulting room. *International Journal of Psychoanalysis*, *93*(5): 1–24.

Christou, E. (1963). *The Logos of the Soul.* Vienna: Spring.

Eaton, J. (2011). *A Fruitful Harvest: Essays after Bion.* Seattle, WA: Alliance Press.

Eigen, M. (1985). Toward Bion's starting point: between catastrophe and faith. *International Journal of Psychoanalysis, 66*: 321–30. and in Eigen, M. (1993) *The Electrified Tightrope* (pp. 211–225). Northvale, NJ: Jason Aronson.

Eigen, M. (1986). *The Psychotic Core.* Northvale, NJ: Jason Aronson.

Eigen, M. (1996a). *Psychic Deadness.* Northvale, NJ: Jason Aronson.

Eigen, M. (1996b). Two kinds of No-Thing. In: *Psychic Deadness* (pp. 55–68): Northvale, NJ: Jason Aronson.

Eigen, M. (1998). *The Psychoanalytic Mystic.* London: Free Association Books.

Eigen, M. (1999). *Toxic Nourishment.* London: Karnac.

Eigen, M. (2000). *Damaged Bonds.* London: Karnac.

Eigen, M. (2002). *Rage.* Middletown, CT: Wesleyan University Press.

Eigen, M. (2004). *The Sensitive Self.* Middletown, CT: Wesleyan University Press.

Eigen, M. (2005). *Emotional Storm.* Middletown, CT: Wesleyan University Press.

Eigen, M. (2007). *Feeling Matters.* London: Karnac.

Eigen, M. (2009). *Flames from the Unconscious.* London: Karnac.

Eigen, M. (2010). *Eigen in Seoul Vol. 1: Madness and Murder.* London: Karnac.

Eigen, M. (2011a). *Eigen in Seoul Vol. 2: Faith and Transformation.* London: Karnac.

Eigen, M. (2011b). *Contact with the Depths.* London: Karnac.

Eigen, M. (2012a). *Kabbalah and Psychoanalysis.* London: Karnac.

Eigen, M. (2012b). On Winnicott's clinical innovations in the analysis of adults. *International Journal of Psychoanalysis, 93*: 1449–1459.

Grotstein, J. S. (1996). Bion's "transformations in 'O', the "thing-in-itself," and the "real": towards the concept of the transcendent position. *Journal of Melanie Klein and Object Relations, 14*(2): 109–141

Grotstein, J. S. (2007). *A Beam of Intense Darkness: Wilfred Bion's Legacy to Psychoanalysis.* London: Karnac.

Jung, C. G. (1959). *The Collected Works of C. G. Jung Vol. 9(i): The Archetypes and the Collective Unconscious,* R. F. C. Hull (Trans.). London: Routledge.

Klein, M. (1946). Notes on some schizoid mechanisms. In: M. Klein, P. Heimann, S. Isaacs, & J. Riviere (Eds.), *Developments in Psycho-analysis* (pp. 292–320). London: Hogarth.

Mellick, J. (1996). *The Individual Artistry of Dreams*. Berkley, CA: Conari Press.

Ramprasad, S. (1999). *Grace and Mercy in Her Wild Hair: Selected Poems to the Mother Goddess*, L. Nathan & C. Seely (Trans.). Prescott, AZ: Hohm Press.

Rhode, E. (2008). *Axis Mundi*. London: Apex One.

Salzburg, S. (2003). *Faith*. London: Element Books.

Sat Chuen Hon (2003). *Taoist Qigong for Health and Vitality*. Boston, MA: Shambhala.

Souter, K. M. (2009). 'The War Memoirs': some origins of the thought of W. R. Bion. *International Journal of Psychoanalysis, 90*: 795–808.

Spielrein, S. (1912). Destruction as the cause of coming into being. *Journal of Analytical Psychology, 39*: 155–186.

Sri Aurobindo (1954). *Savitri: Book 1, Part 1*. Pondicherri: Sri Aurobindo Ashram [reprinted Silver Lake, WI: Lotus Press, 1995].

Szykierski, D. (2010). The traumatic roots of containment: the evolution of Bion's metapsychology. *Psychoanalytic Quarterly, LXXIX*(4): 935–968.

Zimmer, H. (1972). *Myths and Symbols in Indian Art and Civilization*. Princeton, NJ: Bollingen.

CHAPTER TWO

Distinction–union: a Buddhist reflection on the great embrace

Mark Epstein

Over the course of his career, Michael Eigen (2011a) has developed the notion of a "distinction–union structure" to describe the subjective appreciation of the interpenetration of self and surround. Based on Winnicott's (1988) notion of an essential aloneness predicated upon good-enough environmental support, Eigen (2011a, p. 10) has written of how this interdependent conjunction has an ongoing psychic life.

> The environmental support our aloneness gets is necessary and remains part of our sense of aloneness all through life. We may not cognize it clearly, but it lives inside us, part of an indistinguishable nexus of support that feeds a sense of existing.

Eigen has called the background feeling of primary aloneness "boundless, unknown support," and, like Winnicott before him, has proposed that when there is damage to this system early in life, the personality pays a price. Wounded aloneness, akin to Michael Balint's concept of the basic fault, is one way of describing the toll the self pays for environmental, or relational, failures.

While Eigen's concept of a distinction–union structure emerged from his immersion in psychoanalytic thought, a similar notion exists in the realm of Buddhist psychology and philosophy. One of the core tenets of Buddhist thought is the self's lack of inherent existence. While this principle is often misunderstood to mean that the self does not exist *at all*, this is not what the Buddha's insight meant. Zen Buddhism has insisted that this particular misunderstanding (of self as absence) is akin to being trapped in a "demon cave." The Buddhist view of self–selflessness is much more nuanced than is usually assumed. It affirms that the self does not exist in the way we usually understand it (as a concrete entity, for instance) but it does not claim that it has no reality. Self, in the Buddhist view, is relative and relational, contingent and contextual. It can never be extracted from its environment. Indeed, the heralded experience of selflessness or emptiness, as reported by Buddhist masters over the centuries, is always accompanied by a fresh and poignant appreciation of the situational matrix in which the subject is embedded.

Some years ago, I began to teach about Buddhism and psychotherapy with two colleagues, Sharon Salzberg and Robert Thurman, and shortly thereafter I was made aware, in the context of this teaching, of a Tibetan–Mongolian version of Eigen's distinction–union structure. Sharon had been a friend since 1974, when I first began studying Buddhism. She had already been to India, discovered the wisdom of the Buddha, and was about to begin teaching intensive meditation retreats in this country when we met. Several years later, she co-founded the Insight Meditation Society in Barre, Massachusetts, where I have always gone on retreat. When I began my therapy practice, I would often refer to her patients who wanted to learn about meditation and around this time she moved to New York and began teaching Buddhism in the evenings to working New Yorkers who wanted to learn about it. Having her in New York City made the process of referral all the more easy. Robert Thurman was someone I had admired from afar. I had first observed him in action in the mid-1970s when he translated for the Dalai Lama on his first trip to the West. Thurman had ordained as a Tibetan Buddhist monk in 1964 with a Mongolian lama living in rural New Jersey and had gone on, at the lama's insistence, to become a professor of religious studies, first at Amherst and then, in 1988, at Columbia. I met him when he moved to New York and Sharon and I began to teach, at his invitation, at Tibet House in lower Manhattan shortly thereafter.

The first talk I ever gave with Bob centered on everything I had already learned from his writings and talks. I went through, point by point, each of the difficult Buddhist concepts he had elucidated for me. It was from Bob that I learned that meditation by itself was not enough, that trying to meditate without a clear idea of its purpose was like a blind man wandering about in open country with no idea of where he was heading. It was from Bob that I had learned that the root of the Sanskrit word for emptiness, *shunyata*, derives from a word meaning *to swell*. The metaphorical meaning of the word implies the swelling of a seed or the swelling of a pregnant womb. Buddha's emptiness was a full emptiness, one rich with potential, one big enough to hold the entire world of possibility, not an absolute nothingness the way I might have imagined it. And it was from Bob that I had learned about the Tibetan Buddhist concept of injured innocence (Epstein, 1995) as the psychological state most conducive to finding the self that Buddha said did not exist in the way we imagine. This became one of my favorite Buddhist notions. To understand selflessness, the cornerstone of the Buddha's psychology, one had to first find the self as it exists, as we actually feel it, and then examine the feeling closely. It does not work to just write the self off, to try to convince oneself that it is an illusion. When a friend or loved one accuses you of doing something that you know you did not do, when they treat you in a way that you know you do not deserve, a strong feeling of *me* arises. The thought that often comes in such a situation is something in the order of, "How could she do that to *me,* how can she treat *me* this way?" In the Tibetan tradition, this occasion is a golden opportunity to zero in on the self that normally drives us. In more heated states of rage or desire or jealousy the feeling of *me* is obscured by the overpowering intensity of the emotion, but in these periods of hurt feelings—of injured innocence—there can be enough room left for a modicum of self-observation. Bob could make these concepts ring true and I did not tire of listening to him or reading his work. He always deepened my understanding.

One of my favorite lines from Bob came out one day when he was reminiscing about his old Mongolian Lama explaining the nature the Buddha's teachings about self. "It's not that you're not real," he exclaimed to Bob at one point. "Of course you're real! But the problem with you is that you think you're *really* real." It was this extra quality, of *really* real, that the Buddha suggested was at the root of much self-imposed misery. Bob called this extra quality the intrinsic identity instinct, or the intrinsic identity habit, and described it as the way we each, secretly and unconsciously, feel ourselves to exist *absolutely*, apart from everyone else and the world. In psychodynamic terms, an equivalent might be found in the concept of annihilation anxiety, or annihilation dread. We are all protecting our insecure sense of ourselves, our feelings of existing independently and autonomously in the midst of so many other independent and autonomous people. Even as infants, we fear our vulnerability and dependence and contort our minds to protect ourselves. The various mechanisms of defense, such as splitting, depersonalization, and dissociation, outlined in psychoanalytic thought, derive in good part from this effort at self-protection.

As the Dalai Lama (Gyatso, 1984, p. 70) once explained it, "This seemingly solid, concrete, independent, self-instituting I under its own power that appears actually does not exist at all." Those adjectives used by the Dalai Lama are important. They seek to convey what Thurman's Mongolian teacher was getting at when he used the phrase *really* real. Much of our psychic energy goes into sustaining this assumption of being solid, concrete, independent, and self-sufficient. What would we be without it? To my mind, the work of Michael Eigen aims directly at this question.

"What does one do with the emotional knot or core that is compressed pain, ecstasy, hate, domination, submission, caring, sex, hunger, fear, worry, grief, madness and the drive for truth?" he asks.

"All of these fuse to a dense navel, congealed ball, fist. The knot can be radioactive, malignant, demonic, longing, aching for the freedom of good moments, hoping against hope it won't stuff good moments with rot" (Eigen, 2001, p. 86). Eigen's view parallels that of the Buddha. Both agree that our true natures are obscured by our instinctive habits of thought. Dread keeps us from knowing our full potential.

One day when the three of us were teaching, Thurman reached impulsively for a volume of his called *Essential Tibetan Buddhism*. His sudden move was not entirely unfamiliar. His book contained a range of materials, essential texts in an amazingly rich Buddhist tradition, most of which Thurman had translated into English for the first time. He knew them well and often referenced them to make a point. On this particular day, he was talking about *Mahamudra*, the experiential knowledge of the union of appearance and emptiness. *Mahamudra* is traditionally translated as "The Great Seal," but this translation is imperfect as the original meaning is quickly lost when rendered into English in this way. "Seal" refers not to a marine animal, but to a wax seal, the kind used to close letters in times gone by. The idea is that appearance and emptiness are one, that they are tightly bound, inseparable, each making the other possible. A better translation than "Great Seal", said Bob, might be "The Great Embrace." At the center of many Tibetan paintings, in a *yab-yum* display that confounded their first Western beholders, is often to be found copulating couples, representing the union of compassion (male) and wisdom (female). Their wisdom is the wisdom of emptiness (of *shunyata*) and their compassion is the altruistic expression that pours out of their true understanding. Sometimes called "Bliss–Void Indivisible", these depictions of intercourse also represent the union of ultimate and relative realities. The implication is that the awakened state found by the Buddha does not exist apart from our everyday world, that the compressed knot of emotional pain described by Michael Eigen is also the ecstatic bliss of orgasm and enlightenment. While Freud dwelt on the psychopathology of everyday life, Buddha was busy describing its perfection. Enlightenment is one and the same as this world of suffering, he said. It is revealed when our habits of obscuration, our fears of annihilation, are relinquished.

In Tibetan Buddhism, the stages of realization that come from meditation are sometimes compared to the process of falling in love (Epstein, 1998). It is said that the bliss of sexual union with a cherished partner is the closest we can come in everyday life to knowing the underlying nature of reality as grasped by the Buddha. Looking, smiling, embracing, and orgasm are used to refer to the different layers of realization. But this is not the only allegory that the Buddhist traditions have employed. The smiling face of the mother as she engages with her baby is another important example, another version of "The Great Embrace." It was this notion that inspired Thurman on this particular day. He realized he had translated a poem about it, one that I had never bothered to look at, buried, as it was, on page 209 of his text (1995), deep in Chapter Six, in a chapter entitled 'Practicing the liberating wisdom.' I prided myself on having read most of Thurman's body of work, but I had not made it all the way through this one and the poem took me completely by surprise.

But there it was, "The Discovery of Mother Voidness: A Song of Enlightenment" by the great Mongolian Lama Jankya Rolway Dorje (1717–1786), written at the sacred mountain Wu Tai Shan in Shensei province of China in the aftermath of his awakening. His name meaning "playful *vajra*" (or thunderbolt—a common Tibetan symbol of the wisdom that comes through the transformation of anger), Rolway Dorje's verse was in a long line of "enlightenment songs," whose function is to express (in Thurman's words) "joy and appreciation in the euphoria and lucidity of just having attained a comprehensive freedom from ageless suffering and anxiety" (1995, p. 311).

The Buddha began the tradition of enlightenment songs by spontaneously breaking into ecstatic verse after his enlightenment. "Oh, housebuilder," he exclaimed, "you have now been seen. You shall build this house no longer!" The Buddha was referring here to the intrinsic identity instinct, the unconscious tendency to impute an extra solidity to people and things. His "house" was his identity, the self that he believed existed "absolutely", separate and apart from the rest of the world. The "housebuilder" was his "thirst", "craving" or "clinging", his need for control, coherence, stability, permanence, or some kind of absolute, unchanging, and fixed reality. He was able to see within himself that which created both the illusion of his own isolation and the dread of annihilation. Many hundreds of years later, in the midst of the Manchu empire, Jankya Rolway Dorje composed his own such verse, paralleling that of the Buddha while opening another approach to the Great Embrace. It was this alternative approach that Bob was reaching for when he remembered the eighteenth century poem.

In an extended digression, Bob had just been talking about how his mother had once been a promising actress, Bette Davis's roommate in drama school, who had chosen, with some un-worked through ambivalence, to have children rather than pursue a career in the theater. Bob had always felt somewhat responsible for her unhappiness, he admitted. She had continued to have her Shakespeare coach to a weekly Sunday lunch, however, and, in accord with British theater tradition, had turned those meals into readings of Shakespearean drama with the children at the table assigned the most ambitious roles. Bob had grown up reading Shakespeare, and he used his oratorial skills to good effect in bringing this obscure poem to life. Sharon and I, along with our audience, sat transfixed as Bob began to recite.

"O Thatness of profound Relativity—O Wonder!" he began, as the old Mongolian Lama began to peek his way through Bob's late twentieth century veneer. The turquoise lariat he wore dangling around his neck seemed suddenly more Tibetan than Navaho.

> *May the Guru who nakedly reveals this as it is,*
> *His kindness irrepayable, be enthroned in my heart!*
> *I will speak spontaneously whatever comes to mind!*

I was struck by the last line—"I will speak spontaneously whatever comes to mind." It startled me a little, evoking, as it did, the psychoanalytic tradition of Freud, whose technique of free association rested on just this activity. They already knew about free association in the 1700s in Mongolia, I thought? I waited for what might come next. What would a newly enlightened Lama spontaneously declare?

> *I was like a mad child long lost his old mother,*
> *Never could find her, though she was with him always!*
> *But now it seems I'm about to find that kind old mother,*
> *Since Big Brother Relativity hints where she hides*

It was difficult for me to listen too carefully once Bob had belted out the first several lines of this verse. Something was choking up inside. "Like a mad child long lost his old mother, / Never could find her, though she was with him always." My mind kept repeating the phrase. I had not lost my own kind mother but that did not stop me from relating to the notion of a "mad child." Winnicott (1992, p. 571) once wrote that there are two categories of people in the world, those who "carry around 'having been mad'" and those who do not. By "mad" he meant crazy, not angry, but there was a strong link between the two in his thinking. "Having been mad", he proposed, meant there was once "a breakdown" at the dawn of an individual's life, a breakdown in the dynamic parent–infant environment that supports and facilitates development. It is not usually the infant that breaks down in this scenario, at least not initially, but it is the maternal function (whomever is doing the child-rearing) that falls prematurely away. Here was a Buddhist monk alluding to the same phenomenon.

When Winnicott wrote his little formulation about "having been mad", he was summarizing his life's work for a 1967 meeting of a society of British analysts called the 1952 Club. He passed around mimeographed notes before speaking, notes which have survived, that provided an outline of his essential ideas. Those who carry around having been mad, he explained, experience themselves in certain classic ways. He listed the following:

falling forever
de-integration
disorientation
depersonalization, etc.

Winnicott liked to infer what failure must have felt like to a person not yet consolidated enough, or mature enough, to symbolize, or contain, or understand, what was happening when the infant–mother bond was challenged. It had to be preserved non-conceptually, he reasoned, at least originally.

"Panic," he specified in his outline (p. 572), is a "defence against unthinkable anxiety." By defense, he meant a more tolerable substitution, a way of coping by creating an emotional event that can be known or communicated. We know what panic is, even if it threatens to overwhelm us. And we panic with the hope that someone will rescue us, or at least notice us. As a creative construction, panic conveys a sense of the unthinkable while still being within the realm of the mundane. But panic, felt Winnicott, is never just panic. It is a defense *against* something worse, a way of both approaching and pushing away something for which there is not only no words, but no thoughts. The thing that panic defends against must have happened before thinking did. Thus, it remains an unthinkable anxiety: a madness carried around by its unsuspecting progenitor.

Thurman was evoking all of this for me while reading the Mongolian verse. As I listened to him continue, I began to wonder how Winnicott would have responded to this poem. Rolway Dorje's song was making the two come together for me.

I think, "Yes, yes!"—then, "No, no!"—then, "Could it be, really?"
These various subjects and objects are my mother's smiling face!
These births, deaths, and changes are my Mother's lying words!
My undeceiving Mother has deceived me!
My only hope of refuge is in Big Brother Relativity!

The poem, as Bob explained, takes the smiling face of the mother as the prototype of the awakened mind. A mother feels her infant to be the best of her and regards him thus. Her gaze is the exact opposite of the killing egotism that rules much of our inner life, wherein we seek to destroy whomever threatens our pre-eminence. The mother is the most highly evolved of our mammalian species; through learning to nurture and develop life within her own body, she has achieved a capacity for empathy and compassion that the rest of us are still searching for. This verse describes the perplexity of the monk as his understanding dawns. He has been searching for something outside of himself, imagining enlightenment as some kind of external achievement, or as some kind of perfection, as a place to be journeyed to or a state to be achieved. As he awakens, he starts to get glimmers of enlightenment in the everyday. He wonders if it could really be so and begins to see that his habits of mind have kept him removed. As he begins to nakedly experience reality as it actually is, he feels the presence of his long-lost mother all around and through him. A world of objects comes alive as a dynamic flowing body of love. The world that was threatening him with its births, deaths, and changes bursts open as his mother's smiling face. An ancient story of the Buddha giving a sermon by silently holding up a flower springs to mind. Only one elderly monk understood and smiled. The Buddha saw the smile and indicated his approval. A non-verbal mind-to-mind transmission took place. "This monk knows my mind," the Buddha acknowledged. For Jankya Rolway Dorje, the entire world became the Buddha's smile and the Buddha's smile became the mother.

For me, as I listened to the Shakespearean overtones of Thurman's booming voice, the smiling face of Winnicott rose to meet me. I was having several thoughts at once. Myself as a mad child; Bob feeling responsible for his mother's frustration; Winnicott writing of falling forever and carrying around having been mad; the Buddha holding up a flower on Vulture's Peak when already awakened. And then I started to wonder. Did part of my attraction to the Buddha's thought lie in the way that it spoke, subconsciously, to those who carried around having been mad? Could that early loss be reverberating in the Buddha's teachings? And was Winnicott, in focusing for the first time in psychoanalytic history on the effects of early disruptions in mother–infant bonding, approaching a Buddhist perspective through the doorway of a good-enough mother's ordinary devotion? I felt many worlds converging as I listened to Thurman start on the next verse:

But the sole chance for freedom is just old Mother's love;
. . . these various changes
Are but the changes of the unchanging Mother!

For a moment, the Great Embrace of *Mahamudra* was not only the union of appearance and emptiness, of relative and ultimate realities, of the mother and father in sexual union, or the ordinary devotion of the mother–infant couple. It was also the romance between Winnicott and Buddha, a romance that, for the moment, seemed to exist only in my own mind, but one that I hoped could continue reverberating as the teachings of the Buddha came to rest in the West.

And reverberate it has, most particularly in the recent work of Michael Eigen. "Winnicott writes of essential aloneness," Eigen has written (2011b, p. 19).

> Now that's a strong term. Essential aloneness. He feels that we are essentially alone. He says the baby is supported in an alone state by a not quite cognized presence. That is, we are supported. When we are supported well we are supported in an alone state without quite realizing we are getting support. That's why if therapy goes well, patients may feel they've done it all by themselves and the therapist did very little. The patient didn't know it was the therapist who helped. Well. That's a very good kind of help.

Eigen, like the Mongolian Lama before him, affirmed that our essential aloneness is supported by an unknown boundless presence: by the smiling face of the parent. For many people, aloneness can be wounded and can seem oppressive, as it would to a mad child long lost to his old mother. But there is another experience of aloneness waiting in the wings, one that can be divined with proper support and guidance, one that is part of our birthright. "Never could find her, though she was with him always!" sang the newly enlightened Lama. Eigen (2011a, p. 16) has said something similar in his description of the distinction–union structure. "To be permeable and distinct, connected and separate, in union yet distinct, is part of our plasticity and persistence, part of the mystery, difficulty, and creative challenge of our nature. Can we make room for ourselves?"

Eigen's depiction of self as a distinction–union structure is an important bridge between Buddhism and psychoanalysis. It brings the seminal contributions of Winnicott into a conversation with the ancient wisdom of the Buddha, enriching our understanding of both while making it more possible to, in his words, make room for ourselves.

References

Eigen, M. (2001). *Ecstasy*. Middletown, CT: Wesleyan University Press.

Eigen, M. (2011a). *Contact With the Depths*. London: Karnac.

Eigen, M. (2011b). *Eigen in Seoul* (Volume Two): *Faith and Transformation*. London: Karnac.

Epstein, M. (1995). *Thoughts Without a Thinker*. New York: Basic.

Epstein, M. (1998). *Going to Pieces Without Falling Apart*. New York: Broadway.

Gyatso, T. (1984). *Kindness, Clarity, and Insight*. Ithaca: Snow Lion.

Thurman, R. A. F. (1995). *Essential Tibetan Buddhism*. New York: Harper SanFrancisco.

Winnicott, D. W. (1988). *Human Nature*. New York: Routledge.

Winnicott, D. W. (1992). *Psycho-Analytic Explorations*, C. Winnicott, R. Shepherd, & M. Davis (Eds.). Cambridge, MA: Harvard University Press.

CHAPTER THREE

The work of Michael Eigen: into the heart of psychoanalysis

Marlene Goldsmith

Introduction

Michael Eigen brings us into the living pulse of his psychoanalytic vision and praxis. We experience the vicissitudes of patient and analyst in all their anguished, despairing, sacred, and ecstatic dimensions. Eigen reveals multiple facets of the inner world of both, where nothing is univocal and experience is prismatic. Psychological processes and person-to-person affective engagement constitute dynamic unfolding events that take precedence over static states and content. Emotional pain, evolving struggle, and ambiguity, erase categorical thinking. Eigen does not attempt to create a systematic theoretical paradigm with well-differentiated concepts. Such systems erase the raw aliveness of experience. Theoretical concepts often deform the phenomena they are meant to study, providing ill-fitting categories that cannot accommodate the multi-faceted, a rational nature of psychic events. His purpose ". . . is less 'explanation' than appreciation and the growth personal encounter brings" (Eigen, 1986, p. 84).

Heart, as used here, refers both to the core matter of psychoanalysis (the heart of the matter), and to the passion, lifeblood, and humanity enlivening this subject matter (a heart of flesh). Filled with wonder and a love of psyche, Eigen's evocative, poetic writings endow psychoanalysis with a heart in both senses of the word. His view of the boundless unknown, feeling, faith, and emotional transformation comprise its central heartbeat, pumping fires of life into the bloodstream of psychoanalytic vision and discourse. How they do so will be described below in four separate sections, each section concerning one of the four core phenomena. I would like to stress, however, that the latter are all interwoven; they have been separated for the purposes of discussion. The four constitute reciprocally informing structures that participate in one another. One cannot be discussed without touching upon the others. Occasionally, one or more will be referred to before a fuller discussion in its primary section.

The infinite boundless unknown: source and background support of existence

An essential dimension of Eigen's vision is the "infinite boundless unknown". Elsewhere, it has been referred to by many other names, God, the absolute, the One, Consciousness, and so forth. It creates us and forms the ineffable background support of our lives. Bion, a psychoanalyst with whom Eigen dialogues extensively, refers to it as O or "infinity" (Eigen, 2011a, pp. 3–4, 10). O is our fundamental reality, in which inscrutable transformations "work and influence us, even structure us". Through their workings, we undergo endless development and growth. Unknown processes assure our psychic momentum and flexibility. Although unfathomable, we live these processes and they participate in our growth. They shape and re-shape us, sometimes warping us (2011a, pp. 1, 4–5, 59).

Our relationship to O is fraught with ambiguity. O can appear frighteningly deformed or sacred. We often feel helpless as it washes through our lives, our psychic capacities of "perception and awareness" insufficient to assimilate its enormous intensities. Out of the dread it arouses, we transmute O into a monster. Discussing the demons and monsters of Buddhist art, Eigen mentions their relationship to "deformations of vision owing to lack of capacity to take too much intensity of experience" (2012, p. 122). We are painful, sometimes disastrous, disturbances to ourselves. Our psyches produce more than we can digest, often with distorted or even violent consequences. Eigen iterates throughout his work that we must become "partners" with our capacities to prevent such outcomes.

Despite our ambiguous relationship to O, the origins of our creativity and very existence emerge from its ineffable depths. O is our very being. Certain scientists also share this view. According to David Bohm, the physicist Eigen refers to in *Contact With the Depths*, "We are expressions of creative processes that permeate the universe" (2011a, p. 3). Our creative sense in living and working arises from an unseen order that is one with reality and lacking in differentiations.

O quickens our lives. A primordial "O-sense" presses for creative expression. It gives rise to the materials necessary for this expression: paint, stone, language, musical instruments, etc. (Bion in Eigen, 2012, p. 102). Expressive action, palpable engagement with artistic materials, creative movement through inner and outer worlds, embodiment of emotion in works of art, all these issue from O. In my view this demonstrates how the unknown engages us sensually in a sensual world. O permeates and fires our psychosomatic existence. It touches the quick of enfleshed feelings, issuing in a heartfelt expression of beauty.

According to Eigen, some acquire "a taste for the mystery itself" (2011a, p. 72). In stillness we wait to be touched by the unknown, longing to fill our hearts with the unutterable peace, rapture, and beauty communion brings (2011a, p. 35). We open out from our heart to the unknown heart of existence, aching to touch the ground of our being.

O is not only peaceful. Just as it creates us, it can deform us, wreaking havoc. Bion writes of a destructive force that goes on functioning after all existence has been destroyed (Eigen, 2011a, p. 5, 59). At times when we feel estranged from O and desperately alone, in these moments we reach out, broken-hearted, in anguish, hunger, despair, and misery.

Waves of emotion permeate our relationship to O. Within the psychoanalytic context, Bion views O as unknown emotional reality. Although wordless, imageless, and ineffable, this unknown is the primary of sessions. The psychoanalyst brings a radical openness to her work. Concern lies with the unknown rather than with the known. Indeed, unknowing becomes a method. Eigen writes an entire chapter on the phrase "I don't know", in order to dignify and celebrate it

(2011a, p. 31). In it, he discusses Bion's definition of the psychoanalytic attitude as faith; that is, entering the session without memory, desire, understanding, or expectation. Patience and waiting without intention characterize work with unknown emotional realities. The therapist waits with a ready, open heart. Often wordless, transformative processes occur without the therapist's knowledge. Eigen writes, "One may sense something, an intimation, a felt change without knowing what it is. Something is happening we say. Something is happening we as yet have no words for" (2012, p. 119). Once known, more of the inexhaustible unknown emerges.

I envision an open heart of attentive aliveness at the core of the psychoanalytic attitude. We wait with an alert sensitivity to what might emerge. Unknown wordless stirrings in the form of vague sensations or intuitions thrum through the heart's chambers. These constitute bodily sensations that further enhance aliveness and enrich open sensitivity.

During sessions, the psychoanalyst becomes the unknown boundless other of background support. Such support allows the patient to "relax into" herself. It provides the silence, or "Sabbath point of the soul", that Eigen views as essential for processing affects, although he adds that "You don't have to be silent for silence to happen" (2011b, pp. 24–26).

By referring to this silence as the "Sabbath point", Eigen emphasizes its sacred quality. Affects are processed within its holy stillness. Silence penetrates both patient and therapist, deepening such feelings as awe, respect for suffering, love, tenderness, and compassion. Sharing sacred stillness, an experience of the heart, is transformative for both.

As with so many of the phenomena Eigen addresses, a paradoxical quality characterizes the therapist's presence. Not all is peaceful in sessions "Because we are traumatizers" (2011b, p. 28). When a person puts herself at risk and allows dependency to grow deeply, pain emerges. Her heart will be broken. The practitioner will fail her. For Eigen, wounded trust is inevitable in human relationships.

> The person is going to go through hell. And you're going to go through hell together . . . and you come through as human beings together. You don't go through dependency perfectly, you get hurt, but you go through in a better way than you did before . . . and it was worth it. (2011b, p. 28)

Coming through a perfect therapy does not heal. What heals is *how* both partners come through therapy. Even though it is a hardship, even though patient and psychotherapist traumatize one another, they survive one another. Neither one is immune and neither one abandons the other. The psychoanalyst communicates wordlessly, by her presence, that she can tolerate the patient's intense suffering, rage, shame, terror, and so forth. Cycles of "spontaneous recovery, spontaneous traumatization, spontaneous recovery" repeat themselves, establishing a "rhythm of recovery". The patient learns she can survive her therapist, her therapy, and her life (2011b, pp. 28–29). Despite the psychotherapist's traumatizing presence, she has been there, paradoxically, as the unfathomable boundless other of background support.

Paradox marks much of Eigen's writing. He demonstrates repeatedly that our psychic existence is multi-dimensional, encompassing opposites that do not cancel one another out. I believe this co-existence of opposites leads to a synthetic approach rather than to analytic, categorical thinking. Our view becomes flexible and broadens. We need not erase one or two or more contradictory dimensions operating at the same time.

The boundless unknown itself is a paradox. It is the ground of our being, that which gives birth to us. Its forces circulate in and through the bloodstream of our psychosomatic being. Without its holy pulse, we would not exist. Moreover, we are O. It is the heart of our being; we could not be closer. Nevertheless, O remains ineffable, a reality forever beyond our grasp, the paradoxical unknown heart.

Feeling: a foundational psychic phenomenon

For the purposes of this chapter, I use feeling, emotion, and affect interchangeably. Eigen never explicitly differentiates them. I believe they comprise a unitary phenomenon, shading into one another with broad areas of overlap, distinguishable but not separable.

* * *

Eigen describes the emotional background of our existence as ". . . unknown infinity with a million faces (experienced/filtered through dread, agony, rage, joy) . . ." (2012, p. 112). Our affects have both mystical and cosmic underpinnings (1986, p. 211). In this sense, I understand them as connecting us to other realms of existence. The emotional unknown, coursing through our palpable emotions, endows them with an unfathomably mysterious resonance. Inasmuch as unknown infinity is an emotional background, feeling becomes primary to the foundational dimension of our being. As will be shown below, it is the source of many essential aspects of the psyche.

At the heart of our psychic existence lie terror, dread, and devastating collapse. A cataclysmic feeling courses through the psyche. It has been there since its birth, when a permanent wound was inscribed into psychic foundations, one we will never escape. According to Bion, the psyche undergoes a constitutive catastrophe just as it begins to form. In this way, a catastrophic element becomes part of its nature, but also a thread binding personality together. "We are catastrophic beings and our sense of being [so] . . . is often part of our most intimate feeling" (Eigen, 2012, p. 41). Eigen calls our feel for this damage a "catastrophic sense" (2011a, pp. 65–66).

I understand Eigen to be saying that we are tragic beings, struck by a paradoxical, evolving catastrophe that damages then knits together our personality. However, for Eigen we are not just tragic beings. Feeling, in its multi-dimensionality, also plays a role in the emergence of ethics, beauty, space, and the dream.

Ethics and beauty are deeply interrelated. In discussing the divine flow of energy through the *Sephirot*, or Kabbalistic Tree of Life, Eigen comes to the place where *Tiferet*/beauty holds sway. It is the middle or heart of the tree.

> The association of heart and beauty is profound. We are deeply touched by the beauty in life, its association with time, loss, poignant longing, the ache of being . . . I feel that beauty is one root of ethics, a sense of wanting to do right by life, to do justice to that which can so arouse such depth of feeling . . . (2012, p. 82)

For me, the heart carries an intimate connection, literally and figuratively, with life and death. Its pulsing keeps us alive; its failure to do so results in death. It also holds connotations of being the source of all feeling. Beauty, through its linkage to the heart of the tree, takes on multi-dimensional meanings. It touches us in the heart of our existence, where life, death, and feeling throb. In turn, our hearts are filled with beauty's inextricable connection to our ephemeral existence and the related feelings of longing, ache, and loss. From the heart of the tree to our heart and back again, a deep empathy, gratitude, and, as Eigen points out, desire for justice, emerge. Ethics is our response. Through it we validate and honor that which moves us so completely.

The psychic phenomena of space and dreaming have deep connections to feeling. Being filled with, or emptied of, emotion makes possible our sense of external space. "Originary space is affective space" (Bion, in Eigen, 2007, p. 29). Citing Bion, Eigen writes that the core (or heart) of our dreams is emotional experience and not manifest content (in Eigen, 2011b, p. 2). Varying emotional currents conjoin in the dream, which is "a magnet for emotions", drawing them in "to express and digest them". Dreams aid in forming emotions and slanting how they are born (2011b, p. 3). Although not explicitly articulated by Eigen, emotions more than likely give birth to, and shape, the images of the dream in a reciprocal exchange. Once again, two terms, emotion and image, co-constitute one another as part of a larger unfolding pattern, the dream.

A co-constitutive dynamic also exists between the body and affects. Eigen describes an inextricable, reciprocal relationship between the two. Each is inscribed in, and forms, the other. He writes that "... affective attitudes mould the body and vice versa" (2011a, p. 58). He speaks of "sensation–feeling blends". Sensation is a type of feeling he refers to as "felt sensation", and feeling is a type of sensation he calls a "feeling sensation" (2012, p. 87).

As I understand Eigen, sensation is not a static, mechanical process devoid of significance. It incarnates feelings. The latter's inchoate meanings are one with it. In turn, sensation gives feeling palpable vibrancy. According to Eigen, sensation plays a part in "feeling feelings." As such, it plays a constitutive role in making the lived experience of feeling possible (2012, p. 113).

Eigen is not a dualistic thinker. Once again, he envisions a dynamic, unfolding structure containing distinguishable, but not separable, dimensions. Feeling and sensation form a unitary phenomenon.

Feeling constitutes the foundational dimension and primary agent of change in the psychoanalytic endeavor. Affective attitudes are a "raw material" that shape us even as we shape them, "creating richly textured possibilities of being" (2007, p. 21). In psychoanalysis, they become the medium for creative work. Indeed, the O of sessions is unknown emotional reality. Eigen writes that "Psychoanalysis is . . . an act of creation, an incessant shaping, re-texturing, fine tuning of affective attitudes" (2007, p. 12). For him, it is far more important to get the feel of the patient and session than their meaning (2011a, p. 39).

Patients bring to sessions their murderous, suicidal urges; they come saturated with despair, rage, disappointment, terror, agony, dread. Many emotionally murder the therapist, whose job it is to survive and reconstitute (2011b, pp. 40–42). Patients also suffer the affective impact of the therapist. In and through feeling, both make contact.

> The view behind the work . . . hinges on spontaneous interaction of two beings, person to person, psyche to psyche, self to self . . . The ordering is not from a higher place but from a psyche to psyche reordering, reshuffling, growing from interacting affective attitudes. We are permeable beings and affect each other. Over time, contact leads to changes. (2011a, pp. 29–30)

Essential to healing is the emotional life shared by the therapist and patient in the immediate present. The emphasis changes from *the what* of interpretation to *the how* of process. Critical to advancing in treatment is the quality of how the therapist and patient come through cycles of mutual affective impact. By repeatedly surviving and feeling themselves and the therapist reform in new, positive ways (the "rhythm of recovery" referred to above), patients learn they can endure their most terrifying feelings.

Eigen expects no less of himself than he does of his patients. The therapist opens to as full a range of her humanity as possible, to the tragic, wounded, cruel, helpless, tortured dimensions of herself. She moves through cycles of unbearable agony with the patient. Contact with "some abject nucleus" of her own becomes crucial, as the following example will demonstrate (2011b, p. 53).

Eigen relates the story of a supervisee who wove herself around a life theme of perfection. She wore elegant clothes along with perfect make-up. She was a competent, lovely person. Her patient, on the other hand, felt herself to be an ugly mess. The supervisee could not empathize with the patient's level of self-denigration. As Eigen sat with the therapist, he realized ". . . that her patient was going to kill herself unless the therapist could begin, even a little, to get in touch with the abject part of herself that was totally shut out" (2011b, p. 53).

The supervisee needed to be "under" rather than "over" the patient. This change meant finding a "feeling tone" of humility and losing some layers of "rightness" (2011b, p. 53). Her attitude of perfection aggravated the patient's self-denigration and aroused serious self-annihilation tendencies. The situation demanded affective change from the therapist in order to avert tragedy. She needed to acquire a feel for self-hatred and self-loathing. Eigen stresses that the therapist must develop the ability to sustain and process negative feelings. As she does, subtle shadings of negativity will emerge. "The work is very much like cataloguing and exploring varieties of fecal odors . . . And yet, if the therapist is respectful of the patient's illness . . . sometimes light also comes" (1986, p. 196).

Eigen's approach to therapy is not for the faint of heart. Intellectual understanding expressed through interpretation ignores the heart of the matter. The therapist works from a deep affective resonance with the patient's negative feelings. At times, it will be necessary to cut through layers of defense to find these feelings inside her, then stay with, taste, and explore the felt reality of their existence. Moving through this process brings about the needed change of heart. Both patient and therapist are touched to the quick and transformed in Eigen's approach.

This affective quality of the work, together with Eigen's emphasis on process rather than content and ineffable events, calls for an evocative language for psychoanalysis. Theory, explanation, and narrative cannot represent what occurs in sessions. These complex, wordless domains of experience require poetic, descriptive, intuitive, and expressive writing (Eigen, paraphrasing Bion, 2011a, pp. 16–17). Words, for Eigen, resonate with affect and wordlessness. All three are inherently related and give rise to one another. Words open "gateways to the wordless" and "create feeling" at the same time that "feeling creates words." He proposes that words and feelings arise from ". . . a deeper synchrony in our beings [that] . . . leads to both feelings and words, word feelings, feeling words" (2011b, p. 42). They are vibrant and alive, pulsing with wordlessness. "Words are a kind of emotional blood. For writers, words are a life blood. There is soul in words." However, they are also "soul killers." Eigen points out how a sharp maternal tongue mediates death; rage reverberating through words

"... intimidates, chills, tries to strip the other of power. To castigate, to reduce to obedience, to freeze ... A murderously wordless affective attitude vibrates through the mother's spoken words" (2007, p. 46). The child comprehends this attitude not only through explicit words, but with a wordless sensing, which is more important (2011a, p. 70). For me, Eigen reveals the paradoxical, multi-dimensional nature of the word, its spoken, inchoate, and affective valences as well as its dynamic potential to create feelings and provide openings to wordlessness.

Evocative language need not be inexact or undisciplined. The poet and mystic both exercise precision and rigor in creating successful evocative languages. The depth psychologist, in developing her own style of evocative expression, "... is obligated to think as clearly as possible, but it is ... thinking rooted in a specific sensibility. A certain tension between clarity and evocation must be maintained" (1986, p. 22).

And what, precisely, of Eigen's style? I experience a wordless but palpable aliveness radiating throughout Eigen's writings, an aliveness that comprises, at the same time, a dynamic momentum. The latter draws me in and carries me forward with deep, concentrated interest. His words, poetic, evocative, and emotionally vibrant, render vivid images, thoughts, and felt sensations that co-create specific psychological events. What follows is an example in which he describes the therapist experiencing the detritus resulting from the catastrophic origins of psychosis.

> Some of these bits and pieces might pop up and hit you in the therapy room, and you might try to talk about them and make sense of them. But you might be running before you have a ball. The bits and pieces of exploded personality floating in the room might not be redolent with meaning so much as flotsam and jetsam of an extended SOS signal, like a vanishing scream over time. (Eigen, 2002, pp. 151–155).
>
> You might be speaking to the wind as the piece you address continues to rush away. It just happened to pass through your office at that moment. (Quotation, including Eigen's citation, in Eigen, 2012, p. 19)

Eigen, here, describes the struggle a therapist might undergo as she meets the patient's detritus and tries to make sense of it; not once does he overtly state this topic. It is accomplished through the wordlessness of metaphor and evocation. The "bits and pieces" that might "hit you," presumably, refer to being emotionally struck by the patient. The struggle continues with your attempt to talk about this event meaningfully. This attempt might end in more struggle, a struggle in which you "might be running before you have a ball" with sense making. The word, "running" is packed with wordlessly inflected meaning. The talking did not go very well. In fact it went so badly, you might be in urgent need of distancing yourself emotionally as a protection from further emotional blows. The detritus you thought had meaning is actually an SOS, communicating that the patient is in mortal emotional danger. As you try to respond, your words find no substantive response from the patient. You might as well be talking to the invisible, insubstantive "wind". The SOS disappears as quickly as it arrived.

There are several aspects of the passage that endow it with aliveness. Phrases such as "pop up and hit you", "flotsam and jetsam of an extended SOS", "running before you have a ball", "vanishing scream", and "speaking to the wind", all suggest actions moving through time. They give rise to vivid sensual images involving vision, hearing, touch, or some combination thereof. They pull the reader in, as does the pronoun, "you". Through this pronoun, we identify with the therapist and are carried along, tasting and living through the struggle. Eigen's words reverberate with wordless reality.

I would like to share another example from the same work that shows a variation of Eigen's style, in which rhythm and sentence structure co-create meaning. It concerns our response to the unknown.

> It seems monstrous; it seems divine. Or it exceeds all categories. In the *Bhagavad Gita,* Krishna makes a monstrous appearance, yet is in all things and more—is all things. In part, the "monstrousness" has to do with human perception and awareness being unable to take full dosage of divinity/reality. (2012, p. 122)

This is such a beautiful rendering of Eigen's point. The writing is poetic in intensity and evocative through use of images, which for me include both the holy book, *Bhagavad Gita,* the god, Krishna (understood as an aspect of O), and his monstrous advent. The passage maintains psychological focus throughout. I include the book because the name conjures a sense of holiness, images of battlefields, and the characters of Arjuna and Krishna speaking with one another. The writing is highly rhythmic as he tells of qualities of the unknown, especially the shorter phrased sentences near the beginning, one following the other, each having a similar pace or beat in their first three words. The semi-colon both lightly links and separates the two components of the first sentence. Through doing so, it demonstrates the closely related although opposite sides of our experience of the unknown, divinity and monstrosity. The two components have the exact same number of words and almost identical rhythm. One phenomenon (monstrosity) is actually the other (divinity), differentiated only by our faulty capacities. The form of the writing wordlessly demonstrates this situation: two differentiated aspects of one sentence. The second sentence, although remaining short, is slightly longer. Its first three words carry a similar rhythm, but then the sentence opens out, just as the unknown does, to carry us into the unfathomable notion of exceeding all categories.

The long sentence following is also rhythmic. The first part of the sentence has a descending rhythm and mood, which complements the very slight ascending qualities of the second, which begins with the word, "yet". The final words before the dash, "and more", create another ascension in affect in the form of a rhythmically paused anticipation. We descend with the weight of Krishna's monstrous advent and ascend with the verbal experience that, despite it, he is "in all things"; in fact, "is all things". The phrases once again bring forth the repetition of rhythm and number of words described above. The dash that institutes a pause creates a marked emphasis on the last three words. The repetition of rhythm and words, together with the anticipatory pause, evokes in us the wonder of Krishna's divinity. Except for its initial short phrase, the final sentence, reads continuously with no pronounced breaks. The long and uninterrupted rhythmic flow parallels what the sentence is about: a large dose of divinity. It is through language such as this that Eigen conveys the aliveness of his vision and expresses the emotional heart of his work. Through the wordlessness of image, word phrasings, and rhythm, we are carried into the monstrousness of Krishna and the horror/wonder of his being in/being everything—"and more". Eigen reaches out and touches us with his heartfelt words; he evokes an experience of divinity, monstrosity, and incapacity at the same time that he delineates its significance as a specific psychic event. This writing, as well as the example above, seamlessly embodies his subject matter and pulses with wordless realities. Eigen style speaks a language of the unknown, despite the latter's ultimate inscrutability.

Eigen's approach does not characterize feeling as a self-enclosed, solipsistic psychic event; rather, feeling reaches out beyond itself, connecting us to self, world, and others. It generates change in psychotherapy, co-constitutes the nature and wordless meaning of words, and helps to create ethics, the experience of space, and the dream. With its origins in the unknown emotional background of existence, feeling constitutes a bridge to the foundation of our being, while embodying this foundation in its nature. It makes speaking from the heart possible at the same time that it constitutes this heart in all its joy, suffering, dread, and longing.

The primacy of faith

Faith plays a primary role in psychic functioning for Eigen. It is rooted both in the unknown and an attitude of radical openness to it, having no pre-conceptions or hidden intentions. Faith is patient, attentive, and clear, approaching "... pure receptiveness ... an alert readiness, an alive waiting ..." (1986, p. 136). It is an "intuitive organ" through which we have intimations of unknown forces and nameless transformations. It is wordless and imageless, as are the mysterious phenomena ont o which it opens (2011a, pp. 71–72). Yet, it is powerful, the only experience capable of meeting psychic catastrophe and "absolute destruction", which goes on functioning after all has been destroyed (2011a, p. 5). We engage faith with our entire being, with all of our heart, soul, and might (1993, p. 109). For Bion, it is a way of living and being fully alive to reality here and now, no matter what that reality brings (in Eigen, 2011b, p. 62).

Belief plays no role in faith. Faith is deeper than belief, which precipitously structures processes that remain unknown, distorting them (2012, p. 43). It prevents the "experimental exploration, imaginative conjecture, experiential probes" sustained by faith. In faith, we allow what is before us to resonate in its nameless inscrutability. We give it time and space without forcing meaning. Belief blinds us to the unknown with its premature connections and organization (2012, p. vii).

Faith founds the conditions that make psychoanalysis possible. As noted earlier, the ultimate reality of psychoanalytic sessions is unknown emotional truth. Psychoanalysts have faith that such truth is possible and necessary for psychic growth. Although the emotional truth "may be unknown and unknowable . . . nothing can be more important than learning to attend to it." Paradoxically, unknowable truth is the psychoanalyst's focus of attention. Her faith that something valuable will come from that focus opens a working place for truth (1993, p. 124).

Faith constitutes a founding dimension of psychoanalytic practice. As shown above, it embodies the psychoanalytic attitude. According to Bion, such faith is ". . . a state of being without memory, expectation, desire or understanding" (in Eigen, 2011b, p. 62). It is a profound openness to unknown emotional reality, in which we let go of self, mind, and the processes supporting them (2011a, p. 5).

Faith helps to found practice in yet another aspect. The therapist engenders, and becomes part of, the "faithful atmosphere" in sessions by tending to the unknown, respecting its truth, remaining open to impacts and responses, as well as digesting experiences that occur during sessions (2011b, p. 64). I believe Eigen is describing an atmosphere that facilitates the trust and safety necessary for engagement in therapy; if all goes well, the patient's own faith in therapy grows. A reciprocal, wordless exchange develops, in which both participants co-create the "faithful atmosphere" of the work.

Eigen points out that nothing can save us from the pain of existence. We are wounded at the center of our being (2007, p. 29). As seen above, hurt is an inevitability of being with others, as is the torture we undergo through producing intensities we cannot tolerate. For Eigen, this suffering is like a crucifixion alternating with resurrection. Annihilation of self precedes its rebirth, as periods of intense pain alternate with relief. We experience this cycle over and over again. It is a basic rhythm of existence, which he calls a "rhythm of faith" (2007, pp. 109–110).

Eigen frequently approaches different moments of experience as part of a larger evolving pattern. This more inclusive view allows him to delineate aspects of experience and their role in an unfolding context that might otherwise be missed. The "rhythm of faith" incorporates moments of crucifixion and resurrection; the "rhythm of recovery", referred to earlier, consists of periods of traumatization and reconstitution. The decentering terms of each cycle unfold into restitution during an overarching evolution in which both participate.

As I understand Eigen, faith, like feeling, is not a self-enclosed phenomenon, existing only between God and myself. Faith opens us beyond ourselves to the self, world, and others. It is creative and active. It sculpts a receptive inner space, an open heart. In therapy, it sculpts the practitioner's attitude, which, in turn, makes possible the emotional space for the work. Alert readiness, rather than passive inertness, characterizes its nature. As noted, faith is not rational. Neither is it irrational. Faith is arational. It opens in order to "let be" and "stay with", allowing the unknown to resonate in all its nameless, unfathomable reality. It concerns reality, but one existing outside the bounds of rational order, as do all of the phenomena significant to Eigen's work.

Emotional transformation

I would like to begin this section with an example of emotional transformation taken from Eigen's practice. In *Contact With the Depths,* he relates his work with Abe, a severe alcoholic who spiraled through periods of drunkenness and sobriety. Eigen never chose sides in this process. He was a quiet presence. As therapy progressed, Abe became alarmingly withdrawn, removed from his life, and increasingly silent in therapy. Eigen feared he would kill himself; he and Abe were at an utter loss during sessions. Eigen did not know that Abe's drinking was subsiding. During the eight months of Abe's descent, Eigen waited, remained patient, and stayed with the mutual experience of being lost. Apparently, Abe did the same. Then he began reporting feelings of a "radiant, compressed I-point" situated in his chest. It was "ineffable, mysterious, pulsating." He saw it as his I. The feelings associated with it held a sense of peace, comfort, and radiant thrills. It was "a core of pulsating aliveness" at the center of his existence (2011a, pp. 6–7).

The healing unknown had facilitated this emotional transformation. In reflecting on Abe's therapy years later, Eigen recognizes himself as having been a supportive background presence. This support allowed an unconscious bond to form between them. Within this bond, mutual impacts took place. Abe and Eigen were permeable to one another in a way that enabled the assimilation of good feelings. Positive affect radiated from and through one porous heart to the other. Permeability and unconscious background support had been damaged for Abe just as his personality formed. He was the target of a violent alcoholic father and an abusive, although occasionally warm, mother. Beginnings spelled disaster for him. Through Eigen's wordless affects and attitudes, he experienced that beginnings could be sustained, and have a creative outcome (2011a, pp. 7–10). Permeability and unconscious background support need not constitute a source of pain.

Essential to Abe's emotional transformation was his being in the presence of a quiet, non-judgmental background support, who differed dramatically from his parents. It enabled him to develop the trust and faith necessary for opening to Eigen. For me, Eigen incarnated a particular variation of unknown background presence that Abe desperately needed. I believe that how the therapist embodies and channels background support is critical for emotional transformation.

As just seen, both Eigen and Abe stayed with their being lost in sessions. Eigen proffers that an intense staying with unsolvable emotional problems (i.e., "To suffer suffering") changes how we experience them. Staying with, a form of unknowing, unlocks new domains of the psyche. The individual's capacities, such as their intelligence and personality, undergo demands from emotional problems that force development and new directions to emerge (2011a, pp. 111–112). In the case of Abe, a joint suffering through his silent withdrawal in therapy facilitated a radiant experience of I. In effect, Abe underwent crucifixion and rebirth, the "rhythm of recovery" referred to earlier. For Eigen, repeated experiences of this rhythm are crucial to therapy (2011b, pp. 28–29).

Earlier we saw that Eigen addresses a devastating fact of our existence. We are permanently, pervasively wounded. However, in and through that very suffering, he finds hope. By staying with our wounds, we change our relationship to them. As I understand it, "To suffer suffering" is not a passive, but a creative, transformative, *act*. While Abe and Eigen felt lost, much was happening between and inside them, even if unknown to both. Unknown emotional transformations unfolded in darkness, ungraspable but potent, forming a generative unknown. Even in our suffering, even in our brokenness, an inscrutable hope lives. Eigen shows us despair without leaving us in it. In so doing he unveils the paradoxical, prismatic, multi-layered nature of psychic events.

Summary remarks: Eigen's contribution

Eigen has given psychoanalysis a heart. He has established the centrality and founding nature of the boundless unknown, feeling, faith, and emotional transformation (the heart of the matter), as well as restored the latter to their passion, lifeblood, and humanity (a heart of flesh). His work transfigures the psyche as traditionally set forth in psychoanalysis. Rather than being impelled by libido, the psyche is created and continues to evolve in and through the unknown, undergoing lifelong rhythms of devastation and reconstitution. Feeling, faith, and emotional transformation, as indissoluble dimensions of the unknown, comprise foundational aspects of psyche's nature. Eigen does not view these phenomena in a one-sided or sentimental manner. He sees creation and destruction at play in them. We are tragic beings, wounded to the quick, and yet from our wounds emerge creativity, personal transformation, even joy.

He contributes a new and heartfelt mode of writing as a viable language for psychoanalysis. The evocative, poetic style of his work forms a coherent unity with its subject matter, expressing ineffable feelings, unspeakable wounds, wordless communications, living moments, etc. As I read him, I feel the freedom and creative evolution of his vision occurring in the moment; at the same time, his words bear psychological specificity and clarity.

Paradox, multi-dimensionality, and the reciprocal constitution of even seemingly opposite terms characterize Eigen's approach. He sees the doubleness inherent in psychic phenomena and brilliantly turns rational thinking on its head. He is not an atomistic thinker, but envisions phenomena as part of larger unitary and open-ended structures, in which they are distinguishable but not separable. Structures are in process, dynamic and evolving. His domain is arational reality, where he cultivates intuition and unknowing as methods. Rather than using linear, cause–effect thinking, Eigen works in terms of cycles, rhythms, and wider patterns. As he indicates when discussing the work of Deleuze and Guaterri, energies can run like the roots of a rhizome, "every which way", without start or end point, tangling round one another, doubling back, in all manner of random directions that no diagram will ever capture (2012, p. 83). Neither can Eigen's work be fully captured in an essay such as this one. The unknown and the wordless permeate his words. It is essential to read him to feel the heart beating in his writings.

References

Eigen, M. (1986). *The Psychotic Core.* London: Karnac, 2004.

Eigen, M. (1993). *The Electrified Tightrope,* A. Phillips (Ed.). London: Karnac, 2004.

Eigen, M. (2002). *Rage.* Middletown, CT: Wesleyan University Press.

Eigen, M. (2007). *Feeling Matters.* London: Karnac.

Eigen, M. (2011a). *Contact With the Depths.* London: Karnac.

Eigen, M. (2011b). *Faith and Transformation.* London: Karnac.

Eigen, M. (2012). *Kabbalah and Psychoanalysis.* London: Karnac (Kindle edn).

CHAPTER FOUR

Eigentime: time in the writing of Michael Eigen

Evan Malater

A commonly repeated complaint of the contemporary beleaguered psychoanalyst may be symptomatic of a failure to come to terms with time—as if time itself is evaded, repressed, dissociated, and projected. We constantly hear of patients who only want a "quick fix." These are apparently the same people who have failed to realize that "change takes time," who need to be constantly reminded of the virtue of patience, like demanding children in a car who constantly ask "Are we there yet?" It is not that this portrait is entirely unfounded or to deny that there are cultural forces that support a demand for immediacy; however, the aspects of truth contained in this description mask a deeper evasion—somehow it is always someone else who wants a quick fix, someone else who needs to be counselled on patience. Maybe it is we who need to slow down, to ask what is meant by these complaints. Does psychoanalysis really take time? What can this possibly mean? Why are we so opposed to quick fixes? Is it the quickness or the fix that so upsets us? Would we allow our patients to wish for a slow fix? What is worse, the demand for quickness or the desire for a fix, slow or quick?

To say that someone wants a fix is to say that he wants something. When does he want it? He wants it now. As if the time of wanting is really ever otherwise in its essence. Wanting is always the time of wanting now. Wanting is always the want of a quick fix. Our dream life goes to work on what we want. A dream is a quick fix. An overly determined condensed and displaced quick fix, but a quick fix nevertheless. The dream does not defer its fix for a dream to come next week or a dream eventually to be dreamt in ten years. The dream dreams it now.

All of which is to say that time is apparently tied to desire. We hesitate to explain what we mean by time and what we think of desire; it all seems so readily apparent. But to say one needs a quick fix is to theorize something about desire's effect on time that needs to be further interrogated. It is here that the work of Michael Eigen becomes crucial. Fittingly, there is not one work or essay on the topic; rather, time in all its dimensions threads in a non-linear way through his writing, here as a musing on theory, there as a moment in a clinical encounter. Unravelling Eigen's writing on time is a bit like grabbing a snake biting its tail and attempting to straighten it out. As the result would be predictably hazardous, my approach will not be to domesticate or untangle the various writings into a systematic treatise, but, rather, to name and encounter the multiple levels of time without removing the necessary simultaneity, paradox, and contingency which make this writing so vital. To take up Eigen on time is to encounter a topic prone to the most ethereal abstraction and smash it up against the impact of bodies and desires. It is to ask what Eigen thinks about time, but, more than this, to ask what he or any analyst *wants* (or does not want) from time. Accordingly, I will describe several key dimensions of time in Eigen's writing with an aim of articulating the desire of the analyst in and towards time. I will consider Eigen's thinking on time in relation to other key themes of his writing, including psychosis, trauma, and faith.

Bad beginnings and psychotic time

In the beginning there was *The Psychotic Core* (1986). Of course, this is only a nominal beginning and we shall see that Eigen has many beginnings. In his seminar, he once commented that one could write a whole study on the various notions of beginnings in Winnicott's writing alone. Nevertheless, as beginnings go, the foundation of Eigen's writing career on the precarious ground of psychosis seems appropriate. With this work, he not only staked his own claim to the importance of understanding psychotic thinking for psychoanalysis, but also made a strong case that psychosis was always central to psychoanalytic theory, starting with Freud.

In the psychotic beginning, there is psychotic time. There is the paranoid–schizoid Kleinian baby with its rageful attacks on a bad breast. There is no continuity in time between the good breast taken in the mouth and the cruelly depriving bad breast. A hallucination of the absent breast marks the space in time between the presence of a breast and its absence. It will be a long time before there is one breast and one mother.

From the beginning, time is measured and shattered by the vicissitudes of desire. In Eigen's telling, time is never a blank neutral medium, rather, it is a filled with sensuality up to and including the sensuality of deadness. There is the sight, smell, and feel of the hallucinated breast. There is the rhythmic sucking sound of a small mouth on a nipple, the sound of satiation, the essence of a quick fix. At the same time, in psychotic time, there is always a baby screaming, a scream without start or finish. For some, Eigen notes, life is one extended scream and time is nothing other than this one scream. We can imagine the one scream had its own beginning and, indeed, a fair amount of Eigen's work revolves around tracing the beginning of an endless scream. We can imagine the scream coming from the mouth of the no longer satiated baby, a baby's scream that becomes a Bion patient, an Eigen patient, a patient whose every word is a scream, whose every silence is a stifled cry. In his attempts to trace the beginnings of the endless scream, Eigen often turns to Winnicott's cruelly mathematical formulation of an x + 1 moment in time which marks the breaking point where the mother's absence goes from awful to unbearable. In time x, there was still a possibility of rescue and consolation from a caring other. X + 1 is a moment in time where the scream became endless and inconsolable; it is the moment after the breaking point. For such a person, we may imagine that we can find the time before hallucination failed, a time where it was still possible that there would be another quick fix coming, but such a thought could itself be hallucinatory or, at best, wishful thinking. We may never know if there ever was such a beginning.

Yesterday, a new patient came to me complaining of crushing loneliness and failure to fit in. I asked if it had always been so and he told me, "In preschool I was the most popular boy in class. I don't know why." The good start that short circuits, aborts, goes bad is a recurrent theme for Eigen; there are enough references to bad beginnings, short circuits, and aborted efforts to fill a book.

The book on good beginnings gone wrong would begin with so much promise, but by the middle chapters, things have gone wrong. Nobody knows what the wrong thing is. After stating that something is wrong, the book goes on for chapter after chapter, asking "What has gone wrong?" Time becomes the repetitive asking of this question. The book on good beginnings gone wrong ends unfinished. For many, the unfinished book of good beginnings gone wrong becomes a template. A template becomes an automatism to kill the painful novelty of time. One's life becomes a series of unfinished projects, a library of unfinished books.

Trauma time and repetition

If Eigen starts with the psychotic, at the same time, to put psychosis into an ordered sequence is to erase the psychotic in psychosis by assigning it a number when, in fact, the psychotic may erupt at any time, beginning, middle, or end. There is a close relation between the realm of psychosis in Eigen's writing and the topic of trauma. In some ways, trauma is related to the psychotic as another form of constitutional excess.

In Eigen's writing, moments in time become marked by the presence of deforming impacts that strike at certain points in the developmental rhythm of a person's formation. The placement of the trauma has implications that include the fear and unconscious re-enactment of catastrophe in the beginning, middle, or end. There are endless variations of catastrophic sequences. Trauma time may be punctuated by catastrophes of presence or catastrophes of absence. Mixtures of presence and absence create unique sequences according to traumatic templates that unfold in life and congeal into the time of transference in psychoanalysis. Transference is a kind of freezing in time. But how might the analyst inhabit time for him or herself through psychoanalytic understanding?

In "On time and dreams" (1983) Eigen presents the following dream of a patient:

> Doris was to board a boat. A fluid, shaky rope ladder connected the boat with shore. The ladder moved easily and rapidly, sensitive to every nuance of one's movement. Doris could have gone across. For her the ladder was a challenging possibility. However, she was with a group of people, including two old ladies who were supposed to be her grandmother and great grandmother. The two old ladies kept falling off the ladder into the water. Doris and others kept trying to help them across it without success. At last sharks started to come. A man placed a pacifier in his mouth as a decoy for the sharks to bite on. Doris imagined this man a capable uncle who would really help. The dream ended with everyone still in the water. (1983, p. 211)

Much of the paper involves a conflict between the patient's interpretation of the dream and Eigen's. The conflict centers on the old ladies in the dream, the grandmother and great grandmother. In Doris's view, the dream shows how she is now, unlike in the past, both able to offer help and ask for help. However, Eigen is not convinced by this and instead sees the old women as parts of the past, loyalties that inhibit the demands of the present moment. His interpretation is that it may be best to let the old women go; they are a part of her that no longer serves her needs. If she keeps helping them she may never get on the boat. Eigen shakes up the patient's conventionally adaptive interpretation (which could be summarized as, "I can both meet the demands of my family and find my own happiness") in order to present a challenge to a habitual sense of repetitive time that is soldered together by unquestioned internalized loyalties.

In questioning the patient's interpretation, Eigen demonstrates that conventionally adaptive conceptions of the new are often thinly disguised versions of old paradigms. The patient is seen as resisting the potential for something that would represent a break in repetitive time through her conscious interpretation according to familiar patterns. Eigen sees the patient's version of the new as reductively linear: in the past, something was missing which is now present—the ability to ask for help at the same time as giving help. The new is a gentle and gradual modification of something old, a supplement. Eigen's intervention has a kind of violence through its insistence that the new that is trying to emerge in the dream is, in fact, a radical break with the past.

Similar questions regarding the possibility of change and the new are found in the writing of French philosopher Alain Badiou in relation to what he calls the Event. For Badiou (2005), the Event is an unpredictable rupture outside of law, the creation of something new in art, politics, love, or science. The new, while exceedingly rare, can emerge at any moment. The Event has an enigmatic relationship to the ongoing work of those dedicated to truths in their respective fields (art, science, politics, or love. Psychoanalysis is situated as a truth of love). The time devoted by these workers to uncovering the new is not irrelevant to the emergence of the new; however, there is no lawful formula to predict its arrival. The Event, when it comes, is sparked by what, retrospectively, seems to be a random, contingent occurrence. Accordingly, it would be meaningless to assert that the creation of the new "takes time." Likewise, in this sense, the arrival of the new in psychoanalysis does not take time. The new is a rupture of repetitive, conventional time.

Nevertheless, Eigen often writes, the impacts of psychoanalysis do "take time" to be processed and digested. How can we reconcile these two positions? Here, we are confronting the enigmatic relationship between the gradual, "working through" and the "emergence of the new." The example of the dream suggests that, from the psychoanalytic point of view, the new comes with a dramatic break in unconsciously internalized demands of archaic objects. While the example here demonstrates such a shift in the form of a dream, it also suggests that the ongoing work of receiving the new that is struggling to come forth involves a confrontation with the analyst in the transference. In this example, according to the dream imagery, Eigen is both the familiar old lady and the sharks threatening the patient with a catastrophic loss in the precarious waters of the unconscious. The leap into a new time does not take time. It is a leap that may or may not ever occur. It may take time to hear and debate what Eigen is saying. After all, what kind of analyst recommends throwing your grandmother to the sharks? For a long time, Eigen could be a grandmother-hating murderer. And yet, in a momentary leap, everything could change. In the wake of such a leap, who would the patient be? Who would Eigen be?

In a footnote to "On time and dreams," Eigen addresses the need for a more precise understanding of time, in particular regarding the timelessness of the unconscious. He writes,

> It is at this point ambiguous just what Freud's attribution of timelessness to the unconscious means. He referred to the enduring quality

> of repressed events. But his descriptions do not situate unconscious processes beyond time's net entirely. It is possible (likely) that modes of time besides usual clock time characterize unconscious mental life. The meanings and operations of time/timelessness in unconscious events remains a fertile area of exploration. (1983, p. 219)

With this statement, Eigen refines the general description of time in the unconscious from "timelessness" to "modes of time besides usual clock time." The analyst and the patient in session are neither timeless nor ruled by clock time. Nevertheless, clock time remains, an encroaching presence on another kind of rhythm. In Eigen's paper, "A basic rhythm" (2002), what remains in the absence of clock time is a time warped by the rhythm of desire. Perhaps we can say that time is nothing but this rhythmic warping in and by desire. In order to describe these rhythms, Eigen locates the notion of rhythm in the writing of three analysts: Elkin, Bion, and Winnicott. It would be tempting to ground the notion of non-clock time in a simple analogy to the rhythms of the body through heart and breath, but, with Elkin, Eigen starts instead with a theory that posits an initial state of *disembodied* connection. "Since primordial self and other are experienced before a coherent body image develops, they have an immaterial, ineffable quality" (2002, p. 722). Inevitable disruptions caused by unmet desire for food, presence, and voice cause a sense of distress that cannot yet be mapped on to a body. "In time the other's ministrations take hold and primordial consciousness is reborn" (2002, p. 723). Here, Eigen's use of the common term "in time" is deceptively straightforward. "In time" encompasses the passage from disembodied connection to the infant's awareness of being a body in relation to other bodies. "In time" also evokes the notion of help coming "in time," whereas the alternative, coming too late, creates rhythms of absence and dread.

Writing this paper on a Sunday afternoon, I take a break. I have been reading Samuel Beckett's *Watt* (2006). After a few pages, I put the book down and fall into a pleasant nap. In a dream, I saw no one, but felt one dream kiss placed on me by an invisible presence. How funny to be in a dream of Elkin's disembodied other. I know I will have to add this to my writing, but am not ready to get out of bed, so I open up the Beckett book. Continuing from where I left off, I find the following:

> I was sitting on the step, in the yard, looking at the light, on the wall. I was in the sun, and the wall was in the sun. I was the sun, need I add, and the wall, and the step, and the yard, and the time of year, and the time of day, to mention only these. (Beckett 2006, p. 202)

Beckett's writing dissolves the difference between object, time, self, and environment. To be "in time" here is to be in the sun, which contains the wall, which contains the I of the speaker, all of which are aspects of not one time, but many (the time of year, the time of day, "to mention only these"). Through Beckett, by way of Eigen and Elkin, we can say that psychoanalysis *is* time, as it is the couch, as it is the light coming through the window. It is the time of day and the time of year. It is the voice of the analyst saying, "We have to stop," because there is always this regular clock time, the time our ever-frustrating patients lack the patience to bear. Even the patient whose life is an endless scream sometimes coheres in regular, linear, consensual time. It might be only in retrospect that we say of someone that his or her life is one long scream. For now, we must proceed with our regularly timed sessions, wondering and hoping whether this scream will, after all, turn out to be just a long interruption of a more desirable life trajectory. In the meantime, there are still seasons, birthdays, holidays, morning and night, rent to pay, and weekends to dread. Consensus time prevails—the time of eternal scream is an attempt to describe an aspect of something frozen, but, for most, frozen time exists along with "regular clock time."

Returning to my reading of "A basic rhythm" (Eigen, 2002), which has enacted its own rhythm of interruption, sleep, dream, reverie, and return, I resume with Eigen's discussion of Winnicott. Time, here, is in part the rhythm of the body, its needs for feeding, for touch. The rhythm of bodily needs meets the rhythms of presence and absence of the maternal other. A child is hungry but his mother is not there—until she is there. Finally, in another register, there is the rhythm of the unfolding development of a new being, quite fragile at first. Fragility ensures that there is a rhythm in time where beginnings are weighted with urgency and anxiety. A failure or absence that can be tolerated at a later time is catastrophic for the unformed and vulnerable baby. The basic rhythm is a polyrhythm: the rhythm of the body as it is met by a responsive other while, on another time scale, there is the slow unfolding of a developing being who is quite dependent on the presence of a caring other in order to continue in time. Where in time is the analyst? Not, says Eigen, as interpreter, but instead as the one who holds the map, who knows the rhythm of breakdown and recovery, while risking immersion within its multivalent dimensions.

Finally, with Bion, Eigen adds another elemental rhythm where the presence of the other takes on a much less benign aspect. If Winnicott features a faltering other who comes too late, Bion's other is a necessarily murderous presence. Faced with the murderous other, one might well prefer the damage of absence. To say one has survived murder is to say that time and body has ended. Whatever continues is that which can continue in the absence of a body. It points to a time before and after a body began, a time before birth, a time after death. Throughout this article, Eigen is tracking a sense of time inseparable from the violent impact of desire and its inevitable failures. The basic death and rebirth rhythm through Bion culminates in Eigen's description of the murderous other as one who has identified with annihilation itself. Time is an object such that one may identify with time itself, time as an object. To identify with annihilation, the ending of time through taking on the role of murderer, is to becomes both time itself and its ending. Eigen writes, "For an instant the murderer has the intoxicating illusion that annihilation itself is putty in his or her hands. One manufactures annihilation, has power over it, and imagines annihilation helpless" (p. 732). One can be the one murdered, the one who comes through murder, the one who murders, and, finally, one can be murder and annihilation itself, time and its destruction.

Faith and time

Time, then, for Eigen, is inseparable from an inevitable confrontation with murder. In other words, it is a matter of life and death and the analyst's relation to time, far from being an abstract speculation, is also a matter of life and death. Perhaps this is why it may be valuable to examine the analyst's assumptions regarding time, both in terms of everyday "common sense" notions as well as through formal theoretical concepts.

While Eigen does not explicitly link desire with time, he does stress the centrality of faith, "the area of faith" that sustains the analyst in the face of the inevitability of recurrent murderous confrontation. Just as

Bion says, the analyst cannot "know the O of which the patient is an evolution: he can only be it" (1983, p. 27); likewise, the analyst does not know or understand time, but through faith, the analyst becomes time.

In relation to these considerations, what does it mean to speak of the analyst's "desire" in relation to time? Does not Bion (1983, p. 34) define an "act of faith" as something "peculiar to scientific procedure," which, moreover, is only possible through a "discipline" that prescribes "the avoidance of memory and desire"? What, then, is the relationship between faith, desire, and time in psychoanalysis?

In the book of interviews *Conversations with Michael Eigen* (Eigen & Govrin, 2007), Eigen speaks of one if his earliest memories, estimated to be from when he was somewhere between eight and eighteen months. Eigen recalls making the connection that the voice of a radio announcer ("Now it is Nine O Five, time for the Breakfast Show") "dovetailed with the position of the hands and the numbers of the clock." The presence of a voice and its connection with the image of a clock fills a painful void left by his mother's absence at work each day. The time of mother's absence was felt as

> the feeling that she couldn't (didn't want to) be with me and had to get away, the suffocated feeling she was escaping and the tear through my body. My bearing it, hardening, making do. I learned to tell time in my crib, putting together the hands of a clock in my field of vision with morning radio shows. (p. 85)

Already, in this early memory, time is warped and seeped with desire and longing. There is the time of mother's absence and the time of mastery through knowledge. In the absence of mother's hands, an infant stares, transfixed by clock hands, hypnotized by the radio announcer's voice, a technological presence with no body whose announcements accompany what Eigen describes as a "hardening" and a "tear through my body." He remembers "the suffocated feeling" that, beyond describing his own feelings, suggests the possibility of a state in which feeling itself is suffocated.

In the present time of the interview, Eigen expresses his difficulty in continuing to speak of these memories, "There is more I am afraid to say because it sounds crazy or impossible" (p. 85). Is he afraid to sound crazy as an adult imagining that he was able to tell time at the age of one? Or is he afraid to elaborate an already present craziness in relation to time in the one-year-old version of himself? Despite such ambiguities, it is clear that he has been formed by an orientation to clock timed as a saving grace: "The birth of clock time in my early infancy grew out of trauma time, providing an external frame of reference for acute agony, outside time to organize inside time, primal emotional time/timelessness" (p. 86).

It is worth pausing to take in the complexity of this comment and the multiple registers of time it includes in one sentence: the infant who is said to already live in "clock time" that emerges through "trauma time" to provide an "outside time" that may organize the agony of "inside time". Compare this with Eigen's reading of Winnicott in his classic paper "The area of faith in Winnicott, Lacan and Bion" (1993a). One of the achievements of this paper is to rescue Winnicott from the sentimental and simplified reading by which he is taken to be the gentle common sense teacher of "good enough" and soothing blankets. Instead, Eigen writes, "Transitional phenomenon are not primarily tranquilizers" (p. 111). The transitional object is not essentially an object clutched in fear that allows one to calm down and continue. Instead, the transitional object is an experimental phenomenon that starts from a position of subject–object interpenetration. The child is not a formed subject whose soothing blanket helps him to learn to be patient while his mommy is gone. Winnicott's concept is much stranger: Mommy, blanket, and child are all unformed and elaborated into being through the use of the transitional object.

As Eigen turns to Winnicott's concept of object usage, the sense of time continues to be radically paradoxical. Again, this is not the simplified narrative of a child finding how mother tolerates his aggression and continues to love and be forever present as a good internalized object. Eigen's emphasis is not on the reassurance and triumph of the persistent mother's love, but, rather, on how the mother, in surviving the child's psychic attacks, is seen as other, different, and outside the realm of control. If there is a faith that comes from this, it is not the faith of patience and tranquility based on taking in the goodness of the mother, but, rather, in the felt realization that the other (of time, parent, world, etc.) is not knowable and cannot actually be "used" in any way. Both love and destruction survive and sustain each other, neither triumphs or overcomes; yet something continues. As Eigen writes, "It is a sense of the real that explodes all adaptive and manipulative attempts in principle" (1993a, p. 113)

"The recoil on having another person" (1993b) shows precisely what the manipulative use of time looks like. Eigen notes that the paper "relates moving towards or away from the other to time experience" (p. 22). The patient is a man with a tendency to use and discard friends once they have yielded to his attention and are no longer exciting objects to be attained. In working with this patient, Eigen writes, "Patience seemed poor, if inevitable, counsel and would perhaps provoke him to terminate therapy" (p. 22). Instead, the analysis reveals that what appears to be a desperate need to grab and possess the other belies an overly literal attempt of the patient to secure the experience of approach and openness through an object. It is not exactly a lack of patience that is at stake, but a misunderstanding of one's own desire, here especially seen as a misunderstanding of a desire related to time—the patient tries to possess the time of openness and an eternal approach through having the other. Through the time of psychoanalysis, he begins to see that what he needs is to be in the time of openness, forever approaching another who is never fully known. He needs the possibility of approach. Eigen indicates that this process operates via the transference. In relation to time, one could say that the patient tries to capture the other as known through transference, but finds instead an other who can only ever be approached. By embodying multiple dimensions of time, the analyst allows that the other who can only ever be approached is something more than a carrot on a stick.

Finally, although an account like this allows for no obvious points of ending or conclusion, perhaps we can say that underlying and overlying all these papers and commentaries, there is another time, the time of writing, in which Eigen (2012) asks, "Do you ever feel you are being created by the future of the session? Something without bottom or sides or top? The session is creating you?" Through Eigen's work and writing, psychoanalytic time may be this warp sustained by the rhythms of desire and non-desire, by body and non-body, held by the practice of something that still dares to go by the name of faith.

References

Badiou, A. (2005). *Being and Event*. New York, London: Continuum.

Beckett, S. (2006). *Watt* in *Grove Centenary Edition*, Vol. 1. New York: Grove Press.

Bion, W. (1983). *Attention and Interpretation*. New York: Jason Aronson.
Eigen, M. (1983). On time and dreams. *Psychoanalytic Review, 70*, 211–220.
Eigen, M. (1986). *The Psychotic Core*. Northvale, NJ: Jason Aronson.
Eigen, M. (1993a). The area of faith in Winnicott, Lacan and Bion. In: *The Electrified Tightrope* (pp. 109–138). London: Karnac, 2004.
Eigen, M. (1993b). The recoil on having another person. In: *The Electrified Tightrope* (pp. 21–24). London: Karnac, 2004.
Eigen, M. (2002). A basic rhythm. *Psychoanalytic Review, 89*, 721–740.
Eigen, M. (2012). Future as unknown presence (even if it is absent). *The Candidate, 5*, January, digital journal, www.thecandidatejournal.org.
Eigen, M., & Govrin A. (2007). *Conversations with Michael Eigen*. London: Karnac.

CHAPTER FIVE

Tropisms of creative faith and destructiveness in the works of Michael Eigen and Martin Heidegger

Brent Potter

Introduction

> One can become dead to oneself by trying to be too alive;
> unembarrassed affirmation of passivity;
> let the warp touch you;
> give each other room not to be;
> we swallow a lot of death in order to live
>
> (Michael Eigen, 2013)

Eigen (2006) states,

> The problem of faith and destructiveness is basic to the human condition. Many sessions I write about are felt to be crises of faith. Faith in the face of destructiveness. Can faith survive destructiveness? In what way? How? (p. 1)

Interpersonal–intrapersonal, deception–destruction implies simultaneous deceit and damage inflicted upon self and others. The lines of differentiation and origin blurred, all emanating from a single source, a kind of int(e)r(a)personal deceit–damage to self-and-others. The effect produced in examining such things is more like staring into a fractal, than about binaries of me–you, self–others, in–out, present–past. Exploring these phenomena of psychic reality requires an abiding contemplation upon these typically self-similar patterns, where self-similar means they are the same from near as from far. Psychic "fractals" may be exactly the same at every scale, or, they may be nearly the same at different scales. They represent infinite curves that can be perceived as winding through psychic space differently from an ordinary line, having dimensionality. Such phenomena invite metaphors of origins, ever-shrinking zero-points, circulatory systems, permeable boundaries.

The circulatory system and immune system serve the identical, yet complementary, purpose: to keep the body alive. The circulatory system does this by carrying oxygen from the lungs to every organ and cell in the body. The immune system does this by identifying foreign materials before they can harm the body. The connection between the circulatory system and immune system lies in the fact that the immune system travels through the entire body, inside the circulatory system. Eigen (1999, 2001) delineates and differentiates the many ways people are poisoned by what nourishes them, damaged by the very bonds that sustain them, that give them life. Proximity to toxicity is immanent, inevitable, since it is often difficult, if not impossible, to discern interpersonal and intrapersonal poison from sustenance. It is as if there is an int(e)r(a)personal *pharmakon*, poison-cure, of self-and-others; a null point of differentiation, ground zero.

Eigen (1986) points out that, in many ways, Freud's work can be considered a phenomenology of psychosis, the undifferentiated "substance" of the psyche. For Freud, the id constitutes the seething cauldron of emotional realities where the rules of paradox and common sense do not stand, where being and time are condensed, annulled, and expanded. The superego is often the source of persecution gone awry, spiraling into self-torment, self-flagellation, on the way to self-annihilation. The ego is simultaneously a hallucinatory organ and adaptive agent with anti-hallucinogenic properties. One of the earliest activities of the ego is hallucination. For example, the ego as an agent of wish fulfillment, attempting to extricate disturbance by making believe it is not there in some way, wishing it away, and/or filling the imagined absence with fantasy. A problem with hallucinating disturbance away is that one tends to pretend oneself away as well. There is a vanishing tendency that dispels itself as well as anything in its path. Freud spoke of flooding as a primal trauma. And one way an individual deals with emotional chaos is by trying to wish it, hallucinate it, out of existence. One risks hallucinating oneself out of existence, too. Psychotic states form the foundation and background of Freud's structural concepts. Freud's conception is of a system in motion, circulating. The superego may press back and tyrannize the ego (ego-dystonic) or align with the id and the ego to sanctify fantasies and behavior (ego-syntonic). When the superego partners with the ego and id, the psyche's musing and concordant behavior go unchecked by any moral filter. In contrast, guilt and shame produced by ego-dystonic dynamics need not always result in neurosis. It can, for example, produce the effect of inhibiting self-and-other damage; "I really shouldn't do that again. I remember it hurt his feelings. I felt terrible." Id, ego, and superego emerge and take shape, moving, processing, fusing—differentiating from the primary source. The undifferentiated zero-point (psychosis) and the force working towards it (Thanatos) are the primary substrates, the contexts, meaning, and ground, of psychological life.

One of psychoanalysis's most important contributions to understanding the human condition involved the various ways it explores relationships between idealization and violence (Eigen, 1986, 1992, 1993). Klein adds variations to this theme and also links idealization to deadness. Klein takes for granted the infant's natural tendency to idealize the good object, whether it is inner or outer. This tendency seems to be an in-built, spontaneous one. When frustration and anxiety mount, the infant takes refuge in the internal, idealized good object. The infant seeks to burrow into, hold on to, and enfold itself with its sense of well-being and goodness. The idealized good object is a buffer against death force agents, internal persecutors, bad states. If persecutory fear becomes too great, idealization may be overused to defend against or balance it. In extreme instances, the ego become a shell around a split-off idealized core, which is working overtime to blot out the onset of horrific states, whether invasion by split-off anxiety, menacing presences, or persecutory affects–objects–ego bits. Ego functioning becomes vastly thinned and curtailed in as much as its focus is increased on contact with the idealized core.

Klein takes off on Freud's picture of the infant hallucinating a breast when it is hungry: hallucinated fulfillment takes the place of painful hunger and no breast. She imagines that the infant hallucinates an ideal breast (an ideally good state) while omnipotently denying frustration, pain, persecutory feelings, and bad states. For Klein, denial equals annihilation in the unconscious, and bad states are tied to an image of a bad object—the frustrating, absent, persecutory, or unfulfilling object. Thus, what is denied and annihilated is not just a state or an object, but an object relation and, more, the ego's capacity for a living object relation.

Eigen (1985) points out that it is difficult, if not impossible, to find where the "split" from, or "break" with, oblivion happens. Whatever the point may be, it is akin to the primordial and violent growth processes of Nature: actions of dividing or splitting elements into two or more parts (fission) and simultaneous movements of joining two or more things together to form a single entity (fusion). Following Bion's imagery, Eigen notes a tremendous force and presence inherent in these dynamic processes of cleaving, splitting, dividing, merging, amalgamating, melting. There is a kind of "Big Bang" or, rather, a series of catastrophic "nuclear" explosions that grant the building blocks, the necessary materials, enabling psychic reality to come into being. The "substance" of thoughts are non-substantial, the crude materials which have to be metabolized before they can become a part of the thinking process. The force and presence of such things grip the subject with catastrophic intensity. They can be described as raw affective state, fusing/fissioning of imago–sensation–perception for which the personality has no context, no frame of reference. Without a "container" they travel dispersed throughout the infantile psychic reality, charged with a kind of horror and dread. Bion knew that in tending to dreams and psychotic processes, he was witnessing, catching sight of, the origins of psychic reality. The "radioactive" fragments and bits from the primal cataclysmic explosion (or explosions) carry into the present. They are remnants of psychic origins.

Eigen's and Bion's work here is reminiscent of the "Animism, magic and the omnipotence of thoughts" section of Freud's *Totem and Taboo* (1912–1913) or, perhaps more accurately, his (1919h) "The 'uncanny'". In it, his questioning concerns early moments of human deadness–aliveness that reverberate later, "awakening feelings . . . when there is intellectual uncertainty whether an object is alive or not, and when an inanimate object becomes much like an animate one" (p. 233). Freud is clear that the haunting, uncanny feeling emanates from the *prima material* of the psyche: ". . . this uncanny is in reality nothing new or alien, but something which is familiar and old-established in the mind and which has become alienated from it only through the process of repression" (p. 241). What is consistent is the uncanny feeling, permeated with horror and dread, of mysterious origin. Sometimes, he ascribes the origin to "intra-uterine experience", he mentions the demonic and, in the end, simply refers to the primal source as "hidden":

The layman sees in them the working of forces hitherto unsuspected in his fellow-men, but, at the same time, he is dimly aware of them in remote corners of his own being. The Middle Ages quite consistently ascribed all such maladies to the influence of demons, and in this their psychology is almost correct. Indeed, I should not be surprised to hear that psychoanalysis, which is concerned with laying bare these hidden forces, has itself become uncanny to many people for that very reason (p. 243).

Heidegger (1927) finds, too, that these long forgotten fragments of the original creation haunt the present:

> In its who, the caller is definable by *nothing* "worldly." It is Da-sein in its uncanniness, primordially thrown being-in-the-world, as not-at-home, the naked "that" in the nothingness of the world. The caller is unfamiliar to the everyday they-self, it is something like an *alien* voice. What could be more alien to the they, lost in the manifold "world" of its heedfulness, than the self, individualized to itself in uncanniness thrown into nothingness? "It" calls, and yet gives the heedfully curious ears nothing to hear that could be passed along and publicly spoken about . . .
>
> The call does not report any facts; it calls without uttering anything. The call speaks in the uncanny mode of *silence*. And it does this only because in calling the ones summoned, it does not call him into the public idle chatter of the they, but *calls* him *back* from that *to the reticence of his existent potentiality-of-being*. When the caller reaches him who is summoned, it does so with a cold assurance that is uncanny and by no means obvious. (pp. 255–256)

More recently, Ogden (1992) finds hints of these hidden forces in primitive organizational patterns he dubs the autistic–contiguous position. Ogden proposes this stage as coming before Klein's paranoid–schizoid stage. It is a sensory-dominated, pre-symbolic mode of producing experience. Anxiety in this imago–sensation–perception mode consists of an abiding, ineffable shock of the dissolution of boundedness resulting in feelings of leaking or liquefying into ceaseless, formless space. Similar to Freud's notion of "the uncanny", the person in this stage experiences an onslaught of autistic visceral sensory experiences, his or her mind struggling to break down such things into nutrients that can be used for thinking. Bion's (1962) conceptions of beta prime elements, bizarre objects, and nameless dread reflect the underlying sense of uncanniness not uncommon in everyday experience. Such a feeling, in some instances, may leave one with the nagging feeling of being an orphan of the real, haunted by ghosts of abandoned meaning. In the end, difference remains between oneself and the zero-points and, however minuscule, it is infinite.

Bion's work is filled with many micro-analyses of how this evolution is prevented or goes awry. It must be emphasized that the distance element that seems both threatened and inherent in the sense of catastrophe is not simply our observing capacity. More is involved than the capacity to know. In psychoanalysis, at the levels at stake, knowledge can be part of the disease. A capacity as deep as, or deeper than, the sense of catastrophe must be called forth if healing or profound maturation is to occur. Bion's solution is radical, for he shifts the context of discourse to the relationship between destructiveness and faith.

In giving thought to F in O, Eigen (2011a) posits the "background support of primary aloneness, *boundless unknown support*" (p. 10). I imagine this surmising is akin to Grotstein's (2000) notion of "background presence of primary identification", "a sense of comfort that someone stands behind us in our effort to face the world ... safety ... [an] environmental mother as differentiated from the object mother" (p. 18). According to Grotstein, this background presence furnishes the setting of the dream and of thoughts of the thinker while awake. It is the primary background of all things, Grotstein maintains, from thoughts to the laws of natural science, to the mystic sense of unity with God. The sense that Grotstein relays is one of a more "present" presence of the "I" experiencing of the background presence. Eigen's boundless unknown support of aloneness is just as powerful, and adds qualities that are subtle, supple, quiet, still. This boundless background presence is part of the background sense of existence. It provides a basis for emergent trust and faith. If we cannot trust the environment to uphold our being (*ex-sistance*, literally *standing-out-against*), then we are in jeopardy. And a sense of jeopardy does indeed pervade our existence.

F in O is faith in the midst of catastrophe. We are linked together by faith and also linked by catastrophe. The environmental support of our aloneness is necessary and remains part of our sense of aloneness all through life. We may not realize it clearly, but it lives inside us, part of an indistinguishable nexus of support that feeds a sense of living. It is not unusual for primary support to be injured, even maimed. Addiction is one price we pay for wounded aloneness. Eigen (2011a) points out that addiction is a literalistic response to wounded aloneness: "Since a drug, object, or behavior pattern substitutes for this support, the experience needed for repair is missed. A substance or compulsion takes the place of going through the steps of addressing the wound aloneness bears" (p. 21). From his perspective, addiction extends beyond alcohol and drugs to food, sex, money, power. In a sense, war is an addiction that seeks to mimic, replay, and bring to awareness how catastrophic it felt as an infant when the world fell from under us, when the self fell apart or died for a time, perhaps a very long time. War mimics a transient and macabre wholeness state, melding catastrophe with ideal hopes, wholeness incessantly blown up (Eigen, 2011a).

Heidegger, too, explores in detail the strategies people use to compensate for wounding to the fundamental background nexus of support (Being). He finds symptoms in our everyday contemporary life as well as their addictive qualities. Eigen finds addiction to be a literalistic way of contending with wounded aloneness–support. In a similar fashion, Heidegger explores our contemporary efforts to explain, predict, control, and consume. It is not technology itself that Heidegger finds problematic, although it certainly can be, it is the perspective that if we busy ourselves, preoccupy ourselves with everydayness, that we can obfuscate thinking itself and ignore our wounded relatedness to Being. Heidegger goes to great lengths to point out that we, the thinking–meditating beings, are engaged in a destructive attack upon meditative thinking. He points out that instead we cogitate, memorize, structure, order, engineer. In opposition to meditative thinking, he calls this calculative thinking. Calculative thinking is addictive and destructive. Heidegger (2002), argues that "our whole human existence everywhere sees itself challenged—now playfully and now urgently, now breathlessly and now ponderously—to devote itself to the planning and calculating of everything" (pp. 34–35). Our everyday attitude of fascination with the newest and best technological gadgets, media innovations, television, fashion, advertising, cars, houses, celebrities, health fads, and politics represent a kind of hallucinosis in the service of evading reflective space, contemplation, psychological and spiritual growth: "Nowadays we take in everything in the quickest and cheapest way, only to forget it just as quickly, instantly . . . [M]an is in *flight from thinking*" (Heidegger, 1966, p. 46). Like Eigen, Heidegger's work produces the dizzying, almost disabling realization that what we suspected was true all along; we have been (collectively and individually) living in, participating in, the winning lie.

While the technological perspective does yield wonderful, even life-saving things, it has spiraled out of control. The technological perspective, unlike faith, has addictive elements. First, it is a perspective of mastery and control. While there is nothing inherently wrong with mastery and control, there is a temptation to fall into narcissism and fantasies of omnipotence. The opposite resides in the attitude of faith. In this attitude, one takes accomplishment with a healthy sense of pride and also with gratitude towards the circumstance and people that made such accomplishments possible. In regard to faith in Being/O, there is an inherent humility. This is missing in ego-hero consciousness. There is an addictive trend towards increased inflation, even megalomania. Second, taking flight from existential–psychic reality, especially attacking existential–psychic reality, necessitates further flight/attack. The more we take flight from or attack reality, the more dependent we become upon such anti-reality strategies and ways of being. Like substance dependence, there is an increasing reliance upon the "substance" to contend with the multifaceted aspects of communal and emotional realities and a concordant shrinkage of repertoire for spontaneous, creative modes of engagement. The truth is replaced with compensatory fantasies of power and control. The increasing reliance upon the "one way" to take up life results in a kind of int(e)r(a)personal *alexithymia*, a marked dysfunction of relatedness to the existential–psychic realities of self-and-others. Individual and collective anti-reality strategies leading to *existential–psychic alexithymia* necessitate an ever increasing amount of distance from emotional awareness, social attachment, and interpersonal relating. The more int(e)r(a)personal difficulty in distinguishing and appreciating emotional life, the more *alexithymic* the condition. It is a vicious, never-ending cycle of increasing deadness and decreasing aliveness. The word arrives via the Greek *alexo* ("repel") and *thumos* ("soul, as the seat of emotion, feeling, and thought"). Third, the hallucinated all-powerful ego, literally a superego, becomes increasingly fascinated with its own "reality". The world can only appear as disparate, "out there" somehow, and as a conglomeration of useful things to be used. The world and all things contained in it become leveled down to their usefulness (or lack thereof) to the ego. This is, not coincidentally, reminiscent of Descartes's view of humans as thinking things situated squarely on one side with the world "outside" as *res extensa*, a mathematical space, calculable in forces, adrift with the litter of soulless objects. All psyche, all mind, all consciousness, and all that is living condensed within the human brain organ, putting nature at the disposal of the human will. This forges dependency between an ego, consumed with itself, and the world "out there" as a mass of things to be consumed.

Heidegger sees every aspect of contemporary life, not only machine technology and science, but also art, religion, and culture understood as the pursuit of the highest good, as exhibiting clear marks of the ruling essence of technology that holds sway in the dominion of man as self-conscious, representing subject. In every domain of human life is to be found the contrasting of subject and object and the reliance on evaluating judgment of the subject as crucial. The presencing of everything has been cut at its origins. There is a "world picture" or a "world view" that can only be spoken of in our contemporary age. For the phrase "world picture" means that the "real" in its every aspect and elements is now "taken in such a way that it first *is in being* and *only* is in being to the extent that it is set up by man, who represents and sets forth" (Heidegger, 1977, pp. 129–130). It is interesting, especially today, to read,

> Hourly and daily they are chained to radio and television. Week after week the movies carry them off into uncommon, but often merely common, realms of imagination, and give the illusion of a world that is no world. Picture magazines are everywhere available. All that with which modern techniques of communication stimulate, assail, and drive man. (p. 48)

The world and others become constructed in accordance with the hallucination that they are purely useful things, ready to use. It is a process of leveling differences down to self-sameness, as if the world becomes a mock-up of our own hallucinated ego: "It seems as though man everywhere and always encounters only himself" (Heidegger, 1966, p. 25). In the process of anti-thinking and constructing a compensatory hallucinated "reality", there is an insidious loss of perspective and increased danger.

The human being is summoned, claimed in the very hallucinosis, even though such awareness is unconscious. Humanity's obliviousness to that claim is itself a manifestation of the hallucinosis of calculative thinking. An aspect of the calculative thinking (Heidegger), −K (Bion), and addiction (Eigen) that adds to the obfuscation and obliviousness of those caught in its grip, is the promise of improved life, happiness, serenity. On a collective level, technology's promise of comfort and abundance has taken its toll on natural resources and also the psychological and physical wellbeing of people. From these promises there

> arises a completely new relation of man to the world and his place in it. The world now appears as an object open to the attacks of calculative thought, attacks that nothing is believed able any longer to resist. Nature becomes a gigantic gasoline station, an energy source for modern technology and industry. (Heidegger, 1966, p. 50)

Heidegger (2003) describes, under the influence of technological "thinking", "The circularity of consumption for the sake of consumption" as "the sole procedure which distinctively characterizes . . . a world which has become an unworld" (p. 107). Again, from today's context, it is interesting to ponder how things have developed since Heidegger stated this in a lecture given in 1935:

> The spiritual decline of the earth has progressed so far that peoples are in danger of losing their last spiritual strength, the strength that makes it possible even to see the decline [which is meant in relation to the fate of "Being"] and to appraise it as such. This simple observation has nothing to do with cultural pessimism—nor with any optimism either, of course; for the darkening of the world, the flight of the gods, the destruction of the earth, the reduction of human beings to a mass, the hatred and mistrust of everything creative and free has already reached such proportions throughout the whole earth that such childish categories as pessimism and optimism have long become laughable. (Heidegger, 2000, pp. 40–41)

The obliviousness of the technological perspective as well as the addiction to calculative thinking makes one wonder when humanity will hit "bottom".

Bion amplifies Freud and goes further. He describes the psychoanalytic attitude as being without memory, expectation, desire, or understanding. A radical openness he calls faith. Heidegger arrives at a similar place in his thinking, accenting the necessity of meditative thinking, a faithful abiding to the things themselves and openness to mystery. Bion expresses this special kind of faith as F in O, where O is unknown/unknowable, ultimate reality. For Bion, O, in this context, there is an emphasis on psychic reality, ineffable, infinite. "The fundamental reality is 'infinity', the unknown, the situation for which there is no language—not even that borrowed from the artist or the religious—which gets anywhere near to describing it" (Bion, 1992, p. 372). This has echoes in Heidegger's thought on Being:

> After all, not only is the enowning of timing–spacing–thinging deeply ineffable, but the things themselves (including us) that are gathered in it are also extraordinary and ineffable in their very ordinariness. Being, enowning, timing–spacing–thinging, things, us, saying–showing: every last one, by any name, is a magical display of radiant, ineffable emptiness. (Stenstad, 2006, p. 191)

Bion points towards the essential inextricable link: "I am his other self and it is called a dream." In this same section, he refers to a crisis of faith, a crisis that requires going beyond "disjuncture" and "self-sameness", a kind of int(e)r(a)personal love, a capacity for care of self-and-others. Heidegger (1927) literally links words with hyphens to stress the fundamental interconnected "circulatory system" of Being:

> By reason of this *with-like* Being-in-the-world is always the one that I share with Others. The world of Dasein is a *with-world.* Being-in is *Being-with* Others. Their being-in-themselves within-the-world is *Dasein-with.* (p. 155)

The words are designed, I suspect, to catch us off guard, to make us stumble a bit, to shake up the order of everyday busy "thinking". Heidegger does this, in part, to draw attention to the same fundamental unity to which Bion gives thought. The word "Dasein", too, bespeaks the same essential unity. Heidegger's work is in the service to giving essential thought to Being (Sein). He calls the human being, there-being (Dasein). Dasein is not unlike its source. A drop of ocean water is no less "ocean" than the water mass from which it comes. We are all Dasein. We are all O.

We cannot catch existential–emotional transformation in the act. Again, we cannot know Being/O; we *are* Being/O. In one compact section, Bion (1970, p. 46) writes,

> Although O (infinity) is inaccessible to K it is perfectly accessible to T in O. The analyst has to become infinite by the suspension of memory, desire, understanding. The emotional state of transformation in O is akin to dread as it is represented in the formation:
>
> Like one that on a lonesome road
> Doth walk in fear and dread;
> And having once-turned round moves on,
> And turns no more his head;
> Because he knows a frightful fiend
> Doth close behind him tread.

The "frightful fiend" represents indifferently the quest for truth or the active defense against it, depending on the vertex.

In this situation, what is known and unknown is mysterious. Bion goes deep into the dark waters peering, calling this bare perspective "faith". Eigen (2011b) amplifies Bion:

> Faith supports experiencing and exploration of experience. Faith is deeper than belief. Belief often functions as premature organization, closure of faith. One way faith goes beyond belief is by enabling unknown transformation that opens reality, transformations we may sense but are unable to pin down. (p. 7)

The inextricable interconnectedness inherent in faith (F in Being/O) implies that a crisis of faith is a "crisis of 'I' and 'You', or 'We' and 'They', a crisis that requires going beyond opposition and symbiosis . . . to a love that terms like 'love of God', and 'absolute love' only hint at, a love of reality that requires a language for the infra- and ultra-sensuous" (Eigen, 2011a, p. 42). Faith pares psyche, opening it for a brute connection and *metanoia* (transformation). It is a fountainhead of emotional experience seeking its own level and depth: circulating, undergoing, transmuting, changing, becoming. In Bion's framework the life of meaning goes deeper than language. As Freud (1900a) observed,

> When the whole mass of these dream-thoughts is brought under the pressure of the dream-work, and its elements are turned about, broken into fragments and jammed together – almost like pack-ice – the question arises of what happens to the logical connections which have hitherto formed its framework. What representation do dreams provide for 'if', 'because', 'just as', 'although', 'either–or', and all the other conjunctions without which we cannot understand sentences or speeches. (p. 312)

It is one way that meaning can be organized. Heidegger goes deeper, asserting that language itself is listening to Being. "Man acts as though he were the shaper and master of language, while in fact language remains the master of man" (Heidegger, 2003, p. 267). The inextricable unity with Being is not caused by human speech, but is instead "handed over . . . from Being" (Heidegger, 1978, p. 217). Humanity brings the manifestation of Being to language and maintains it in language through discourse (speech, thinking, writing). While humanity constructs, to a degree, what is proffered, "language . . . is appropriated by Being and pervaded by Being" (p. 237). Briefly, yet powerfully, stated, "Language is the house of Being. In its home man dwells" (p. 217). We are guests in Being/O. Emotional truth, existential–psychic reality, is not confined to language, and neither does it have a static basis. Its evolving quality spreads out in all temporal directions. We open ourselves, clear a living space, to encounter it. Our interpretations strive to express what (in faith) we trust our conduct and considerations to touch: a *gesture of presence impacting self-and-other*.

Love transforms gratitude into loyalty to our selves and unconditional faith in the other. That is how love steadily intensified its innermost secret.

> Here, being close is a matter of being at the greatest distance from the other—distance that lets nothing blur—but instead put the "thou" into the mere presence—transparent but incomprehensible—of a revelation. The other's presence suddenly breaks into our life—no soul can come to terms with that. A human fate gives itself over to another

> human fate, and the duty of pure love is to keep this giving as alive as it was on the first day. (Heidegger, 2004, pp. 4–5)

Eigen (2011b) speaks of an

> enfleshed infinite, an immediate infinite, infinite immediacy: from an infant's response to its mother's face, to our response as grownups to each other. An infinite immediacy that embraces, that upholds within it as its nucleus an infinite distance, intimate distance that calls for respect as well as caring. To see and sense as a form of giving. (p. 4)

Like Heidegger, Eigen's writings combine the most radical genuineness and paradox, a movement from "either–or" to often subtle shades of "both–and". The subject who is attentive to evolutions of O is decentered from himself or the other. Eigen further amplifies Bion by describing the growth in O where there is a movement from projective (existential–psychic reality as "out there") to introjective (integrated existential–psychic reality) states. The latter depicts an organic unfolding that spontaneously arises within a fundamental openness toward Being/O. We find ourselves in growing toward Being/O. The transformations impacting directly self-and-other that happen as a matter of direction are not themselves the principle mode or intention. What is vital is one's comportment, the way of knowing and being with whatever one may be contacting. For Heidegger and Eigen, the essential attunement is the perpetual pursuit of Being/O.

Here we come full circle to the areas Eigen and Heidegger so eloquently point towards—creative faith *vs.* destructiveness. Eigen (1992, 2011a,b) accents creative faith birthing through moments of self-and-other opening, peak moments whose impact seems (and is) "whole" in the moment, but fade. Strikingly similar to Eigen, Heidegger and colleagues (1989) write,

> It is a rationalistic misjudgment of the essence of the personal stream of life, if one intends and demands that it vibrate in the same broad and sonorous amplitudes that well up in graced moments. Such claims grow out of a defect in inner humility before the mystery and grace-character of all life. We must be able to wait for the tautly intensities of meaningful life—and we must remain in continuity with these moments—not so much to enjoy them as to mold them into life—in the continuing course of life, they are taken along and incorporated into the rhythm of all future life. (p. 14)

These are intense, orienting moments in life that interrupt the regular flow of life; they are qualitatively different in some way. The new orientation is characterized as a "vehement life," wherein one becomes committed to "one's own unique . . . spiritual direction" (p. 14). Such graced moments make it possible to experience self-and-others with genuine understanding. They disclose the direction of one's life as something that is not quantitatively "there", like an object, but is, rather, something that must be truly lived. Life is to be lived, experience to be experienced. As with Heidegger, Eigen points out that these moments are fleeting and come to constitute a rhythm in life. "They may seem total at the time, but as their effects linger, more has to be done. They are like seeds that need farming, nurturing, work" (Eigen, 2011a, p. 30). Not all moments of existential–psychic rebirth come to fruition; rather, they may be partially born or even aborted. The process continues. We keep trying to get it right. "Thus rhythm is not necessarily a homeostatic thing. There are rhythms that destroy homeostasis, break new experiential ground" (p. 124). Even partial birth and aborted grace moments may themselves become opportunities for further growth, compassion, and receptivity. Addictive, destructive ways of knowing and being in the world, we hope, recede as genuine aliveness (F in Being/O) comes through the deepening rhythm of creative faith and destructiveness.

In appreciation

It is with great respect and admiration that I offer this chapter in honor of Michael Eigen, who has been a guide and mentor for roughly the last two decades. From my initial contact with him, to his work as external reader on my dissertation committee, to the present, he has been more than generous with his time and support. His amplifications, particularly in the realms of Winnicott and Bion, and originality of thought have greatly influenced me. I am grateful and honored to know him.

References

Bion. W. R. (1962). *Learning from Experience*. London: Heinemann.

Bion, W. R. (1970). *Attention and Interpretation*. London: Tavistock.
Bion, W. R. (1992). *Cogitations*. London: Karnac.
Eigen, M. (1985). Toward Bion's starting point: between catastrophe and faith. *International Journal of Psychoanalysis, 66*: 321–330.
Eigen, M. (1986). *The Psychotic Core*. Northvale, NJ: Jason Aronson.
Eigen, M. (1992). *Coming Through the Whirlwind*. Wilmette, IL: Chiron.
Eigen, M. (1993). *The Electrified Tightrope*, A. Phillips (Ed.). London: Karnac, 2004.
Eigen, M. (1999). *Toxic Nourishment*. London: Karnac.
Eigen, M. (2001). *Damaged Bonds*. London: Karnac.
Eigen, M. (2006). Faith and disillusionment: an interview with Dr. Michael Eigen. *DharmaCafe*. [On-line.] Available at: www.dharmacafe.com/index.php/life-cycles/article/faith-and-disillusionment-an-interview-with-dr-michael-eigen/
Eigen, M. (2011a). *Contact with the Depths*. London: Karnac.
Eigen, M. (2011b). Beauty and destruction: can goodness survive life and what would that mean? *First Humanities Forum*. Lecture conducted from Busan, Korea, November.
Eigen, M. (2013). Personal communication, July 26.
Freud, S. (1900a). *Interpretation of Dreams. S. E., 4–5*. London: Hogarth.
Freud, S. (1912–1913). *Totem and Taboo, S. E., 13*. London: Hogarth.
Freud, S. (1919h). The "uncanny". *S. E., 17*: 219–256. London: Hogarth.
Grotstein, J. (2000). *Who is the Dreamer Who Dreams the Dream?* Hillsdale, NJ: Analytic Press.
Heidegger, M. (1927). *Being and Time*, J. Macquarrie & E. Robinson (Trans.). San Francisco, CA: Harper & Row [reprinted London: Karnac, 1962].
Heidegger, M. (1966). *Discourse on Thinking*. New York: Harper & Row.
Heidegger, M. (1977). *The Question Concerning Technology and Other Essays*. New York: Harper & Row.
Heidegger, M. (1978). Letter on humanism. In: D. F. Krell (Ed.), *Basic Writings*. London: Routledge.
Heidegger, M. (2000). *Introduction to Metaphysics*. New Haven, CT: Yale University Press.
Heidegger, M. (2002). *Identity and Difference*. Chicago: University of Chicago Press.
Heidegger, M. (2003). *Philosophical and Political Writings*. New York: Continuum.
Heidegger, M. (2004). *Letters 1925–1975: Hannah Arendt and Martin Heidegger*. New York: Harcourt.

Heidegger, M., Blochmann, E., & Storch, J. (1989). *Martin Heidegger, Elisabeth Blochmann: Briefwechsel, 1918–1969*. Marbach am Neckar, Germany: Schillergesellschaft.

Ogden, T. (1992). *The Primitive Edge of Experience*. Lanham, MD: Rowman & Littlefield.

Stenstad, G. (2006). *Transformations: Thinking after Heidegger*. Madison, WI: University of Wisconsin Press.

PART II

REFRACTIONS

CHAPTER SIX

Psychic aliveness: on "being murdered into life"

Marian Campbell

Introduction

Michael Eigen opens one to the ideas of Freud, Winnicott, and Bion in such a way that, while I have always revered these masters, it is in reading Eigen that I am beginning really to see and hear and taste and feel in words what my blood knows or wants to know about psychic aliveness. I say this with all the awe, trepidation, and hope appropriate to a yearning for the transformations in O that can be the breath and blood and anguish of an analytic relationship.

A great gift given me as an analyst, an analysand, and a human being is Eigen's articulate conviction of the value, no, not even value, just the necessary "isness" of deadness and meaninglessness, and the indispensability of psychic rhythms and movement to feeling real in the relentless face of O.

Eigen has written extensively about psychic deadness (1996) and on Bion's idea of "being murdered into life" (2004, p. 31). I should like to use the following case material from an analysis in which images found and created give living testament to the neither awake-nor-asleepness of psychic deadness and the anguished, yet miraculous, murdering into life that a sensitive analytic relationship can midwife.

Case material

E is a single (divorced) professional woman in her late thirties with a childhood history characterized by both excellent academic achievement, and severe early emotional neglect and sexual trauma. She works in an academic setting where she is competent but unfulfilled. E referred herself for an open-ended analysis, consisting of thrice-weekly sessions. For the first six months E was punctual, polite, cooperative, articulate, and clearly intelligent. She spoke quite lucidly about her history and assured the analyst that she had already dealt with the sexual trauma in previous therapies of which she had had a few since her early twenties. However, there seemed to be something sanitized and rigid about her tendency to intellectualize, her pseudo-maturity, and the lack of real relatedness to her own feelings and to the analyst in the room. It was not that she did not have emotions, or that she found the world meaningless, but, rather, that she felt she could not tap into that meaning, that she was living behind glass walls that left her always merely looking in. Eigen mentions that deadness can often be seen in people who are "filled with emotions and meaning but somehow remain untouched by their experiences" (1996, p. xiii).

Although E was able to become more intimately involved during her sessions as the analysis developed, she seemed unable to sustain the sense of intimacy between sessions and would arrive at the analyst's door each session with a renewed awkwardness and caution. It was as though she was never sure that her welcome was secure or that the analyst would even be there. The second half of that year saw the emergence of her sexual trauma in fragmented nightmare images, from which she woke up in distress, and body memories, in the form of mostly lower abdominal physical symptoms. The severe emotional poverty in which she had grown up, a single child with anxious, depressed parents, also slowly began to be pieced together. Yet, it was as though E could not really make experiential contact with these fragments. She was able sometimes to draw them and even to bring some poetry she had written when she was younger, but her feelings remained split off and she had not yet shed a single tear in or out of sessions. Then about a year into her analysis, she started bringing a sequence of Christian iconography to which she had become drawn. E was irreligious but had an interest in art and symbols. Interestingly, unbeknown to E, her analyst was quite familiar with Christian imagery. Brought over the course of a further three years, these images illustrated, held, and catalyzed a deep and intense psychic process.

It is specifically the idiosyncratic sequence of the images discussed below that fascinates me as it appears to illustrate something in which I am very interested, that of psychic rebirth, especially after trauma, taking the form of being "murdered into life" (Eigen, 2004, p. 31). Work with the images over time was that of repeated looping and circling, of dead ends, of forgetting and returning. But the basic sequence begins with the Virgin and Child (Figure 1), and the Annunciation (Figure 2) as a prerequisite for, and a sort of heralding of, the birth; and then moves to the *dead* Christ *before* reaching the crucified Christ—and then back to Annunciation and Birth. It is as though E had to become aware of her own psychic deadness and, paradoxically, *live* it with the help of another, before she could experience the murderous pain behind the deadness. According to Eigen (1996), varying degrees of deadness are present in any psyche, but in E's case of severe childhood trauma, a pervasive deadness of which she was hardly aware as it had become so familiar to her had descended to obliterate the realities of O, which had been too overwhelming, especially for a child whose parents could hardly process their own realities, and, in fact, looked to E to comfort and enliven *them*. E's pervasive sense of O was of an oppressive weight that she tried in various ways across her life to enliven and lighten to no lasting effect. E knew only of the horror of O, although she could see that for some people it was also the source of life. She hoped for herself only that she could ferret out a small and inconspicuous space in the world where she could avoid contact with O as much as possible in order to survive in some meagre safety and comfort. Of course, she did not yet know this at the beginning of her analytic journey.

The Virgin and Child *and the* Annunciation *(Figures 1 and 2)*

The sequence into which patient and analyst were drawn began with images of the Virgin and Child in all their interesting variety. E soon realised that the Annunciation preceded the virgin birth; an

Figure 1. The Virgin and Child.

Figure 2. The Annunciation.

insemination/conception of some sort was necessary and E felt strongly that it needed to come to her from without, at least outside of consciousness. She felt the need, she said, for *grace*.

On a concrete level, E was very conscious of her need to make decisions regarding child-bearing as she was nearing forty. Her analyst was perhaps more particularly aware of E's psychological task of birthing herself after a lifetime of being oppressed and squashed by the perceived realities of her life. Reiner (2012) muses that the "miracle" of the Virgin birth "metaphorically represents that empty space in which something new mysteriously forms". The images carried a dual yearning for things E had no idea of how to achieve for herself: on the one hand, a literal baby birthed to a currently single woman; on the other, "the mental child of one's contact with O" (Reiner, 2012, p. 141).

Anne and Mary

E next started becoming aware of the Catholic emphasis on St. Anne, Mary's mother. She began collecting iconic pictures of the Marian Trinity—Anne, Mary, and the infant Christ (Figure 3). The question of whether it was a real or symbolic baby to be birthed, or both, was slowly superseded by the beginnings of a cautious recognition that one needed to have been mothered first in order to mother. E's child-self had received the barest mothering from her biological mother and father and had been largely mind-mothered by her intellect and precocity.

It struck E that pictures of the young Mary before the annunciation often depicted her in blue and *white*, whereas the woman Mary, post-annunciation, was often depicted in blue and *red*. The colour red, also present in the mature Anne's dress, became symbolic to E of fertilisation and womanhood (creativity, aliveness), and the subjective need for some sort of transformative energy or power became ever more urgent.

In this time, E, while driving to work one day, suddenly thought of the tearing of the temple curtain in the Gospels. She discovered a Google image of it in fierce blues and reds (see Figure 7). She felt that the glass behind which she lived needed to be shattered, that the solid veil in her very soul needed to be penetrated, to be torn and shredded by something life-bringing, but it felt an impossible hope. She was reminded, intellectually, of the crucifixion in direct association with

Figure 3. The Marian trinity.

the tearing of the temple curtain, but she could not identify with this spurned, childhood religious image and felt that, really, she had already been crucified through the traumas of her life until then. Both images dwindled from her attention and her sense of dull, thwarted need remained.

In the meantime, E continued to explore different versions of Anne, Mary, and the "annunciation" where beauty and light came upon you and bestowed you with life. Her searching, however, also led to darker ideas such as the Black Madonna and Mary Magdalene. The drawing by Picasso (Figure 4) was a version of the "annunciation" she found particularly disconcerting—it was ravishment rather than the spiritualized, angelic annunciations of before. She was hooked by these new themes, but unsure why. For the analyst, these darker images held an inkling of the impact still to come—and it was soon to

Figure 4. Drawing by Picasso.

arrive.

The "daggerman"

So far, the images seemed to hold E and to move her process along to some extent, but as though the pictures were enough in themselves, she was relatively inarticulate about their emotional meanings or, rather, she could articulate emotions, but did not seem to be *feeling* them. The analyst seemed much more emotionally impacted upon by the implications of the pictures. Also, the images which she had fastened to her wall at home seemed to be "mothering" her more, or in a more magical way, than the actual relationship with her analyst.

It seemed that, as yet, E had only an intuition of what still needed to happen psychically. The concern was whether E could use these images as symbols to represent emotional reality or to get rid of it.

According to Eigen (1996), if an individual does not have the attitude and capacity to struggle for rebirth, the symbol of rebirth may simply become a sign that the person is out of her depth, in psychic trouble. Bion and Winnicott are less concerned with the symbols themselves than with the processes that give rise to symbols (Eigen, 1996). It seemed that although E's need for, and preoccupation with, the images arose from the unconscious psyche, she was almost exclusively using secondary processing to control their meaning. She was right that something had to happen that was outside of her control, outside of the control of secondary processing. At least part of what E needed was a greater capacity for, and trust in, primary processing. For this, she would need what Eigen calls "flow and contact with flow" (1996, p. 53), or alpha functioning.

A significant turning point occurred after the production in pastels of the image depicted in Figure 5. The "mother and child" are illuminated by sacred candles in what the patient described as a cathedral. E's desire for mothering, her desire to give birth/"birth", and some form of "faith" or "reverie" are clearly depicted in the Madonna and child image and the sacred setting. But a dark, threatening "daggerman" intrudes between the image of the mother and child and her own petrified child-self, lying curled up on the floor. She did not know who the man was, but he felt familiar and so did the terror he inspired in her. He was like an inescapable, dark emptiness in the shape of a villain.

Again, E was unable to express the poignant, terrified feelings captured in the drawing she showed her analyst. But her analyst's eyes filled with unshed tears as she said that the picture was very moving, that it was terrible how the "daggerman" was violently preventing the child from contacting the parts of herself and the analytic relationship that she yearned for, and that the analyst thought that she might have been crying the tears that the patient herself could not yet cry. The patient was slightly awkward and surprised, yet she heard the echo of distant knowledge that something, as yet unreachable, *was* crying inside. Kogan and Jaffe (2010, p. 1233) describe this as an analyst who can "work as a living container that feels the scratch of experience: the analyst consciously experiences something which the patient cannot feel and succeeds in expressing it in thoughts and words stemming from what he feels himself." Of course, E did not immediately, or even soon thereafter, start feeling and crying, but she

Figure 5. The mother and child and the "daggerman".

went home somewhat changed inside, having had a new experience with another human being.

The drawing also gave an important message to the analyst at this time: in colour, both Anne/Mary and the child-self are wearing blue and *red*—the colour E associated in the images of Mary with fertilisation. Bearing in mind that one does not facilitate an impending regression lightly, the patient's unconscious seemed to be giving some indication in the drawing that the traumatized child is paradoxically also identified with fructifying. And the religious setting seemed to confirm a sense that this patient, despite her damage, had the soul's desire for truth, her truth (Grotstein, 2004).

St. Anne and the "frozen child"

Shortly after the imaging of the "daggerman", E brought the image below (Figure 6), which is apparently of Anne and Mary. Anne is holding a candle beside the heavily swaddled, sleeping Mary, her hand cupping the flame to prevent it guttering. It has the atmosphere almost of a vigil. There are blues and reds in the colour reproduction.

E seemed to be becoming aware of the presence of the analyst to a child still lost in the absence of her mother. E felt that the baby Mary was frozen and not dead and that Anne was waiting, protecting, and hoping. She seemed cautiously more receptive to her now more conscious need of the analyst's mothering.

In *Psychic Deadness* (1996, p. xix), Eigen says of Ferenczi, "I mention Ferenczi now because he stands as a beam of light, explicitly

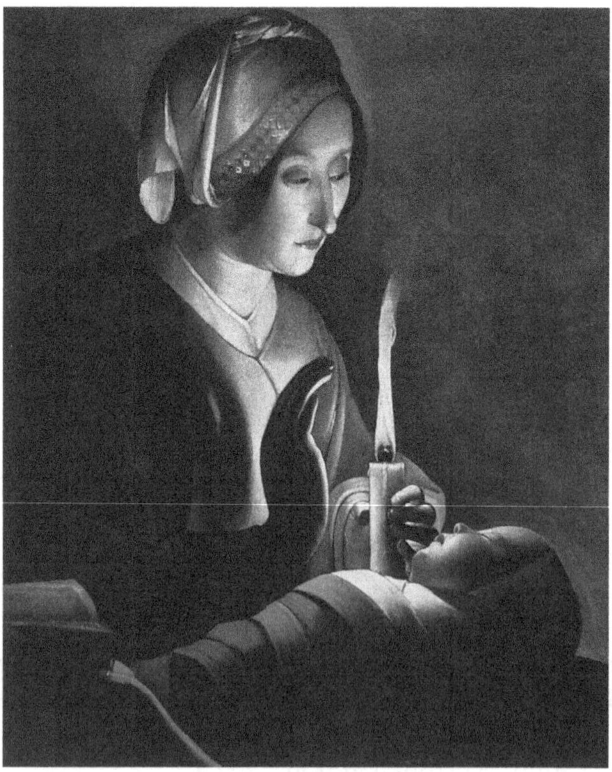

Figure 6. Anne and Mary, the "frozen child".

emphasizing the importance of the analyst's love in counter-acting destructive forces." Eigen also says that for the mother/analyst to seduce the baby/patient into life, the latter must have some "capacity to use another person for growth" (1996, p. xix). As mentioned above, various things had already hinted that E seemed to have this capacity and to cling tenaciously to the hope the analyst held out, despite how threadbare that hope sometimes seemed. E seemed to know there were other selves to be found besides the "frozen" self in which she was incarcerated.

> We might say that in this *pre*conception of a self, there is a self already in the process of being conceived, a self that is 'pending', or held in abeyance until it can be realised through the relationship with another sentient being. In the absence of such a person, the infant in the proto-mental phase is, in a sense, *Waiting for Godot*, a seemingly timeless wait in an infinite universe for someone who might or might not make sense of these truths he does not *know* but which, inherently he is, and which he instinctually yearns to have developed through his capacity to think. (Reiner, 2012, p. 144)

However, it was to be an excruciating time for patient and analyst. E found it impossible to stay in her sessions, yet impossible to leave. Sometimes she left early in despair; sometimes she left early in mute rage. Sometimes she could manage the full session, but always left feeling it was not enough. Always, after leaving early, she would call, a child's voice saying, "I'm sorry, please don't be angry, I don't know what to do." Sometimes she could cry on the phone, a child's sobs, but never in the actual session. She felt helplessly unreachable. The following is an extract of what she wrote at the time:

> "The place of the dead babies knows my name. It knows my dark name which probably no-one else would want to know. I don't know what the name is in words but I feel it calling in my body. And then I lie around it to contain it and be contained by it. Her [the analyst] words can't touch me in the visceral places where I am owned. Sitting with A [analyst], freezing just millimetres outside the lamplight of her warmth. Gnawing hunger, tears as close as vomit in my throat. Shroud of angry words. I cannot stay, I cannot leave."

I think that E was being played by the growing "possibility of being there to undergo the murder that made it impossible to be there" (Eigen,

2004, p. 28). She seemed simultaneously to be trying to avoid the place of trauma and moving toward it. Despite everything, E kept working toward increased feeling, vacillating between disbelief that there was anything to feel and unconscious fear of annihilation by impact.

E had been an unplanned baby, growing up in a home where her parents were physically present, but emotionally and psychically absent for their child. They literally did virtually nothing, enjoyed very little, and struggled to survive, let alone feel alive. The child E had wandered around the quiet house, trying to find substance in touching the heavy old furniture, eventually returning to her room to read endlessly, or just to lie on her bed, in her own body's bubble. Sometimes she remembered these fragments and it always brought her some relief to contextualize her otherwise "psychotic-seeming dead baby" experiences, although she often questioned the veracity of her memories, as though they were fabrications rather than memories, which is probably what they were; these childhood experiences of E were both so familiar and so traumatic that they had most likely not been captured in explicit memory, but, rather, had formed an experiential substrate of unconscious knowing.

It was around this time in the analytic process that E's attention returned to the tearing of the temple curtain mentioned above.

Interestingly, in colour, the image depicted in Figure 7 uses a blue curtain against a red background to surround the gleaming tabernacle—again the blues and reds E associates with fructification in the annunciation pictures. She seemed to be yearning "to experience one's power and energy ripping through suffocation" (Eigen, 2004, p. 30).

Again, E dabbled with a few images of the crucifixion but still they did not move her at all. She could increasingly remember her past, but not the pain; and she could, at times, imagine into the aliveness she would like to feel in the future, but the present hung, a dead weight across her way.

Then she found Hans Holbein the Younger's *The Body of the Dead Christ in the Tomb* (Figure 8).

Dead self in the tomb

Holbein's dead Christ resonated deeply and scarily with E and her consciousness of a frozen child was expanded into consciousness of a "dead" adult. It led her to produce the drawing in Figure 9.

Figure 7. Image associated with the tearing of the temple curtain.

In this drawing, E's adult self is "dead" on her bed, which has turned into a tomb. It is a macabre sort of Sleeping Beauty scene. She is wearing blue only, unfructified by the red of blood and life and feeling. The shadowy figure with the dagger reappears, threatening to kill her should she dare to try to awake to life. It is an arresting scene: the "daggerman," it seems, controls not only E's traumatized child-self, but also her familiar, daily adult-self. Both "daggerman" drawings seem like evil parodies of the annunciations she had been collecting: a daimonic male figure is again poised across from the unfertilised female, but here he is intent on blocking transformation rather than

Figure 8. The Body of the Dead Christ in the Tomb by Hans Holbein.

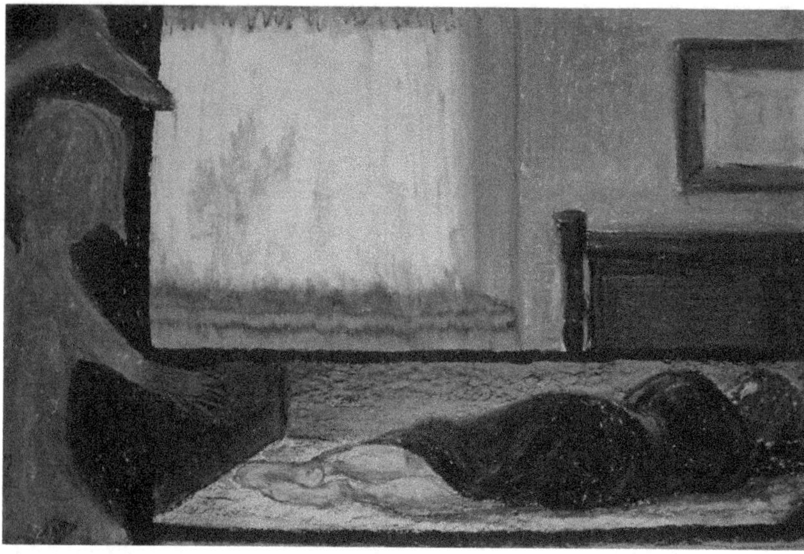

Figure 9. E's depiction of her "dead" adult self.

bringing it. And it seems that he is succeeding. The figure looks peaceful, hypnotized even; she is certainly not trying to get out. She is incarcerated, but safe, and shows none of the fear the child-self in the cathedral shows. Kristeva (1989) writes about the intimacy of black melancholy that the sufferer can feel more attracted to this dark inner "Thing" (p. 145) than to life or people. E's journal entry above had already alluded to just such a relationship:

> "*The place of the dead babies knows my name.* It knows my dark name which probably no-one else would want to know. I don't know what the name is in words but I feel it calling in my body. *And then I lie around it to contain it and be contained by it. Her [the analyst's] words can't touch me in the visceral places where I am owned.*" (My italics)

This was a traumatic recognition for E. She had so far allowed a remarkable engagement with a dead baby part of herself, made possible partly because she felt she had been excavating a *past* self, intruding on the present, but not really her. Now she was faced with the impact of the past on her *present self*, from which she could not so easily dis-identify.

This image holds none of the romance associated with the fairytale of Sleeping Beauty or the myth of the annunciation. Yet, there are hints of hope: in the background is a lighted window with what looks like green leaves behind the glass. The brightness of the white-curtained window in the light reminds one of the light of the tabernacle behind its torn blue curtains, and the window-sill is red, E's colour for fructification.

E allowed herself the recognition that this was a "true" image of the nothingness of her current psychic deadness. Unwitnessed by human presence, this absence had turned into a persecuting presence, a concretized no-thing keeping her stuck, immobilised. Indigestible, it was the opposite of the no-thing from which something can be born, a tolerable absence or empty space to which something can be added, from which experience can evolve (Eigen, 1996). Rather, this deadness felt like a suspension of experience from which E could neither fall asleep nor wake up (Bion, 1962).

Occasionally, when E could find the words to speak in sessions, she began describing herself returning home from work—where she continued to perform well, or from friends with whom she could be intelligent, funny, and caring—to lie with her face to the wall, often on the hard floor, without eating or even moving for hours. She described the need to curl around herself so as to prevent falling through herself—this last life-preserving intention was all she had energy for. Her mind was blank, her body was concentrating on saving her last bit of herself before freefall. Her fantasies, when she was asked to try to describe her inner world, were of the Vodacom advertisement from a number of years before where a baby floats in space, except that, for E, the bubble-like spacesuit isolates her from the human world rather than protecting her from space, and she is not smiling as she hangs there, unconnected to anything or anybody.

The analyst continued to feel the desperate oscillation and unbearable tension between disconnected lifelessness, in which the patient felt absolutely lost to her, defeated by the vacuum, and, at times, the frustrated, angry pleading in her eyes for some sort of transformative help. It was painful and helpless-making, and it had to be borne. E made barely a gesture or movement on the couch, and often the session was borne in an atmosphere something like Eigen's unbearable "silent scream . . . an explosion that no one can hear because it occurred and goes on occurring in a place where there is no Other" (1996, p. 7).

E was sometimes able to reflect that she was aware that there had been pockets of this dead place throughout her life, but now it was amplifying as she acknowledged the gravity of its existence for the first time, as she allowed herself to experience it consciously and to bring it to another human being. It was impossible for her to maintain her fragile connection to her analyst between or within sessions, but, in the midst of all the overwhelming despair, the patient–analyst team managed to maintain a capacity for hope: partly because of the power of the images to act as containers for experience, titrating the raw experience, but largely due to the fact that this time the Other was both present and alive, or able to become alive again after deathly impact. Eigen (1996) describes such deadness as "something transpersonal in the force field that wipes everything out" (p. 14) in sessions, something bigger than both analyst and patient. A dead analyst could be in danger of identifying and falling with the patient. E had little sense of her own continuity of being but she started to feel her analyst's capacity for survival and repair. E's analyst fought to be able to stay with E in her dead spaces, knowing both may be stuck, but trying to have faith in meaning *and* meaninglessness, and in the potential for "movement between the digestible–indigestible" (Eigen, 1996, p. 19) to be stimulated and sustained. In this way she tried to "dream the patient while awake in sessions, . . . making the patient real, taking the patient in, making the patient's life and destruction part of her psychic bloodstream" (Eigen, 2004, p. 32).

E slowly began to detect the possibility of seeing deadness no longer as "nowhere," but as a legitimate "somewhere." With the help of her mother/analyst, E seemed to be learning to "process what cannot be processed with a processor that cannot process it" (Eigen, 2004, p. 32).

The crucifixion

From the deadness described above, E slowly returned to the idea of the crucifixion (Figure 10), but produced her own image—a portrait drawing of herself on the cross (Figure 11). The colours blue and red figure sharply in the colour drawing. The crown of thorns is also a crown of red flowers. There is red blood running down her hair. And she has found a voice, she is clearly shouting out—to O? An improvement in the quality of E's capacity to process experience through the

Figure 10. The cruxifixion.

Figure 11. E's portrait of herself on the cross

trough of deadness seemed to be leading to the transformations in O she yearned for, but it felt like crucifixion rather than life. In *Cogitations*, Bion wrote that the return of feeling feels like murder (Eigen, 2004, p. 27).

Previously, E started retrieving or making memories. Then she fell into the deadness of cut-off feelings. With the above drawing of her screaming on the cross, E began to experience fragments of intense feeling—of pain, and rage, and loneliness, and a wretchedness that was only wordless, physical sobbing—seemingly unconnected to any memory. Again, she needed her analyst to make meaning of what seemed like madness, to midwife a murder–birth with no guarantees other than faith in the rhythmic movement of the psychic life–death–life cycle. E seemed another step further in her reaching to Winnicott's X (1992, p. 128), the trauma at the beginning of personality formation, "a terror too terrifying to experience is a truth needing digestion, a moment searching for someone to endure it, if only a little, or a little at a time" (Eigen, 2004, p. 26), a living moment searching for someone to experience it.

These living moments were crucifying, murderous: as E's frozen psychic equipment thawed, the flow of metaphoric life-blood felt excruciating. Eigen describes it thus: "To have blood may be more frightening than not having blood. In the former, one risks trauma all over again. In the latter one is protected by hopelessness; one is already dead" (2004, p. 27). E and her analyst soon discovered a pattern where each little chunk of E's felt experience was followed by a backlash of numb deadness, compulsive reading through the night and day, and a feeling of disconnection from her analyst.

It became very clear what the deadness and the "daggerman" were protecting E against: not only the childhood pain of her mother's absence and the trauma of abuse, but also the adult pain of the devastating long-term sequelae of sexual and relational trauma and the frustration of allowing a hunger for mothering in an analytic relationship that could, by its very nature, never fulfill all that E had not had as a child and never would have.

Initially, the "daggerman" protected E. As a child, she could not possibly have digested the impact of her reality at the time. But this protection took on a life of its own, it became a killing force in the psyche, a "daggerman", cutting apart the psyche, splitting events from memory and memory from feeling. This dispersal of affect diminishes feeling until feeling is eventually lost, as are impulse and desire (Eigen 1996, 2004).

On the other hand, E's "daggerman" also had a teleological significance, because his appearance in her drawing eventually led to this: recognition of psychic process, a cutting together, a possible annunciation.

The use of symbols

I should like to return to the idea of images as containers. The positive teleological potential of the images E used was realised because she and her analyst managed to use them as transitional objects, as it were, rather than as fetish objects (Winnicott, 2005). At first, E's relationship to the images was primarily intuitive. She seemed to use them to represent what she could not yet feel and to communicate this to the analyst. However, they became conduits for effective primary processing, acting together with the analyst to metabolize the unbearable and indescribable. When primary processing is damaged, as was the case with E, it can become part of the problem and perpetuate damage to the psyche. For example, the image of E's "daggerman" could have atrophied as a container and the drawing would then have functioned to keep her in her tomb, consolidating the lie that escape would be more annihilatory than being "dead". There is a knife-edge, as it were, between the creativity and destructivity in symbols. The daggerman's lies brought the bloodless murder of psychic paralysis; his living presence brought the bloody murder of near annihilation through impact with O. E and her analyst somehow managed to "symbolize destructive processes that stop symbolization" (Eigen, 2004, p. 34).

It is noteworthy that E's symbols were of a deeply religious nature, despite her not being Catholic, or even Christian. This reminds me of Eigen's musings that religion can hold something about O without being O (Eigen, 1997). The attitude that risks opening oneself to murder/life/reality Bion called faith (Eigen, 2004; Reiner, 2012). It is also possible that the sense of the sacred, of reverie and awe in these religious images helped to represent and hold the integrity and faith with which E engaged in this process and the grace that pulled the analytic dyad through.

Movement and faith

What followed E's crucifixion was not a momentously glorious resurrection, but a sense of having come through and being more all right (Bion, in Eigen, 2004, p. 31), of being more open to herself and to the world, of feeling a little less alienated from life. She is learning to allow impulse and desire a little more space to develop, instead of immediately deadening either for fear of disappointment and danger. She is beginning to develop the nuanced taste for the instinctual rhythm of being alive (Eigen, 1996), rather than the wilful structure she had previously relied on to cope for so long in the world, squeezing as much blood out of the stone of her life as possible, thinking she could overcome the incapacity toward fuller life by her own effort. E has learned through experience that you have to risk madness and terror to reclaim the realness of your life, which is how Winnicott's X is related to Bion's O (Bloch, 2009). She is beginning to perceive that living is more about movement than destination and that rebirth happens continually and deadness may even be nourishing (Eigen, 1996).

There is no once-off rebirth. The images E used are one cultural representation of humanity's attempts to grapple with how to live in the impersonal face of the life–death–life cycle of the psyche. Impact is happening to us all the time—of the O of ourselves, of another, of ultimate reality. Becoming alive is murderous, but "Bion invites us to practice getting murdered, ultimately being enlivened by it" (Eigen, 2004, p. 31).

Faith, then, for E, is no longer a passive waiting for an angel to bring her the child of her life and joy, but an opening to experience, even if through murder. She was waiting for grace to descend from the outside, but is learning that facing into her own truths as they evolve, even the truth of deadness and meaninglessness, satisfies her soul's hunger for realness and relatedness.

The "daggerman" has not gone away completely. He regularly tells her that she will come to harm, that she is heading for disaster in her new faith, and that then she will be alone and solely to blame for her destitution. But E no longer wants to do such violence to experience. She is dreaming of "the faith Bion has in mind . . . the need sensitivity has to taste life, to feel impacts and digest them in ways that lead to more life" (Eigen, 2004, p. 9).

In Auden's poem "Age of Anxiety (19)" he describes a collective that would rather die in fear, dread, and illusion than be crucified by the transforming realities of the present moment. E has moved from Auden's collective to Denise Levertov's *Kyrie* in "Mass for the Day of St. Thomas Didymus" (2002, pp. 130–131).

> We live in terror
> of what we do not know,
> in terror of not knowing,
> of the limitless, through which freefalling
> forever, our dread
> sinks and sinks,
> or
> of the violent closure of all.
>
> Yet our hope lies
> in the unknown,
> in our unknowing.
>
> O deep, remote unknown,
> O deep unknown,
> Have mercy upon us.

References

Auden, W. H. (2011). *The Age of Anxiety: A Baroque Eclogue*, A. Jacobs (Ed.). Princeton: Princeton University Press.

Bion, W. R. (1962). *Learning from Experience.* New York: Basic Books.

Bloch, S. (2009). Personal communication.

Eigen, M. (1996). *Psychic Deadness.* Northvale, New Jersey: Jason Aronson.

Eigen, M. (1997). Musings on O. *Journal of Melanie Klein and Object Relations, 15(2)*, 213–226.

Eigen, M. (2004). *The Sensitive Self.* Middletown, CT: Wesleyan University Press.

Grotstein, J. S. (2004). The seventh servant: the implications of a truth drive in Bion's theory of 'O'. *International Journal of Psychoanalysis, 85*: 1081–1101.

Kogan, I., & Jaffe, R. (2010). 'There is a remedy for everything but death': to bear witness, to recover and transform psychic experiences of annihilation. (Panel report.) *International Journal of Psychoanalysis, 91*: 1231–1235.

Kristeva, J. (1989). *Black Sun: Depression and Melancholia*. New York: Columbia University Press.

Levertov, D. (2002). *Selected Poems*. New York: New Directions Books.

Reiner, A. (2012). *Bion and Being: Passion and the Creative Mind*. London: Karnac.

Winnicott, D. W. (1992). *Psycho-analytic Explorations*, C. Winnicott, R. Shepherd, & M. Davis (Eds.). Cambridge MA: Harvard University Press.

Winnicott, D. W. (2005). *Playing and Reality*. Oxford: Routledge.

CHAPTER SEVEN

Eigen's transformational esthetic: wounded nourishment, primary process work, and the purple period

Loray Daws

In the beginning: Eigen's stirring psychoanalytic attentiveness

> Madness is both innate and a form of adaptation. It is a desperate response to emotional pain and the stress of life. But it is also part of the way we are innately structured, and it has a developmental timetable of its own. In sum: the ego is sane and mad. In his letters to Jung, Freud called the ego a clown, but it is a dangerous and precious clown, attached to truth, compromise, and delusion. Its polarities may support one another or tear a soul to pieces; they usually do both. (Eigen, 2004a, p. 10)

Eigen's oeuvre remains a committed psychoanalytic quest in mapping new psychological vistas, carving out uncharted psychic territories while remaining faithful to our analytic forefathers as creative instruments for orientation. Throughout his prolific writings and teachings, Eigen's mental cartography and analytic geolect never fails to read organically—pulsating, alive, present, and open, touching, tasting, and probing the inner world with much respect and ethical sensibility. Given this, there are many Eigenesque vertices to follow, many thoughts to thicken, expand, and play with. For the purposes of the current chapter, I will limit my focus to Eigen's (1999) main trauma statements and their relevance to the therapeutic praxis of "unwanted patients" (Eigen, 1977). In doing so, I hope to emphasize not so much the "hard to reach patient", but, rather, the "hard to reach *interface* between therapist and patient" and the importance of Eigen's notion of primary impact work (2004c). Eigen's rhythm of faith, its relationship to Jeff Eaton's (2005) work on the obstructive object, as well as Eigen's inherent relational ethic in remaining a "welcoming" other to the necessary beta-element impacts (and its transformations) will serve as further organizing principles.

Developing a rhythm of faith

Psychoanalytic experience, suspended momentarily from all ontological and epistemological discourse, personifies a language of possibility, a unique vision of human idiom and psychic growth. In service of our most private sense of self, communicable or not, psychoanalysis provides, through its language and technical setting, the creation of a potential space distinctly suited for our instinctual aesthetic, our inherent generative capacity, our continual *unfolding* of Being (Bollas, 1978, 1979; Eigen, 1981, 1983, 1985, 2004d, 2007; Ogden, 1985a,b). Within psychoanalytic thought, the various vertices of reparation, reclamation, and restoration of self are compassionately and faithfully transcribed by various schools of thought. Eigen's aesthetic, immersed in differing languages of possibility, appears fuelled by a seemingly simple yet richly organizing principle, a unique "rhythm of faith" (2004d, p. 33). Eigen himself summarizes the rhythm of faith as death and rebirth, breakdown and recovery, and the sense of being murdered as one comes alive:

> Here I suggest that part of the rhythm Freud intuits has to do with a kind of psychic pulse, an opening–closing linked with death–rebirth (Elkin), breakdown–recovery (Winnicott), coming alive–being murdered–feeling all right (Bion) . . . For Elkin one is born through a merciful Other after suffering boundless horror. For Winnicott trauma breaks personality as it forms, dread of breakdown persisting as an undercurrent associated with new beginnings . . . For Bion it is as if one is murdered every time one tries to come alive. (2004d, pp. 33–34)

Within this rhythm, Eigen has created a unique psychoanalytic songline[1] (Chatwin, 1987), a primordial contact and growth "thesis" able to organize many psychoanalytic phenomena and clinical thoughts, carrying our psychoanalytic yearnings forward and onward towards Faith ("F") in Ultimate Reality ("O").

Eigen's songlines: sojourns into the primordial self

As hinted at in the opening paragraphs of this chapter, Eigen's psychoanalytic reverie makes special mention of our nourished and traumatized selves when he writes, "(1) In the beginning there is nourishment; (2) in the beginning (almost) there is trauma, and (3) in the beginning there is nourishment–trauma" (1999, p. 145). Parents provide a historical soma–psychic potential long before a child's awareness of its own facticity. Preconception, pregnancy, birth, and, thereafter, parents' pre- and post-Caesurian idiom (Daws, 2009) both enliven and constrict reverie-cycles and potentialities. Eigen's rhythm of faith maps the vicissitudes of the nascent self's continual struggle towards growth, the various "impacts" of an "other," the sensitivity and poignancy of ego-grasping, the facticity of damaged bonds, the infinite implications of entropy and psychic deadness, our psychotic core, as well as our inherent vitality and sensitive self potentiality. Nestled in rich psychoanalytic soil and "clinical probes," Eigen carves and "re-visions" sensitive phenomenological descriptions of mothers and fathers as both alpha and omega functions (Williams, 1998), that is, our necessary symbol makers and signifiers which either undo or enhance (usually both) our psyche, our coenesthetic–interoceptive–proprioceptive–kinesthetic–perceptual–cognitive–affective capacity. Notational Eigen (2004c), in true Bionian fashion, represents the evolution of the psyche as the constant conjunction between the nascent self (autochthony) (Grotstein, 1997), the maternal and the paternal (alterity) (Grotstein, 1997), and being in a/the world (cosmogony) (Grotstein, 1997). Within such potential psychological soil, each individual is continually engaged in psychic movement and the building of his or her own unique rhythm of faith, as well as the very forces that constitute its reversal. Eigen's rhythm reworks and "re-envisions" the infinite variations and permutations of moments of growth–collapse, nurture–trauma and its resulting artifacts. In my reading of

Eigen, special attention is given to the very artifacts, the "trauma globs" that remain in need of "transmutations" into "useable feeling/imagining/thinking flows"[2] (1995, p. 113). That is,

> [r]aw, unprocessed and unprocessable trauma globs [which], together with shards of aborted, deformed thoughts–affects (scraps of failed psychic movement), agglutinate and further block possibility of movement. One may depict this state as stagnant, as a graveyard or garbage heap—a dead or inert or wasted psyche. The psyche is at once dead and radioactive; its deadness takes on a poisonous life of its own, contaminating and destroying whatever comes near . . . (Eigen, 1995, p. 113)

Whereas many may shrink from such a psyche and its implications, similar to oceanic dead spots, Eigen has spent decades forging a language of vitality, of resurrection and redemption. Being unable, even "crippled", reflects a damaged psychic processor, unconscious or otherwise, although held by Eigen as being *constantly* in search of a container for its transformation. The reader may rightly note that even such a search may not be in the service of growth, only in the service of an ongoing fateful tragedy. There are clients who can only allow us to bear witness to their inner holocaust, and our embryonic science and grasping may prove unable to be the very object and presencing they so desperately need.[3]

However, Eigen does provide us with an esthetic of faith, reminding the analyst of the inherent need for human contact and the need to protect the "divine/vital spark" in another (Hornstein, 2000). To repeat, Eigen's trauma globs, the signifiers of the wounding, obdurate,[4] and obstructive object (Eaton, 2005) subvert psychic potentiality through both malevolent hypo- and hyper-transformations. Overflowing with projection, it is both frightened and frightening. In the descriptive language of Eigen (2004c), Eaton (2005), Williams (1998), and Symington (2002), attempting to live with such an endopsychic state of affairs creates various patterns of body–mind–self–other madness, keeping alive the original traumatic impact of the intensifier (a consequence of trauma/trauma in psychic form), the petrifier (hardening, stony, obdurate, aghast, panic), and/or the liquefier (submission, passionate refusal) (Symington, 2002). The continual parent-child, unconscious, psyche-to-psyche impact leaves in its wake the very artifacts, debris and residues, and toxic breadcrumbs (the principle of sedimentation of Symington, 2002) that are either *represented* or *managed* through states such as psychic deadness (Eigen, 2004c,d), stasis and entropy, megalomania, being too good, and, finally, through (the principle of) hypostatization, wherein the very activity, thought, and feeling that is "hated" is displaced on to a figure who serves as the receptacle of the activity, its feelings and behaviors, thereby emptying psychic capacity and creating a role and mask-like adaptation in interpersonal life (Eigen, 2004c; Symington, 2002).

The obstructive–wounding–obdurate object remains unable to accept, or serve as midwife to, the nascent self, and the dilemma is clinically seen in acting "out" and "in," dreams of internal saboteurs, and even in the relentless concretizing of all inner life, inciting terrible frustration and mental pain in the analytic couple (Freedman et al., 2011; Frosch, 2012; Kogan, 2007). These infinite variations of soul murder and soul blindness locked in deadly grip are central to Eigen's work, as is the very possibility of a new beginning in which the rhythm of faith can guide us in finding ways into this catastrophe (Eigen, 2014). Eigen's rhythm is an open invitation to the sense of self that is left behind given the wounding object, one that can be viewed as ontologically "true" and salvageable. Where it is indeed possible to work within ("with" and "in") such states of mind saturated with trauma globs, stagnation, and radioactive waste, it is believed that the internalization of a *welcoming object* may touch and even salvage the most vital and enlivening dual-track rhythm of breakdown and repair, making psychic growth ever possible (Eaton, 2005, 2014; Eigen, 1981, 1985, 1999, 2001; Grotstein, 1997).

Presencing Eigen's clinical chamber

"The patient, in a way, reads himself in the therapist's being and vice versa" (Eigen, 2001, p. 5).

Through rich metaphor and organic language, Eigen's clinical narrative enlivens damage, its malevolent transformations, and our potential nature in holding these transformations. As psychological phoropter, Eigen's vision subtly shifts to find the most needed lens, metaphor, and language to enhance the reader's view of trauma-nourishment. Eigen remains clear that tolerating and transforming wounded nourishment and its impacts while feeling present, receptive, willing, and psychoanalytically able remains a daunting undertaking.[5] Many passages see not only the client being held, but also Eigen remaining open to his own reactions, limitations, and inner primary-process working, his own "recoil on having another person" (2004b, p. 21). I have found that Eigen "lends" himself the very respect, care, interest, and demands he communicates to his analytic co-worker. One only has to read the transformation of Dee (1986), a twelve-year-old epileptic schizophrenic, to appreciate Eigen's contact with the primary process of another. Clearly, for Eigen it is a matter of living: "I must confess I am a primary process lover. In an important way, loving the flow of primary process meanings has made my life worth-while" (2004c, p. 142).

Akin to a medieval sin-eater, Eigen remains "being" with another in a way that cultivates an ability to take in the most damaged of the other (into one's "psychic bloodstream"), and, as such, bring to pass a waking dream of the other's conscious and unconscious wounding object. Eigen's Elkin–Winnicott–Bion rhythm serves as Ariadne's thread to the psychoanalytic attitude and the "sense"–"ability" inherent in his presencing and analytic touch:

> In analysis the patient experiences the analyst variously as a traumatic force or wounding object, supportive background presence, vehicle of wisdom and stupidity, auxiliary dream-worker, agent of faith. The experiential arc described here constitutes a rhythm of faith. For Elkin faith evolves and is sustained as the primordial self is nursed through despair and stupor, quickening into life with the Other's help. (Eigen, 2004d, p. 34)

Faith held by Elkin, as for Winnicott, is the consequence of good enough midwifery of the primordial self in despair due to a wounding object and its obdurate sequelae. A good enough psychic midwife is expected to *initiate* the "breakdown–recovery rhythm" (Eigen, 2004d), and within such a rhythm there remains an inherent faith in the other's ability not only to experience agony and anxiety, but also to develop trust in "one's ability to come through the trauma–recovery sequence, and experience one's own generative capacity. Gradually one's experiential reach is able to encompass blends of intrusiveness/obtrusiveness/abandonment/support that is part of inter-subjectivity" (Eigen, 2004d, p. 34).

For a Bionian Eigen, the rhythm of faith includes the symbolization of affective damage, "going through the murderous object that psychic birth evolves—as process of opening the worst and coming through" (2004d, p. 34) the dreaming of this very catastrophe, the reworking of radicalized states of mind, not through entropy and delinking, but by being truthful within our destruction and our catastrophes. In Eigen's writing, the seemingly obtuse and mathematizing Bion suddenly comes forth as a form of radical openness towards the self and other dealing with catastrophe. Clearly, Bion, Elkin, and Winnicott's writings (as read through Eigen) are not just theories, but creative and imaginative suggestions for developing a kind of *thinking heart* needed to accomplish psychic growth after it has been exposed to wounding experiences. Bion left a legacy in his writing of how to develop such a mind, Winnicott, the therapeutic space within which psychic birth can take place, and Elkin, a faith in the object and analytic project. Together, a powerful analytic trilogy woven by Eigen into a coherent, therapeutic songline. The rhythm of faith also implies, by definition, being more than a technical observer, an "objective other" repeating abstract notations and inferences (as important as they are); rather, it is a "welcoming" and an "allowing" of another into one's (or *a*) psychic life so that the other evokes and intermingles with one's own discourse, one's private idiom with its own developmental vicissitudes. Patient–analyst "with-ness" (Eshel, 2005, 2010, 2013, see also Chapter Nine, this volume) or presencing (Eshel, 2013; Marcel, 2001a,b) refer to the capacity to hold, think, feel, dream, and tolerate mutual impacts, to allow one to be reached, and to be available:

> A therapist may or may not get the message, but he tries to stay with the situation until it begins to reach him. To talk about reaching the patient before the therapist is reached can be premature. The therapist speaks from a place he is touched, which includes his own incomplete, ongoing bonding process, with its incessant dream-work. . . . As a therapist, it is necessary to go even deeper into strangulated states—not only to observe, but to feel the closing in on oneself, collapsing, enduring mutilation, becoming aware of rotten, ruptured areas of one's own life. . . . [But] often one finds damage to self, tied to embedded damaged objects that are now part of self. It is not possible to remove the damage to self by removing the damaged object (e.g. residues of a depressed or psychotic or abusive parent): the damage is done. But one can help a person to open new channels to process the damage, enabling new states of self to evolve. (Eigen, 2001, pp. 3–4)

We all actively wish away damaged bonds, catastrophic impacts, poisonous residue, and various other "irritants", even, at times, relying on the psychoanalytic discourse *per se* to rid the self of the containing function it was originally designed for (Eigen, 2001; Slochower, 2006). The reasons for the latter are complex, deeply personal, and painfully exposing to the analytic couple, not to mention the profession. Eigen frequently mentions how analysts at times try to get rid of their patients, hoping to make life and the encounter more "peaceful," but it remains a problem that is only postponed. Patients and the difficulties faced may be too much, necessitating foreclosure. For Eigen, there is a price to pay for both avoiding and working with trauma nourishment. Tolerating the developmental enclaves and failures and our most wounded selves within our patients, ourselves, and our psychoanalytic interactions remains a creative activity, a human feat in and of itself. It is held throughout Eigen's work that as welcoming other (alpha functioning) (Eaton, 2005), one may serve the needed auxiliary support, processing affect, and enabling emotional digestion, even when it entails deep contact with the colicky parts of life, having to manage emotional shingles,[6] or meeting a self that is enslaved and entombed. It should also be mentioned that Eigen (2004d) forewarns that coming alive has its own risks; that is, aliveness carries the burden of possible re-traumatization. Irrespective of this, all growth, limited though it may be, is expected to bring forth the very capacity to not only re-experience wounded-nourishment and its vicissitudes, that is, the various endopsychic, interpersonal, and communal/cultural forces of self-estrangement, but also a renewed hope that the native self may germinate. The latter is seen in Eigen's use of Bion's notion of alpha function as laboring disability, and the intimate conjunction between self-creation, I "feeling", and the moment of destruction (meeting the wounding–obstructive–obdurate object):

> Alpha function, then, labors with a chronic disability, injured by the injury it works with. Yet it is driven to process damaging forces as part of the way it heals itself, risking further injury by seeking health . . . To assemble anything means to assemble what destroys one. . . . The fact that dreaming destruction is a bit of alpha work against all odds is one reason, I believe, why Bion says the analyst must dream the patient while awake in the sessions . . . The analyst's anxiety/resistance is about dreaming the patient, making the patient real, taking the

> patient in, making the patient's life and destruction part of one's psychic bloodstream. To constitute a living person within oneself is to constitute what is destroying this person as well. The analyst must dream what destroys the patient's dreams, and since the analyst may or may not be much better at this than the patient, the analyst turns on two people becoming partners in evolution, doing work all humanity must come to do. In other words, part of the long term work involves becoming real to ourselves and each other and the profound ethic this implies.[7] (2004d, p. 32)

It is with this notion of alpha function as laboring disability, the welcoming of the wounding–obstructive–obdurate object through or within the rhythm of faith, that I now turn to a case.

Psychoanalytic dialogues with an educated "hobo"[8]: on "negatosis" and the memory of justice

Pete[9] was referred to me by his physician with a principle diagnosis of bipolarity. It is, to her credit, due to her sensible and respectful undertaking of Pete that he remains alive today. Pete initially consulted his physician to request euthanasia, as he felt life to be too unbearable to continue living. After many months of containment and discussion, Pete agreed to meet with me. Despite Pete's diagnosis and many "barriers," he seemed eager to make use of the therapeutic space and used the first year to simply "download." Severely neglected and embattled, Pete barely seemed able to contain severe "fits" of anger and disappointment—a need to "let rip" alternating with a severe clamping down on himself. His mental anguish was palpable and his struggle, soon to be discovered, was lifelong: a self-nucleus without a psychic skin—his nascent self an exposed nerve living without a protective shell. Desperate for a container, Pete fought this very need as well. Given a life of deployment and betrayal, it paradoxically ensured his very survival.

It is difficult to accurately describe the first year of therapy and, as I write, I am aware of snippets and fragments emerging haphazardly, despite copious notes and flowing angry narrative—a truly painful gestalt, which was stitched together over time enabling us to achieve greater analytic reciprocity. Many years of unthinkable frustration-turned-fury, objective injustice, and self-imposed loneliness pervaded

Pete's existence. This mental pain was not always contained, or containable for that matter, and many times Pete's immense self-discipline and "hermitage" failed him and he would spill over. Pete was "known" to be "difficult", writing to officials in a "poison pen";[10] once, when confronted with a typical bureaucratic letter,[11] Pete threatened to set himself on fire. This in turn led to police action and hospitalization. Initially, Pete's fury ceaselessly pounded my more moderate sensibility, and our early sessions felt like psychic concussive blows. The latter was made worse by my desire to argue and stave off (if not strangle) his preoccupation with contemporary "egotopia," to take on (in the worst sense of the word) his utopian *naïveté*. This left me feeling disconnected from Pete, a self-containment unable to ensure a co-mingling; there seemed minimal ways *into* Pete's experience and, as such, a lack of any tenderness and welcoming qualities.

It took months within myself to both hold, reorientate and rework this so as to become aware that thoughts and feelings were experienced as something that irritates our common boundary, and, in doing so, disallowing a natural osmotic process in our interaction. I also became increasingly aware that my words, although imbued with logic and structure, were akin to baby shaking. It dawned upon me that Pete, although verbally gifted and very able, was speaking, true to Ferenczi's child, from within a different language and psychological era. Pete's so-called "ranting and raving" was more akin to the *period of purple crying*[12] wherein the child's crying is largely misunderstood, trapping the other in (reciprocal) experiences of incapacity and rage. I felt like such an analytic co-worker, so to speak. It was also during this time of discovering the concept of the period of purple crying that I remembered, and returned to, Eigen's notion of "impact and movement" (2004c, p. 143) and the importance of remaining true to another's impact, the "primary raw datum" (2004c, p. 143) that is in need of "holding" and "nursing." I will return to Eigen's concept and my inner work shortly, as for the moment I feel Pete's inner life and history needs greater presencing.

Pete's heartache can be traced back to his family of origin, being a child in a family that could only stimulate a need for escape. Dipping into his historical narrative would frequently activate a gnashing of teeth and clenching of fists. His mother was recalled as suffering from a psychotic disorder and was hospitalized after the birth of Pete's eldest brother for over a year. Pete was aware that his mother experienced some relief in provoking anger, mentally pinching family members, and binging on alcohol. Pete's relationships with his siblings were also complicated. Two estranged brothers and a sister who was "struck" with their mother's "illness", all seemingly unable to develop bonds of affection and mutual support. As Pete discussed his background, his voice frequently and unexpectedly softened, especially when he spoke about his sister and mother being ill. Being continuously aware of, and alert to, their mental anguish, it was as if he had a special empathic, marsupial enclave reserved for them. This seemed to me an impossible feat, given his years of immense neglect and his mother's constant shaming and over-stimulating of him. In contrast, Pete had no contact with his brothers and had only reconciled with his father a few years before his death. Pete's father, a career militarist, was described by Pete as a man known for his capacity to enforce order with a combination of insensitivity and respect for power and dominance.

As a parental couple, Pete's parents personified irritation, their union a mixture of eruptions, ruptures, anger flare-ups, and frequent verbal and physical fights. Pete mentioned that as a young child he could "feel" the "rise" and had to escape, a feeling both he and I frequently identified with leading to unnecessary withdrawal between us, which further aggravated his feelings of neglect. The parental soon became, in true analytic fashion, the external world; a world that failed to ensure a sense of safety; a damaged and damaging psychic envelope devoid of nourishment, soothing or support; a world bent on destruction and harm. In short, a world one could only "drop out" of. Some of Pete's earlier recollections accentuate this:

> I was seven when I decided that adults were crazy and were going to kill us all with their nuclear bombs and stupidity. I think I was traumatized by "nuclear attack drills" in 1962. I was frightened walking to and from school. After seeing JFK murdered on TV (I was home with the measles) I was convinced I did not want to be part of the lunacy, as to me he was a prince of the earth—he had just saved us all from certain death. I had dropped out then and have fought the rest of my life to drop back in with limited success. When I was 11 years old I was riding through northern Ontario with my parents and as I looked at the expanse of Tundra forest I was struck with the thought of how I would love to just walk into it and build a life there away from the crazy chaos of my family and our society.

> I was depressed already. Then the "other" voice spoke and said that sooner or later they would come and bother me there too. I was not schizophrenic. It was my own voice. I am aware I have two minds working at odds and it never stops. It can be paralyzing. I was wracked with anxiety and grinding . . . fighting off the grinding, relentless *negatosis*[13] leading to burnout inevitably left me feeling the failure, a quitter, and in deep shame and self-recrimination. I get wiped out. I got to the point I did nothing, as I could not see when it was good enough. I was constantly harassed by that negative side and eventually to complete mental paralysis. *I would stare out the window and in a second four months or more would go by—my time slippage.*

Pete's negatosis and "in–out program" (Guntrip, 2011; Katz, 2004; Klein, 1995a–f; Pearson, 2003) was even more evident as an adult in his inability to work for more than eighteen months at a time. During these periods, Pete would actually *over*work and *over*achieve, which was followed by an increasing negatosis and inability to sleep or experience any rest, even in his sleep.

After many years, we managed to piece together the fact that if Pete did not anesthetize his negatosis he could "feel the rise of an inability to have a night and day—working all night and day, no reprieve, dreams filled with my day, slights turning into menacing probability. A cycle of work, doping, and passing out until total withdrawal" (also see Eaton, 2005). Relating and doing, and being with others only enlivened the rise of the obdurate state of mind; day residue became ghost-line manifestations, used in an encapsulated inner drama of fear and attack. Similar to Chronos, "it" would devour his sense of self, his temporal capacity, until Pete had to symbolically "die"—that is, walk away and live a separate, isolated life ("my hermitage") for many years. This isolation, if not desolation, was heightened by the fact that the "taking in" and reliance on any good experience was tenuous, if not felt as "impossible":

> I could not internalize good; *the negative side would not allow it.* The energy to stave off the negative and to achieve the positive was too much, I could not penetrate the wall, settle the anxiety; I would just walk away. I turned to alcohol and chain-smoking to battle the constant negative mind, to remain focused on the positive. I was never without it, the anxieties over my inability to trust and to connect with my many friends, and my inability to internalize their love for me. Having moved as a child every couple of years in an army family had made me unable to fully allow myself to

> connect and to bond with new people, knowing it could end at any moment. Children did not get warning of an impending move. It just happened. Dad—a distant Master Warrant officer—expected us to be good soldiers, rigid and intolerant. I lived in *fear* of both my parents, feared living.

It remains a source of constant surprise to me that despite a tormenting childhood, an inability to enjoy a professional career, a failed marriage (a true trauma for Pete), extreme poverty, and living on the streets, Pete did seem to salvage his "sensitive self," his own rhythm of faith, mainly in service of his own utopian society and dream. As anti-"Ego"-topian (and in true Foucauldian logic), Pete's master–slave dialectic (Klein, 1995a–g) found support in the concept of parrhesia, compelling him to speak the truth even at the expense of his own freedom. Pete seemed to have an immense intolerance of malice, deceit, and betrayal, in both himself and in others. This inevitably complicated his relationships with those close to him, his co-workers, and his life in general, as any sign of moral impropriety would evoke much anger, disappointment, and result in eventual withdrawal. The master–slave dialectic permeated his existence and his utopian rhythm remained his only sustenance and connection to the world. As such, in the therapeutic encounter, I had to learn over time to become deeply appreciative of this impact, and his parrhesia as a variation of adult crying and reaching, his utopian demand as a form of ego-play in which he could master his cumulative trauma (Khan, 1960, 1963, 1971, 1972). It was a primary impact in need of time and a rhythm of faith and recovery (Eigen, 2004c). As previously mentioned, I held in mind (at times clung to) Eigen's description of impact and movement:

> [The] core ingredient . . . is the impact of the patient on the therapist. Impact is primary raw datum. It is the most private intimate fact of a meeting. *The therapist may hide yet secretly nurse the deep impact the patient has on him.* To put the impact into words too soon may spoil its *unfolding*. An impact needs time to take root and grow. It occurs instantaneously, but needs the analyst's faith, time, and loyalty in order to prosper. (2004c, p. 143, my emphasis)

With Eigen's words as songline, I could focus more on what made me an obstructive object, supporting an awareness of moments of inability to be a welcoming other. Open to accepting his grasping, it may come as no surprise to the reader that it created a different way of relating. Being reached by Pete brought forth a sudden and surprising shift "in" and "for" us as analytic co-workers. A natural rhythm transpired between reaching out, being touched, and reaching out and touching. Thematically, parrhesia transformed into painful crying, into allowing me to emotionally witness the "injustice" behind his parrhesia/crying. Pete simultaneously wondered about his cumulative experiences anew, as well as his feelings about being in an unjust world, the impact it had on his life and relationships, and its impact on me. The transformation took me by surprise and only strengthened my resolve that Pete needed a unique space, an interpersonal and intrapsychic event of letting his perspective be, as painful and as impactful as it may have seemed on my psyche. Pete needed to be allowed to externalize, to project, so to speak, before he could feel himself in a different way. Logic, perspectivism, and interpretation alone would not do it. Not that the change was just smooth sailing; any attempt at interpretation would evoke a noisy reminder (parrhesia and symptoms of photophobia) that we were not in the "area" of his wounded self (primary *I*-feel), necessitating a retreat and self-protection. Theoretically, I understood this as the difference between feeling "held" and feeling "handled" by me. His language would also support me in feeling his psyche and current self-state. Words such as "things nick at me . . . pick at me" would alert me to Pete's experiencing a laceration of sorts, feeling bruised and tender due to the impact of his immediate environment (endopsychically and interpersonally).

Countertransferentially, and by identifying with the projection as a way to understand his communication, I experienced many feelings in response to my, at times, "crude" handling of his being, my missing of his "area" of reach, akin to spoiling a doodle in its "coming alongness". During this time of allowing his injustice to reach me, I also recalled Grotstein's notion of "memory of justice":

> Transcendental Bion seems to be clearly stating that the infant must project in order to survive and that mother must absorb, contain, translate, transform, and communicate in order to establish the model for thinking which the infant is then able to undergo only because of mother's observed capacity. Further, the infant must project into

> reality, and herein lies an extraordinarily intuitive point that Bion has lit upon. Projective identification never occurs in a vacuum. There must always be an external realization, which *justifies* the projection so that the projection can take place. Mother must frustrate, err, disappoint, etc.—seemingly purposely so as to justify the projective identifications into reality—and mother must acknowledge these "goofs," as must analysts, so that the *Memory of Justice* can be restored . . . (Grotstein, 1987, pp. 69–70)

With time, in the slow process of restorative being-with-each-other, I became increasingly aware and appreciative of Pete as an extremely perceptive and astute human being, painfully in touch with many necrophilic human tendencies (in Erich Fromm's sense). Pete was indeed in need of a receptive other, who could, over time, "experience" his "capacity" to "influence" another, to feel another not as "a" and/or "in-" reaction to his being, but part of a growing mutual play space. Treating his verbalizations as undreamt dreams, that is, as his own unique language and grammar of coming into being/collapse, although seemingly through the predominant use of beta elements (initial parrhesia), I became attentive to his immense and sensitive reaching capacity, his hopeful gesture within anger and shaking of me so as to rediscover and rework his obdurate/obstructive object. A "soft fascination" transpired when I allowed myself to "have" his "thought" for "thought."

Within this, I also became aware of my own naïve and simplistic understanding of his presenting complaints and initial anger bursts. Even my notion of Bion's container–contained allowed for a more cubistic understanding, permitting me to re-envision the accepted thesis wherein it is held that the therapist's *reworking of psychic material (from a client) may be viewed as more advanced than the client's*. Given our training, focus, and analytic instruments (models of mind, analytic techniques), as well as the asymmetrical nature of therapy, this may indeed be true on a certain level. Given my contact with Pete and following Eigen's rhythm of faith and devotion, I became aware of a further possibility—to serve within myself, between Pete and I, as well as within Pete, as a guardian to the conjunction of alpha and beta elements and functioning. Beta elements in search of alpha functioning—to be alpha-betized remains an inextricable conjunction; an alpha function without beta elements is no language at all. In Winnicottian discourse, there is no such thing as an infant without a mother.

Mothers can, thus, also read their handling, their own discourse, in the infant's internalization of their alpha-betized elements.

Thus, I became aware that I needed Pete to influence me, to allow a certain measure of him to impact my view of the world in such a way as someone asking, "Can you see it too?" As I comprehended something of the latter, the fact that it had meaning, a natural Goldilocks principle developed—a mutual play between, and searching for, a habitable "intra"- and "inter"-world. As we moved through a year of unloading (uploading for me!), I also became aware of my own contribution to his mental pain. As mentioned earlier, there were many moments during which I had to modulate my reaction, my need to argue, cajole, and re-educate through interpretation of his difficulties. I came to see through his eyes (by definition, not the final truth) a certain version of the world, and it thickened my understanding of themes such as slavery, control, and punishment (I would not always interpret this). I also came to understand how it shaped his inner ecology of failed dreams (frequent nightmares since childhood) and dreams of being bitten by animals (personifying my/the world's logic of chasing him down and biting him with our comments). Seeing, feeling, and hearing his touch and being was rewarded, so to speak, with Pete allowing himself to be more present.

The following serves as a note of the latter processes, a feeling between us concerning deprivation, privation, the obstructive object, being abandoned in a world without instruction, as well as his need for welcoming qualities and Winnicottian "play", the royal road to the Real Self.

Pete: Christmas is difficult, I grit my teeth, bear through; you know, like that soldier that shot himself, I want to blow myself away. What is the point? The sense of despair. After Xmas I pick up again, I will be more positive [laughs] . . . ok, *approach* being more positive, I lament . . . as a kid, my house, you know it was like World War Three. I got so excited on Xmas that I actually threw up, manic to get what I really wanted, a chemistry set! But no one to help me, I got what I want, but I could not do it. I was eight years old, my parents were not there, either in books or just being crazy, usually not doing anything with us, never did much with us, but they also had this expectation—you should know things without instruction! I could not read the instructions—I get blocked, even now. As a kid I never knew, I could do it in partnership, never alone. Same in adulthood. So I never desired, but I see it in others, to have a boat for example, I would like to go out on one, but not what it takes to have one! Therefore I always thought I was lazy, stupid, too much work given the cost, then the negatosis, lament not having anything, but I don't want it actually. I even hate shopping, I don't buy my own clothes, too overwhelming, too many choices, crushes me for a while, despair, but a fact of life for me.

Loray: May I muddle a little, Pete? You state a desire, but it is dangerous, a mind-blowing event, as it means there may be at once gifts but also no one to help you in a partnership with instruction. You feel abandoned in a feeling of inability with angry, crazy, unavailable others.

[Pete becomes emotional; I wait.]

[He nods.]

Loray: This also makes you feel foreign in the world's and others' "way" of "getting" [a frequent complaint he ascribed to ADHD]. People "get it" to "get it", leaving you feeling even more unable, without instruction, as if they know the instruction. Without instruction you are beset with anxiety, frustration, and it activates the negatosis. With no partner in thought you can only feel either at odds with the world or odd in the world. The negatosis turns this pain you experience into "must have knowns." You were not allowed time to make "use" of a partnership, you were punished, had to be an ideal but it stretched you too far. Maybe that is why you push yourself so hard in eighteen-month cycles, and feel so depleted?

[He is silent and emotional.]

Pete: *You are there* . . . I also fear getting into trouble, I am interested but worried getting into trouble; I am alone in my thoughts. I can't remember much of my home life, as I lived outside. I have been *roaming* since I was five, only went home to eat. I was never *"seen", I was never lost in play, as I would suddenly be told I did wrong, punished,* always concerned to do something wrong, can't enjoy, it all seems like trouble . . . but I daydream, a lot, I take myself OUT, where I was, there is no give and take in my world, there is always in the back that negative, that fear . . . that *fear that I will not be welcomed.* I foresee trouble, I am always on guard, I don't like to think of it as fear, but it's fear.

Over the past few years, Pete has slowly allowed himself more play, more room(s) to be (in), and, as such, a deepening openness and spontaneity in his own unique self-formulation within which resides both an expression of catastrophe and hope/faith:

> "When I allow myself to desire, to want, I get so anxious, it's so difficult and tormenting for me. I would rather be depressed and suicidal than have that anxiety ... But I have so much more now, so much. I am better in many ways. My relationships are better. I am doing better. This is difficult for me ... not switching enthusiasm into indifference, drudge, boring ... I am developing a good ego-part that expands the "rooms" I can be in in the world. It was just me in my room, but I have a room at my girlfriend's, at work, my kids, the doctor's room, here with you ... rooms I am *welcomed in*."

Every good experience/nurturing experience is, as described by Eigen's rhythm, also linked with further historic and contemporary traumata, nurture-trauma, presently actively embraced and present for dreaming. Within this, Pete frequently feels "parts" of him come alive as well as other parts that have to die off in order for him to become more open. I also seem "able" to meet Pete more successfully, at times with stupidity and misunderstanding, although our rhythm of faith repairs much quicker. Lacerations and nicks have become scratches. There is also a greater expression of hope. The following serves as a spontaneous hint of the latter:

> "There was a woman that didn't know she was going to have a baby. She was squatting to use the bathroom, it was one of those you get in the Middle East, anyways ... it popped out! Poor kid got stuck in the shit pipe. It took two doctors to safely remove the child from the shit pipe, although it took them many, many, many hours! Kid is OK, considering, but can you imagine what that was like! Giving birth and then the child gets stuck!"

I hope the reader will agree that this is a rich and meaningful communication from Pete to me, and even to and for himself. Themes of surprise and denial of the child, unexpected birth, and resulting stuckness invite many interpretations. The content of interpretation is not as important as the *invitation* (irrespective of whom we relate to internally as organizer, whether Freudian, Kleinian, Jungian, or the like). As a spontaneous mental gesture, I was aware of a sense of "disaster" averted and, with the two doctors, *my* immediate thought, privately held and nourished, was that my "partner" in the fecal baby rescue was Michael Eigen.

Conclusion

I would like to end this chapter with a quote from Bertrand Russell (1872–1970), which relates indirectly to Eigen's main clinical method and psychoanalytic ethos as touched upon in this chapter. In his autobiography, Russell wrote of an experience he had in 1901, articulating the "region" so thoughtfully mapped by Eigen's many works. That is, Russell describes a brief moment wherein contact with the depths enabled the nourishment of a "soul space," enlivening a transformational perspectivism able to touch unendurable loneliness. I do believe that Eigen's work has supported me in applying psychoanalytic thinking and being in service of such a "region," and continues to provide me with a language and framework that cultivates both presencing and dignity;

> Suddenly the ground seemed to give way beneath me, and I found myself in quite another region. Within five minutes I went through some such reflections as the following: the loneliness of the human soul is unendurable; nothing can penetrate it except the highest intensity of the sort of love that religious teachers have preached; whatever does not spring from this motive is harmful, or at best useless . . . and that in human relations one should penetrate to the core of loneliness in each person and speak to that. At the end of those five minutes, I had become a completely different person. For a time, a sort of mystic illumination possessed me . . . I found myself filled with semi-mystical feelings about beauty, and with an intense interest in children and with a desire almost as profound as that of the Buddha to find some philosophy, which should make human life endurable. A strange excitement possessed me, containing intense pain but also some element of wisdom. The mystic insight, which I then imagined myself to possess has largely faded, and the habit of analysis has reasserted itself. But in something of what I thought I saw in that moment has remained always with me. (1998, p. 149)

Notes

1. I am deeply indebted to Dr. Judith Pearson (2013) for introducing me to this concept and its relationship to psychic orientation within schizoid states.
2. This reminds of the South African statesman Jan Smuts, who, in describing the concept of holism, held that "dead" material can support life in nature, that is, compost (Savage, 1998).
3. Biblically, this is akin to the apostles falling asleep in Gethsemane, as Jesus struggled with unimaginable terror. Remaining "awake" to an impending catastrophe is, in itself, a developmental achievement.
4. The reader can access Eigen's original thoughts on what I refer to as the obdurate object in *The Psychotic Core* under the theme of "self-hardening" (1986, p. 201).
5. See Eigen's *The Psychotic Core* (2004a, pp. 201–202) for such a reflection on "phobic structures" embedded in our psychic life.
6. Even after one is no longer symptomatic, the *herpes zoster* virus may hide in the nervous system and be "activated" under stress or as a result of a compromised immune system, creating lesions and pain. Toxic nourishment may work similarly.
7. Also see Antonino Ferro's description of "respect for the patient's text" (2002, p. 89) and note 14 (p. 113) on the use of the "special liquid" in the treatment of narcissistic states.
8. This is the client's own description of himself.
9. The client kindly gave permission to use his experiences and therapy as educator. Some details have been changed to protect his identity.
10. Much later, I saw his hope that he could be proven wrong, that good existed "out there" and would undo his childhood mistrust.
11. As I got to know Pete, his needs and particular states of mind, reading the letters sent to him left me feeling desolate, an inner reality Pete has struggled with since childhood.
12. *The Purple Period* is named for the acronym PURPLE: "Peak of crying (P)", that is, a baby crying more than a week; "Unexpected" (U) in that the crying can come and go without reason; "Resist" (R) all soothing no matter what the mother attempts; "Pain-like face" (P)—they look in pain even if they are not; "Long lasting" (L), that is, lasting for five hours a day or longer; and "Late afternoon and Evening" (E). See www.purplecrying.info/.
13. A client I treated was exposed to extreme negative paternal parenting and referred to his father's approach as "optic rectomitis", creatively and evocatively linking the digestive track with the visual. His father could

only "see" his "shit", him as "a shit", giving him constant "shit", leaving him chronically "bummed out".

References

Bollas, C. (1978). The aesthetic moment and the search for transformation. *Annual of Psychoanalysis, 6*: 385–394.

Bollas, C. (1979). The transformational object. *International Journal of Psychoanalysis, 60*: 97–107.

Chatwin, B. (1987). *The Songlines*. New York: Elisabeth Sifton.

Daws, L. (2009). Dreaming the dream: in search of endopsychic ontology. *Issues in Psychoanalytic Psychology, 31*(1): 21–40.

Eaton, J. E. (2005). The obstructive object. *Psychoanalytic Review, 92*(3): 355–372.

Eigen, M. (1977). On working with "unwanted" patients. *International Journal of Psychoanalysis, 58*: 109–121.

Eigen, M. (1981). The area of faith in Winnicott, Lacan and Bion. *International Journal of Psychoanalysis, 62*: 413–433.

Eigen, M. (1983). Dual union or undifferentiation? A critique of Marion Milner's view of the sense of psychic creativeness. *International Review of Psycho-Analysis, 10*: 415–428.

Eigen, M. (1985). Toward Bion's starting point: between catastrophe and faith. *International Journal of Psychoanalysis, 66*: 321–330.

Eigen, M. (1995). Psychic deadness: Freud. *Contemporary Psychoanalysis, 31*(2): 277–299.

Eigen, M. (1999). *Toxic Nourishment*. London: Karnac.

Eigen, M. (2001). *Damaged Bonds*. London: Karnac.

Eigen, M. (2004a). *The Psychotic Core*. London: Karnac.

Eigen, M. (2004b). *The Electrified Tightrope*, A. Phillips (Ed.). London: Karnac.

Eigen, M. (2004c). *Psychic Deadness*. London: Karnac.

Eigen, M. (2004d). *The Sensitive Self*. Middletown, CT: Wesleyan University Press.

Eigen, M. (2007). *Feelings Matter*. London: Karnac.

Eigen, M. (2014). Personal communication, 3 April.

Eshel, O. (2005). Pentheus rather than Oedipus: on perversion, survival and analytic "presencing." *International Journal of Psychoanalysis, 86*: 1071–1097.

Eshel, O. (2010). Patient–analyst interconnectedness: personal notes on close encounters of a new dimension. *Psychoanalytic Inquiry, 30*: 146–154.

Eshel, O. (2013). Patient–analyst "withness": on analytic "presencing", passion, and compassion in states of breakdown, despair, and deadness. *Psychoanalytic Quarterly, 82*: 925–963.

Ferro, A. (2002). *In the Analyst's Consulting Room*. New York: Routledge.

Freedman, N., Hurvich, M., Ward, R., Geller, J. D., & Hoffenberg, J. (2011). *Another Kind of Evidence: Studies on Internalization, Annihilation Anxiety, and Progressive Symbolization in the Psychoanalytic Process*. London: Karnac.

Frosch, A. (Ed.). (2012). *Absolute Truth and Unbearable Psychic Pain: Psychoanalytic Perspectives on Concrete Experience*. London: Karnac.

Grotstein, J. S. (1987). Making the best of a bad deal: on Harold Boris' "Bion Revisited". *Contemporary Psychoanalysis, 23*: 60–76.

Grotstein, J. S. (1997). Integrating one-person and two-person psychologies: autochthony and alterity in counterpoint. *Psychoanalytic Quarterly, 66*: 403–430.

Guntrip, H. (2011). *Schizoid Phenomena, Object Relations and the Self*. London: Karnac.

Hornstein, G. A. (2000). *To Redeem One Person is to Redeem the World: The Life of Frieda Fromm Reichmann*. New York: Free Press.

Katz, J. (2004). The schizoid personality disorder. In: J. F. Masterson & A. R. Liberman (Eds.), *A Therapist's Guide to the Personality Disorders, the Masterson Approach: A Handbook and Workbook* (pp. 91–110). Phoenix, AZ: Zeig, Tucker & Thiesen.

Khan, M. R. (1960). Regression and integration in the analytic setting: a clinical essay on the transference and counter-transference aspects of these phenomena. *International Journal of Psychoanalysis, 41*: 130–146.

Khan, M. R. (1963). The concept of cumulative trauma. *Psychoanalytic Study of the Child, 18*: 286–306.

Khan, M. R. (1971). Infantile neurosis as a false-self organization. *Psychoanalytic Quarterly, 40*: 245–263.

Khan, M. R. (1972). Dread of surrender to resourceless dependence in the analytic situation. *International Journal of Psychoanalysis, 53*: 225–230.

Klein, R. (1995a). Evolution. In: J. F. Masterson & R. Klein (Eds.), *Disorders of the Self: New Therapeutic Horizons, the Masterson Approach* (pp. 3–12). New York: Brunner/Mazel.

Klein, R. (1995b). Description. In: J. F. Masterson & R. Klein (Eds.), *Disorders of the Self: New Therapeutic Horizons, the Masterson Approach* (pp. 13–32). New York: Brunner/Mazel.

Klein, R. (1995c). Developmental theory. In: J. F. Masterson & R. Klein (Eds.), *Disorders of the Self: New Therapeutic Horizons, the Masterson Approach* (pp. 33–44). New York: Brunner/Mazel.

Klein, R. (1995d). Intrapsychic structures. In: J. F. Masterson & R. Klein (Eds.), *Disorders of the Self: New Therapeutic Horizons, the Masterson Approach* (pp. 45–68). New York: Brunner/Mazel.

Klein, R. (1995e). Establishing a therapeutic alliance. In: J. F. Masterson & R. Klein (Eds.), *Disorders of the Self: New Therapeutic Horizons, the Masterson Approach* (pp. 69–94). New York: Brunner/Mazel.

Klein, R. (1995f). Shorter-term treatment. In: J. F. Masterson & R. Klein (Eds.), *Disorders of the Self: New Therapeutic Horizons, the Masterson Approach* (pp. 95–122).

Klein, R. (1995g). Intensive, long-term treatment. In: J. F. Masterson & R. Klein (Eds.), *Disorders of the Self: New Therapeutic Horizons, the Masterson Approach* (pp. 123–42). New York: Brunner/Mazel.

Kogan, I. (2007). *Escape from Selfhood: Breaking Boundaries and Craving for Oneness*. London: International Psychoanalytic Association.

Marcel, G. (2001a). *The Mystery of Being, Volume I: Reflection and Mystery*, G. S. Fraser (Trans.). South Bend, IN: St Augustine's Press.

Marcel, G. (2001b). *The Mystery of Being, Volume II: Faith and Reality*, G. S. Fraser (Trans.). South Bend, IN: St Augustine's Press.

Ogden, T. H. (1985a). On potential space. *International Journal of Psychoanalysis, 66*: 129–141.

Ogden, T. H. (1985b). The mother, the infant and the matrix: interpretations of aspects of the work of Donald Winnicott. *Contemporary Psychoanalysis, 21*: 346–371.

Ogden, T. H. (1988). On the dialectical structure of experience: some clinical and theoretical implications. *Contemporary Psychoanalysis, 24*: 17–45.

Pearson, J. (2013). Personal communication, 19 May.

Russell, B. (1998). *The Autobiography of Bertrand Russell, Volume 1: 1872–1914*. London: George Allen.

Savage, H. (1998). *An Introduction to Holism*. Pretoria: Wessa.

Slochower, J. A. (2006). *Psychoanalytic Collisions*. Mahwah, NJ: Analytic Press.

Symington, N. (2002). *Patterns of Madness*. London: Karnac.

Williams, G. (1998). *Internal Landscapes and Foreign Bodies: Eating Disorders and Other Pathologies*. London: Routledge (Tavistock Clinic Series).

CHAPTER EIGHT

Becoming a welcoming object: personal notes on Michael Eigen's impact

Jeffrey L. Eaton

Introduction

At the end of his autobiography *All My Sins Remembered: Another Part of a Life* (Bion, 1985) the English psychoanalyst Wilfred Bion describes an extremely painful memory. He is sitting in his garden with his infant daughter. His wife has died in childbirth. His daughter calls out to him and, feeling "numbed and insensitive" (1985, p. 70), he refuses to answer her or to go to her. She begins to cry and to crawl toward him across the lawn but he ignores her. He even feels angry that she is persecuting him. Finally, the child's nanny picks her up and comforts her. Bion feels, he reports, astonished "to find such depth of cruelty in myself" (Bion, 1985, p. 70).

Hatred of pain is spontaneous and often deeply entrenched for many unconscious reasons. However, by rejecting pain, we inevitably amplify it. The habit of rejecting pain spreads it, moment by moment, person to person, family through family, creating patterns of suffering that can last for generations. Bion seems to be warning that rather than finding relief when we go dead to pain, we open a door to even deeper forms of pain, like cruelty inflicted upon innocent others.

Bion's work inspires another way of being with pain. Instead of turning away from it, we learn how to turn toward pain. Bion questions how we can face pain, tolerate it, explore it, and communicate about it. We can try to *reverse* the habit of rejection by *welcoming experience*. If we can cultivate, expand, and sustain a disciplined and compassionate attention to the truth of our own suffering, we might learn to observe how pain can keep transforming in unpredictable ways. However, none of this is possible without first resolving to welcome experience.

One of the main inspirations I have found for the plausibility of becoming a welcoming object is Michael Eigen's example. There are many beautiful themes in Eigen's twenty-some books. It is impossible to briefly describe the dozens of different strands of Eigen's work that cumulatively create a vision of human resilience, faith, and creativity. But to make a concise formulation, Eigen encourages his readers to grow the capacity to welcome *any* kind of experience.

Perhaps what impresses me most is Eigen's constant recognition of the complexity of forms that life forces take. Eigen is somehow consistently able to describe in vivid personal language the myriad ways life impulses evolve, get tangled, or even strangled, and yet still continue to grow in the midst of sometimes undreamable and unthinkable suffering.

A poem by Rumi (2004, p. 109) provides a model for the attitude inspiring my reflections on becoming a welcoming object.

The Guest House

This being human is a guest house.
Every morning a new arrival.

A joy, a depression, a meanness,
some momentary awareness comes
As an unexpected visitor.

Welcome and entertain them all!
Even if they're a crowd of sorrows,
who violently sweep your house
empty of its furniture.

Still, treat each guest honorably.
He may be clearing you out
for some new delight.

The dark thought, the shame, the malice,
meet them at the door laughing,
and invite them in.

Be grateful for whoever comes,
because each has been sent
as a guide from beyond

Rumi beautifully evokes an ethic of "welcoming". When I read this poem, I picture Eigen sitting in his leather chair in his modest Central Park office underneath the picture of a seagull that adorns an otherwise bare wall. There is perhaps no deeper need than to be welcomed by another and no greater pain than to be rejected, ignored, or exiled. Every lifetime involves the never-ending oscillation, lived out moment by moment, of the tension between welcoming and rejecting, being welcomed and feeling exiled. We are always searching for shelter in welcoming spaces and the relief and promise of contact with other welcoming hearts and minds.

A deep commitment to the power of welcoming runs like an underground river through all of Eigen's work. Welcoming is the action that openness to experience makes possible. Eigen's sensibility is infectious because he helps to welcome so much, and because he shares so much of the harvest of his own experience. He really seems to believe in the presence of "the guides from beyond" who arrive with necessary messages for those willing to clear a space and to learn how to listen.

Eigen's welcoming attitude helps me to recognize these guides from beyond as communications from my own "sensitive self". The unconscious is not a thing but a living, flourishing process that touches and shapes everything. Eigen describes unconscious momentums and intensities. He opens a space to pay attention to life's embryonic aspects. He makes room for complexity, and does not shy away from describing the arrogant, prickly, grimy, poisoning processes that can kill awareness from the inside out.

Here, there is always another side, always another view. Take another look, Eigen encourages. Destructive influences have their place amid sun, seed, soil, and rain. Life survives and keeps renewing—or "coming through," as he likes to say. We struggle toward the light, and spread thoughts like seeds along the way.

At a basic level, the capacity for welcoming, if it is to foster sustainable creativity, must involve opening beyond interpersonal concerns. After we have learned how to begin to open to others and to the world, we must learn how to turn back again, move inward more thoroughly, and to rediscover shattered, scattered, and alienated aspects of ourselves. We have an impact on ourselves as much as on others. We need new ways of sensing, tracking, and exploring self↔world intercourses that are embedded in self↔Self expansion and evolution.

At the core of Eigen's work, in conjunction with his attention to destructive forces, is a luminous affirmation of the wonder of human experience, especially emotional experience. Over decades, his work has drawn attention to, and celebrated, a deep feeling that Buddhists call the preciousness of human embodiment.

Inspired by openness, we can ask, in an honest and compassionate way, and with a practical spirit: How well do I welcome my own experiences? What quality of relationship do I offer to my own thoughts, intuitions, emotions, fantasies, wishes, desires, and dreams? How well can I play with my own life experiences? How free am I to meet myself? In my view, Eigen's "welcoming" is part of the function of the mystic part of the personality, ultimately opening up to welcoming the presence of what Bion (1985) terms O and all its turbulent reverberations.

Welcoming the breath

In 1977, Eigen published a short paper titled "Breathing and identity" (Eigen, 1993, pp. 43–47). In it, he makes several intriguing observations. For example, he suggests that "the therapeutic use of the body in the West has largely been assimilated to the paradigm of appetite" (1993, p. 43). Eigen says that our conception of the self as based on the model of appetite is quite different from a view of self that could be derived from paying attention to the experience of breathing. "Appetite . . . is a more ambivalent experience," writes Eigen. "The rise of appetite involves more acute and insistent sensations than [does] the flow of breathing". In contrast to appetite, "Breathing goes on constantly at a fairly steady pace with momentary and periodic variations . . . it is not experienced as a disturbance under normal circumstances" (1993, p. 45).

A psychology looking only at what interrupts is incomplete or unbalanced. Eigen (1977/1993) shifts attention from what intrudes (sensations of lack or wanting) to what sustains (the background flow of the breath, a sense of plenitude, even gratitude). He highlights the intriguing question of what a psychology that placed breathing in the foreground would feel like.

Breathing is one of our first unconscious linking devices. Breathing links inside and outside, mind and body, and even self and other. Breathing creates a basic rhythm. This basic rhythm emerges and is elaborated unconsciously in the body's experience of self, other, and world. As Eigen says, breathing is *"a bodily form for communion and relatedness in life"* (1993, p. 45, my italics).

Dreaming is to the mind what breathing is to the body. Dreaming involves other forms of linking and, like breathing, dramatically sustains and enhances different qualities of experience. Without the capacity to dream, we slowly suffocate emotionally. A shallow relationship to dream life is like not knowing how to breathe from your belly. One strand of a basic rhythm, then, is how mind dreams the body and how affective bodily life energizes mind and dream.

Welcoming the body

A body exists in time against a dual background of sensation and infinity. Sensation orients us, and, according to Bion (1985), traps us in the familiar moment. Our identification with our bodies makes us believe that the moment has tangible boundaries or shapes. In fact, the moment has no edges. Instead, every moment is like the universe itself, a moment of growth, constantly expanding. Our senses, however, cannot register this sort of space, or, if they do, we might feel a kind of panic, like the person whom we call psychotic.

Intuiting the radical openness of the moment brings us into touch with another aspect of basic rhythm: the fear of breakdown, the too-muchness of experience that is felt both in mind and body.

Attention to any moment reveals how many rhythms can evolve. In his recent book *Kabbalah and Psychoanalysis* (2012), Eigen mentions the "in-out rhythm of the breath" (p. 6), which he links with Taoist ideas and a larger theme of *expansion↔contraction*. Breath is linked with life and death. Breathing in, expanding, links with life energy, while breathing out, contracting, evokes an eventual "last breath" and the inescapable reality of death.

Of course, it is not just lungs that expand; minds expand and contract, too; perceptions widen or become narrow, tolerance deepens or stays shallow. Pictures of the world change and transform with a fluidity that rides on the rhythm of a *breathing↔dreaming* process in experiences of body–mind–self.

From his earliest work, Eigen has emphasized the relationship between self–other and body–mind dynamics. In *Coming Through the Whirlwind* (1992) Eigen writes,

> Either mental or physical aspects of life may be more or less prominent in experience at any time. They may interweave and blur but they are never identical. The "I" may distinguish itself from or identity with either mind or body at a given time. . . . Their relationships are typically subtle and complex, since each is apt to be experienced as both self and other in a variety of ways. The boundaries between shift, so that there is latitude in what may be considered mind or body as conditions change. (p. xiv)

Eigen tracks what he calls "a kind of biography of body self/ mental self in heart-to-heart, mind-to-mind encounter" (1992, p. xv). Perhaps, as much of my clinical work is spent with difficult to reach children, I have become attuned to the creaturely expression of encounter with others. I long ago started to pay attention to what Eigen calls a "basic pathological psychic structure of our day" (1992, p. xv). He describes this as "a detached, covertly transcendent, steel-like mental ego vis-à-vis an explosive–fusional body ego" (1992, p. xv). This formulation has opened up a lot of windows for me in my work with autistic states in children.

One of Eigen's special qualities as a writer, supervisor, or therapist seems to be how much room he has *to play* with experience. Play, according to Winnicott, has its origins in the freedom to express deep bodily aliveness. In my own training (mainly Kleinian), it was hard to imagine interpretation as a form of "spontaneous gesture" or play.

Eigen's example, among others, helped open up a certain kind of rigidity that can influence both body and mind.

Eigen has a knack for following the phenomenological trail of different flavors of emotional experience. He will wonder why something is so present, or so missing, so intense, or barely detectable. He notices slight shifts in qualities of experience and encourages new spaces for speaking as well as for silence. In this way, Eigen becomes a kind of midwife creating space for surprises, for welcoming a new idea, exploring new energies, and dabbling in novel perceptions. Eigen not only tracks how bodily impulses in the patient might emerge, he freely draws on his own bodily aliveness, simultaneously opening up space to explore the impacts of mind-to-mind and body-to-mind encounters, expanding a generative transforming field.

Welcoming "emotional storm"

Few analysts are more creative than Eigen in describing the turbulence of self–other and self-to-self impacts that emerge through the evolving adventure of psychoanalytic dialogue. Some of Eigen's most moving writing comes through exploring the theme of impact as it emerges from "emotional storm" (Eigen, 2005). Throughout his work, Eigen reminds the reader that part of being human involves growing the equipment to process the experience of being human. We can never process everything, sometimes not even enough. One way to define trauma involves the impact of experience that damages or disables emotional processing equipment. Eigen believes in *a basic rhythm, a rhythm of breakdown and repair*. He writes,

> The sense of trauma-recovery and breakdown-repair is a basic emotional sequence that informs and colors our lives. It is part of a basic faith and trust that meets many challenges. Nevertheless, even when the sequence comes out well—on the side of repair, recovery, reconciliation—something inside of us does not altogether let go of the breakdown. We keep one of our many inner eyes on it. The fact that we are beings subject to emotional breakdown does not go away. (Eigen, 2005, p. 18)

We are creatures that have to contend with catastrophe. Some people are more sensitive, some more resilient. Some people turn away, others plunge into the black hole. Eigen keenly describes how we need each other to help grow the capacities for making sense and meaning of our lives, even as these same human relationships can be the sources of so much psychological wounding and even emotional crippling.

Eigen writes that "Emotional storm is not pathology. It is part of reactivity, permeability, responsiveness—part of what happens when people meet" (2005, p. 21). He continues,

> We need to grow with impacts, or around them, and let a sense of what it feels like to be together to develop. The sense of what it feels like to be together is what makes us—all of us—partners. To not cultivate the feel of another is a kind of soul murder. The evolution of the human race depends on not aborting the feeling of another. (2005, p. 21)

Bion, Buber, and Levinas, among others, are in the background of this ethical sensibility. I find the attitude of the welcoming object epitomized in Eigen's voice in passages like this:

> Primary emotional storm, vulnerability, permeability. The first thing to do is to acknowledge it. Grant it space, time, recognition, honor. Note it: we are in and part of an emotional storm. It is us and we are it—partly. Don't pull the plug by violence or collapse. It is enough to begin with a sense that emotional storm is happening. The simple fact: impact is happening, impact is happening, impact is happening. No need to sanitize or soundproof it. We are struggling to build our capacity to bear being with another human being, to bear to build one's own responsiveness, reciprocal responsiveness. (2005, p. 19)

Welcoming a sensitive self

Although Eigen does not write about autism in any great detail, I have, nonetheless, been inspired by his way of working and have used his ideas to develop a space in myself to welcome the emotional storms that inevitably emerge in the psychoanalytic process when treating children with autism. Autistic children are among the most sensitive selves in certain kinds of ways. I regard the analyst's attitude as a crucial variable in creating a setting with an atmosphere that makes communication with a difficult to reach child eventually possible.

Eigen's example has helped me to open my imagination to getting to know and sometimes even "becoming" my patient's experience. I strive to embody a new and tolerable presence in each encounter so that we can discover each other and begin to interact, in whatever form may be possible.

Without lively interaction we cannot build and expand what Francis Tustin called "a rhythm of safety." Discovering an interactive rhythm of safety helps to consolidate a sensory floor for experience. With such a sensory floor, a child can begin to attend to the world around him. When this is possible, the capacity to harness emotional interest and invest those emotions in actual others begins to emerge. Finally, a sensitive self with many different aspects begins to be expressed through the analytic process and it becomes possible to explore all sorts of emotions and impulses together. This shared experience involves tolerating intensities, recognizing and describing patterns, and ultimately fosters symbolization of personal experience. A whole new kind of learning process begins to take center stage from session to session.

The process of discovering a sensitive self coming alive amid autistic defenses often involves a literal movement from screaming to dreaming. The complexity of this process is impossible to describe briefly. However, I would like to evoke something of this movement by sharing a "moment of growth", one of many, in my experience with a boy whom I will call Steven.

I met Steven when he was seven. He had been diagnosed with autism at the age of three. His parents were struggling now with his violent meltdowns, which could last as long as an hour. These events involved screaming, hitting, kicking, biting, and, on some days, smearing his feces on his bedroom walls.

Early in our work, I was lucky to discover that Steven was able to draw. The complexity of Steven's experience as he drew was fascinating to observe. For a long time he didn't say much to me. But he made many different kinds of sounds as he drew.

His noise-making was often very animated. He oscillated between excited nonsense sounds, squeals, musical jingles, snatches of cartoon narratives, and occasional very polite, sculpted statements. I began to realize that each "scene" that he was drawing was accompanied by a kind of emotional soundtrack. There were also long stretches of concentrated silence.

Over time, Steven tolerated my sharing feelings and questions evoked by the impact of his drawings and sounds upon me. At some point, he confided that there was "a secret movie inside" that was completely private that no one could ever know about.

The moment of growth I want to describe occurred over a series of sessions in our third year of twice-weekly meetings. By this time, Steven had decided to allow me to become an audience and to share in the elaboration of his secret movie.

Steven had created an entire world externalizing and developing his secret movie. He made paper figures, cut them out, colored them, named them, and then staged interactions among the different characters. He created different worlds by making scenes, like movie backgrounds and stage sets. Gradually, these worlds evolved into three-dimensional productions. For example, he drew a swirling portal that looked like a Jackson Pollock picture, and, not satisfied with the effect, cut a door in the paper so that it could actually fold open. Then he could move a paper character through the portal into a new dimension.

One day, Steven introduced the character of a giant monster dog. This dog was much larger than the paper children who were the heroes of his secret movie. The dog had mean eyes, sharp fangs, and a giant scar over half its body. I was told he was sent to terrorize the children by an evil figure who dominated a parallel universe called "the shadow world."

The atmosphere I felt during this unfolding drama made a deep impact on me. I felt in a new and different way how Steven's screams were now becoming dreamt through the materialization of this mean dog and his *sharing* it with me. I said to him, "I think by sharing your secret movie you are letting what used to be screams become dreams now, like this monster dog." I also said, "I think you used to feel such a pressure to keep this all to yourself because you were afraid that to let it out would ruin everything." Steven searched my face with his eyes, almost like an infant trying to fathom the expression on his mother's face.

In our next session, Steven said, "Remember the monster dog?" He said, "I want to do something to it." He took the figure of a little boy, an important character in his secret movie, and he made the monster dog eat the little boy. Then he showed me how the boy travelled through the insides of the monster dog. I thought of Jonah being swallowed by the whale, but didn't say so. Then Steven began to hum "All You Need Is Love," by The Beatles. Then he sang the words to "All You Need Is Love." He turned the monster dog over and began to color the blank reverse side of the paper.

He made a heart with the word "Love" written inside. He then drew a picture of a tree and two flowers followed by a bubble right behind the dog's eye and filled it with a rainbow, a sun, and a smiling moon. He then drew a peace sign. In the dog's feet, he drew a heart, a tear, a girl's face, and a math equation. In the dog's tail, he drew a devil's face, an angry face, a swastika, a lightning bolt, and then a lock with a key.

Instead of fangs, he made the dog's teeth smooth. The creation of this drawing took the entire session and we did not talk about it as he was making it. Throughout the entire session I had many intense feelings, including suspense, anticipation, and even a sense of dawning awe.

In the following session Steven said "Do you still have the dog?" "Yes," I replied. "And I'm very curious to find out about all the changes you made in the dog during our last meeting." "Yes," said Steven, "they are very important."

When Steven looked at the dog again, he began literally to shiver with excitement. He started to sing "All You Need Is Love" again. I noted out loud how excited he was to see his creation again. I said it stirred up so much in his mind and in his body. He took this comment, I guess, as a shaming one and tried to pull himself together. I said that he seemed to feel I was criticizing him, which I said I had not meant to do.

He said he would tell me about the dog. The little boy, he said, had gone inside the dog to bring him love. At first the dog had wanted to either spit the little boy out because he was poison, or else to chew him up completely and poop him out. The evil master in the shadow world did not want the boy to stay inside and change the dog from evil to loving. But the little boy had refused to be stopped. His job was to save the dog and to change the dog from the inside out. The little boy sang to the dog "All You Need is Love" and the love began to spread out inside the dog, first of all changing his heart.

As the love spread through the dog, connecting his eyes and brain with his heart and his legs, new things appeared. There was a new heart for the dog that changed the way he could feel. A new brain changed the way he could see. A peace sign calmed the dog down.

I asked Steven what the symbols in the dog's feet meant. The heart meant more love to help the dog move. The tear represented the dog's sadness, which he could now feel because he had been so evil. The girl's face represented the dog's love for his mother. And the equation represented the dog's new-found confidence in being able to learn.

I was deeply moved by all this, and said so. Then, I asked about the dog's tail. Steven explained that you can't make evil, anger, and meanness just go away. He said that was how the dog was born and that is just how it is. It can't be changed. But, since the dog has love inside of him now, those things can be locked in the tail so they can't get out and spoil the love that connects everything else.

Steven turned the dog over again and showed me how a rainbow was reflected in the dog's tail because the evil was safely confined. He said, "What you see from the outside is the love."

Welcoming the unwanted

My experience with Steven provides one example of how psychotherapy can sponsor a surprising process of transformation that begins with welcoming unwanted experiences.

Welcoming unwanted experience has been a strong theme in Eigen's work from his earliest writing. His essay "Working with 'unwanted' patients" (Eigen, 1993, pp. 25–42) impressed me deeply when I read it many years ago. The essay describes some of the challenges of working with patients that others might consider not only undesirable, but also untreatable. Eigen offers this reflection on working with difficult patients. He writes,

> Perhaps one of the most far-reaching contributions of psychoanalysis to the concept of human relations is its theory of the way in which the helper uses the full range of his thoughts and feelings to further his understanding of the one he helps. The analyst learns to become sensitive to his positive and negative states as a source of intelligence about himself, the patient and the varied forms their relationship assumes. If this is difficult with people with whom one easily feels good, how much more so with someone whose type of ego deformation is seriously off-putting. (Eigen, 1993, p. 39)

Part of the difficulty in welcoming a patient's unwanted experience is linked to the pain of welcoming unwanted states that arise in ourselves, states that are often troubling, even shocking, but that, nonetheless, record the emotional impact of our "contact with the depths" evoked by another person's suffering.

In looking over Eigen's many books, it is my sense that few analysts have sustained such a continuous concern in their writing with the forces of affirmation and growth alongside a deepening exploration of factors that combine to destroy awareness and truncate lives. One of the powerful lessons derived from Eigen's example is that he never turns his back on the reality of human destructiveness.

I register a generosity of spirit, as well as the toughness and courage, demonstrated by Eigen's willingness to focus so much attention on multiple forms of suffering. It is hard to really appreciate, much less to describe, the myriad forms of darkness, violence, perversion, and damage that can emerge within an individual, a couple, a family, a group, or a nation. Violence demands attention, yet there is nothing easier or more common than to turn away from it.

Evidence of destructiveness is everywhere in daily life. Violence can be so intimidating that it becomes unspeakable. Daring to speak is one of the most important acts in re-establishing a human dimension otherwise often crushed in the aftermath of violence. Eigen helps find words for violence, trauma, damage, and forms of extreme distress. The value of this particular dimension of his work can not be underestimated. We need real language to sustain the possibility of thinking, exploring, fathoming, and working through violence and the suffering that it sows.

Eigen describes many intensities and pathways of destructive impulses, actions, thoughts, wishes, and deeds. Over the years, he has introduced a new lexicon to help think about such unwanted experience. He speaks, for example, of psychic deadness, toxic nourishment, damaged dreamwork, and annihilated selves. Naming and describing painful states of unwanted experience, as well as sharing detailed and moving stories about people he has worked with, helped, and learned from, encourages his readers to risk noticing, approaching, contacting, and listening deeply and carefully to the violent others alive within ourselves and our own experiences.

Eigen has written movingly about what he calls "killers in dreams" (2005, pp. 120–153). He writes, "Not all people survive themselves.

Killers in dreams portray aspects of the pressure that personality exerts against itself, that life exerts against itself" (p. 137). He also observes,

> To kill, not to kill, to kill *and* not to kill, a kind of unconscious pulse gives rise to the feeling that life is threatened, precarious, saved in the nick of time. We escape the knife—once more, but not always, not forever. Relief after fright creates a powerful rhythm in emotional life. Shock, fear, threat, danger—coming through, survival, renewal. A basic rebirth sensation partly involving living through dangers, especially our own dangerous natures. When this works decently enough, the destructive urge adds spice to life, makes for drama and suspense. (Eigen, 2005, p. 137)

Eigen encourages an improbable conversation with the bullies inside myself. Anyone who welcomes their dreams over decades will notice the presence of delinquents, sadists, fire-starters, serial killers, murderers, and psychopaths. Not only do these figures populate newspapers, films, novels, and television programs, they enter our dreams and, by doing so, disturbingly color the perceptions of our daily lives.

Some people turn off the news because it is so disturbing. How much more troubling, then, to refuse the news of your own dream life because it feels too traumatic, violent, and wounding.

According to Eigen, we should seek to know and work on some of the annihilating aspects within ourselves. After a while, as we adjust to the atmosphere of a nightmare, or accept the presence of a fragment of a very bad dream oddly coexisting with brighter emotions, scenes, and images, we become gradually familiar with a congregation of destructive and damaged objects seeking an audience within us.

Letting our demons bring news from dream life helps to diminish our fears in the long run. Such figures frighten us when they first arrive, but that is perhaps because they feel unwanted and we refuse to welcome them. There is a beautiful story about the Tibetan saint Milarepa. A great master, he was still plagued by demons who arrived to destroy his quiet mountain retreat. Then, instead of fighting the demons or fleeing from them, Milarepa invited them to sit with him and to have tea. As soon as he sincerely welcomed them, their power over him disappeared and they vanished.

Properly welcomed, our negative emotions no longer arrive as alien, split-off, denied, or disowned threats. Doing the work of welcoming the unwanted in ourselves is a vital practice to prepare to welcome the unwanted that others so urgently need to speak about and find an audience for.

By welcoming unwanted aspects of experience, we break the spells we have lived under for sometimes very long periods of time. We emerge into new relational spaces as well as into new qualities of mental space. One may even begin to harvest the fruits of a darker wisdom from those inner experiences of violence, cruelty, and murder-dread. Eigen gives a creative example of this in his chapter on "Killers in dreams". He asserts,

> Rising energy vis-à-vis a lower energy threshold can be translated into killers in dreams, and, vice versa, a fall of energy after adaptation to a higher energy level can be represented as a threat to life. On the other hand, too much control, toning down, cutting off energy flow can find expression as a killer in dreams. Dream killers spontaneously give expression to changes in energy (from high to low, low to high) or control (too much, too little along a severity-diffusion continuum). (Eigen, 2005, pp. 124–125)

Such insights are stunning. They seem possible because Eigen is willing to get to know unwanted states of mind and is not hypnotized by the cobra-like aura of destructiveness. Neither does he concretize destructiveness and treat it as an unchanging or unchangeable power. He's keenly attuned to the flux and flow of process, and this kind of attention to the many-colored strands of experience leads to a de-concretizing attitude that slowly expands possibilities for thinking and feeling, lessening intimidation and anxiety.

The Buddhist teacher Stephen Levine often said that if the pain of the world made a sound, we would all be deafened by its roar. Fear of pain and hatred of it spreads and amplifies misery, isolation, helplessness, and hopelessness. Eigen writes extensively about the necessity of comprehending how and why psychic numbness and deadness appear as outcomes of living in a damaging world.

Eigen respects the way people take paths of numbness, deadness, denial, and self-attack. His method, though that is probably too formal a word, is to show up as a beacon of auxiliary awareness, encouraging the gradual expansion of attention, welcoming faint signals of life, hope, interest, novelty, desire, truth, rage, as well as any of the many kinds of aliveness that can emerge from the inertia of living within long-established bunkers of psychic survival.

Most of all, Eigen encourages a keener witnessing of the mystery of constantly changing experience itself. Paying attention to mystery, suffering, not-knowing, getting to know, becoming—these are all factors in the way healthy growth can be detected in what otherwise appear to be barren or poisoned psychic landscapes.

It is a tall order to learn to play with destructiveness. But, that is the sort of evolution that Eigen suggests is possible. Such transformations arise from the deep faith Eigen has in the possibilities of communication with unwanted aspects of experience. His radical generosity has been to share so much of his own experience in the form of writing and teaching in a way that cracks open ordinary psychoanalytic knowledge and exploration.

Welcoming the future

I still remember the excitement I felt when stumbling on to a copy of Eigen's early book *Coming Through the Whirlwind* (1992) while browsing one day at a local bookstore on my lunch hour. I could barely put the book down to return to my work. Today, I think Eigen's books will remain small, potent, largely hidden treasures, expressions of his unique sensibility that others will continue to discover and value over time.

By writing as fully and openly as he has, Eigen's work has become a meaningful act of resistance to the corrosive effects of the widespread denigration of meaning in our culture. By his own assessment, Eigen sees the emergence of what he calls "an age of psychopathy" (2007). He defines this as the intentional manipulation of psychotic anxieties for the purpose of gaining, consolidating, and exploiting power. It is one thing to offer information, and quite another to risk sharing your own critical wisdom. Such openness is a much needed antidote to the superficial flood of images that saturate daily life as well as to the claustrophobic states of mind that people can become trapped in through their many unconscious identifications.

Eigen's work offers countless glimpses into the amazingly complex and idiosyncratic processes that can evolve between patient and analyst. He is able to evoke the many ways analyst and patient sometimes triangulate O, bringing body, mind, heart, and soul together to expand consciousness of self–other–mind–body–God and world.

In my own work, Eigen has helped me to begin to recognize that over time screams are able to be dreamt. The silent scream can eventually be heard, and the scream that never stops screaming can become part of a larger rhythm of breakdown, repair, discovery, and gratitude.

Our dreams take us beyond what we believed we could tolerate. Gradually, we learn to work with the oscillation of opening and closing, welcoming and rejecting, screaming and dreaming. Each day, with the encouragement of others, we grow a little beyond what, yesterday, was thinkable or bearable. Without encouragement like this, we would be lost.

In his book *Rage*, Eigen writes,

> Let us pray for a safe, healthy, productive life for all. But we can be sure that whoever and wherever we are, the same old human problems will rise to greet us, and we will have ourselves to face not just at the end or the beginning of the day, but throughout our lives.
>
> It is one of the great paradoxes of living that we do change when we focus on what can't change. Sometimes we will hold hands. Sometimes we will travel alone. But we will never stop moving toward a beginning when it comes to what we do with ourselves and each other. . . . We have a lot of evolving to do. (2002, pp. 178–179)

References

Bion, W. (1985). *All My Sins Remembered: Another Part of a Life.* Abingdon: Fleetwood Press.

Eigen, M. (1977). On breathing and identity. *Journal of Humanistic Psychology, 17*: 35–39. Reprinted in: *The Electrified Tightrope* (pp. 43–47). London: Karnac, 2004.

Eigen, M. (1992). *Coming Through the Whirlwind: Case Studies in Psychotherapy.* Wilmette, IL: Chiron.

Eigen, M. (1993). *The Electrified Tightrope,* A. Phillips (Ed.). London: Karnac, 2004.

Eigen, M. (2002). *Rage.* Middletown, CT: Wesleyan University Press.
Eigen, M. (2005). *Emotional Storm.* Middletown, CT: Wesleyan University Press.
Eigen, M. (2007). Guilt in an age of psychopathy. *Psychoanalytic Review, 94*(5):727–749.
Eigen, M. (2012). *Kabbalah and Psychoanalysis.* London: Karnac.
Rumi, J. (2004). *The Essential Rumi,* C. Barks (Trans.). (p. 109). New York: HarperCollins.

CHAPTER NINE

Being with-in, "wherever you find yourself with a patient"

Ofra Eshel

> "Wherever you find yourself with a patient, you have to go. We wish things could be otherwise, could be easier, but we have little choice when light shines through the ruins of injury. I think that is a very Kabbalistic model"
>
> (Eigen, 2005, p. 41)

It is to this simple, yet profound, singular voice at the core of Eigen's writing that I would like to dedicate this chapter, in particular because of its great significance to me in my psychoanalytic work, as I strive and struggle to go through the ruins and heal the brokenness of a human(e) psyche.

A theoretical–clinical context

I first became acquainted with Eigen's writing at the end of the 1990s, when I "discovered" and read his evocative paper "The area of faith in Winnicott, Lacan, and Bion" (1981), and then his early books, one by one: *The Psychotic Core* (1986), *Coming Through the Whirlwind* (1992), and *The Electrified Tightrope* (1993). I was enthralled not only with his ideas, but the distinctively authentic way in which he expressed them, his stirring uniqueness. This grew stronger and deeper over the past dozen years, with the unfolding of my own exploration into the dimension created by the analyst/therapist's[1] *presence* and the ensuing *patient–analyst interconnectedness, or "withness"* as a fundamental dimension of analytic work that extends the reach of psychoanalytic treatment to more disturbed patients.

Central to this dimension is the analyst's "being there", or "presencing", within (with-in) the patient's experiential world and within the grip of the analytic process. I first developed this approach with regard to massive acting out, acting in, and enactment, arguing that the fate of these acting situations in the therapeutic work is determined largely by the analyst's willingness and ability to give him/herself over to "being there", staying within the intense impact of the acting situation and communing with it (Eshel, 1998a,b). Later, I expanded these ideas to the treatment of difficult-to-reach schizoid, narcissistic, and severely perverse patients, and to various difficult treatment situations (Eshel, 2001, 2004a,b, 2005, 2009, 2010, 2011, 2012, 2013a,b).

Essentially, "presencing" is the analyst's deep acceptance of the necessity of becoming an embedded, elemental, and sustaining functioning presence within the treatment process, thereby experiencing, withstanding, processing, and gradually transforming, *from within*, the repetitive cycle of pathological self-other relations and defenses. "Presencing" may develop into its full potential in the treatment of difficult-to-treat patients, and in difficult treatment situations and enactments. It is a primary quality of presence, or deep availability, that focuses on experience-near attunement, receptive capacity, holding, containing, and protection, rather than proffering interpretations of the analytic relationships and, especially, of patient–analyst separateness. I believe that while "presencing" involves the above capacities and functions, the experience of "presencing" is a quality that is superordinate to these capacities and functions and must be considered an aspect of the analytic experience in its own terms. It concentrates primarily on the ontological (being) quality of the analytic experience that is lived through with the analyst, rather than on epistemological and interpretive qualities. The analyst gives himself over to becoming part of the patient's ongoing emotional reality and mental processes.[2] Patient and analyst *"live an experience together"*

(Winnicott, 1992a, p. 152). This very elemental quality of the analyst's "presencing," with its profound ontological implications, engenders a new possibility for being and experiencing, where that possibility had been missing or foreclosed.

Through the analyst's "presencing with-in" (and the often evolving therapeutic regression, in Winnicott's and Balint's sense), patient and analyst enter another realm of experience—that of patient–analyst interconnectedness, or "withness." The patient is able to transfer/project unbearable, split-off inner experiences into another psyche that is there to be used as an area of experiencing, processing, and transformation. Patient and analyst, thereby, forge an emergent new experiential–emotional entity that goes beyond the confines of their separate subjectivities and the simple summation of the two—an entity (unit or being) of interconnectedness, "withness," or "t(w)o-getherness." *Two-in-oneness.* Treatment, thus, *creates* psychic reality, and a different kind of knowledge, experience, and powerful affects that come into being when the analyst interconnects psychically with the patient in living through the process. It is a shift in emphasis from the unveiling of meaning and relationships within the patient's already existing scripts to *a process of being and becoming,* as a consequence of the experience of patient–analyst living the experience t(w)ogether.

It is in my endeavor to grasp, delve into, and convey the true nature of the analyst's "presencing" and interconnectedness that Eigen's singular writing greatly helped and enriched me. I have often experienced in his writing this quality of being with-in, with its different elemental feel and different implications, and with its potential to engender markedly new possibilities from those we conventionally embrace. Eigen writes, "This collapse into being with another, the deepest states of the other—isn't this something of the kind of sensitivity that gives our annihilated states a home?" (Eigen, 2006, p. 38; also cited in Eshel, 2013b).

I have quoted the following passage from Eigen regarding the treatment of a difficult patient, because it conveys ideas that are closely related to my "being there within, presencing":

> Little by little, I see him [the patient] seeing me out of the corner of his psyche. He is aware that I am there, whoever I am. I am someone not talking him out of himself . . . He cannot get rid of the him-in-me with

> words. He is perplexed and curious about being part of my inner life . . . It is something new to bump up against another's quietness and find the quietness moulded around himself . . . He is a growing presence in a living being. (Eigen, 2001, pp. 134–135; also cited in Eshel, 2005)

However, within my notion of interconnected "presencing," where "him-in-me" and me-in-him begins or ends, nobody knows.

In addition, in order to describe the getting in touch with primary relatedness and formative experiences of being and becoming that the ontological quality of analytic "presencing" enables, I have referred to his telling words on reaching out to "starting points [at] the depths of being":

> Yet one *can* dip into the storehouse of possibilities, shift attitudes, and rework one's sense of what it means to be an experiencing subject . . . a new experiencing of it, can set into motion a change, a lightening and deepening of relating to self and others that runs down one's backbone *to the very toes of being*. One senses work going on in the *basement*, a *placeless place* where elements of personality mix and re-form. (Eigen, 1993, p. 266, original italics and mine, respectively; also cited in Eshel, 2012).

Into breakdown, catastrophe, and the last scream: the return of the dissociated

In recent years, I have developed this dimension of patient–analyst interconnected being and experiencing even further. I venture to propose *patient–analyst interconnectedness or "withness" as the only state of being that can meet and transform catastrophe and breakdown* (Eshel, 2009, 2011, 2012, 2013a,b). This draws heavily on ideas from Winnicott's posthumous writings and Bion's late works, with Eigen's evocative rendering of them that powerfully captures, illuminates, and deepens them in his distinctively unique way.

To begin with, Winnicott's later papers "Fear of breakdown" (1986; written around 1963, but published three years after his death, in 1974), and its continuation, "Psychology of madness" (1989a), assumed great importance for me. In these two papers, Winnicott addresses the disastrous impact of being broken down at the beginning of one's life. It is that extreme primitive agony of early breakdown that Winnicott also calls madness X, and Eigen, later, refers to as agony X (1999, 2004). This early breakdown was so unthinkable and "indescribably painful" that it could not be experienced, and a new massive defence organization, which the patient displays as an illness syndrome, was organized against it. Consequently, the individual becomes imprisoned in a dissociated, ever-present "unthinkable state of affairs that underlies the defence organization" (Winnicott, 1986, p. 174), which cannot get into the past tense, and is feared and compulsively sought after in the future. It is, thus, an ongoing catastrophe, then, now, about to happen; an endless impact on one's being.

Winnicott is describing here a profound inner struggle. In those depths of unthinkable agony of early breakdown or madness are buried both the traumatic experience and a "*basic urge*" to experience it and, thus, "to be recovered in experience . . . remembered in the reliving of it" (1989a, p. 126, original italics) in treatment. This evokes the dread of breakdown or of the return of the original madness, but also evokes the patient's great need to reach to this original, unthinkable state of breakdown, to risk re-experiencing and reliving the early agony, this time in treatment, with the analyst and his or her different holding and "auxiliary ego-supporting function," which will make recovery possible.

Eigen thoroughly reworks this theme with his own touch:

> Since breakdown occurred while personality was forming, one did not have capacity even to experience what was happening. One lacked ability or equipment to undergo original madness as it occurred. One could not be present at one's undoing. The intensity was too much to bear. One would have to experience breakdown of life, mind, self, psyche before one could be there long enough to experience it. Yet an underlying sense of what one dare not, could not tolerate experiencing remains as a defining fact, all the more powerful as a potential fact.
>
> . . . It can be [only] experienced but not remembered. It is recoverable by experiencing breakdown moments in therapy. It is not a matter of recovering repressed memories, but living in the present bits of what could not be organized enough to be repressed. (1999, p. 174)

Eigen merely makes a reference here (1999, p. 174) to the madness in the words of Winnicott's patient into the third hour of a three-hour session, and its connection to loneliness (I think Eigen was not fully aware of its significance at the time). In my view, it is a touching moment: "She said: I've been trying to show you *me being alone* [the first two hours of the session]; that's the way I go on when alone, though without words at all, as I don't let myself start talking to myself (that would be madness)" (Winnicott, 1971, p. 73, original italics).

Eigen (2002, 2010, 2012a) extends the unexperienced breakdown or madness to the scream that was not screamed or experienced in Winnicott's (1989b) description of a patient with psychosomatic skin disorder. In her treatment, "the great non-event of every session is screaming . . . the scream that this patient is always not experiencing" because in childhood, her crying went unmet, "the child cried and the mother did not appear" (Winnicott, 1989b, p. 116). Therefore, for Winnicott, the scream that his patient "is looking for is *the last scream just before hope was abandoned.* Since then screaming has been of no use because it fails in its purpose." The emergence of the patient's scream, both in a dream and in her waking life, "only becomes possible as a result of the analysis, in which hope about screaming returned and is recaptured from the time before she became ill . . . it is the only way to correct the failure of [her] last scream to work" (Winnicott, 1989b, pp. 116–118, original italics).

Eigen (1998, 2002, 2012b) takes the theme of the scream even further, amplifying it through Bion's late writing, with added Kabbalistic import:

> In psychosis Bion (1970) depicted an explosion (trauma), with bits and pieces of personality floating in space at accelerating velocity, going further and further away from each other and further from the point of explosion . . . The bits and pieces of exploded personality floating in the [therapy] room might not be redolent with meaning so much as flotsam and jetsam of an extended SOS signal, like a thinning, vanishing scream over time . . . Even so, the vanishing debris might have value as passing signals of a catastrophic process that began long ago and still goes on . . . Feel the impact . . . something like: I am catastrophe in process. My personality is catastrophic. Something awful has happened, is happening. I am undergoing a state of disintegration . . .
>
> Maybe part of what needs to happen is to sit with the explosion, hear the SOS. [As in] a Kabbalistic exercise, listen, hear the scream. There is

a scream inside . . . Stay with the scream, an inaudible scream of your patient's being . . .

The scream is a sign of distress that cannot be addressed by the screaming one. A distress the adult or baby cannot solve, an unsolvable disturbance . . . But you are prepared to stay with the scream for decades, to sit with the unsolvable disturbance, providing a background support for something to grow over time . . .

For Bion, the attitude, state, and disposition with which we meet catastrophe is Faith. Not "k", not knowledge . . . F in O, where O signifies unknown ultimate reality, especially, in psychoanalysis emotional reality, [and] Faith includes the discipline of being without memory, expectation, understanding, or desire. (Eigen, 2012b, pp. 19–21)

I feel that Eigen's rendering of Bion's late work, over the years, from his 1981 paper to his latest book, *Kabbalah and Psychoanalysis* (2012b), paved my way into Bion's later radical, ground-breaking conceptualization, and helped me to incorporate other perceptive contributions regarding this complex conceptualization (Grotstein, 2007, 2010; Ogden, 2005; Vermote, 2013). It constitutes analytic work that necessitates Faith in O and Transformation in O, when dealing with the most non-thought, unknown, undifferentiated zone of psychic functioning. Rather than epistemological exploration (knowing), the focus here is on the unknown and unknowable ultimate emotional reality-O, the primacy of being at-one with the reality of the patient, and a lived, new experience. In this zone of analytic functioning, Bion's enigmatic words acquire their full meaning:

With this [O] the analyst cannot be identified: he must *be* it . . . at-one-ment with it and evolution . . . that is common to analyst and analysand. . . . In practice this means *not* that the analyst recalls some relevant memory but that a relevant constellation will be evoked during the process of at-one-ment with O, the process denoted by transformation O→K. (Bion, 1970, pp. 27, 30, 33, original italics)

This is an amalgamation of Winnicott's and Bion's powerful ideas, with Eigen providing his singular inspiring contact with their depths: breakdown and madness, catastrophe and the last scream, being-with, Faith, and at-one-ment with the patient's innermost emotional reality. It may be seen as their *"transformation in O→K"* within Eigen's writing. All these have infused themselves into my analytic work and thinking, into the unfolding and deepening of the dimension of analytic "presencing" and patient–analyst deep interconnectedness, or "withness." In particular, I came to see this as the only way of being, which in treatment can meet and transform catastrophe, breakdown, and the scream that is dying out. For, as Eigen writes, when you listen to the scream inside—and I would add, when you are there, with-in—the scream becomes "louder and louder." Staying with the scream provides "a background support for something to grow over time" (Eigen, 2012b, p. 20).

This brings to mind the repeated, desperate, sputtering scream of the woman in Samuel Beckett's short play "Rockaby" (1981); the unmet, withering, last scream of a lonely woman, rocking in her chair, "for another, another like herself, another creature like herself, a little like . . . for another, another living soul, one other like herself, a little like . . ." until she relinquishes hope and surrenders unto death and communion with her dead mother. I feel here the yearning for an interconnected presence that can allow this traumatic repetition to take on the transformative experience of being-with "another like herself," and living through the screaming t(w)ogether. This tortured scream embodies "the failure of her last scream to work," until hope is abandoned.

Furthermore, I would dare to argue that the analyst's being within, along with the emergence of deep patient–analyst interconnectedness or at-one-ment, is the only state in treatment that can meet and transform the scream that died out into the "*last scream just before hope was abandoned*." It is the only state that can transform the dissociated breakdown and the state of no-hope and catastrophe into risking, in treatment, relived catastrophic experiencing before it became frozen, lost, terminal, dead. Recently, a patient of mine said, most movingly, that in the first several years of treatment we searched for, found, listened to, and deciphered the black box of his breakdown, while now we hear the black box just before the breakdown, in an unsettling, intense state of dread and hope. I believe that only patient and analyst "t(w)ogether" (Eshel, 2012, 2013a,b) become able to experience, tolerate, and go through the anxieties that were unthinkable in their original setting; the analyst, thus, bears and experiences with the patient and for the patient the relived breakdown, madness, screaming. "Someone must feel it in order for us to embrace it as reality" (Eigen, 2004, p. 65). The catastrophic change (Bion, 1965) thus *becomes a catastrophic chance*.

I shall now present a detailed clinical illustration from my early therapeutic work, which epitomizes these themes in a most extreme way.

Case illustration

"If thou wilt go with me, then I will go; but if thou wilt not go with me, I will not go" (Judges 4:8).

The patient I describe was in treatment with me for over ten years, separated by two intervals, so that, taken together, it spanned a period of more than fifteen years. The following account focuses on the first two years, and mainly the second year, of the first treatment period (a four-year period).

Referral for treatment

Reuben was referred to me for compulsory intensive psychotherapy in the state psychiatric hospital where I was working. He was hospitalized in order to undergo intensive psychotherapy, based on a court verdict and by order of the Commissioner of Prisons, in lieu of being sent to prison. Reuben was thirty years old, good-looking, beginning a doctoral degree. He was sentenced to five years imprisonment for sex offenses involving four girls aged twelve–thirteen over a period of three months, beginning when his second wife left him. According to the evidence, in each incident he would invite the girl into his car with the excuse that he was searching for an address, take her to the same place, force her to engage in oral and anal intercourse, masturbate in front of her and take her back home. Thus, when he brought the fourth girl back home in his car, the police were waiting, and apprehended him.

Before the trial, he was interned in the psychiatric hospital for approximately five months for observation and preparation of a psychiatric expert opinion for the court. During this period, his smiling, cooperative manner was regarded by the hospital staff as superficial. He expressed no feelings of remorse or guilt about his behavior towards the girls in spite of great pressure to do so. He claimed that he did not remember what he had done, was unable to remember the girls' faces, could not explain his behavior, and asserted that it had not been premeditated. But he also insisted that he had only committed indecent acts and not actual rape. By contrast, he repeatedly expressed concern about his future, lest the hospitalization and his emotional state cause his intellectual ability to deteriorate.

The summary of the psychiatric expert opinion submitted to the court stated:

A. The accused is capable of following the court proceedings and participating in his defense.

B. At the time of the alleged incident, the accused was not mentally ill, but mentally disturbed, and as such, knew right from wrong. He acted under a strong, unconscious urge which, given his illness (compulsive states in a state of depersonalization), was hard to resist. However, at the time of the incident he was not suffering from a mental illness.

C. Although he is capable of serving any sentence, it seems to us that in this specific case there are strong grounds for allowing the accused to serve all or part of his sentence incarcerated in a psychiatric hospital, so as to permit intensive psychotherapy.

The psychological evaluation included in the expert opinion emphasized Reuben's rigid defense system and massive use of intellectualization, rationalization, and dissociation for dealing with feelings of abandonment and rejection in interpersonal relationships, and its collapse into vengeful, perverse destructiveness. The evaluation also stressed the need for intensive psychotherapy.

During this period, there were two unsuccessful attempts at psychotherapy, the first with a private psychologist (brought in by the family), who, after several sessions, felt she could not continue treatment because the patient was emotionally "flat" and "full of resistance." The second attempt was by the hospital's ward psychologist, who felt, as well, that it was impossible to form a real therapeutic relationship. After the court sentence, and after the patient, under court order, had been sent back to the hospital for psychotherapy, I was asked to take the case. There was great concern that since Reuben had already been sentenced, even his superficial willingness to undergo psychotherapy would disappear.

Background

Although Reuben had apparently grown up in harsh emotional circumstances, when he spoke about his life at the start of treatment, everything was always "fine", and he "got along well with everyone."

Reuben was the second of two children. His sister was two years older. An older brother had died when he was two months old. Reuben's parents were born in Germany. They left Germany before the Second World War, moving to one country and then to another (when Reuben was about three years old). Their financial state was sound, but family relationships were very bad (which Reuben claimed he knew nothing about until his mother revealed this in the hospital). His father had frequently been away from home on business, and also had relationships with other women. His mother made extended visits to her family in Israel, when Reuben was four, six, and eight years of age (at age eight, when they stayed for half a year, she placed him in a religious kibbutz, despite his secular upbringing), but when Reuben was six, the children remained with the father. When they returned from the last visit, Reuben's father complained of feeling unwell, was diagnosed with cancer, hospitalized, and died half a year later. He was forty-two years old at the time, and the mother was thirty-six, "beautiful and imposing" (in Reuben's words). Reuben's mother sold their house and belongings, discovered that there were many debts, and immigrated to Israel with the children that same year. Reuben was ten years old at the time, and from then on he no longer lived at home. The mother lived with her older brother, a businessman to whom she was particularly close, and she placed Reuben and his sister in a residential institution for underprivileged children. Two years later, she moved into a flat of her own, bringing the sister, who was an outstanding pupil, back home, claiming that she was too gifted to be left in an institution. Reuben, on the other hand, remained at the institution and was a most unmanageable pupil. During those years, he visited his mother only during vacations, and she and her brother (the businessman uncle) visited him only sporadically.

At age eighteen, Reuben enlisted in the paratroopers, an elite army unit. After finishing his army service, he worked in construction for a while, lived with his mother, and took his matriculation exams. He then went to a university in a different city, fought actively in the Six Day War, and married a girl who had been an unsteady girlfriend from his earlier military days. The marriage was unsuccessful; his wife left him after a year and a half, and later they divorced.

After the divorce, Reuben completed his bachelors and masters degrees. He met a girl who was a student at a university in another city, and became immediately and rapidly involved. In spite of a crisis during their second year together, they decided to marry. She switched universities, continuing her doctoral studies in the city in which Reuben was studying; they married, and he, too, started doctoral studies. After the marriage, great tension developed between the couple. Reuben's wife claimed that he was irritable and detached and he also interfered with her studies. After less than three months, she suddenly announced that she wanted to leave and move into the student dormitories. An attempt at marriage counseling was unsuccessful, and the counselor recommended a temporary separation. During this period, Reuben became very restless, was unable to concentrate on his work and studies, and frequently went to his wife at her dormitory and work, pleading with her to return to him. *It was on the way back from these visits that the incidents with the girls began, until he was caught with the fourth girl.* After Reuben was transferred from prison to the psychiatric hospital for observation, his wife demanded a divorce.

The above information was provided mainly by his mother, uncle, sister, and wife. During the interviews, Reuben's speech was emotionally flat and fragmented and he remembered almost nothing of his childhood before age ten, until his father's death and the family's immigration to Israel. In fact, his clearer memories were only from the time he was placed in the youth institution, stating repeatedly that it had been a "good time" of mischief, never mentioning the abandonment and neglect, or the fact that his sister had been returned home while he had not. He stressed that he had never been envious of his sister and admired her for her academic achievements. He also stated that he was not envious of his cousins (the children of his businessman uncle), who lived at home in luxury whereas he remained in a youth institution. Reuben did stress his successful army service. As for the "action" he saw in the war, he remarked that even though there had been many casualties on both sides, he had felt nothing, that "they ate breakfast alongside the dead bodies."

Concerning his marriages, Rueben mentioned that his first marriage had been unimportant and he saw no need to think about it any further. He regarded his second marriage as very important, but was unable to explain what had happened between him and his wife that led to the break and her wish to leave. He had tried to ignore the tension that had developed between them after their marriage and go on as if nothing was amiss. As mentioned, he remembered almost nothing about the "incidents with the girls", and he was unable to understand what had happened to him.

Given the compulsory circumstances of the treatment, his level of personality organization, and way of providing information, Reuben's willingness and capacity to undergo dynamic psychotherapy and to relate reflectively and affectively to his inner world and relationships seemed to be minimal.

The treatment

The first two years of treatment—four times per week (face-to-face) intensive psychotherapy—were marked by frequent disruptions in verbal communication, ranging from Reuben's general difficulty in speaking to lapses into complete silence. During the first year of treatment, these silences would last an entire session, or several consecutive sessions. In the second year, the silence was long and extreme, and lasted for over four months.

I will now describe these ruptures in communication, especially the long silence in the second year, and the breakthrough after two years of treatment.

The first session was laden with anxiety. Reuben shifted restlessly in his chair until he almost fell off, gazed at pictures on the wall, asked "Have to undress already?", and spoke in a vague, fragmented way about his relationships with his two wives and his mother, and about the "incidents with the girls." Beginning with the second session, he became withdrawn and barely communicated.

The sessions dragged on heavily; he would not speak spontaneously, and when he did speak, it was mostly to answer my questions in a stultified, dull way. Often he would not answer at all. Over and over he would say, "Again your annoying questions," immediately followed by "Are you angry?" Or he would say that he had not heard my question, and that his ears were ringing. He claimed that when he was in the army, a bazooka had been fired right next to his ear, causing it partial deafness. It was evident, however, that his hearing problems increased when the questions were more difficult for him to deal with. Later on, he began suffering from pain in his abdomen, hugging his stomach, his body contorted; he worried that he had an ulcer, until medical tests were conducted, which turned out negative.

After two months, Reuben gradually began to talk in a more detailed, emotional way. And then the silences burst forth. Any openness or emotional relating on his part was immediately followed by great tension, by angry outbursts at me that lately what I say "annoys" him and that I "distort things", by having difficulty remaining until the sessions ended, and by silences. He would sit tensely, his hands tightly gripping the arms of the chair, his face contorted, half crying, half shouting: "I don't know what's happening, I can't talk to you." When I said that the difficulty was perhaps rendered by our talking and connection, he smiled sadly and remained silent until the end of the session. In the next session he spoke, but in the sessions that followed the difficulty in speaking continued and worsened. He would speak little during the sessions, sit silently, his fingers fidgeting nervously with his lips and the tip of his nose, or he would draw squares on the sheets of paper that were on the table, applying great pressure on the pencil, filling in the squares with crisscross lines resembling prison bars. Sometimes, he would begin by writing his name in a flowery hand, then completely cover it with criss-crosses, or he would surround himself with objects, as if erecting a wall around himself (a pack of cigarettes, an ashtray, a matchbox and a pencil), covering his mouth with his hand, while his eyes watched alertly. He would sleep a lot before the sessions, and go to sleep immediately afterwards; during the sessions he would say that he was tired, that he had only just gotten up, that he could not concentrate, and that he could not think on his own between sessions. Questions about his thoughts or feelings only intensified his silences. My interventions and suggestions concerning these reactions evoked great tension and anger. Nonetheless, at the end of the sessions he would leave slowly, saying, "It's hard to come and hard to go."

It was at this time that the issue of recollecting the "incidents with the girls" resurfaced, after not being referred to since the beginning of treatment. Reuben began inquiring into the possibility of taking hospital leave one afternoon a week to study, and was told that it would not be granted until he gained a better recollection and understanding of what had occurred with the girls, in order to increase his self-control. In the session with me, he iterated that he could not recall what he had done, and repeated what he had already said in the same vague, partial (only the ride in the car to and from the place), affectless manner. He again stressed that he was certain there had been no rape, repeating that he could recall nothing else, and fell silent. But at the end of the session, when I told him that the session was over, he burst out, saying I should stay with him until evening so that he would remember, that I end the sessions whenever I feel like ending them, that he always has to come and remember and talk when I want him to, and not when he wants and is able to, that I dominate him, and he left very angrily. The following session he arrived quieter, saying that he understood and accepted that hospital leave was conditional upon his remembering and understanding the incidents with the girls, and since he wanted to be granted the leave, and was also interested in relieving himself of the matter but could do nothing more, he requested an injection of Pentothal. He was insistent about receiving the injection the next morning. I told him that it was not just a matter of providing information, but of his ability to recollect it on his own and with another person, of struggling with inner obstacles to knowing. Therefore, it was important that he remembers on his own, rather than a passive, forced remembering induced by Pentothal. Then suddenly, for the first time, he told me a dream he had dreamt in the youth institution when he was eleven–twelve years old. He was pursued by wolves, and running, fell softly into an abyss ahead of him, an abyss with beautiful, shining stars alongside it. He came to the following session feeling relieved that the idea of using Pentothal had been dropped, but there was no progress in his recollection of the incidents with the girls. He said that there are things that psychologists might want people to know, but people will *break down, go crazy.*

At the end of the first year of treatment, I took a four-week vacation. Soon after I returned, a lengthy silence began which lasted over four months. This silence was directly related to Reuben's relationship with me. When I returned from vacation, he was awaiting me excitedly at the gate of the hospital. During the sessions, he spoke about strong feelings of "loneliness and distress", of his fear of becoming dependent on me, of needing me, and that without me he felt great emptiness; he poignantly recalled a tree at the institution, under which he would sit alone and cry, and then spoke again of having no control over his relationship with me. Then, his tension and anger mounted; he asked himself over and over again, after the sessions, why he had told me all these very personal things, and had no answers. He left a session before it ended, saying in the next session that it had been because of a dream he had dreamt several days earlier, which he remembered in the previous session. In the dream, he causes my husband's death, comes to my house, and I, totally unaware, greet him joyfully, looking softer than usual in a skirt and blouse. It is a one-storey house with antique furniture and a door of pale wood, and many people are there. Reuben said the dream was terrifying because in it he causes death in order to get closer to me, and also because he has harmed me and I don't even know it. He said that he recounted the dream in this session and not the previous one because that session had been towards the evening, and now it was early afternoon. He then said anxiously that a dam had suddenly burst and his fantasies were beginning to run wild. I talked about the difference between fantasy and reality, thought and action. I said that if all the people killed in fantasy were to be dead, the world would be full of dead people. He appeared somewhat calmer. (Parenthetically, I would add that, unlike other interventions in this treatment, today I would not have offered this interpretation because it was too experience-far from his acute sense of impending danger and dread of his destructiveness.)

In the following session, he said that he remembered something connected to one of the girls, which he had not remembered earlier: When he took her home, the girl asked him, "Right, nothing happened to me?" and he answered, "Nothing," and, feeling extremely uncomfortable, brusquely opened the car door for her to get out, without looking at her.

At the next session, he said that he told me too many thoughts, fantasies, that he had reached his limit. And then silence reigned for over four months.

During these many sessions of silence, Reuben sat very tensely, pulling apart paper clips and breaking them, tearing up paper that was on the table, breaking pencils and a ruler—first taking apart its metal ends and then bending and breaking the ruler into small bits. Then, he spent hours burning matches. He would light a match, and when it was almost all burnt, would get hold of the other end until the entire match was burnt and black, then place it in the ashtray and light another. My attempts to speak to him, to relate to his fidgeting with objects and playing with fire, to offer interpretations or help him speak, were received with absolute silence or with sharp cries of "Don't nag," "Don't fuck my mind," "You're pretending." It was only when I said I felt he wanted me to disappear, because in his world I had become very frightening, that he said, "You finally understand," but then went silent again. He sat hidden, with his leg up on the chair, his hand over his mouth as if to hold back the words, with only his eyes peeking out tensely, saying it was boring. The next time that he said it was boring, he pointedly took out a newspaper to read, but his eyes did not follow the lines. Then he took a day's hospital leave in place of our session, leaving the hospital a few minutes before the session was to begin. At each session during this long silence, he would repeat just one sentence—standing at the door, before leaving, he would ask or point out the day and time of our next session: "You'll come on . . . at . . . o'clock."

What stood out during all of these sessions was that, despite his seemingly complete detachment and fidgeting, he was inexplicably very sensitive to my every movement, and if I shifted in my seat or looked elsewhere, he would suddenly shout, "You're fed up, I can see that you're fed up with me and this whole treatment."

As for my own reaction, I was surprised at my abiding patience with him during these continuous hours of silence. At times, I was anxious about his emotional state, occasionally I became impatient with his detached, obdurate, and provocative reactions, but mostly I sat quietly, engrossed patiently and resolutely with him and in that massive, intensive "something" that was going on inside him. Waiting in silence.

Reuben came to the session following the one he had missed for hospital leave looking pale, a rash covering his face. He began by saying he was tired, depressed, in a bad mood, and couldn't sleep, attributing it to our meetings. He said he wanted to stay at a distance from me because relating to me, especially his feelings and fantasies was difficult, and he also wanted to try things on his own, so that he wouldn't have to tell me everything. He said; "I'm afraid it'll get burnt." Reuben did not explain his fear further, but suddenly appeared more relaxed. He then said, "But you aren't leaving yet", and sank limply into his chair, appearing to be sleeping quietly until the end of the session. After the session, he resumed talking, and spoke continuously for hours about the youth institution, his feelings of abandonment and rejection, terrible earaches at night, physical abuse, and his aggressiveness. He said fearfully that he was "destroying the only home he had ever had, the idyllic picture", but still continued talking. After another hospital leave, he spoke emotionally about his feelings when he visited his rich uncle and family, that they were all very disturbed, hiding within great aggression towards the uncle, and if this aggression were to surface, they would lynch the uncle. In the following session, he spoke again about the hidden, overall aggression that he felt was aimed at his uncle. He tried to think it through, when suddenly he became very pale, grabbed the table, and said that the entire world was spinning. He asked to leave and return to the ward, insisting on it, even though I said that he had begun feeling bad here and we would wait together until the dizziness passed. When he refused to remain, I offered to accompany him to the ward. As we walked, he glanced sideways at me, with a kind of wonderment and excitement. Upon arriving at the ward, I bade him farewell and left.

At the next session, Reuben spoke about trivial matters, not mentioning the previous session, but something seemed to be bothering him greatly. Towards the end of the session, he said that he wanted to tell me something important—that when home on his last hospital leave, he had wanted to remember the incidents with the girls, that it was as though it was resurfacing; but in spite of everything, he could not remember. He thought that if he were to drive the route he had taken with the girls, he would remember, but was afraid to do so alone. Would I be willing to travel the route with him? I thought for a while. I then suggested that we talk about it again and together try to recall the details during the two and a half months left until the end of this year of treatment. And, if we do not manage to remember, I would travel the route with him. This was a difficult promise for me to make. I think of it as an act of faith.

For two months, we spoke about the girls: four girls with no face, no shape. In detail, step-by-step, we reviewed his leaving the house, the clothes he had worn, the route he had taken, but each time we got stuck at the point where he saw a girl on the way, stopped the car with a screech, asked how to find an address, and subsequently remembered nothing except the desolate place where he had taken them, and that afterwards he had taken them home. It seemed that in treatment, too, each time he stopped with a screech at this point.

Little by little, he was able to recall the face of one girl, the clothes of another. During these two months, many things "happened to him". He lost his wallet with his identity card and driving license. He arrived for treatment with a large scratch on his forehead—like the sign of Cain. He also formed an intense relationship with a nurse at the hospital (who, two years later, became his wife).

As we approached the end of this (second) year of treatment, and I was beginning to think that he would not manage to remember in this way, making it necessary to take the ride he had proposed, Reuben inquired towards the end of a particular session when treatment would end. As I began to answer, he cut me off and asked if it were possible that I might suddenly decide to end the treatment and leave. I answered that I would not. Then, at the beginning of the following session, Reuben said that he had completely remembered the incidents with the girls, and asked if I would like to hear it. And he talked for an hour and a half without a break, describing girl after girl, what he had said, what he had done, "pouring" it all on me, and when he finished speaking he looked completely drained and I felt as if I had been run over. I said only that it had been difficult and that we had taken a big, important step. The following day, Reuben said that the previous day he had feared I would think him a monster and would tell him to leave and never come back, but when I spoke of the importance of what he had told me, he felt I was holding out a hand to him.

Even though difficulties in speaking and shorter lapses into silence still occurred afterwards in treatment, this had been a momentous breakthrough in the wall of silence that Reuben had erected around himself. This was the first time he had dared open up and reveal harsh, darkened matter from his hidden, secret world, exposing himself to the very frightening dread of being rejected, hurt, abandoned, and dominated by another person. I am referring to breaking through the silence and not the non-remembering, as one could perhaps argue that he remembered more than he claimed to remember, and it was only then that he recounted it. Even so, I felt that it was a precious, profound, and crucial step. For, throughout his life, Reuben had used disconnectedness, shutting down, and dissociative–autistic encapsulation as the main defensive means for coping and surviving devastating emotional situations. Loneliness, neglect, and abandonment had been inflicted upon him from an early age, both emotionally and physically by his mother's narcissistic, rejecting attitude, and by the absence of the protective presence of his father (even when his father was still alive, and certainly after his death). His feelings and needs had always been completely ignored. Consequently, his personality had "to be built round the reorganization of defences following traumata, defences that must needs retain primitive features such as personality splitting" (Winnicott, 1989c, p. 260). Over the years, behind a façade of niceness and smiles, he developed a closed emotional world, suspicious, aggressive, hidden, and disconnected. Trusting another person was, thus, a betrayal of his elemental self-protection and the defence strategies that had been crucial to maintaining his sanity and his very survival. It meant the unraveling of his constantly being on guard against emotional connection and the ensuing alarming experiences of dependence, neediness, loss of power and control, rejection, abandonment, breaking down—the evoking of longing and dread. In addition, remembering and telling me the incidents with the girls were a confession and acknowledgment of guilt in the most concrete way.

The extent of this emerging trust and inner change were further revealed on three occasions when Reuben *chose* to be in treatment. The first of these was after three years of compulsory treatment in the hospital, when he was granted amnesty and was free to leave the hospital and treatment. Continuing treatment clearly expressed his wanting the treatment and it meant financing it himself from his own savings at a time when his financial state and employment opportunities after being released from the hospital appeared extremely uncertain. He deliberated, but said in his characteristic way that he had to exceed the three-year period in treatment with me, because his relationships with women always broke up after three years. He remained in treatment for another year, and ended it after four years, on the eve of his wedding. He said that he now had to invest and concentrate emotionally on his marriage, and I accepted and respected it.

Two and a half years later, he returned to treatment because of deliberations over having a child, and treatment lasted a further three and a half years. After another two and a half year break (and after a second child had been born) he again returned to treatment because of feelings of distress, restlessness, and a vague sense of problems with himself and in his relationship with his wife, and treatment lasted another three years.

I feel that Reuben's returning to treatment at a time of distress, rather than following his familiar, impulsive, lonely, destructive pattern of behavior, was an enormous change, a venture of trust in the therapeutic relationship. It was something which would have been unimaginable several years earlier, and it was forged during those first difficult years of our living through, t(w)ogether, the depths of long, dark silences and violent inner struggle. Treatment managed to offer an alternative to his rejecting, shattering self-and-other world, and to the breakdown of communication, hope, and sustaining emotional contact.

Concluding thoughts

"This collapse into being with another, the deepest states of the other—isn't this something of the kind of sensitivity that gives our annihilated states a home?" (Eigen, 2007, p. 151).

I would now like to consider Reuben's difficult treatment in light of these stirring words of Eigen's regarding the analyst/therapist's *collapse into being-with* the patient. I feel that these words compellingly capture the very nature of what I have been describing over the years as the analyst's "presencing" and withnessing, or interconnecting psychically, with the patient. In particular, I would like to think about the incredible therapeutic power and, at the same time, the complex emotional meaning of *this collapse into being-with* the patient's unbearable states of breakdown and madness, catastrophe and the failing last scream before, and even more so after, hope was abandoned, which are inherent in difficult treatments. Here "collaps[ing] into" these states is an especially harsh undertaking.

Reuben's treatment illustrates these processes in a provoking, extreme way. On the one hand, there was Ruben's split-off, impenetrable psychotic state, foreclosed from psychological work, which remained an ominous threat to his sanity and very being. This found massive, harsh expression in his non-remembering and disconnectedness from the "incidents with the girls"; a closed-off, mad, profoundly destructive and perverse area inside him. On the other hand, my abiding interconnected presence with-in/within gradually became a great critical force, which bordered on the concrete. Reuben opened his dark world of secrets following my consent to go with him on his drive to reconstruct the "incidents with the girls," a starkly real commitment to his request, which, having been made, ultimately did not have to be carried out. This ensued after he tested and verified the reliability of my presence during many hours of total silence and aggressive detachment, session by session. It was only within my *sustained and cumulative presence* that his mute cry and need for help, which had no means of expression, and his desperate dread of abandonment, could be absorbed and eventually become a new and powerful experience—a critical mass that could overcome the horrors of dependency, emotional connection, and neediness.

But, over the years, I have come to realize the extent of my *being and becoming*[3] with-in Reuben's split-off, psychotic areas. I was letting myself *become part* of his emotional reality and mental processes so as to become the missing functioning part there. It is this more complex, more difficult, and more disturbing aspect of *becoming* that I would now like to consider. For, within Reuben's treatment, and particularly within the battle for his recalling and ability to relate "the incidents with the girls," I was with him, utterly interconnected to his struggle, his deep inner foreclosure, and the dissociative processes that enable such an inner state, in him–in me; to their breaking through. This extreme being with-in and becoming found particularly powerful expression when I told Reuben, in response to his request that I join him on his drive to reconstruct the incidents with the girls, that "we would talk about it again and together try to recall the details during the two and a half months left until the end of this year of treatment. And, if *we do not manage to remember, I would travel* the route with him." (I rechecked my old notes to ascertain that I had indeed said these spontaneous words then, as a young therapist, before I had begun to conceive of and formulate this later way of thinking.)

It was not merely that "the analyst keeps moral judgment out of the relationship" (Winnicott, 1992b, p. 285). I did not think about, or relate at all, to the harrowing experience and anguish of the girls he had hurt, the extent of their hurt, what they had undergone. A sort of blind spot, a shared blind spot; indeed, a *"collapse into being-with- him"* there.

Would the process that took place in Reuben's treatment have been possible without my profound "collapse into being-with" him? I think not. For it is impossible to venture alone into the horrifying, dark, split-off and silenced collapse into madness. Only this joining of the analyst's psyche provides it with a place to be, a place to shatter oneself, to experience[4] the horrid breakdown, to be held, contained, lived through, and saved: a place that is beyond good and evil.

> One would have to experience breakdown of life, mind, self, psyche before one could be there ... to experience it [breakdown/ madness]. Yet an underlying sense of what one dare not, could not tolerate experiencing remains as a defining fact. (Eigen, 1999, p. 174)

I suggest that the analyst's being there, with-in, and "becoming" at-one with the patient's intolerable emotional reality enables, in treatment, a fundamental therapeutic functioning and a new possibility of being, experiencing, and transformation.

In the context of psychoanalytic writings, this seems closely related to more radical post-Bionian approaches:

Early on, Grinberg (1991, 1997) proposes a transformation in the analyst, which enables him to reach a "state of '*convergence*'" with the patient's unbearable emotions:

> The receptive attitude of the analyst reveals itself by his *consent* to be invaded by the projections of the analysand's psychotic anxieties and by his ability to contain them so as to be able to *feel, think and share* the emotions contained in such projection, as if they were a part of his own self, whatever their nature (murderous hate, fear of death, catastrophic terror, etc.). (1991, p. 21, original italics)

Grotstein (2010) maintains that, unlike the treatment of the healthier personality, the course of treatment of the split-off, "castaway patients" "involves the indivisibility of the transference↔countertransference in the analyst's reverie, his or her capacity to '*become*' the patient's anguish ... Bion terms this phenomenon 'transformations in O within the analyst'" (2010, p. 25, original italics).

Vermote (2013) has recently formulated an integrative model of psychic functioning for dealing with the unknown that discerns three distinct zones of psychic functioning with varying degrees of differentiation, different major psychoanalytic models, and clinical implications for the analyst: Reason, Transformation in Knowledge, and the third zone, transformation in O, when dealing with the most non-thought, unknown, undifferentiated zone of psychic functioning (Winnicott, Milner, late Bion, late Lacan).

Eigen's singular writing over the years (1981, 1998, 2011, 2012b) expounds on Faith in O and Transformation in O, which I have summarized earlier. But, in order to conclude, I will return to Eigen's captivating words with which I opened this paper:

> Wherever you find yourself with a patient, you have to go. We wish things could be otherwise, could be easier, but we have little choice when light shines through the ruins of injury. I think that is a very Kabbalistic model. (Eigen, 2005, p. 41)

I think that is also the very essence of "presencing" and interconnectedness, and Eigen provides me with simple, profound words that touch and convey its very nature. Perhaps only such a fundamental process of *being with-in* can stand a chance.

Notes

1. For simplicity's sake, throughout this paper I will use "analyst" to refer both to analyst and therapist, unless I am describing a particular patient–therapist situation.
2. In this context, I would like to refer to Bollas's (1987) distinction between two fundamental genres of transference: One involves the patient and his objects; the other derives from a receptive capacity (in both analyst and patient). It is a state of being in which the analyst functions as a part of the patient's mental process, which facilitates the creation of new internal objects and self experiences. "The psychoanalyst's countertransference task within this transference is to allow himself to be assumed by the patient and not to interpret unless the patient needs it" (p. 256). I find that working with this kind of countertransference is closely related to my idea of "presencing."
3. I use here the words "being" and "becoming" to refer to Bion's conception of at-one-ment and the analyst's "being" and "'becoming' O", the unknown and unknowable emotional reality of the patient, that goes beyond the analyst's projective–introjective identification: "With this [O] the analyst cannot be identified: he must *be* it" (1970, p. 27, original italics). The clinical importance of the analyst's "becoming" has recently been elaborated by Grotstein's perceptive writing (2010) on infantile trauma and chronic resistance. According to Grotstein, the treatment of the split-off, "castaway patients," unlike the treatment of the healthier

personality, requires "the analyst to experience his own inner version of what the analysand is suffering from; to '*become*' the analysand's anguish and agony" (p. 25, original italics).

4. Here, I intend experience in all its meanings: from the Latin *experiri*—to try, test, prove; and to undergo risk—from the Latin *peritus*, cognate with the word peril, meaning risk, jeopardy, or danger.

References

Beckett, S. (1981). *Rockaby*. In: *The Complete Dramatic Works*. Tel-Aviv: Tel-Aviv University, 2007, pp. 501–510.

Bion, W. R. (1965). *Transformations*. London: Maresfield Library/ Karnac.

Bion, W. R. (1970). *Attention and Interpretation*. London: Maresfield Library/Karnac.

Bollas, C. (1987). *The Shadow of the Object: Psychoanalysis of the Unthought Known*. New York: Columbia University Press.

Eigen, M. (1981). The area of faith in Winnicott, Lacan, and Bion. *International Journal of Psychoanalysis*, *62*: 413–433.

Eigen, M. (1986). *The Psychotic Core*. London: Karnac. 2004.

Eigen, M. (1992). *Coming Trough the Whirlwind*. Wilmette, IL: Chiron.

Eigen, M. (1993). *The Electrified Tightrope*, ed. A. Phillips. London: Karnac, 2004.

Eigen, M. (1998). *The Psychoanalytic Mystic*. London & New York: Free Association Books.

Eigen, M. (1999). *Toxic Nourishment*. London: Karnac.

Eigen, M. (2001). *Damaged Bonds*. London: Karnac.

Eigen, M. (2002). *Rage*. Middletown, CT: Wesleyan University Press.

Eigen, M. (2004). *The Sensitive Self*. Middletown, CT: Wesleyan University Press.

Eigen, M. (2005). Interview with Micha Odenheimer. *Another Country* [Hebrew: Eretz Acheret], *26*: 36–42.

Eigen, M. (2006). The annihilated self. *Psychoanalytic Review*, *93*: 25–38.

Eigen, M. (2007). *Feeling Matters*. London: Karnac.

Eigen, M. (2010). *Eigen in Seoul* (Volume One): *Madness and Murder*. London: Karnac.

Eigen, M. (2011). *Eigen in Seoul* (Volume Two): *Faith and Transformation*. London: Karnac.

Eigen, M. (2012a). On Winnicott's clinical innovations in the analysis of adults. *International Journal of Psychoanalysis*, *93*: 1449–1459.

Eigen, M. (2012b). *Kabbalah and Psychoanalysis*. London: Karnac.

Eshel, O. (1998a). "Black Holes," deadness and existing analytically. *International Journal of Psychoanalysis, 79*: 1115–1130.

Eshel, O. (1998b). Meeting acting out, acting in and enactment in psychoanalytic treatment, or: going into the eye of the storm. *Sihot—-Dialogue, Israel Journal of Psychotherapy, 13*: 4–16.

Eshel, O. (2001). Whose sleep is it, anyway? Or "Night Moves." *International Journal of Psychoanalysis, 82*: 545–562.

Eshel, O. (2005). Pentheus rather than Oedipus: on perversion, survival and analytic "presencing." *International Journal of Psychoanalysis, 86*: 1071–1097.

Eshel, O. (2009). To be "included" in the silence: on the silent patient and the analyst's "presencing." *Sihot—-Dialogue, Israel Journal of Psychotherapy, 23*: 221–235.

Eshel, O. (2010). Patient–analyst interconnectedness: personal notes on close encounters of a new dimension. *Psychoanalytic Inquiry, 30*: 146–154.

Eshel, O. (2011). Do I dare be an analyst of a severely perverse patient? On being within ("presencing"), daring (passion), and caring (compassion). Paper presented to the conference of the Leonard J. Comess Fund at the New Center for Psychoanalysis in Los Angeles, California, May.

Eshel, O. (2012). A beam of "chimeric" darkness: presence, interconnectedness and transformation in the psychoanalytic treatment of a patient convicted of sex offenses. *Psychoanalytic Review, 99*: 149–178.

Eshel, O. (2013a). Tustin's "diabolon" and "metabolon" revisited: further clinical explorations. The Frances Tustin Memorial Prize, the 18th Annual Frances Tustin Memorial Lectureship in Los Angeles, California.

Eshel, O. (2013b). Patient–analyst "withness": on analytic "presencing", passion, and compassion in states of breakdown, despair, and deadness. *Psychoanalytic Quarterly, 82*(4): 925–963,

Grinberg, L. (1991). Countertransference and projective counter-identification in non-verbal communication. *European Psychoanalytical Federation Bulletin, 36*: 11–24

Grinberg, L. (1997). Is the transference feared by the psychoanalyst? *International Journal of Psychoanalysis, 78*: 1–14.

Grotstein, J. S. (2007). *A Beam of Intense Darkness: Wilfred Bion's Legacy to Psychoanalysis.* London: Karnac.

Grotstein, J. S. (2010). "Orphans of O": the negative therapeutic reaction and the longing for the childhood that never was. In: J. V. Buren &

S. Alhanati (Eds.), *Primitive Mental States* (pp. 8–30). London: Routledge.

Ogden, T. H. (2005). Reading Bion. In: *This Art of Psychoanalysis: Dreaming Undreamt Dreams and Interrupted Cries* (pp. 77–92). London: Routledge.

Vermote, R. (2013). The undifferentiated zone of psychic functioning: an integrative approach and clinical implications. Paper presented to European Psychoanalytical Federation Conference, Basel, Switzerland, March 24.

Winnicott, D. W. (1971). *Playing and Reality*. London: Penguin.

Winnicott, D. W. (1986). Fear of breakdown. In: G. Kohon (Ed.), *The British School of Psychoanalysis: The Independent Tradition* (pp. 173–182). London: Free Association Books.

Winnicott, D. W. (1989a). The psychology of madness: a contribution from psychoanalysis. In: C. Winnicott, R. Shepherd, & M. Davis (Eds.), *Psycho-Analytic Explorations* (pp. 119–129). Cambridge, MA: Harvard University Press.

Winnicott, D. W. (1989b). Additional note on psycho-somatic disorder. In: C. Winnicott, R. Shepherd, & M. Davis (Eds), *Psycho-Analytic Explorations* (pp. 115–118). Cambridge, MA: Harvard University Press.

Winnicott, D. W. (1989c). The mother–infant experience of mutuality. In: C. Winnicott, R. Shepherd, & M. Davis (Eds.), *Psycho-Analytic Explorations* (pp. 251–260). Cambridge, MA: Harvard University Press.

Winnicott, D. W. (1992a). Primitive emotional development. In: *Through Paediatrics to Psycho-Analysis* (pp. 145–156). London: Karnac.

Winnicott, D. W. (1992b). Metapsychological and clinical aspects of regression within the psycho-analytical set-up. In: *Through Paediatrics to Psycho-Analysis* (pp. 278–294). London: Karnac.

CHAPTER TEN

Michael Eigen: rich impacts

Margaret Fetting

Introduction

Michael Eigen identifies the importance of registering impacts. He refers to this as the most intimate fact of meeting with each other, and our experiences. The first three sections of this chapter explore his impact on my personal and professional growth and development. The next sections provide the reader with an understanding of how I use the "theoretical soundings" that Eigen has studied over the years for thinking about the psychic life of a person with a substance use disorder (P/SUD). A psychoanalytic attitude risks waiting in faith, instead of the more traditional approach of intervening to redirect the P/SUD's behavior. The final sections explore a case study that illustrates how I borrow Eigen's "tapestry of ideas" to inform my clinical intuitions with a problem drinker.

Eigen-full

I have read and studied Michael Eigen's work for quite some time. I found him twenty-one years ago. His "insides talked to my insides," and I never left him or his work.

He began an opening, a blossoming of self that deepened my capacity for experience, radically expanded my view of living, took my clinical work and teaching to new depths, and emboldened my writing. I felt I was in a different world, but one I yearned for as an "unthought known," or the dispositional knowledge of my true self that had not yet been thought (Bollas, 1989, p. 10). My days of living in suspended animation were finally over (Phillips, 1994). Dr. Eigen touched me with relief, pleasure, and courage. I wanted to stay in touch with this humble man and prolific psychoanalytic writer who shared his "vague, mutant intensities drifting randomly, threads, currents and cracks without clear notation" (Eigen, 2004, p. 93). I wanted to read more of this man who listened to "a bell inside him" (Eigen, 2013).

Eigen sends his hopes to his readers:

> I like to think I've encoded in my writings, the message that it is okay for people to be and develop in their own way, to develop their own bell, that we mutants [he includes Winnicott and Bion here] are real and have a very real contribution to make, and that the world would be poorer without us. (Eigen, 2013)

Eigen continues, "People have had the experience, in reading my writings, of hearing their own voice in a deeper way, of feeling they had a right to be in their own particular way" (Molino, 1997, pp. 119–120). The clanging of "something is always wrong" (Eigen, 2009, p. 73) began to dim ever so slightly inside me, and I immediately paired up with this sensitive thinker.

I wait for Eigen's publications. I read them, study them, and rummage around in them over time. I search for solace, sanity, and clinical wisdom. While reading, I feel as if I belong in my skin and also to some place in the world. I always feel comfortable inside an Eigen book. He provides a kind and rigorous place for my struggles, and a safe and stimulating home to return to again and again. His writing is full of faith, hope, and he gifts us with a real opportunity. Heinz Kohut refers to this opportunity as the Zeigarnik phenomenon—the wonderful, delightful, human tendency to complete interrupted tasks of development if given the chance to do so (Chessick, 1992, p. 152). Reading early Eigen books offered me this chance, and his prolific generosity continues to build upon this opportunity.

Winnicott cautions, "Do not assume that we all live a life" (cited in Bollas, 1989, p. 26). Eigen's books and his being strongly encourage each reader to take responsibility for this daunting and lonely choice. Eigen's rigorous investigations into living make me feel secure. I ruthlessly use his ruthless use of himself. He passionately asks that we make room for all the deeper processes of our psyche and take their movements seriously; that we stay true to our psychic struggles and wait them out, and that we become "better versions of ourselves," for the sake of ourselves and our world (Eigen, 2011b, p. 12). I am attracted to Michael Eigen's faith.

Eigen has wrestled, and continues to wrestle, with the works of Freud, Jung, Kohut, Klein, and, most passionately, it seems, with Bion, Winnicott, and Lacan. He affirms, "In a way, I am a Winnicottian–Bion analyst, which means I am not sure what psychoanalysis (Psa) is, and I am always discovering what it can be" (Eigen, 2013). Eigen's exhaustive inquiry into the works of Winnicott, Bion, and Lacan bequeath a gift to all readers. He becomes our "good object" link to these sometimes exhausting and dense writers and we soon feel equipped, inspired, and drawn to study them in our own time and in our own way. Eigen advises, "Grapple with Bion's sentences, but the realities they touch ought not get lost" (Eigen, 2013).

Gifted are the people who create a body of work, as well as a following around their natural proclivities. As Eigen shares his thoughts and feelings on some of the psychoanalytic greats, an impression starts to build. His sensitivities, intensities, perceptions, and literary style soon capture the readers' minds and also awaken their hearts. We become enamored with the mind, soul, and heart of this persevering artist and his impressionistic–expressionistic, evocative psychoanalysis. Eigen's words and ideas provide tastings that lavish, satisfy, and later linger. Evan Malater eloquently captures what Eigen does: "Instead, his approach in writing and speaking is not to simply speak about this [or that], but to actually create a space through language that allows one's essential questions to be pursued and held" (Malater, 2013). Through all this, Eigen asks that we deepen our own journey, not follow his.

Eigen seems to have become that "living" internal object that many of us needed as we prematurely unmoored ourselves from our "dead" object homes, drifting at sea, surviving with the little nourishment that was our daily bread. In the drifting and destruction, I hope, we eventually found more aliveness to grow into, more to use. Reading Eigen moors and gives more, if you stay with all that he offers and provokes.

In over my head, but not out of place

I knew very little about psychoanalysis when I read my first Eigen book, *The Psychotic Core* (1986). Rogers referred to it as, "phenomenologically vivid" (1989). Eigen says he contributes "a working orientation that does madness justice" (Eigen in Rogers, 1989). I knew I was in over my head, yet I did not feel out of place. So, I began living in and with his sentences, breaking them down, pulling them apart, connecting them to my history, as well as bringing them into my teaching and clinical work.

Eigen passionately shares and re-shares with his readers the "tapestry of ideas" that inform his clinical intuitions (1996, p. xvii). This exhaustive, yet not experientially exhausting list of "theoretical soundings," in no particular order, includes: psychic deadness; our psychotic core; the butchered and bleak qualities of psychotic landscapes; meeting catastrophe with faith; waiting, resting, and resetting and also the rhythms of breaking down and building up inherent in mental life that run amok or are aborted; our self-disappearing nature; staying with experience, letting it build; "I don't know"; a psyche that cannot do away with its states, but can make room for more states; a psyche that is too much to bear; working through the wormhole; rhythms of passivity and activity; "something is always wrong"; one never recovers from being human; winning lies; emotional truths; self-disclosing meaning; double movements; our embryonic psychic capacities; contact from the depths with self and others; beta buzz as mindless, hallucinatory globs, gestated by alpha function into an alive, affective thinking process that may include partial lies; the annihilated self; the human irritability associated with widespread psychic indigestion (Eigen, 1986–2013). These are just a few.

Eigen and impact

A sentence in *Psychic Deadness* caught my attention early. "A core ingredient in the kind of work I have in mind is the *impact* of the patient on the therapist" (1996, p. 143). As has been mentioned, Eigen's work tends to be impressionistic–expressionistic, evocative psychoanalysis, one in which subject-to-subject impact is central. The word impact appears in many, many sentences in most of his twenty-two books. In 1996, he spoke of it as core to his work, and his fidelity and reverence for impact remains to this day.

Impact as core—what does this mean? The quotes below are mostly Eigen originals, some combination of Eigen originals, or some combination of Eigen and Fetting. I hope these register with the reader.

- The most private, intimate fact of a meeting between two people is impact. Keep dipping into the impact someone is having on you, the sensations, feelings, imaginings and thoughts that grow from mute impact. If we are lucky, we let the other's impact play on us; we feel it, dream it, think about it, and let it give rise to creative musings. We give the other's impact time. Wait until the reality at hand finds voice, and then you might have something helpful to say to a patient or a loved one (1996, p. 195).
- Impact is the primary raw datum; the therapist may hide, yet secretly nurse the deep impact the patient has on him. Let it unfold, better not to put words and share it too soon. An impact needs time to take root and grow. It occurs instantaneously, but needs the therapist's faith, time and loyalty in order to grow. In some instances it may be years before an impact can be revealed, and by that time the patient has a different impact, although some of the original impact remains (1996, p. 143).
- The therapist in the beginning speaks away from the impact while collecting history, facts, to keep things going. One plays for time and protects and nurses the impact (1996, pp. 143–145).
- One must make inner sacrifices and adjustments to hear another person or really feel heard. This requires a mutual resonance, speaking, listening, feeling and working imaginatively with the impact of each other's being (1996, p. 210).
- If you use upper story thinking you might miss the session, miss the patient's impact, and miss the response the patient needs in order for something more to happen. If distracted in any way, remember; always return to impact (2011b, p. 17).
- Most often impacts are shocks, the shock of one personality impacting on another. Sometimes the impact is pleasant,

sometimes not; often it is mixed and usually mute. A monolithic shock soon becomes variegated, having many different forms. As one lives with the shock, one comes to know different parts of it. One becomes more familiar with its colors, tonalities, textures and tensions. There are blue, red, white and black shocks, and sometimes we see stars or hear ringings or voices or music (1996, p. 144).

- One's personality may contract or constrict itself around the shock of the other, the point of impact. If the shock is great, stiffening may be widespread. One goes blank and waits. The mind may race to get its bearings. If the shock is unpleasant the mind may freeze. It takes moments to realize that the danger is psychical, not physical, so that the primary process may come out of hiding and work (1996, p. 144).
- If the shock is wonderful, even the shock of joy, one cannot open enough; sound carries. If the shock is horrible one cannot close fast enough, sound flattens. Sometimes the shock comes through, sometimes one wades through layers of numbness to get the taste (1996, p. 144).
- Much depends on the therapist's ability to sustain the buildup of the patient's impact until the realities at hand find voice. An inability to achieve this build up may murder the experience of the patient's psychic death (the painful surrender to vulnerability/weakness, need) and perhaps the possibility of life as well. An interpretation may kill or support the growth of experience, including the experience of violation and dying out of self. The therapist's processing of the patient's impact provides new psychic experiences (1996, p. 145, 147).
    - It gives the patient a sense of being taken seriously; "I must be of value."
    - The patient experiences the therapist's metabolizing catastrophic bits of affect that the patient could not due to lack of psychic equipment (thus starts the process of building his missing psychic equipment). He eventually starts to feel less of a menace to others.
    - The patient learns by the therapist's acceptance that he is not disgusting, not extremely indigestible, nor entirely digestible.
    - Feeling this registering from the therapist allows the patient to begin to link up with himself.

- The therapist allows the patient's empty depression to wash over him, no matter how confusing and difficult to experience. Empty depression reflects the relative emptiness of self, paucity of psychic structure and lack of good internal objects" (Kohut in Fetting, 2012, p. 103). The patient is relieved; "someone can be with my feelings of nothingness."
- Someone wants to hear, support, and process my experience(s) and inner struggles.

Registering impacts has become a core clinical ingredient in my work in the substance use disorder field. It nurtures a "here and now" alive contact between the therapist and patient. As a result of feeling so deeply heard and contained, the patient soon feels "allowed" to initiate and investigate his own path of transformation from destructiveness to more aliveness. This provides a radically different experience for the P/SUD in treatment. He is prepared to be *caught, controlled, and directed* by a family member or even a therapist.

Waiting on impact contrasts sharply with the panicked sense of urgency that dominates the SUDs field. "All we have to do is listen" and wait out impact until we have something useful to say to the patient. "I play for time", and wait for the relationship to become a trusted container for the patient allowing him to reveal his passionate and obsessive attachments to alcohol and other drugs (AOD) (Eigen, 2013).

A winning lie

The early epiphanies in the addiction field seem to have the ingredients of a winning lie (Eigen, 1996, pp. 201–211). A lie meant to persuade the public that the answer to the disease of addiction, the weak-willed, sinful curse of humanity, had been discovered. The solution for this disease was abstinence.

A winning lie in contemporary culture is a lie that has massive amounts of political and cultural steam behind it. A winning lie is a lie that gets sold to the country to push an agenda, to prove a point, to develop a way of responding to a complex phenomenon, and to shield people from what we do not know and push instead what we think we know.

In addition, winning lies sell. Complexity seems just too hard for humans. We do not seem to have a knack for it, both as individuals and in culture. We surely do not seem to embrace it in our understanding of substance use disorders and its treatment. Sell us the simple; we will buy it and put it to work. Furthermore, winning lies do work for a time. Eventually, though, winning lies fray and the culture reaches for more.

Simplicity obfuscated complexity in the early days of the SUDs field. Abstinence, the disease/medical model, and AA meetings took hold and eventually swept over our land like a tsunami. The country bought into these winning "white" lies and the financially lucrative treatment industry further ensured its protection.

Treatment rensions

In the 1970s, Dr. Ed Khantzian, a psychoanalyst and psychiatrist at Harvard, introduced another idea. His self-medication theory addressed the psychological suffering motivating addictive behaviors. It was not embraced by those who were completely persuaded by, and satisfied with, disease–abstinence model thinking. It was embraced by those who wanted to take a person's psychological distress into account. Today, the industry feels combative and territorial about etiological assumptions and treatment choices. Is it a neuroscience problem, a spiritual or biological disease, or is it an act of self-medication?

Despite these tensions, the American treatment industry continues to develop services for medical detoxification and in and out patient rehabilitation treatment for the early days and stages of recovery. AA and other groups provide ongoing support.

There is a decreasing treatment interest in making contact with the individual's psychological suffering driving these destructive behaviors. *DSM-V* refers to addiction as a behavioral, cognitive, and physiological disorder (American Psychiatric Asssociation, 2013). Traditional talk therapy is considered to miss the point, enable the patient's behavior, while psychoanalysis, with its emphasis on deep listening and experiencing, is considered inappropriate for the addict or problem user. Evidence-based protocols and psychopharmacology are the treatment approaches in good currency and have captured the concrete thinking of medicine, rehabilitation centers, and insurance companies. Currently, most residential and day treatment programs, as well as outpatient therapy, are licensed and funded only if they offer services that include evidence-based outcome research. The emphasis is on short-term intervention to address behavioral changes.

Despite this outpouring of services, relapse rates are gloomy, usually in the range of 50–90% (Caron Treatment Center, 2013). "Addiction treatment narcissism has prevented people from seeing and noticing that things are not going very well" (Eigen, 2011b, p. 8).

What can Eigen and psychoanalysis offer the patient in addiction treatment?

My clinical practice, teaching, and writing in the SUDs field have been highly influenced by Eigen and psychoanalysis. A psychoanalytic attitude listens and waits. It adds merit to a field that tends to be overzealous, over-controlling, possessive, too directive, and prematurely reassuring. Eigen challenges,

> There are those [SUDs] patients who respond to the faith that underlies the analytic attitude. There are those wishing to open to the moment, with all its uncertainty, rather than foreclose on a chance for more experiencing [with a didactic behavioral directive]. There are those that begin to view life more truthfully and are finally able to extend the horizon towards all possible solutions. And then there are those who fall back on the status quo [relapse] and try to remain inured to the call of the more or another. (Eigen, 1999, p. 190)

Eigen's theoretical soundings, especially his concept of registering impacts, allows the clinician to be guided by the P/SUDS felt impact, not the clinician's sense of what is right for the patient. This is a radical shift in the treatment of addicts and a radical shift in their experience of treatment.

Eigen reminds us that faith is the open attitude that allows impacts to register. Listening with faith allows the treatment provider to stay true to impact, and helpful responses may follow. "Faith plays an important role in transformational processes in therapy. Faith supports experiential exploration, imaginative conjecture, experiential probing" (2011a, p. vii). Eigen and Bion suggest that we meet absolute destruction (of a SUD) with F (faith) and O (openness), faith in the radical openness of the moment. Bion suggests this attitude for psychoanalytic treatment, and I strongly suggest its incorporation into SUDs treatment.

This attitude encourages us to wait with the patient and not abruptly foreclose on his exploration with behavioral commandments and injunctions of dogmatic K (knowledge). *Bion suggests that the transformational process (in SUD recovery) may not happen without risking, waiting in F.* When Eigen is asked about how transformations happen: "I have no idea, except that creating an atmosphere where people [addicts] can just hear themselves sometimes does strange and marvelous things" (1999, p. 221).

What is suggested here is that therapists spend less time trying to possess the mind of a P/SUD and conquer and control his behavior, but instead take in his impact, dream it, feel it, and imagine it. Be with the problem drinker's lack of processing capacity, emptiness, and ongoing punitive persecutions. Let these wash over you and see where they take you. Listen, hold, wait, and back off. Allow the patient to have the experience of being seen and heard. Avoid the imperative toward urgency and the histrionic warning, "They will die if we do not provide direct interventions."

Problem drinkers in therapy

Only recently has our culture moved away from the bifurcated notion that "You are either an alcoholic, or you are not." We are beginning to consider less Calvinistic views about the human desire for alcohol and other drugs as well as the desire for intoxication. We seem more open to alternatives to abstinence. There are four times as many problem drinkers as alcoholics in this country, and we have historically offered them the least amount of services. We have been loath to recognize and respect this drinking pattern (Fetting, 2012).

Today, more and more problem drinkers are seeking out sensitive outpatient or inpatient therapists not wedded to abstinence and are also willing to support an open-ended examination of their troublesome relationship with substances. We welcome "all those who care about their own destructiveness, care enough to struggle with it" (Eigen in Fetting, 2012, dedication page).

Sixty-five percent of my substance use disorder practice is with problem drinkers or marijuana misusers, who acknowledge problems, yet want the pleasures of getting high to be a part of their lives. Thirty-five percent of my practice is with people who have come to value abstinence from alcohol or prescription medication as the best choice for them.

Rather than directly control, possess, or try to conquer either profile, I am interested in exploring the user's relationship with his self-medicated drug of choice. I listen in faith as he explores his individual, familial and cultural meanings around AOD. I wait in patience and offer a suggestion or two if my experience can provide value. In those early days of treatment, when the patient's anxiety about losing AOD is extremely heightened, registering a problem users' impacts and giving them a chance "to let down", fosters a hope (Eigen, 1999, p. 49). "I will be listened to here, not told 'You are in massive denial and need abstinence.'"

The following case study demonstrates how I use some of *Eigen's tapestry of ideas* to think about and work with the psychic life of a SUDs patient. For me, it begins and continues with my ongoing struggles to be clinically still enough to allow my natural desire to register impact take sway. This skill allows me to make more contact with what lives under the problem behaviors. When I do this, I find myself suddenly more interested in dreaming about Lindsay's *self-disappearing nature*, her confusion while untangling the *winning lie*, her *lack of capacity to turn catastrophic beta buzz into alpha thinking*, her *inability to register impacts*, her *false self horns*, and her habituated self-medicating need for alcohol (Eigen, 1995–2014). I am not focused on getting the patient to abstinence.

Lindsay: getting our bearings

Lindsay is a forty-three-year-old mother of two. I was recommended to her by a former student who noticed and said to her, "You seem tense and overwhelmed." Lindsay's initial impact felt child-like—confused, but determined to figure things out, determined to know. She also felt frightened of, and frustrated by, one of her children, her husband, and fretful about her own life. I felt her sense of catastrophe in living; she seemed overwhelmed by her own psychic indigestion.

Bion and Eigen say it best, "There is a catastrophe in progress, life is a catastrophe, and I am a catastrophe. Help me! Help me!" (Eigen, 2011b, p. 47).

Lindsay drinks too much wine every night, sometimes says too much, and often remembers too little. She wakes up alcohol-foggy, but is determined to attend to her maternal and familial tasks. Lindsay looks forward to, and counts on, her glasses of wine every night. She starts salivating at 5 p.m. and promises herself a "better night of drinking." Lindsay drinks two to three glasses to recover from the persecution of the "daily shoulds" that she carries around from childhood. "My father felt perfect, meticulous. I just wanted his approval. I still do. My mother made the most beautiful homes, nothing looked out of place. I just wanted her approval. I still do." Eigen captures her childhood: "There was a history of neglect, a mixture of over- and under-stimulation, the usual story of emotional poverty in a luxurious setting" (1996, p. 3).

Over time, I proposed some traditional supports: group meetings, talking to a friend, talking to her husband. "Why should I have to go to meetings for my alcohol? I have my shit together." She bashfully shares her drinking worries with her husband as she prepares dinner. He says, "You don't have a problem," as he opens a bottle of wine for the two of them. Her friends drink every night, too. A few friends also acknowledge, "My drinking is problematic." Most need alcohol to "work through" mismatched marriages, social pressure, the stresses to keep it all together, envy and jealousy. Alcohol helps Lindsay and her friends feel a sense of imaginary intactness (Eigen, 1999, p. 222). My sense with Lindsay is that she is overwhelmed and in over her psyche with most things. She lags behind her impacts; she lives in a state of psychic indigestion (Eigen, 2013).

Traditionally, addiction thinkers believe that if Lindsay's drinking is not arrested now, she will progress into the disease of addiction. Directives about AA meetings, sponsors, steps, and motivational protocols are the standard of care in addiction treatment. These are so helpful for many, yet, increasingly, more protest the "one size fits all" approach.

I have learned from Eigen that "if the [SUD] needs you to say something, then you say it. You can say it as a supportive thing, a challenging thing, a stimulating thing, and an interpretation, whatever is needed." Eigen has wisely offered SUD clinicians, "You do what you need to play for time, so that links can be formed over time in therapy" (2011b, p. 8).

When I register and imagine Lindsay's youth, I dream of a child who lived in a stupor or dull state. No one helped her or taught her how to process and emotionally digest what was happening around her. Lindsay did not get the chance to explore or elaborate on the impact of her parents, her sibling, her friends, or everyday experiences. No one waited with Lindsay in faith until she felt comfortable in the face of what seemed overwhelming to her psyche. Eigen captures the P/SUD's early plight, "One gives up noticing emotional realities if one is unable to achieve anything fruitful by noticing them. Yet these realities exert pressure" (1999, p. 147).

After years of living in a thumb-sucking trance, Lindsay found alcohol. It provided relief for her lack of the capacity to live in an experience, register experience, let experience build, and learn from it. She missed out on "getting a little better at working over impacts and letting impacts work on [her] so that [she] could get something more out of living" (Eigen, 2004, p. 142).

Lindsay's soul went on the run, and she lived with a sense of self-sufficiency that convinced her that the impacts of self and others could be overlooked. She found a way to escape impact, push it aside, and compulsively discharge the tension of this emptiness with AOD. Phillips captures a key struggle for SUDs patients so accurately, "Hell is not other people but one's need for other people" (1994, p. 45). The therapist's challenge is to develop an interest in accepting this need, a need that brought devastation and psychic retreating beginning in infancy and early childhood (Steiner, 1993).

It took about thirteen months for Lindsay to feel safe enough in our relationship to not want to self-disappear; "When we make ourselves disappear, try to make pain disappear, we enter a state of madness" (Eigen, 2011b, p. 72). Over time, we created a capacity to be alone together with her madness.

"Addiction is a substitute for those who cannot wait for time's unfolding" (Bion, 1992, p. 299). Over time, Lindsay created some capacity for stillness. She soon began more deeply exploring and reflecting on her relationship with her neurotic processes, her relationship with alcohol, and what happened in her family that drove her repeatedly to search for relief in the nightly over-use of this psychoactive drug.

Beta buzz, alpha, and partial lies

Parents, and later the therapist, ideally act as containers able to think through the undigested catastrophic experiences of the infant–child that Bion names "beta elements." Bits of nameless, formless, catastrophic "beta buzz" (Fetting in Eigen, 2013) are reworked by maternal alpha functions and turned into moods, images, narrative in dreams and myths, and reveries (Eigen, 1996, p. 142). Turning this nameless dread into thinking or dreaming is a developmental triumph; "One of the best kept secrets about thinking is how ecstatic it is" (Eigen, 1998, p. 24).

Eigen recently intrigues us:

> Sometimes alpha lying or lying-truthing works to suppress or rein in beta impacts and helps clear some space for possible processing. One might even regard beta elements and their buzz as a purer truth that can only be partially processed with the help of partial lies. (Eigen, 2013)

Many people can live and even thrive with these partial truths/partial lies.

Contrary to popular belief, P/SUDs are not good liars. Khantzian and Albanese have been impressed by the extreme sensitivities of SUDs patients (2008). Without their capacity to buffer life with alpha lying, living feels unbearable, and AOD creates a pseudo-confidence that life is, indeed, doable. Lindsay relied on this confidence for decades.

False-self horn

Eigen (1998), in his book *The Psychoanalytic Mystic*, elaborates on our understanding of a false self. He describes an inauthentic expression of self that has two horns. One horn has toughness to its edge; another horn is driven by a compulsion to please. It seems that an individual's false self expression can rely on one horn or a blend of both (p. 55). Lindsay relied on both.

Lindsay's disposition developed compliance as a way to respond to the pressures she felt to falsify her inner essence. Pleasing people and getting along with others ensured her everyday survival. When compliant, Lindsay discovers that being "easy" for others brought peace to her world. This false self silently screams, "I please, and I placate!" (Eigen, 1998, pp. 56–57). Lindsay's compliant self found safety and security in not being a burden to her mother. She learned to be loyal to her mother's wishes at the expense of her own. Her school peers and friends, teachers, and neighbors took advantage of this willingness to cater to others. She married to serve her partner. She parents to satisfy her children's every wish. Her sense of sacrificial nobility muffles the intensity of her inner despair. Eventually, her compliant expression fatigues and fades out. Lindsay searches for alcohol, or resorts to using her other horn.

Lindsay's disposition also developed a toughness to handle the horror of so much parental misunderstanding. This toughness ensured everyday survival and brought her feelings of temporary triumph. Her false self screamed, "I can and I will!" (1998, p. 55). This sense of bravado persuaded her true self to retreat in silence. It was seduced into protective submission. This shelter permitted a manner of functioning. Eigen reminds us that toughness can be counted on to maintain a sense of aliveness (p. 56). Careers are chosen, marriages are entered, and children are born from this deceptively determined, yet wayward, self-organization. These solutions bring moments of aliveness that can go on for years and decades. Sadly, they are based on self-fraudulence and conformity to social expectations.

Lindsay's true self despaired in exile and, eventually, her horn of toughness also grew weary of its job. She began to live with an empty heart and with frustration at the very core. What was accomplished in work and love could no longer be sustained. In these situations, the fatigue cannot be avoided and, more often than not, one's entire being fades out and goes under (Eigen, 1998, p. 57).

During these times when Lindsay's false-self horns grew weary and could no longer support her, alcohol provided much comfort. She ruthlessly and repeatedly selected alcohol as a reliable source of soothing and reprieve. It reversed ongoing feelings of false self fraudulence and quieted her longings for true self expression in her life. AOD seemed the perfect complement for her painful, prescribed way of living. The possibility of an alternative future was beyond her grasp; "I can live in this world if I am fortified with alcohol." A fated childhood, adolescence, and adulthood are now fated by addictive consumption (Fetting, 2012, p. 249).

Lindsay lives the words of one of Eigen's patients:

> My contact with what people call reality is monitored. I'm not really in the experience. I've committed to a life of caring behavior. I believe people are connected by love, the most precious thing we know about in the universe, but I don't partake of it. I'm excruciatingly sensitive, but I don't feel for another person. I look like I'm feeling and feel that I'm feeling, in the feeling I'm not feeling. It is the most painful of all to not care in the caring, to not feel in the feeling. (Eigen, 2004, p. 106)

Deficits in psychological equipment can be experienced as emptiness (Eigen, 1996, p. 145). Lindsay drinks to avoid feeling this emptiness and lack, and to avoid telling somebody about it.

Impacts in a session

Lindsay and I meet. She sighs and says, "I'm so frustrated with collecting a few sober days then losing them. This whole business about my drinking just feels like a 'should'. I know that my drinking is problematic, I know it is interfering with my sense of peace, my parenting and my marriage, and I know I should stop." I dream her frustrations, her persecutory expectations, and then respectfully ask her if she wants to continue drinking. Does she need it now just to get through life? She did not say yes, but instead says, "I know I should stop. I just want to let the effort go and see where it ends up." I open to her impact of fatigue, weariness, and also hesitancy to voice her way. As a result of this, I decide not to impose my "memory" of her failed attempts at this approach. Lindsay feels me registering her impact, rather than offering a "helpful" suggestion. Lindsay begins to slow down. I sense her softening and wondering, "What is Margy doing here?"

Eigen urges us to give the P/SUD's impact time to build and unfold (1996, p. 210). We offer the psychoanalytic attitude when we dream and wait, and in the process become a feeling person more deeply attuned to the patient's incapacity and overreliance on AOD. This feeling therapist is now felt by the patient, and a connection begins or deepens (Coltart, 2000, pp. 154–157).

The session turns away from solutions and resolutions. Lindsay easily opens up about all her pressures, her tendency to placate her husband, compulsively please her parents, and bear her trying daughter. I just listen and follow and do not mention drinking. I just hear and hold, hear and hold, register her impact. No memory or desire. Lindsay feels me become a feeling therapist at that moment. She moves toward me and I to her. We feel connected. She now has hope, and I renew my faith.

When I listen from this open and receptive attitude, the therapy relationship feels like a space for Lindsay to "let down" in (Eigen, 1999, p. 49). I then feel a person who lives in a chaotic and chronic state of paralyzing absence within a psyche that cannot process its own daily impacts.

Without this internal equipment, Lindsay is naturally oriented toward external objects (AOD) for soothing and survival (1999, p. 138). Eigen provides wisdom:

> The grim paradox is that insofar as [the P/SUD] lacks the capacity to tolerate the sense of catastrophe that saturates [his] psychic reality, [the P/SUD] may heighten external catastrophe [SUD] as a way of objectifying himself. He may finally 'know' himself through this dramatization [addiction]. (1999, p. 138)

A clinician that can reverie the P/SUD's objectification processes will soon feel the patient's sense of lack, confusion, fear, and desperation.

Eigen encourages therapists to respect the patient's (P/SUD's) absolute otherness. They are on their own search. He suggests that we register and follow the (P/SUD's) instructions of living rather than our own. He dares us to give them space to do their best—or their worst (Eigen, 2008, personal communications).

Every week, Lindsay returns not yet satisfactorily understanding how this seemingly, "unsolvable problem is happening to me." Lindsay is frustrated at the core, but she continues to adhere to her struggle. Eigen reminds us, "no faith . . . no path" (Eigen, 2013). As of now, Lindsay and I continue on our faith path together, and try to hold to that which is difficult (Rilke, 1993).

Clinical addendum

It is nine months since I submitted this chapter to the editors. Lindsay is now six months free of alcohol. She fell into a state of conviction while talking to some "mom" drinking buddies. She tells me these days, "Maybe I will drink again one day, maybe I will revisit this option, but not until I finish crying and also strengthening my own psychic capacity for feeling through and processing the impacts of my world."

Closing remarks

History has shown us that we are uncertain about how to live with the ancient desire to escape and expand consciousness with alcohol and drugs. Use of these substances has been embedded in religious ceremonies, used different ways by different classes, and has been privileged for males, sanctioned for females. We have called for temperance and prohibition. Contemporary history has created the terms "addiction" and "disease". Dr. Jellinek, in 1960, casually ushered in the use of the word disease with the following statement, "A disease is what the medical profession recognizes as such." Without convincing scientific evidence, Jellinek changed both the concept and experience of alcoholism to that of a disease (Severns, 2004). We currently live in a culture of recovery and rehabilitation, denial and confrontation. We have gotten lost in the extremes of behavior and the extremes of treatment. In the process, we have silenced the dialogue about the meaning of this ancient drive and offered no real support for those of us who want to enjoy this pleasure throughout our lifetime and also want to seek help to explore why this pleasure often brings us troubles.

Mike Eigen's elaborations on the importance of working with impacts feels a timely and masterful addition to the treatment of substance use disorders. The *DSM 5* (2013) has discontinued the words abuse and dependence and the use of the word addiction is up to the clinician's discretion. A mild, moderate, and severe spectrum of disorders allows for more of a psychoanalytic attitude of waiting in faith with the patient rather than imposing with memory and desire (Eigen, 2013).

Dr. Eigen has gifted the field of psychoanalysis with his loyalty to himself, his soul, his mind, and his psyche. We are graced with the fruits of his disciplined devotion to his own unfolding. He is tireless and we are breathless from all he has contributed to the evolution of psychoanalytic thinking and the development of other fields of treatment as well.

References

American Psychiatric Association. (2013). *Diagnostic and Statistical Manual of Mental Disorders* (5th edn rev.). Washington, DC: American Psychiatric Association.

Bion, W. R. (1992). *Cogitations.* London: Karnac.

Bollas, C. (1989). *Forces of Destiny: Psychoanalysis and Human Idiom.* London: Free Association Books.

Caron Treatment Center (2013). www.caron.org/current-statistics.html.

Chessick, R. (1992). *What Constitutes the Patient in Psychotherapy.* London: Jason Aronson.

Coltart, N. (1993). *How to Survive as a Psychotherapist.* London: Sheldon Press.

Coltart, N. (2000). *Slouching towards Bethlehem.* New York: Other Press.

Eigen, M. (1986). *The Psychotic Core.* London: Karnac, 2004.

Eigen, M. (1995–2014). Personal communications.

Eigen, M. (1996). *Psychic Deadness.* London: Karnac, 2004.

Eigen, M. (1998). *The Psychoanalytic Mystic.* London: Free Association Books.

Eigen, M. (1999). *Toxic Nourishment.* London: Karnac.

Eigen, M. (2001). *Ecstasy.* Middletown, CT: Wesleyan University Press.

Eigen, M. (2002). *Rage.* Middletown, CT: Wesleyan University Press.

Eigen, M. (2004). *The Sensitive Self.* Middletown, CT: Wesleyan University Press.

Eigen, M. (2009). *Flames from the Unconscious.* London: Karnac.

Eigen, M. (2011a). *Eigen in Seoul* (Volume Two): *Faith and Transformation.* London: Karnac.

Eigen, M. (2011b). *Contact with the Depths.* London: Karnac.

Eigen, M. (2013). MEigen Workshop.

Fetting, M. (2012). *Perspectives on Addiction.* Los Angeles: Sage.

Jellinek, E. M. (1960). *The Disease Concept of Alcoholism.* New Haven, CT: Hillhouse Press.

Khantzian, E. J., & Albanese, M. J. (2008). *Understanding Addiction as Self Medication.* Lanham, MD: Rowan & Littlefield.

Malater, E. (2013). Review of Seoul books. MEigen Workshop.

Molino, A. (Ed.) (1997). *Freely Associated.* London: Free Association Books.

Phillips, A. (1994). *On Flirtation.* Cambridge, MA: Harvard University Press.

Rilke, R. M. (1993). *Letters to a Young Poet.* New York: W. W. Norton.

Rogers, R. (1989). Review of The Psychotic Core. *Psychoanalytic Psychology,* 6(3): 367–373.

Severns, J. R. (2004). A sociohistorical view of addiction and alcoholism. *Janus Head*, *7*(1): 149–165.

Steiner, J. (1993). *Psychic Retreats*. London: Routledge.

CHAPTER ELEVEN

Supervision with Michael Eigen: notes on a love affair

Aner Govrin

The supervision excerpt featured in this chapter forms part of the book *Conversations with Michael Eigen*, published in 2007 by Karnac. The supervision with Michael Eigen took place between September and December 2003 in his office in Manhattan and in his Brooklyn home. Seven conversations lasting a total of more than twenty hours were recorded.

The first section of *Conversations* focused on Michael Eigen's seminal ideas, the second section concentrated on Eigen's personal life, and the third section detailed two case supervisions, one of which is cited in this chapter.

After *Conversations with Michael Eigen* (Eigen & Govrin, 2007) was published with these cases, there was a widespread curiosity from clinicians wanting to know how Michael Eigen *actually* supervises. I usually answered that I have written all I had to say in *Conversations*, but people wanted to know more of what kind of supervisor Eigen is. Does he supervise in a way that reflects his poetic writing style?

My aim in this extension is to answer these questions, as well as to convey how my meetings with Eigen affected me as a person and contributed to my growth as a psychotherapist. The supervision session is followed by an epilogue in which I reflect on the impact the supervision had on my work as a psychotherapist, which continues to this present day.

Supervision, 2003 (published 2007)

Aner: Rachel is a married woman, age forty-five. She is a mother to three children from her second marriage. Rachel has been in therapy for five years. She comes twice a week on a regular basis. Rachel first came to therapy because she felt depressed. She cried a lot, felt miserable and barely functioned in her work as a secretary. Rachel also suffered from a compulsion to wash her hands, putting them under the tap for several minutes, especially before cooking or after washing the house with detergents. She feared that residues of detergents remaining on her hands might mix with cooked food and poison her family.

Mike: How long has Rachel been married?

Aner: Rachel married when she was twenty-three. She is a small woman. She has a child-like look; it is hard to believe that she is forty-five. Rachel suffered many catastrophes. Her mother died in a car accident when she was nine. She was sent abroad and was raised by her uncle until the age of seventeen. She returned to Israel when her father had a stroke. Her father died three years later. Before his death, Rachel had to take care of him. For years, she felt guilty because of her parents' deaths. She was in the kitchen with her mother a few days before the car accident. Rachel's mother was cooking and washing the dishes. Suddenly an unpleasant thought "jumped" to her mind: how great it would be if she could replace her mother in the kitchen. After her mother's death, she thought her private thought might have caused harm—the death. She was tormented by guilt feelings. Her memories of her mother are ambivalent. Her mother was not warm or affectionate.

Rachel felt close to her father. He often visited her when she was abroad with her uncle and his wife. He supported her financially. He told her how he liked her looks, complimented her about her talents. When he got sick, Rachel nursed him devotedly, took care of him like a little woman. She cooked, cleaned, and nursed him. After he died, she thought she could have prevented his death if she was more devoted and caring. If only she had prepared better food for him or taken him to the doctors more often, she might have saved his life. For years, she felt depressed and guilty. Rachel also had a young brother, who has been schizophrenic since her adolescence. He has spent most of his life in a psychiatric hospital. After a few weeks in therapy Rachel made good progress and there was an enormous relief in her symptoms.

Mike: How did you do that?

Aner: I don't know. It just happened. I guess it was something in our relationship, a movement, a quiet happening, a blessing. It was really amazing.

But then Rachel began to complain about her mother-in-law. These complaints were more resistant to therapy. She repeated them in almost every session. She felt that her mother-in-law did not welcome her to the family. She felt rejected by her mother-in-law. She thought her mother-in-law wished and prayed for "bad things" to happen to her. According to Rachel, these bad wishes and prayers influenced her life in a profound and tragic way. Her whole miserable situation was because of her mother-in-law's bad spell.

Mike: How often do they see each other?

Aner: In Israel, family ties are very close. They meet very often. The year of crisis between her and her mother-in-law began after she gave birth to her first child. After the birth, her husband put a lot of pressure on her to stay with his family and she agreed—reluctantly. She had some kind of after birth depression, I am not sure how severe it was, but apparently her mother-in-law questioned her ability to be a mother and, according to my patient, refused to help her. The husband's family was in distress. They asked for professional help from welfare services. A social worker was sent. My patient felt humiliated. For Rachel, it was a traumatic experience. In some sessions, she repeats again and again the same story in the same words. She felt awful.

Mike: Why does she think the mother-in-law is against her?

Aner: Rachel thinks that her mother-in-law thinks she owns the son and that she refuses to let go of him. They are competing for the same man, only they are not equal. Her mother-in-law is powerful and bad, her prayers are heard somewhere but Rachel feels weak and helpless.

Mike: What position does the son/husband take?

Aner: The son is a "Nebech". He is passive and weak; anger and conflicts intimidate him. He just wants things to be quiet between the two.

Mike: Isn't it strange that such a passive man has two women fighting about him?

Aner: Yes. He is trying to negotiate between the two. He keeps saying that Rachel sees elephants where there are only flies. Frankly, I don't really know what's going on because Rachel can make false attributions, like her conviction that her mother-in-law's "bad thoughts" had a devastating effect on her life.

Mike: Did Rachel say more about that?

Aner: Well, at first she was ashamed to tell me. Rachel is not psychotic. It's a cultural thing. She knows exactly how it sounds from the outside. She doesn't have a clear idea how these things work.

Mike: What bad things have happened so far?

Aner: She got fired. She has been unemployed for a couple of years and she thinks her mother-in-law has something to do with it. As long as that woman wishes her misfortune, the world cannot be a safe place.

Mike: Is there any other motive, besides the competition with her son, that Rachel attributes to her mother-in-law?

Aner: Yes. Rachel thinks her mother-in-law, whom she likes to call "primitive", envies her attractive appearance and modernity. Rachel feels that her mother-in-law wishes my patient to be exactly like her: primitive, arranging her life around household duties, neglecting her physical appearance.

Mike: What more can you tell me about Rachel?

Aner: She doesn't have any friends. She doesn't like or appreciate women very much. When Rachel did work, she did not get on with the other female workers. Rachel thought that they didn't like her for two reasons: First, she was prettier; second, the boss preferred her. There is always a strong, powerful woman that turns against her, cursing her secretly and thinking bad thoughts. Likewise, there is always a good-looking, nice man who treats her well and favours her. At her work, it was her boss. She felt there was something special between them. Rachel thinks the other women envied her special relations with her boss. The man is always weak compared to some powerful woman who wants to take him away from her. But no matter how strong the powerful woman is, she is always inferior to Rachel because she lacks Rachel's beauty and attractiveness. A few weeks before she was fired, she thought that one of the female workers tried to poison her by putting deadly pills in her tea. She was embarrassed to tell me that because she was not sure if I would believe her. She did not want me to think that she is mad.

Before her marriage, an educated young man fell in love with Rachel and wanted to marry her. Rachel remembers that he was fond of her. She proudly describes how she attracted him and how he liked to smell her body and touch her. She misses him and often has daydreams about what would have happened if she lived with him. Eventually, Rachel didn't marry him because she thought that his family would never accept an uneducated and simple woman like her.

Mike: Tell me more about the therapy.

Aner: From the beginning, Rachel felt aroused and tense in my presence. Our relations became very lively. After the first two years, just after she got out of her depression, she was convinced that I was desperately in love with her. For her, our relationship was a love affair. She thought we must keep it in secret. She did not put on her make-up before sessions so that her husband wouldn't suspect that anything fishy was happening between us. She asked me if I love my wife. She added that she wouldn't dream of taking her place. Though she felt we were having an affair, she was certain that I loved my wife deeply and would never give her up. In one dramatic session, she came to my office and noticed the wires coming out of my computer. She asked me if my wife had installed a recording device so she can listen to our conversations. She is certain that I am afraid of our relationship, that I can't handle it, that it's too much for me.

Mike: What do you tell her?

Aner: I always feel that Rachel is distorting what I say. It is like she hears whatever she wants to. If I say A, she understands B. Now B is always something against her, a criticism. For example, if I say: It was hard for you to realise that your mother-in-law would not welcome you to her family, she'll answer: No, I am not a miserable woman or It's not only in my head, or It's not just me, every woman who marries her husband needs to feel welcomed and accepted by her mother-in-law. Whatever I say, Rachel feels that I attacked or criticised her. She is also extremely demanding. She wants to know if I really love her and then says that she is certain that I love my wife and not her. Sometimes it's hard to bear her. I feel that she wants so much and that she feels I give her so little. Rachel pays me a ridiculously low fee because she is unemployed. Yet she is insulted by the mere fact that she has to pay me. At some meetings, Rachel says that she won't come next week because she doesn't have enough to pay me. Then she adds: You wouldn't consider giving me a discount, would you? I tell her that she is testing me. *If I really loved her I would reduce her fee, perhaps even agree to meet her for free.* But what she really wants to hear is that I really want her to come. It is important that you come, I tell her, you feel so lonely and have no one to talk to. It's not a good idea to skip a session. Rachel enjoys seeing how hard I work for her to change her mind. It's like a ritual in which everyone has to play his part: she says she won't come, I sweat blood to convince her. The drama ends when she finally succumbs and agrees. Sometimes she says: It's important for me to come, but what about you? When I tell her that it will make me happy to see her next week she blushes and hides a little smile.

Mike: Do you spend extra time with Rachel?

Aner: No, 50 minutes are enough and sometimes too much.

Mike: Does Rachel miss appointments?

Aner: Never. She comes even when she is sick.

Mike: How do you like Rachel?

Aner: Rachel is special to me, despite the difficulties. It feels good to nurture someone who is extremely deprived but is willing to be nurtured. Rachel has never had this experience—being the center of a relationship. But, as you can see, she is not an easy patient. I often think of her as ungrateful. Whatever I give her, whatever I do for her, it's just not enough.

On the other hand, I feel that Rachel is afraid of getting too close to me. She keeps saying that I limit her by saying that my relationship with her is purely professional. I have never said that. In reality, she is the one who feels very tense and shy in my presence. She once told me that it embarrasses her to drink water or do anything with her body in my presence. She told me that she would like to be more spontaneous and less reserved when we sit together. She says that if she could just take her shoes off, or jump, or do silly things like a child, it would make her feel good. In many sessions, she expresses an urge to see me more. She says she misses me, that fifty-minute sessions are not enough. She wants us to spend more time together. But of course, she says, insulted, you won't agree to see me free of charge, would you? And, of course, she continues, I wouldn't expect you to. It is always *me* who rejects *her*, because I can live without her.

Mike: If you would want Rachel enough, what would happen then?

Aner: I don't know. Sometimes I ask myself if Rachel hears me at all. I want to shout: *Hello, did you hear what I just said?* Rachel keeps twisting things, as though I am criticizing her and she has to defend herself.

Mike: What stops Rachel from feeling how special she is for you?

Aner: Maybe I'm missing something here.

Mike: Ask her: Rachel, what makes you deaf to what I am saying? What stops you from hearing me? How do you do that? How does that happen?

She is protecting herself. Maybe over time it is possible to explore what that means. [Ask her:] How do you do that? What is it that is doing that? What protects you from yourself? How does that work that you are so good at shutting me out?

Aner: Are you saying that I should confront her?

Mike: No, not confront; raise the questions and bring the matter up. I wouldn't necessarily expect Rachel to answer or even to be able to answer, but at least plant the seeds for the future.

Why do you think there is such an enormous force, and what is behind this force you experience as not hearing?

Aner: I am not sure what it is that Rachel doesn't want to hear.

Mike: Rachel doesn't know what to do with the other's good feelings. Maybe she thinks: As soon as I have good feelings I'll die or the therapy will have to stop. *You can suggest that to her: Maybe you are afraid that if good feelings happen the therapy will have to end.*

Look what happened with her closest bonds as she grew up. Something good signals that a catastrophe is on the way, so she has to protect herself from the depth of a bond. Bonds end up catastrophically, with death and madness, or jealousy. Destructive forces kick into gear once feelings start. Love means catastrophe, bond means catastrophe, feelings mean catastrophe, anything close or significant means death or madness: My brother went crazy, my mother died, my father died. That's quite a background. Rachel is doing very well. Rachel has the right to be insane. She has a psychotic part. I wouldn't expect too much sanity.

How did Rachel feel about her brother's insanity?

Aner: She was ashamed of his illness. She was also afraid that she would be ill too.

Mike: Her whole nuclear family died?

Aner: She doesn't have anyone except her mother's brother. But she is disappointed with him too.

Mike: So Rachel has to protect herself, she is very self-protective. Seeing the other as bad is a way of protecting herself. Sometimes she is right and the other *is* bad. Other times her sense that bonds can be catastrophic spreads and she tries to contain the spread by focusing on specific target figures. It is a battle between spreading catastrophe and focused catastrophe. Why wouldn't Rachel lose her husband and children if she lost everyone else? So the rituals are protective and also show how Rachel feels responsible for her losses. Rachel is afraid that those she loves will be taken away from her. She thinks inside herself: If only I can be good enough, clean enough, pure enough, God won't take them from me. Rachel is afraid her mother-in-law will take you away from her. Her mother-in-law's magic and brutal powers will steal you away.

Aner: Fortunately, we don't know each other.

Mike: It doesn't matter. You don't have to know each other in order for bad magic power to work. You don't have to be near each other. What distance can bad power travel? How far away can badness or evil intentionality or unconscious negative magical force be and still be effective? Does bad power only work when there is literal contact or can it work at a distance too? Bad power can traverse immense distances instantaneously. It can travel from mind to mind, body to body without barriers. Rachel feels there is a bad force in the universe that is working against her and she has to try to defend herself against it. In so far as you are a good force, Rachel has to protect you too.

Aner: If there is one area that the powerful mother-in-law has not touched, it is the therapeutic relation. Until you said that, I felt quite safe.

Mike: (laughs) So far, Rachel kept the bad force somewhat circumscribed. She tells the bad force: you can have this area, but not that area. Rachel is afraid that the bad force will go further and take her children, her husband, and will stop therapy.

Aner: She was scared that she would become mad too, like her brother.

Mike: Yes. I'd like to hear more about that.

Aner: It does not concern her now as much as it did before. But when Rachel was depressed, she thought she was going mad. She wanted me to reassure her that she is OK, which I did. She refused to take psychiatric treatments to relieve her depression and compulsion. Her brother took medication and other psychiatric treatments all his life. Rachel could not bear the thought that they share the same fate. She did not want to end up like her brother.

Mike: Tell me more about the therapeutic process.

Aner: After a session in which Rachel feels close to me, I can almost anticipate the next session. In it she will describe again her compulsive hand washings. In the libidinal session she might say: I know you would never choose a woman like me, I am not the kind of woman you are interested in, but I must tell you, I really think of you a lot, I imagine us doing things together. And then she will add that she would rather not discuss it right now. Then comes the next session, when she focuses on her symptoms: Will this come to an end? Can you help me more than you have already done? In contrast to the previous session she will not mention anything personal. It is as if she is trying to clean the "sins" of the previous sessions.

Mike: They are connected. Rachel is saying If I have strong feelings for you, you will be taken away from me. No matter how much I wash my hands it's not enough to protect you from bad forces. There's no end to washing bad or good or strong feelings away, feelings that I'm afraid of, feelings that disturb me. One never stops trying to wash them away. To wash is to clean and also to get rid of. "To wash one's hands of something" means to drop the matter, to no longer be interested, to let something go, get rid of it, let it fall, drop it out of one's life—a little like sending a scapegoat over a cliff. Get rid of sin, of disturbance, of problems. In America, there is a song that says, "I'm going to wash that man right out of my hair." Which hair, you might wonder, top or bottom or both? Out of one's psychic hair. To wash the psyche clean and create a disturbance-free psyche.

Compulsive washing also defends against loss and damage, tries to undo loss and damage. When Rachel has good feelings or sexy feelings for you, they threaten the relationship. Because they are too much, too exciting, overwhelming, too good or too hot to handle, *and* because they are subject to loss, damage, attack, spoilage. They can be ruined and taken away. Rachel has to spoil her feelings so that she can feel protected. She washes her hands so much when she cooks because she is afraid to poison the food with bad or disturbing or good or exciting feelings. Too much of her will run off into the food, too much will result in spillage, drainage of her insides into the food. Rachel is really afraid. When she gets to the point of thinking, They are laughing at me, they think I'm crazy, I would tell her, You don't have to think it's [hand washing, etc.] sane. Just let it be. Maybe after therapy goes on for a while, it will make more sense. Part of the reason that you have to do this is because you are afraid of losing those who are close to you, so you try to purify yourself, so death won't happen again.

We try to wash sin away; we try to wash death away. We try to wash evil and madness away. We try to preserve ourselves and others by washing away what might infect us. Washing, too, is a kind of self-protective murder since it tries to kill off what is bothering one (psychic dis-ease). Rachel feels that if she doesn't do a good job as a mother and as a wife her family will be hurt and the same goes for you. She has to nurture and preserve her therapy against great odds.

Aner: In what way?

Mike: She has to both nourish you *and* give you her pathology. In a way, it is like feeding a cancer. Rachel has to see that you stay alive and well in face of omnipresent danger. She has to help you survive and flourish in face of the sickness she puts into you. She has to find some way to feel good enough to stay in therapy, to be a wife, to be a mother, to be a patient, because she doesn't feel good enough.

For now, I wouldn't do too much with the mother-in-law. Her ideas about the mother-in-law are pretty fixed. I wouldn't attack them, I wouldn't try to solve them, I wouldn't invest too much on this front, at this point. It's better, at this stage, to support her and, reassure her, saying something like, Oh, that was a lousy thing for your mother-in-law to say. I don't blame you for feeling that way. That is, just acknowledge her feelings. To explore and investigate is likely to feel like rejection, unless she begins to hunger for such activity. Rachel is likely to use anything she learns as a way to feel worse about herself. Right now, she is less curious than frightened, trying to keep threats at bay.

I wouldn't introduce the mother-in-law as a major focus unless she forces you to. I would stay with the things she does to protect the people she loves in her life, acknowledging that she is afraid something bad will happen to them. Look what's happened in the past; you fear you are going to lose those who are close to you; you are trying now to make things better. It's like biblical purification on a stationary bicycle. You keep pedalling and pedalling, trying to clean yourself enough so that God will not do bad things, so that those you love can go on living. What does one have to do to stop God from doing bad things?

Aner: It's a lot of self-blaming.

Mike: Rachel suffered enormous losses . . . She seems to have a fairly rich personality, given what she has gone through.

Aner: You think so?

Mike: Don't you? She has feelings for you; she has all these crazy ideas. You are doing a good job.

Aner: It's good to hear you say that.

Mike: Rachel thinks that you are afraid to feel for her. She feels that you should be afraid of your feelings or you will leave your wife. If you are not afraid of your feelings, what will happen with the two of you? To have feelings means to feel too much. There is boundlessness at work, so she works so hard to keep things bounded. To have feelings is to have uncontrollable feelings, a flood, destructive gratification. Yet you sit with her and you show her that you have good feelings for her. You and Rachel are still with each other. You manage to survive having feelings for each other. But there are always threats. Tell Rachel: You have the right to be afraid. You feel that I am afraid of you and you are afraid of me. Why are you so afraid of that? Maybe that's how human beings are, afraid of each other. We don't know what to do with feelings. No one teaches us what to do. You are left in the forest or the desert to take care of yourself. What do we do with the feelings we have? Maybe therapy is a place where, over time, something can happen. We can learn about feelings, become less afraid of some of our feelings. We can learn to dip in.

Aner: Rachel thinks of our relationship in a very rigid way. She thinks there are just two options: either it is a professional relationship—nothing personal, she is just one of my patients—or it's a romantic relationship.

Mike: Did you point out this dichotomy, either everything or nothing?

Aner: Many times . . .

Mike: Isn't therapy strange? What relationships are like it? We talk about the most personal, intimate things. The therapist invites the patient to say anything and everything. Yet we are still therapist and patient. It is a weird relationship, a different kind of relationship. How is this relationship different from all other relationships? Why did human beings invent such a relationship? If they invented it, it must have a purpose; let's see if we can find out.

Aner: That's much too philosophical for her.

Mike: Then try asking: What do you make of this strange relationship, intimate yet not intimate, close but not close?

Aner: Rachel would answer: It's because of *you*. I want more of you but you insist that it's all professional.

Mike: . . . But do you find that sometimes I am too close, and sometimes I am too far, that I don't get it just right? You are telling me that it is frustrating for you; it is aggravating that I don't get it right. Too close, too far, too cold, too warm. Maybe it takes time for us to learn how to be together.

Aner: I am not sure if Rachel could be at ease with this subject.

Mike: Let it stay unresolved. One lives with a lot that's unsolved. It takes a lot of patience, two people together.

Aner: For her, just talking about such things is a sin. This kind of talk is too intimate, verbal intercourse *is* sexual intercourse. She came to solve her problems, not to have an affair. And yet, she enjoys flirting with me.

Mike: The biggest problem that what we are working with, and what hope to make a little better, is the feeling that all the good things in your life will be taken away from you. Relationships mean catastrophe. Something catastrophic is going to happen. You think all the time while you are living that bad things will happen. You know you are not wrong. Bad things do happen and have happened and will happen. Now, you want to go farther. You want to live in spite of such knowledge. One thing I feel about the washing is that it is a place where you want to make things better. Can you say more about this feeling of trying to make things better?

Aner: Rachel feels that she doesn't cook enough and that her children complain about it. She does not experience herself as a fully nurturing mother. It's amazing how enormously important food is in some cultures. On the other hand, before Rachel worked, she spent many hours in the kitchen like "a good mother" but she didn't enjoy it. It was bad then, and it is bad now. Everything is bad, nothing is good. It's hard for her to acknowledge anything good in her life.

Mike: If she does, it will be taken away. I can feel that there are some things you feel *are* good. You are afraid to acknowledge them, you are afraid to say them, you are afraid that they will be taken away. Only show the bad things. Keep all the good things secret because if someone sees them they will be taken away.

Aner: So for Rachel, good means a pending catastrophe?

Mike: Yes. Lots of damage. The bad is a protective shield. If everything is going to be bad inevitably, then there is not too much of a risk of loss.

Aner: I am worried; I don't see a movement there. I am not sure if change is possible.

Mike: Don't be worried. How long can she stay?

Aner: I don't see an end.

Mike: That's good. That means that she can stand it. Rachel senses something true in the relationship. Don't worry about change. It will happen by itself. It will happen through the interaction over time: a little here, a little there. I wouldn't look for big things. Just stay with Rachel and something will happen. It's already happening. Don't ask if this is going to go away, or if that's going to go away. That's the wrong question. Just keep on going and see what will happen. There will be emotional change—just from being together and going through things.

Aner: I always felt pessimistic about Rachel's life and optimistic about therapy. There is something in her therapy that goes very well and is good for her. But I don't see a similar rhythm in her life.

Mike: Therapy *is* life. Therapy is part of her life, a support, a background. It's a lot. For Rachel, it is an interaction with an interesting man whom she can't have, who is too good for her (laughs), who is above her. Like the daddy she never had. For her, you are someone who is interested, someone who looks after her.

Aner: Once a month, almost in/as a routine, we have a session in which she says that she must quit therapy otherwise she will get used to it and might never leave.

Mike: Rachel might feel that she has to leave because she must protect you from her destructiveness. Then you should say: If this therapy ends, it's not because I am getting rid of you, it's because you are getting rid of me. I am here. I am sticking it out. I'll stick it out if you can take it. But you are the one who can't take it.

If she has to go, make sure Rachel understands that she can come back at some point. Tell her not to let her shame stop her from coming back when she wants to. Give her an escape hatch and leave the door open. You understand that she feels locked in by therapy and has to get away now.

Aner: I understand. I think you are saying that I feel locked in with Rachel and that I have to get away. Not anymore. Being in a dyad with her is suffocating. But now you are in the picture. You hold both of us. That's liberating.

Mike: That's terrific. God bless you. A bond can contain toxic and all kinds of negative elements. If you keep bearing it, things happen. Rachel has to keep purifying herself by washing her hands because she doesn't have an intersubjective washing, a soul washing, a psyche washing.

Aner: Surprisingly, Rachel's hand washing has declined since I've been here in the States.

Mike: (laughs) You are here, she is there. You survive without her, she survives without you. It's less intense, she doesn't have to protect you as much. When you're together, she has to protect you more. Contact heats things up, is more intense, she has to protect you (and herself) more. Overall, you are communicating: You are afraid for me and have to protect me with the washing but our relationship will survive. You don't have to work so hard. Let it go. Your coming to the States, leaving her, is an act of faith, a letting go.

Aner: Some sessions are structured like a drama with a beginning, a peak, and an exciting finale. She opens the session by talking about her symptoms and how awful she feels. She goes on to talk about us. She starts to get excited, smiles a lot—as if she is playing and enjoying. During that phase, she seems less tense. As the session ends, she gets highly aroused. A few seconds before the session ends, she wants to know how I feel about her.

Mike: (raises his voice): You waited for the very end of the hour to ask me the most important question on your mind? I want you to start next session with this question. I want you to practise asking that question earlier.

Aner: I am not sure. I don't feel comfortable saying that.

Mike: You don't have to be so serious about it. Come in and ask her: How do I look like I feel about you right now? Maybe each time it will be something different. Maybe I feel different things about you at different times. Next session when I ask you, you'll see something else.

The point here is to help her get some psychic exercise. Rachel gets stuck on one track. She has an imperative, a command: You should feel one thing for me, whatever that one thing is at the moment, for example, passion and love. Thou shalt feel passion and love. By asking, How do I look like I feel towards you now? And now? And now?, you are creating a counter-demand, or invitation, or counter-current, making waves, creating the possibility of some undulating movement. How do I look now? Is it the same as last time, is it different? What's the same? What's different? Perhaps she will begin to exercise her psyche. A little like artificial respiration. You are trying to stimulate some movement between perceptions, without being too dogmatic or pushy. It is an extended invitation to move around a bit.

Aner: When she asks me that final dramatic question at the end—what feelings do I have for her?—I feel tension in the air. It's like the whole session was built to get to that point.

Mike: A work of art (raises his voice dramatically): All through the session, you worked to get to this point, to ask me this question as you are walking out the door. That's awesome. How did you do that? Save the best for last. *Then you don't need me anymore.*

Aner: I still don't know how to answer.

Mike: (amused) Oh, my God, now that you are leaving? How can I possibly say it all in thirty seconds? How do you think I feel? Next time ask me two minutes earlier.

Aner: That will be the wrong answer for her. I always give her the wrong answer. For her I should be saying: I love you as much as you love me. That's what Rachel expects me to say.

Mike: That's very nice. So say: I love you much as you love me. How do you feel saying that?

Aner: It's not true.

Mike: I have a psychotic patient who often says at the end of sessions, so, am I going to be OK? Am I going to be OK? Tell me I am going to be OK. Sometimes I answer: You will be OK. And he says: No, no, say it like you mean it, say Jay, you are going to be OK. Sometimes I do say, Jay, you will be OK.

I may have my doubts, my fears. I hope and pray he will be OK. In some sense, like a mother, I am conveying that he is OK now. There is something lovable about him. He is a profoundly good person, profoundly troubled, in need, and I do care. When I say, You are going to be OK, Jay, I feel skin form around him. It is quite a moving sensation, to mediate the growth of skin. A second before, it wasn't there, he was raw. He was asking to be in a body with skin, a psyche with skin. My holding back withheld the growth of skin. My giving enabled its formation. It changes one's picture of self and life to realise that words form skin.

You said before that you told Rachel that she would be OK but it is hard for you to say I love you? Aner, don't say something you are not comfortable with. Ask her: how do I look to you? What can you tell about my feelings when you look at my face?

Aner: She is very interested in finding how I really feel for her. I feel trapped. Whatever I say, it's not the right answer.

Mike: You always have the right to reflect. The assumption is that you feel only one thing at a time for her. Rachel may see things in you that you don't want her to see. She may be right about you. She wishes for more or something else. Rachel wants you to love her more, to be more devoted to her, to want her the way she wants you. But you do have your own mind, or at least a mind somewhat independent of her mind. She fears giving either her mind or your mind space. She wants to fill the space with *one* thing. One mind, one thing. Two minds, one thing. But a mind, yours or hers, contains other possibilities. Whatever pressure you feel, you have to keep in mind what a complex person you are. You have to keep on being a complex person, no matter how simplified she wants to make things. There is a force at work to reduce complexity and you must withstand it. Rachel is afraid to see that she is not of one mind. She fears the loss of the love she hopes to have. Rachel does not think that she can have a mind and love at the same time. She is not yet able to let love admit difference; Let love manifest itself in different ways, vary, but something in her sees the writing on the wall and fights it.

Aner: For her it's a multiple choice, it's either A or B.

Mike: If I don't feel the right thing, you won't like it, you will feel rejected. Maybe I feel some of the right thing, some of the wrong thing; some of this, some of that. I feel a mixture of things. But a mixture may not be enough.

I have nothing against saying, I love you too, after a patient says, I love you. But if you feel trapped, you may be being too literal. Maybe Mohamed Ali's "dancing like a butterfly" is a better model. She may be being literal but you don't have to be. You don't have to be confined by literalness. You can give *something* from your heart or mind, but not give your *whole* heart or mind. Or perhaps you *can* be whole-hearted, but in a specific way. She is after something whole. A part of a meal can be a lot, if it is let in and digested. There are a lot of colours on an emotional palette. Perhaps you offer her a picnic and she wants a banquet. But she may get more from a picnic than you think.

Aner: I see now what happened. I have reduced myself to fit into her world. The pressure on me was strong.

Mike: No wonder it was hard for you to say I love you. Of course it's a real feeling, but it's also just another affect expression, part of a larger emotional palette. We're in a kind of emotional gymnasium: working the equipment, working ourselves, jumpstarting and developing ourselves. You tone up muscles. There are ways you tone emotions too. After you say I love you, you can ask, Do you believe me? Do you feel I can feel other things too, a little of this, a little of that? A lot of this, a lot of that? Does my love for you have to be all I feel? A totally exclusive love? Of course, that is what you feel you want; the idea of a total love grips you. But you love your husband, your kid, as well as me. And I love others as well as you.

Well, maybe Rachel can take that in and work it around and maybe not. Whether she does or not, that doesn't mean you should leave your symbolic capacity behind. You can picture a world of larger and more varied and nuanced emotional possibilities. You don't have to sacrifice your sense of what is possible between people because Rachel pressures you into a tight mould. You can go on upholding paradox. We are close and distant. We love and leave each other and go home to our everyday lives, and come back again. We love and keep on being therapist and patient. Our relationship is strange, paradoxical, not one thing. This confuses her. She needs to stretch, in order to take in this complexity: that we are not one thing, that our relationship is not one thing. You can say to her, You are getting confused because our relationship has opposites that pull on each other and you don't know what to do with them yet. You haven't dealt with a relationship like this before. It's a new kind of relationship. It takes a lot of growing into. It's not anything you're used to. Trying to make it one kind of love is like standing in front of a train.

Capacities grow over years. In terms of therapy, we're speaking of years of being together, five, ten, fifteen years. I like the notion of steeping, immersion, steeping in a therapy feeling for years, like soup on a low flame. It is not unusual for me to work with someone for thirty years or more, but I am much older than you and some of my patients and I are growing old together.

My guess is that work with Rachel will take a long time. I would think in terms of the long haul and not get too bogged down in moment-to-moment crises. Do what you need to do to keep going. The main thing is hanging in there for as long as you need to, and to expect that to be a long time. This kind of therapy can't be rushed. You feel pressured into rushing, but that is part of a larger process that gradually absorbs and works with that pressure.

I think, Aner, that you are doing a terrific job. Rachel is connected to you. She has good feelings. She is afraid of her feelings. She is afraid of your feelings. I don't blame her. With this bond, there is a chance that in ten or fifteen years, your contact with each other will make a difference. It already has made a positive change in her life.

Eigen as supervisor—a decade later

During our first sessions, I asked Eigen to explain ideas or notions that I found enigmatic: "Just what do you mean by that? Would you mind saying it again? Sorry, couldn't catch that". At first, Eigen politely cooperated but soon he got tired and began to show his impatience . . . He asked me to let go. I don't think that it was just him not wanting to be interrupted, it was him working, moulding, trying to induce in me a different way of grasping, seeing, getting to something. But I could not resist the temptation to understand it all in my usual way of going about understanding things. I like my world clear, I like to know and reveal the threads of it that are another way to describe this state of mind. I assumed that I could superimpose my own categories of thoughts on Eigen's world. I wanted to navigate Eigen's world without getting lost.

But it was of no use. I was at sea. I got lost again and again. It took me a while to understand that in my attempts to find my way in his thoughts, I was missing much of the surprise, beauty, and living moments of the conversation. It was as if we were in a beautiful green meadow and Eigen was showing me rare and colourful butterflies. The scientist in me awakened. I wanted us to catch each butterfly, dissect it, and examine it so we could fully analyse it. But Eigen was after something else. Eigen insisted in our interaction: "Let them fly, let them be free."

As time passed I learned to enjoy my unknowingness and, instead of making efforts to "understand" what Eigen meant, I began experiencing the feelings and thoughts which his voice aroused in my own mind. I began to interact with Eigen in a real, experiential sense. That takes some doing. In his absence, he felt more real. Eigen's words had been freed and they were doing their business. They became streams of thought in my conscious and unconscious world. I do not practice meditation. I felt, however, that I was in a meditative state of mind when he spoke. I now believe that this is the best way to *read* Eigen, too.

The four months during which I conversed with Eigen were a particularly pleasurable and intriguing voyage into the mind of one of the most fascinating contemporary writers on psychoanalysis. I view Eigen as a writer who belongs to a group of intellectuals that includes the likes of Donald Winnicott, Wilfred Bion, Marion Milner, Adam Phillips, Thomas Ogden, and others whose writing can be considered evocative, creative, emotionally stirring, and reverential rather than strictly "academic". In Eigen's case, the psychoanalytical writing is not *about* psychoanalysis, but, rather, writing that spawns psychoanalytic thinking. My experience was not supervision in the generally accepted meaning of the word. For me, it was a way of getting to know another aspect of his personality and his work as a therapist, and to develop a deeper and more personal bond with him. Over the course of the supervision, the barrier between interviewee and interviewer, questioner and respondent was lifted and, suddenly, I was involved and found myself on the inside.

I felt that I was no longer merely an interviewer writing a book about Eigen, but also a supervisee that had come to him, seeking his experience for two difficult and extreme cases in which I felt that I did not know how to help my patients. In hindsight, I think that these supervisions brought me closer to him, removed barriers, and created an intimacy that was essential to the writing of the book. Eigen was softer in supervision than he had been in the interviews: he was more attentive to nuances, more flexible, he adapted himself to my fears, and he was very tolerant.

Prior to the supervision, I had many questions—I wondered what kind of supervisor Eigen would be. Would he try to understand Rachel as a particular individual before getting to the theoretical conceptualizations that are specifically associated with him, and which he describes in his books? Would the supervision be like his writing, poetic and creative, but also difficult to understand and unsystematic? Or would he instead manage to be more communicative in his role of supervisor? I wondered to what extent he would be able to help me to extract myself from the morass that was my relationship with Rachel if, in the course of the supervision, he became engrossed in poetic, philosophical, or religious thoughts.

I remember that the first thing that surprised me in the supervisions was the extent to which Eigen's approach was practical, dialogic, purposeful, and extremely communicative. In contrast to his writing—or even to the conversations we had had about his ideas—during the two supervisions, Eigen was very focused. He tried to pinpoint the central problems and concentrate on them and them alone. He did not lecture, did not insist on his ideas taking center stage, and did not preach about anything. The strong, intense, bubbly, and always surprising voice that had been present in many of our conversations gave way to a voice that was searching, trying to be responsive and sensitive, attempting to create a dialogue and adapting itself to Rachel's and my needs. He embodied the idea described by Emmanuel Berman (2000, p. 275), that "a good supervisor is less preoccupied with formulating what we should do and more receptive to an exploration of what we actually do and undergo, which may not always be as dictated by his theoretical rationales and goals as we once believed."

In contrast to other supervisions that I have experienced, Eigen did not visualize some other form of therapy, a therapy that could have been, that should have been, or any other imagined, idealized therapy. Eigen accepted what had taken place in the course of the therapy without imposing any kind of "pressure" to change it. Eigen's central outlook was based on letting go of any exaggerated expectations of the patient, of me, of the therapy. For Eigen it was important that the value of the therapy, its vitality, and its achievements be recognized. Eigen regarded the therapeutic relationship as something that should be seen as valuable, perhaps even sacred.

For me, it was a kinder, gentler, supervision. A supervision that moved beyond the aggressive suspicion and anachronistic jargon into a world in which there is more trust, more flexibility, greater openness and, above all, less ideological insistence.

When, with the benefit of hindsight, I now read Eigen's supervision with me in relation to Rachel's case, I notice a number of interesting points. In many places within the text, I find that I am speaking on Rachel's behalf and that Eigen takes over the role of therapist. Seemingly, this is a phenomenon that occurs in practically every supervision dialogue as the supervisor represents the aspiration for change. But what was different with Eigen was the extent of his clinical vocabulary, his lack of fear, his generosity in giving across all boundaries, and his always open, never qualified, position.

When I hear the supervision, I remember how Eigen's talent for acute and perceptive clinical description always amazed me. I think his ability to understand Rachel's psychotic part is due to the great empathy he has with psychosis. At times, his thoughts seem to merge with the very processes he describes.

In Rachel's therapy, I think that Eigen represented a depressive position. I am sure that Eigen would not like my use of psychoanalytical jargon, certainly not of the Kleinian kind, to describe his position in the supervision, but I am doing it in order to explain something profound in Eigen's supervision. Eigen encouraged me to recognize that Rachel is in an inflexible position, a binary state in which some parts of life are utterly and clearly distinct from the rest of life. Since, for Rachel, "love" is a signal of impending catastrophe, she is compelled to leave love detached from her, and not acknowledge it. She has to separate herself and build a wall between all that is good in her life and everything surrounding her. In contrast to the traditionally understood depressive position, Eigen's depressive position does not entail a renunciation. Neither does it mean that you have to come to terms with the fact that you only have a little of everything. In fact, the very reverse is the case. In the depressive position that is manifest in the supervision of Rachel, it is assumed that, instead of getting less, she, in fact, stands to get more and feel that she is getting more. And it is I, the therapist, and not the patient, who needs to engage in the work of acceptance.

The one who had to overcome his fears was me. It was I, not the patient, who was fearful of drowning in them. Eigen's expression of the depressive position is such that he succeeds in ridding himself of the unavoidable incompleteness inherent in therapy, as he finds within this incompleteness the ability to accept the partial as being "everything"—this is yet another paradox, reminiscent of his "presence in absence."

There was no reason for me not to love Rachel as if she was my whole world. My love for her would not destroy my world. That is what Eigen tried to tell me. And I am still digesting what he said.

More than anything else, what helped me was Eigen's saying: "That's quite a background. Rachel is doing very well. Rachel has the right to be insane. She has a psychotic part. I wouldn't expect too much sanity" (p. 103).

Rachel's sanity was suddenly defined by her not being sane. If, given her background, she had been "sane", we would have known for sure that she was psychotic. Perhaps irredeemably, and by the rules of logic that reside in the distressed world of the psychotic, psychosis, according to Eigen, is a sane response.

For me, this one sentence entailed a huge relief that brought with it a greater degree of openness towards Rachel. I stopped being tense and distressed by agitated about her insanity. I stopped trying to "straighten" her out. I had understood her integrity. Now, I was searching for my own.

Eigen's supervision helped me to see both my work with her and Rachel herself in a different light. I began to see Rachel as possessing a richer and far more complex personality than I had seen in her in the past. Prior to Eigen's supervision, the tension of being with her had distressed me. Although I liked her very much, I had at all times been ready to mount a defense against her questioning, her intrusive nature, her binary way of thinking, and the constant necessity to choose, define, set limits, and establish boundaries. I was also troubled by the fact that she was never satisfied, never able to recognize that she enjoyed my presence, even though the expression on her face showed that she was indeed enjoying it. After the supervision, I was far more intrigued by Rachel and more inclined to meet her. In the course of the supervision, Eigen had helped me to re-discover myself.

It helped me to understand what it was that I had deprived her of because of my fears. How easy it sometimes is to swap the fears of the therapist for the anxieties and illnesses of the patient.

While many of his particular insights were revolutionary to my therapy, I still cannot isolate what general aspect of his supervision was most crucial.

Was it Eigen's ability to assist me to find a way out of my own and Rachel's binary mode of thinking? Had he succeeded in enabling me to think my thoughts rather than Rachel's? Was it that he viewed the therapy as a very long-term process, a period of time in which there would be many more things to do? Maybe it was because he himself loved and valued the therapy work I had done with Rachel? Perhaps it was Eigen's capacity to listen and his quickness of understanding that I found breathtaking. Or it may have been his warm and encouraging style. Eigen conveyed the sense of someone with an amazing power to pay attention and a very deep human understanding that was awe-inspiring and deeply moving. Talking with Eigen is talking with a genial, creative, and experimenting mind.

The extent to which the supervision was free of debilitating and burdensome psychoanalytical jargon is something I think that I was unable to convey when describing it in the book. Eigen is able to supervise without even once using a psychoanalytical jargon term. In his supervision, there is a total absence of what Adam Philips (1988, p. 13) termed "the dreary earnestness or mystifying jargon that mars psychoanalytic writing after Freud and Ferenczi."

Perhaps Eigen's way of work can be described as follows: engaging in self-exposure, without using the term self-exposure; feeling the patient, without labeling it projective identification; speaking in your own voice, without reference to intersubjectivity or the third. When Eigen talks or supervises, we have an opportunity to put psychological jargon to one side. We can breathe. His language is fresh, different, surprising, and, at the same time, very direct, purposeful, and extremely clear. The experience of being supervised without the employment of psychoanalytical jargon left a powerful impression on me. Despite the fact that I value the richness of psychoanalytical language and have even written about it in the past (Govrin, 2006), I was amazed at how much *freedom* I gained in talking to Eigen about myself and my feelings without what we said being anchored in theory.

Perhaps Eigen was telling me, and, thereby, therapists like me, what it was that we are afraid of. Because the mind is like a stormy sea; we all like to have our anchors. They start off as theories. They solidify into definitions and we then mistakenly take them to be facts. And these "facts" rise up against us to destroy us or to destroy our thinking. It is not easy to know that you are a captive. Occasionally, I recall the film *The Truman Show* and the moment in it when Truman sails towards the horizon and discovers that his world is made of paper, scenery erected for his comfort, the illusion of consistency. We are required to build houses, decorations, scenery, to turn the horizon into something durable, a real line in the sand that will mark out a boundary. But when I talked to Eigen about my usual concepts, sure of them and them re-assuring me, I felt for a moment like someone who was reaching out, touching his own horizon, and discovering to his astonishment (and to his horror) that this is merely the beginning.

References

Berman, E. (2000). Psychoanalytic supervision. *International Journal of Psychoanalysis, 81*: 273–290.

Eigen, M., & Govrin, A. (2007). *Conversations with Michael Eigen*. London: Karnac.

Govrin, A. (2006). The dilemma of contemporary psychoanalysis: towards a "knowing" post-postmodernism. *Journal of the American Psychoanalytic Association, 45*(2): 507–536.

Phillips, A. (1988). *Winnicott*. Cambridge, MA: Harvard University Press.

CHAPTER TWELVE

Thoughts from Michael Eigen in my work with young Aboriginal mothers

Norma Tracey

In this chapter, I intend to use Michael Eigen's illuminating thinking to bring understanding to those psychic events in pregnancy, birth, and the first year of life, where the most intense experiences of human existence are exposed as the mother–infant couple struggle for survival out of a core of chaos and a sense of catastrophe. I will approach this from the perspective of three concepts Eigen developed out of the work of Freud, Jung, Winnicott, and Bion. The way Eigen evolved his idiosyncratic thinking allowed him also to value the perspective of each person who dares to move outside the norm and construct his or her own ideas.

Emotional, intellectual, and spiritual life

Eigen's faith and its meaning for pregnant women and new mothers underpins my own thinking about the importance of *surviving* this time of chaos and catastrophe by going through it rather than *avoiding* it. A sanity that is superimposed prematurely on chaos stultifies and deadens real growth; if the normal chaos of this period is held, allowed, and traversed, then the mother and infant can grow together through the catastrophe, living through this psychic terrain of "madness" to a place of sanity. Into this I bring ideas of a "new psychic birth" and the kinds of suffering that are inherent.

Eigen's thoughts on the relevance of "a presence", a psychic holding your womb in your mind during this important time, has given the most meaning to my "being there" for the young mothers whose journeys I shall describe. My presence emotionally, mentally, and physically was the healing of a damaged or initial absence of presence, and this meant not flinching or abandoning the chaos until the mother had resolved it in her own way. This meant that the mother could later perform the same role for her infant. With Eigen's theories to inform my work, I wanted to observe, document, and think about how these young Aboriginal mothers and infants traversed this area of both being together and separating out as an inevitable part of becoming.

First contact with Eigen

Travelling from island to island as my husband and I sailed up the East Coast of Australia for a year, I had on board a collection of "to-be-read papers", among them Eigen's "The area of faith in Winnicott, Bion, and Lacan" (1981). I was fully aware of how much this model fitted the depressed mother. I emailed Eigen with a quote from my own work with mothers, which I thought gave relevance to this area of faith. To my astonishment, I received a reply from him within a day. So began a relationship of private emails, and, later, sometimes daily exchanges in the Michael Eigen online chat room, where a group of us shared theoretical and personal conversations and spoke of our ongoing reading of Eigen's many books and papers—with which we often struggled to keep up. His writing is prolific.

Only in this present technological age could one make such a psychic journey over many years with a companion one had never met in person. Eigen gave me the courage to embrace all aspects of my work and to be not just a "good enough" psychoanalytic therapist, but also a total human being with spirituality, passion, and excitement. I admired his freedom of spirit and wisdom and related this to my work with mothers and infants, being myself unafraid to approach the aliveness, and indeed the closeness, to death where motherhood and infancy intersect. He gave a new freedom and dimension to the analysis I experienced with my "good-enough" analyst and my analytic supervisor of many years, both of whom were no longer available to me in my external world.

Eigen's thinking touches your mind, soul, and heart with an immediacy of aliveness. He experiences and shares a passionate quest to find meaning, always accepting the possibility of multiple meanings. You get the sense that Eigen "has to" write, not for the sake of writing, but, rather, for the sake of communicating thoughts. He is never afraid of being and living fully in the moment. His enthusiasm for life has made me unashamed of my own capacity for excitement and the celebration of a creativity that rejoiced in possibilities. In the same way that Eigen encouraged original thought, I was helping Aboriginal mothers to develop their own ways of thinking, to act according to their own intuition, and to know the depths of their own spirituality.

The depressed mother is unable to access the "area of faith"

Eigen's work on faith and catastrophe provided me with a particularly useful way to formulate a framework around what might be happening for the depressed mother. From this, I could identify a difference between Klein and Bion. I began to feel that while both Klein and Winnicott invested the arrival at the depressive position with a kind of "moral" goodness—a sense that the value of paranoia was ignored or passed over—Bion saw the paranoid and the depressive positions as mutually dependent; he understood the act of daring to enter catastrophe, to disintegrate, and to break apart, as the psychic event that gives birth to new thinking. From this I proposed:

> Bion sees it as an innate part of the self's rhythm to fall apart and to come together again. Out of this perception I conceive that the problem of the depressed mother is that she has no faith that if she falls apart she will come together again, indeed she has proof in her past of being unheld and of not coming together. She is frozen in terror and dares not go into catastrophe, so there is no resolution of that catastrophe, no arrival at her own identity. (Tracey, 2000b, p. 187)

There is no capacity for the mother to come in and out of togetherness and separation; she is left at the mercy of raw, unprocessed emotions, which Bion (1963) describes as *beta elements*, "a mixed state in which the patient is persecuted by feelings of depression and depressed by feelings of persecution" (p. 39). This, says Bion, all points to catastrophe.

I further suggested that, possibly during her own infancy, the "holder of the faith", her own mother, had failed her and failed to hold her through catastrophe. This is not difficult to understand within the context of the history of the Aboriginals, who, through colonialism, were stripped of their land, culture, spirituality, community, and family, and sometimes subjugated as far as death. As a consequence, this catastrophe, being too much to tolerate, would have caused dissociation and an emotional deadness in the mother. I discovered that the dynamic between faith and catastrophe was, therefore, itself deadened and stultified. The depressed mother dares not risk madness and therefore cannot reach sanity. She has not traversed the psychic space through loss of faith to a place where true faith can emerge to reside from within. Yet, it is in this important place that faith and catastrophe meet and self is born. Risking unknowing allows for knowing to occur. This hypothesis corresponds with Tustin's work on psychological birth and psychological catastrophe. She writes of a premature rupturing of the "at-oneness" of mother and infant, owing to the mother's failure to be fully there for the infant (Tustin, 1981).

Eigen stresses that, until we are psychically alive, we cannot allow or know the terror of annihilation, and yet the central core of being alive has to do with surviving that terror:

> Beginning becomes like making a massive effort to pass through a force field, an anti-life field, where the "big bang" that destroys all is also the big bang out of which life is born. Hopefully the result is the triumph of Freud's *eros* over *thanatos*. (Eigen & Tracey, 1995–2005)

Unfortunately, this is not necessarily the case. Many Aboriginal mothers, suffering the trauma of their previous generations, do not have a good outcome. Crippled by their own infancy and often by the loss of meaning for a mother who has lost meaning for herself, they are unable to give meaning to their infants. And it is this "giving of meaning" that is integral to attachment and bonding with their infants.

The nameless dread of catastrophe

As Eigen writes, "For Bion there is something terrifying in the very birth of self and the latter's inextricable tie to oblivion that is part of it and that it is part of" (Eigen, 1995). It is this sense of catastrophe that links aspects of the personality. For Eigen, cataclysm is a formative part of our being. He argues that the "first thoughts were non-thoughts" (1993, p. 216), and "[T]hey are catastrophic hallucinatory bits and pieces which seem to function chaotically, that is without reference to one another" (1993, p. 221). Eigen also refers to Bion's remarks on the resulting "feelings of depression–persecution and guilt and therefore aspects of the personality linked by a sense of catastrophe" (Bion, 1963, p. 214). In optimal growth, this dispersed state culminates in the emergence of genuine coherence. The transmuting of such primordial emotions to emotions that can be thought about and thought through (*alpha elements*) heralds the advent and the evolution of self (see Eigen, 1993, pp. 114–119).

Eigen's central thinking focuses on the nameless dread of catastrophe. He writes,

> The nameless sense of catastrophe Bion points to moves between nothingness–somethingness–everythingness. It threatens to hurl the personality into an unimaginable abyss beyond oblivion, a horrific spacelessness in which there is no direction or valence other than horror itself. It fuses chaos and nothingness, scattered noise and blankness. This happens because the personality is in the process of disintegrating, experiencing and representing its disintegration, representing the disintegration of representations, and undoing itself and its representational capacity as far as inhumanely (yet all too humanly) possible.
>
> Yet one wonders if the self is ever fully at one with its sense of catastrophe. (Eigen, 1986, p. 119)

Eigen and the significance of early work with mothers and infants

Over fifty-four years ago, I had the opportunity to work with mothers "in trouble": I was aware of their being unable to hold on in the catastrophe until it was converted into a tolerable living experience, but it was Eigen who gave this added articulation and meaning for me as I moved to working with Aboriginal mothers and their infants. This was in our program at Gunawirra House in Redfern, Sydney, which became our center for pregnant and young Aboriginal mothers, and is where we still work today. While I see some of the mothers in individual therapy, my colleague, Cate Osborn, leads groups for the mothers and infants.

Initially, we were challenged by the fact that the work we were doing was not always considered to be "pure psychoanalysis"; we were seen almost as second-class citizens. Additionally, that it earned us almost nothing meant that it was not financially viable. Even our colleagues, while giving lip service to the needs of greatly disadvantaged people, found the task of actually engaging with them not inviting. By working with a disadvantaged, subjugated people we had somehow become identified with a lower level of competence. Eigen saw this differently and encouraged our efforts at every turn. Later, his encouragement was formalized in supervision by Skype with Jeff Eaton, who had been part of the New York Michael Eigen online group, which extended to many other cities in the USA as well as to South Africa and parts of Australia.

As time progressed at Gunawirra, we began to realize that we were far more than an early intervention service for Aboriginal mothers and infants. The support of Louise Gyler, a Sydney psychoanalyst, was particularly valuable at this time. Recalling the words of my colleague, Cate Osborn, "We recognized that the weight of generations of privation and trauma bears heavily on the hearts and minds of many of these women, in ways that cannot always be known to them" (2012). We saw how the pleasant, warm, and inviting surroundings; the non-judgmental behavior of the workers; our encouragement of the mothers to be fully in charge of their infants; and our focus on supporting the adult, "good" mother in them led to a neutralizing of a paranoid persecutory state—the dread of losing their children to a hostile authoritative entity with which they had no identification.

The ongoing Gunawirra Young Mothers Project has been an attempt to engage with, support, and hold mothers through the first five years of their children's lives, and to neutralize the persecutory aspects of the external world while they deal with the persecutory aspects of the inner-world chaos that is developmentally normal for the time of pregnancy and birth. We realized that this "time of exquisite vulnerability and opportunity for both mother and baby" (Osborn,

2012) was a time when we could use real life to create a situation of love, warmth, and care, and a womb-like supporting environment for a devastated people.

We have never stopped being surprised at how often our predictions of hopelessness were inaccurate and how it was indeed possible to overcome so many of the problems that mother and infant faced. This was in part the extraordinary motivation of mother and infant to get it right for each other.

The Kirra sessions

My first memory of Kirra is of a woman sitting without saying a word and without any expression on her face, an "unheld" baby lying unsupported across her knee. My sense was that both the mother and the infant were moribund. The specialist nurse from the maternity hospital made the referral. She was concerned about the fact that, despite nothing physical showing up on examination, the baby had been losing weight since birth and was not thriving. Cate, our group therapist said, "I am really worried about Kirra's baby. The way she holds her baby, her own vagueness, is quite distressing to observe." My own thoughts were: "How do I work with someone like this? She does not, maybe cannot, even speak."

In the next session, although identical to the previous "non-session", I became aware of just how much Kirra understood about boundaries, confidentiality, and of a special time and space that was hers. I also explained that, while it was the role of the early childhood nurse to take care of the baby, my role was to care for her. The next few sessions were painful for me. Nothing happened. *Nothing*. This was made worse by our anxiety as the baby's weight further decreased. I hung in there, despite being aware of an area of no faith within myself. Then a strange misadventure opened a door. One day, Kirra was forced to take a taxi to the centre when the usual volunteer driver was unable to pick her up. When she arrived, I found her on the front veranda smoking compulsively. She was nervous and shaking visibly. "I nearly didn't get here," she told me. Neither she nor the driver had known the address of the centre. "I was in the cab going somewhere but I had no idea where I was going and neither did he," she said. She then sat down and feverishly put her baby to her breast as if to comfort her baby and herself at the same time. She fed the infant for the whole session. She looked at me unremittingly, her eyes transfixed on my face, digesting me.

What strange event had taken place? Nearly losing me had "found" me? Over the next few sessions Kirra told me about how she had smoked "yandi" (marijuana) and consumed alcohol every day from the age of twelve, and how she had stopped as soon as she found out that she was pregnant. She looked across at me with a steady, unmoving gaze and a smile that didn't leave her face. It felt very much as a mother feels with an infant whose eyes are transfixed on her while feeding from her breast. Her infant's head was fully buried in her breast as she fed him throughout each session. Later, our group worker was to say to me, "She adores you!" While the force of the emotion did not faze me, I was aware of the burden of being loved that intensely. My colleague, Jeff Eaton, described this as a "raw and primitive state of absolute emotion which takes some strength to allow and accept" (2011).

Weeks later, Kirra told me that, every day when she was a baby, her father would rock her on his knee while sitting on a chair on veranda of their home—the same house where she later lived with her mother after pregnancy. Her father committed suicide when she was only six months old, using the tree still standing in the back yard. Had she found in me her father, the love object of her infancy; had his loss been awakened by the birth of her baby; had it opened up a psychotic, autistic core? "I've got this big round thing inside me I can't touch," she told me. "If I do, I might puncture it and it will blow me to smithereens." The baby half awakened. She picked her up and held her very close. The baby fell asleep again. I felt unbelievable grief. I had to feel the pain, hold it, and then give it back to her in small, well-timed doses; I had to make sure that I did not blow her up.

The bough breaks, the cradle falls—catastrophe. Does the mother's love protect from this crash? In primary maternal preoccupation, we think about the mother's love as protecting the infant not only from the dangers without (cold, hunger, and illness), but also from the dangers within: her own hate, anger, murderous feelings, and rage at the loss of the baby from her womb, and at the demands the baby makes on her. Her love forgives the baby for being separate, for being, but her love also protects the baby from internal overflowing emotions, linked with a fear of death and annihilation. Is this what Eigen was trying to help me understand? How, if external catastrophe and trauma have been too much to suffer, can a mother go through this journey with her infant? This is the central question.

There is a massive strength in the drive for life and health, both in the mother–infant couple before the baby is born and in the infant to find that person whom he or she will love with all his or her heart, soul, mind, and strength. From this comes the survival of what I call "the catastrophe in becoming." In my work, I am touched by the incredible effort mothers go through to bond with their babies and the incredible effort babies go through to gain their mother's attachment. Such attachment protects from the terror of death. When the mother and infant cannot negotiate dread, cannot enter into or face it, then, paradoxically, they cannot leave it. We knew an important change had occurred since the taxi drive and the loss of direction and terror of not finding me. We knew this had awakened the loss of her father as the love object womb of her infancy. What we did not expect was the incredible changes that such a re-experiencing of terror would bring to her baby's health.

Kirra's baby's weight went up markedly for the first time since birth. The scales and the weight chart were evidence. The graph went up in a straight line; the baby never lost weight again. In response to this, the nurse looked at me strangely and asked, "What did you do? That baby is alive now and so is her mother." NSW Department of Community Services (DOCS) recently discharged her. She now has a home of her own and Rhea continues to thrive. Mother and Rhea, now a pre-schooler, are still in our group and still in therapy.

Premature escape from the psychotic core: Eigen and the relevance of "being there"

From my experience with Kirra and Rhea, I began to think about how central the mother's faith is to life itself. Without someone holding the faith, one wonders how anyone ever comes into being. This is largely an unconscious process: while it is unspoken and often even unknown to the mother, it is still a faith that life itself is worth having and experiencing, however much risk there is of pain or damage. Mothers must be prepared to risk harm, damage, and even death themselves in order to bring forth new life. Without this capacity, how does any pregnancy even hold, given that there are always these risks?

Eigen sees escape into non-existence as part of a defence. Personal existence is rejected; the person makes an attempt to project out everything that could be personal. Existentialist theory allows us to understand this defence against being; existing means making an attempt to counter a personal tendency toward non-existence. Alluding to Winnicott's (1971) "going on being", Eigen tells us that for the baby "it is the projective world that is 'continuously' destroyed at the same time that the real is 'continuously' born and vice versa, and both of these happenings are necessary for the real as such to be experienced" (Eigen, 1993, p. 115).

Into the garden of good and evil

So many of our Aboriginal mothers like Kirra had suffered from loss, an absence, which our therapeutic presence attempted to counter. It is here that I now come to the center of Eigen's contribution to my thinking. It was the understanding that there is no pure good or pure evil—only people trying to divide them. This insight provided years of contemplation for me, the realization that nothing is pure in itself, and that the easy road of defining good or bad, nourishing or toxic, loving or hateful, simply does not exist. As Eigen notes,

> Emotional nourishment and poisons can be so interwoven that it is difficult, if not impossible, to tell the difference between them. The problem can be so extreme that nourishment one needs to support life is toxic or, worse, one learns to extract what nourishment one can from poisons at hand. (Eigen, 1999, p. xiii)

Bion argues that "[t]he patient feels the pain of an absence of fulfilment of his desires. The absent fulfilment is felt as a 'no-thing'." He adds, "'Non-existence' immediately becomes an object that is immensely hostile and filled with murderous envy towards the quality or function of existence wherever it is to be found" (Bion, 1977, pp. 19–20). For a people who lost their land, their families through the children being stolen and given to white families and institutions, their culture, which was replaced with our so-called superior one, their loss and the meaning of loss was central to all our thinking.

Suffering the suffering: Good Friday–Easter Saturday–Easter Sunday

Good Friday is so much about loss. Easter is about resurrection. They are linked in my mind, with the baby losing the safe place, the warm holding presence of the father, and how in a resurrected state she found him again through me. I began to ask myself and search about this day in between—Easter Saturday.

This now brings me to the center of this chapter. Attempting to make sense of suffering, of total loss in death, I struggled for some time with the concept of Holy Saturday as expressed in the Liturgical Calendar from the Middle Ages down to the present day. Jesus died on Good Friday, but on Holy Saturday he descended into hell, conquered death, and, as a result, rose triumphant. Man's sins were forgiven by this act. The actually of this is not the issue here, for this there is no answer. What is the value, the meaning of an event where—as expressed annually in every church service in the Middle Ages—the altar was stripped, denuded, the tabernacle emptied; no presence! This continues in Christian liturgy to the present day.

I wrote to Eigen, explaining that for me the revelation of Holy Saturday was that at the point of greatest loss—death, abnegation, impotence—Jesus was at his most powerful, triumphing over death. The experience of total loss is at the centre of all our analytic work. Did man have to die to his own personality structure, and face the dark night of the soul, enter the arena of death, before life could be born again from within him? Eigen responded,

> Jesus' suffering is a distillation of our soul's agony. Jesus goes through absolutely, fully, perfectly, what we go through partially. We tend to abort what Jesus goes through fully. Ingrained limits, constrictions, strangulated areas, we pull back, we short-circuit; we make our suffering less than optimal. Still there are times when we do better, when we dare to suffer our own agony, and at that point something opens, changes, and transposes. The story of Job can be seen in this light. The loss of everything leaves agonized suffering with nothing but the God point remaining. Then a new beginning occurs in our psyche, in new life expressing emotional contraction and expansion, the awesome dramas transcribed in the background of our being involving momentous changes of states, like emotional feeling and emptying into boundless pain and joy. Religion is not just another dimension of our

> life; it is a different way of living. Absolute guilt blows a massive hole in reality and opens reality, and Jesus allows us to participate in a realm of total experience, inviting us to go through fully what we at best do partially. (Eigen, 2001)

What is psychotherapy but the process of freeing one from one's own internal shackles, shackles that prevent a person from being who he or she truly is? Analysis helps one see suffering no longer as part of life, but as at the very center of living. Holy Saturday, or our own area of deconstruction that it represents, creates the important link between suffering, death, and mourning—the no-thing space in which we wait for a new beginning

It is release in the therapist, through the surrendering of his or her own memories and desires, that creates an interactive event between therapist and patient which allows release in the patient. The therapist must have the capacity to allow this space for the patient to enter, and the patient needs to be receptive to receiving, emotionally and psychically, the therapist's interpretations. It is the surrendering of defenses that takes the patient into a space where new growth can occur.

What, then, is the task of the "good-enough" therapist in this? The task of the good-enough therapist is to help us surrender in order to be able to return to a space where, as a result of containment, we can bear the risk of losing all faith, hope, and love in the trust that these will be born anew. The therapist's task is to "release" and allow the regression to total breakdown to occur so that we may reach a place where, in Eckhart's (2001) analogy, we are psychically both virgin and wife: the virgin making herself open and available to the new experience; the wife allowing the nurturing, containing, and holding of fruitfulness until there is a pregnancy, a new psychic beginning. This requires daring to move from sanity to insanity and from insanity to sanity. "Madness" is where all creativity can occur. I am not using the words "insanity" and "madness" here in the sense of psychotic, for the psychotic cannot allow disintegration, and therefore cannot have hope for the new birth that occurs only in the absolute depths of chaos and catastrophe. The capacity to arrive in that place is as relevant today as it was in the fourteenth century, where it was central to the teachings of monks; it is certainly at the center of Buddhism and almost every other spiritual tradition.

Looking at this, I was tempted, then, to think about what might effect arriving at this internal space and I was helped greatly in this by Eigen's idea of the "kernel of psychosis," as outlined in his book *The Psychotic Core* (1986). We all hallucinate in our dreams, just as we hallucinate in our daydreams. What I took from this is that all of life contains hallucination—we dream, we daydream. Similarly, every psychosis is characterized by hallucination, but these hallucinations appear not as instances of inward dreaming, but as things in themselves. Speaking of mindlessness, Eigen writes, "Among our earliest defenses is our ability to go blank, even to become stuporous. The mind tries to anesthetize itself in the face of emotional pain" (Eigen, 1986, p. 32).

Inia: The mind struggling to find any sort of relationship

I include the psychotherapy of Inia here because for weeks I did nothing but *be there* for her. Two very strange phenomena disappeared as a result of this. One was her severe splitting. Right in the middle of a session, without any warning, Inia would stop crying and suddenly burst out laughing and make "goo" noises at her baby. The other phenomenon, which disturbed me considerably, was the way she "used" her baby sexually, kissing him on the mouth and involving both the baby and me in a kind of sexual talk, trying to entice me to hold him and flirt with him in a way that was perverse. I avoided this, reminding her that the baby was hers and that I would not ever nurse the baby of a mother in my care. At first she did not understand; she said to me as she left, bewildered, "You are weird!" But I did nothing but be there, not buying into her changes in mood or into her attempts to seduce me with the baby. While both behaviors eventually ceased, what they left behind was unbelievable pain for Inia. At first, this suffering expressed itself in a rage that poured out in sentences directed at me about "you white fellas," this despite the fact that I am many shades darker than she.

Eigen writes:

> [The patient] feared that she was poisoning her baby, and, less consciously, that her baby would poison her. At times she felt poisoned–poisonous within. It is probable that such feelings represented aspects of physical processes that are part of gestation, birth, and development. Normal processes often have toxic elements.

> However, careful exploration suggested dread of poisonous insides was, also, associated with congealed hate. (Eigen, 1999, p. 47)

Our sessions seemed to race by. Inia articulated this same sense to me, complaining, "We just start to get somewhere and it is time to go." I surprised myself at the clarity of my interpretation of this. I replied, "I am so sorry that you are feeling so frustrated by this very real situation, outside, of not being able to move, but it must be worse to feel that such a frustration is also inside you. Your rage is that you cannot move." Her expression of rage then became the whimper of an infant cry. She was completely aware of the meaning of what I had said. Her ongoing response to this moment of realization was painful to observe.

In a further session, she told me, "All my life I have struggled not to harm my children in the way my father harmed me, but I am becoming more aware each day how much I am like him, the person I wished never to be like. Sometimes it feels like I *am* him and I hate myself. Some people might not know they are poisonous to their children. I know because I know how poisonous he was to me."

I became aware of a change in the atmosphere of our sessions;

> The baby is on a blanket on the floor. He gurgles and goos and the mother is enjoying him as a baby. Silence. More silence. We watch the baby together ... she speaks to the baby and gently moves him back on the carpet. I realize how different this is from the way she used to "throw" him around so roughly. She still tries to make him walk at seven months and I am distressed by this; I feel it would be disturbing and intrusive to comment.
>
> We create the space between us.
>
> The baby plays on the floor. Her hate and rage and suffering in her relationship with me frees him, and there is now also love, a love of me. I cannot help but think that the intensity of the love I receive from such patients is no compliment; its intensity is enormous and the pain in it has to be tolerated. It is sensual, but it is also spiritual.

Sandra's journey

I would now like to share the case of Sandra, because it so clearly shows how the defenses work to protect the individual from suffering; how when these defenses break down the personality must deal with experiencing and digesting that suffering; and how a whole new self is possible as a result. I also want to present Sandra's journey with me at this time because she offers such a telling example of the way psychoanalytically informed group work and individual psychotherapy can come together to create a situation where real growth can take place.

Sometimes, the actual trauma of birth can disturb the personality so greatly as to put in place a completely different beginning, one that may not otherwise have occurred. Sandra gave me the feeling of someone who, from birth, was shaped into something to satisfy the mother, rather than something to be satisfied by the mother. Sandra was overly compliant, something I understood to be part of a false self, as the only way in which she could hold on to her mother and survive. Interestingly, she told me that her mother had experienced exactly the same situation with her own mother. Both Sandra's parents were teachers. Her father was well known and respected, but a heavy drinker. Her mother put up with his drinking and suffered it without complaint.

Sandra was one of a new generation of young Aboriginal women who had been tutored and supported to work as professionals in the health system, and she was very capable and proud of her work. She felt effective and valued by all on the rehabilitation ward where she worked. She was part of our mothers' group at Gunawirra House and had one day accidentally entered my office seeking a quiet place for her baby, who was obviously disturbed by the incredible chaos and noise from the mothers, infants, and toddlers who filled the building. She made an appointment for a session with me for the following Friday and saw me weekly thereafter for a year. She was always on time.

Sandra had been essentially emotionally absent for the first three months of her baby's life and was riddled with guilt over this. Session after session we would cope with her intense crying over what a bad mother she thought she was and her confusion at having a baby whom she experiences as having failed her and whom she felt she had failed. Two traumatic events had occurred around the time of her baby's birth. Sandra was diagnosed with pre-eclampsia, a serious condition that can result in the death of both mother and infant. Instead of improving after the birth of her baby, as pre-eclampsia often does,

Sandra's condition remained the same for two or three months. The medication used to treat it anaesthetized her so completely that she could not remember doing anything for her baby during that time. A further serious event occurred just after the baby's birth. It had been an all-night labour and shortly afterwards both she and her husband fell asleep. When they woke up, they looked across to find the baby "blue". They rang the bell for the nurse; the whole place went into action to prevent what could have been a death, a catastrophe. Sandra was full of guilt over this; she had failed as a mother in every way possible.

Speaking of her work and the baby, she said,

> "Yes, I had it so good on the ward with everyone and everything—my work was so valued. There were rules and you kept to them and knew your job; here there is nothing that is predictable. Now it is difficult. I feel unsure and totally unreliable. The baby has really taken my freedom from me and my sense of being in control, too. I've been thinking all last week about what you said and my husband really understood it too, once I explained to him that I had postnatal depression. She had the cord around her throat so that every time I had a contraction there was a danger of something going wrong, and she was a breach birth and they were saying don't push because they were worried about the cord and I was just so ready to have her and then I realised her heart rate was being affected."

Together we realized just how much these events had affected Sandra and how every time she went to free herself or the baby she became aware of how death had become confused with giving life. She said to me, "I kept thinking this can't be happening to me! You told me last time I should continue to come, but there is such a stigma around mental health." However, it was her attaching to me that made it safe for her and her infant begin to play with the idea of holding on and letting go. I am still bemused by those sessions in which the infant played with a teething ring around her finger—letting go of it and allowing the mother to retrieve it—while the mother complained about how imprisoned and enslaved she felt at the infant's refusal to let go. The baby took her own time, and I was stunned on the day that she first noticed me as a person in the room. Another person! At that time I also began to be a real person for Sandra, not just a presence.

Over the months of therapy with Sandra, I became aware of the terror felt by this mother and infant. Reports came from the mother herself and from Cate, the leader in the group situation. Cate reported, as did other professionals working with the group, that the infant's distress at being left by the mother to go to the toilet was like an agonized cry of total loss, with the mother trapped with her own terror and her own desire not to be enslaved. But it has changed over time, slowly but surely, with no great skill from me and no great interpretation, only my presence and my allowing of the transference, both positive and negative.

One day, Sandra was able to say to me, "Yesterday morning Rosy slept with no trouble. In the last two nights she has slept right through. It is mixed up somehow with coming to see you. I said to Ned, 'It is something to do with seeing Norma'; like she's all right when I don't worry. I don't suppose it will last but to have a full night's sleep has been wonderful." I was aware of how so much of what I knew about the fear of falling asleep and the infant's waking in the night was linked with loss and separation.

One can write books on this area and they can even be bestsellers, as, indeed, *Parents of Premature Infants* (Tracey, 2000a) was, but it took the actual work to understand being able to sleep and stay asleep as a fear of attachment, loss, and separation. What we have now is the narrative of a mother and infant, an obviously intelligent infant, who is happy as long as mother is there at first. But now, with time and a lot of pain, both mother and infant are able to let go of each other without the fear that there will be no coming together again. Eigen described this best:

> Distinction–union tendencies enter into many kinds of relationships with each other, antagonistic, symbiotic, parasitic, nullifying, disconnecting, nourishing. We can always ask what one or other of these tendencies is doing at any moment, since both are always co-present. . . . To be permeable and distinct, connected and separate, in union yet distinct, is part of our plasticity and persistence, part of the mystery, difficulty, and creative challenge of our nature. (Eigen, 2011, p. 15)

In summary, this knowing of Michael Eigen over twenty-five years has been a long and intense journey of psychic learning. His invaluable private correspondence, his books, his and other colleagues' discussions in his chatrooms, brought joy and enlightenment for many years. It was not always joyful; sometimes Michael Eigen himself was suffering and able to share it, and sometimes I felt his presence took me to the center of my own psychic abyss. His unflagging support over many years made it possible to present this chapter, of psyche illumination created by his thinking and his encouragement of my own. It was a journey that united my intellectual understanding with a deep spiritual awareness, not being afraid of either as an integral part of analytic thinking.

Acknowledgment

I wish to acknowledge the workers of Gunawirra. Most important to me has been the mentoring and unending support of Michael Eigen.

References

Bion, W. R. (1963). *Elements of Psychoanalysis*. London: Heinemann [reprinted London: Karnac, 1994].

Bion, W. R. (1977). *Seven Servants: Four Works by Wilfred R. Bion*. New York: Jason Aronson.

Eaton, J. (2011). Personal communication.

Eckhart, M. (2001). *Wandering Joy: Meister Eckhart's Mystical Philosophy*, R. Schürmann (Trans.). Great Barrington, MA: Lindisfarne Books.

Eigen, M. (1981). The area of faith in Winnicott, Lacan, and Bion. *International Journal of Psychoanalysis, 6*(4): 413–433 [reprinted in Eigen, M. (1993). *The Electrified Tightrope*: pp. 109–139. Karnac, 2004.

Eigen, M. (1986). *The Psychotic Core*. London: Karnac, 2004.

Eigen, M. (1993). *The Electrified Tightrope*, A. Phillips (Ed.). Northvale, NJ: Jason Aronson [reprinted London: Karnac, 2004].

Eigen, M. (1995). Personal correspondence.

Eigen, M. (1999). *Toxic Nourishment*. London: Karnac.

Eigen, M. (2001). Personal correspondence.

Eigen, M. (2011). *Contact with the Depths*. London: Karnac.

Eigen, M., & Tracey, N. (1995–2005). Private correspondence. Unpublished.

Osborn, C. (2012). Personal communication.

Tracey, N. (Ed.) (2000a). *Parents of Premature Infants: Their Emotional World*. London: Whurr.

Tracey, N. (2000b). Thinking about and working with depressed mothers in the early months of their infant's life. *Journal of Child Psychotherapy, 26*: 183–207.

Tustin, F. (1981). *Autistic States in Children*. London: Routledge.

Winnicott, D. W. (1971). *Playing and Reality*. New York: Basic Books.

CHAPTER THIRTEEN

Studying Bion's work in Mike Eigen's ongoing weekly seminar

Lawrence Wetzler

> "As Gregor Samsa awoke one morning from uneasy dreams he found himself transformed in his bed into a gigantic insect' . . . His numerous legs, which were pitifully thin compared to the rest of his bulk, waved helplessly before his eyes"
>
> (Kafka, 1915, p. 7)

I studied Bion with Michael Eigen for sixteen years and never ceased to experience a sense of wonder, reverence, and awe in response to what he does with the material. I found myself moving into a meditative state during much of our time together and frequently left the seminar feeling as if I had been immersed in a state of prayer. There is a truth beyond words that was evoked for me as I witnessed and participated in these seminars. I experienced Eigen deeply immersing himself in Bion's work, responding to rays of meaning that can so easily be overlooked when one merely reads the text by oneself. It seemed as if Michael Eigen was making love to the text, savouring each of the words on the page, and opening up fields of experience which Bion himself may not have known so intimately.

Eigen stays close to the text, reading a phrase, or perhaps an entire sentence, and then opening up Bion's words with his own clinical and uniquely personal associations, inviting members of our group to respond with their own thoughts evoked by a given passage and/or the fertile associations he may have shared. He might return to the same passage week after week, with further thoughts on what Bion is getting at, expanding meanings intrinsic to the text and the montage of associations evoked, musically repeating a word, a phrase, a given passage, and cross-referencing it with other texts. The experience is rich, dynamic, and moving.

Our focused discussions of the ongoing seminar were elaborated upon by occasional emails, which Eigen sent out to the entire group, communications in which he shared further thoughts on an issue that we had been exploring together. Group members were free to respond to his thinking or contribute their own thoughts to the issues being explored in seminar or via these e-mails. Thus, over and above our weekly meetings themselves, the seminars carried over into our everyday lives.

Having also studied the work of Lacan and Winnicott in Eigen's seminars, I am particularly fascinated with the ways in which the thinking of Bion interfaces with that of Lacan and Winnicott. By bringing together his insights into Kabbalah, Buddhism, and other psychoanalytic thinkers, Eigen offers an incredibly nourishing experience for those who want to journey into the infinity of emotional experience that Bion's work provides. To paraphrase Eigen, there is no exit from oneself, the challenge being entrance into oneself and one's emotional life, partnering with and growing the capacity to work with one's emotional reality. So much of Bion's work addresses this very question.

One of the central issues which Bion addresses is the primacy of emotional experience and how emotional experience itself is a problem, insofar as we have not developed the equipment to metabolize, digest, and process our emotional life. Throughout his teaching, Eigen has come back to the challenge which each of us is faced with when the demands made on us by our emotional life seem more than we can deal with. Echoing the work of Bion, he notes that overwhelming emotional experience can either deform our psyches or stimulate the evolution of the equipment needed to partner with the latter. While he acknowledges Bion's thoughts on the ubiquity of lying to ourselves and to one another, as well as the ways in which cognition can close off as well as open up emotional experience, Eigen also speaks of Bion's notion of faith (F) in the face of catastrophe. Even with our fundamental insufficiency in the face of emotional life, there are "unknown intimacies" which emerge when we allow ourselves to enter into those unknown and unknowing regions of experience. He has noted how, in these moments, the wound that never heals meets the fire that never goes out.

Eigen speaks of psychoanalysis as an evolutionary adventure. He will contrast the ways in which humanity is "aching to evolve" with the ways in which the mind so easily destroys itself in order not to experience the pain of reality, the latter transpiring on a personal, social, and political level. My linking his thoughts on Bion to the ways in which Winnicott and Lacan address similar issues, though from radically different vantage points, has been a transformative and humbling adventure for me, stimulating my own evolution both personally and professionally. ". . . the fundamental reality is "infinity", the unknown, the situation for which there is no language—not even that borrowed from the artist or the religious—which gets anywhere near to describing it" (Bion, 1992, p. 372).

Meditating on these words, I find myself entering into a different universe, opening on to myriad inviting possibilities of thinking and being. Eigen has led us through the wordless landscapes painted by Bion, Lacan, and Winnicott in which language, inasmuch as it allows us to communicate with one another, also distorts, forecloses, and limits our experiences of ourselves and one another. How to find words for an emotional experience? Eigen speaks of words as afterthoughts, after experience, after-births when it comes to honoring one's emotional reality.

In fact, Eigen has described our lives as an extended birth. Echoing Bion, he has noted that we are all permanently embryonic. We remain in this neonatal state, insofar as our lives are also an extended aborted experience. One's psyche destroys itself in order to deal with itself, toning down the too-muchness of an experience in order to respond to emotional impacts. Rather than collapse in the face of a painful reality, one destroys one's mind.

At the same time that something in us wants to know, something in us cannot bear knowing. There is something of human nature that is hostile to knowledge: to knowing ourselves, as well as knowing one another. We deaden ourselves in order to continue living, a theme Freud addressed in *Beyond the Pleasure Principle* (1920g). This is a theme throughout the book where Freud contrasts Thanatos and Eros. Eigen has noted how "one never recovers from being human."

Bion has written on how we create narratives, story lines, in order to contain emotional experience, in order to give a sense of coherence and unity to an experience for which we may not have words. We filter our emotional experiences through the stories we tell to ourselves and to one another. How easily we get caught up in the meaning of our narratives and lose touch with the original emotional experience which may have given birth to these narratives! These narratives can both free us and enslave us.

Truth is something we do not know and may never know. Bion notes how all language is hypothetical, insofar as it brings a sense of coherence to what seemed confusing. However, whatever meaning we may find in our emotional experience is at best partial, and may be only a sliver of something we may never be able to access. Lacan and Freud refer to this as *Das Ding*, a notion at the heart of so much philosophical thought.

Bion speaks of our emotional experience as "being a problem" for which there may be no solution, or in the face of which we may lack the equipment needed to digest the latter. We are called on to live our way into the questions which emotional experience raises, any answers merely opening up further questions. This is living without memory, desire, or understanding, living which protects emotional experience from any narratives we might automatically impose on the latter. As analysts, we are encouraged to be open to the unknown, "the void and formless infinite", to allow for the birth of emotional reality and to be present to "unknown intimacies".

We might thereby begin to appreciate the indeterminate emotion that otherwise gets so quickly interpreted away for its value as the mystery, the unknown, the not-yet, perhaps forever embryonic formless infinite. A place to live from then, thus live from, out of. Something at the heart of creativity and the creative impulse in each of us? For many years, I have puzzled over the following statement of Bion's in his book, *Transformations* (1965).

> The patient's dilemma insofar as he is trying to be co-operative, reparative and creative, lies in his having to choose between "sanity" which

> is powerful, destructive and devoted to exacerbation, on the one hand, and creativeness which is impotent and "insane" on the other. (p. 166)

Perhaps the choice at hand is a choice which all of us are grappling with at some level. Sanity, represented by "the powers that be", is initially described as destructive, devoting itself to exacerbation. Sanity knows precisely what is and what is not. Sanity avoids the unknown regions of experience: prescribing and proscribing what is and what is not, what can and cannot be received and expressed, foreclosing and limiting experience, and ultimately leading to a sense of bitterness and violence. By contrast, creativeness, which opens on to "the void and formless infinite" does not know, is impotent, is lacking, is without, and is experienced as "insane." For the person who wants to be creative, reparative, and cooperative, there is something impoverishing and destructive in choosing sanity. Choosing the path of creativity is a choice to live one's way into the unknown, experiencing one's "impotence" along the way, and venturing into regions of "insanity"—a place beyond the givens of everyday, taken-for-granted, consensually agreed upon reality. As Winnicott (1958, p. 145) has noted, ". . . we are poor indeed if we are only sane."

Towards the end of his writing on Schreber, Freud (1911c, p. 79) notes, "It remains for the future to decide whether there is more delusion in my theory than I should like to admit, or whether there is more truth in Schreber's delusion than other people are as yet prepared to believe." Eigen has repeatedly noted the richness of Schreber's imagery in his descriptions of a reality that remains wordless for most of us. He describes the therapeutic process as being an opportunity to be with one's wordless reality, to create the timeless spaciousness in which the too-muchness of an experience can find the quiescence needed to gestate on the way to being born. The challenge is to "partner" with this "void and formless infinite," rather than aborting what we cannot immediately fathom. Even words can evacuate what we would rather not know, our seeming rationality serving as just another way to deny catastrophic impacts.

Eigen has frequently returned to the words of Sir Arthur Eddington: "Something unknown is doing we do not know what." (Neither Michael Eigen nor I can locate the reference. I found the quote on the Internet.) By cultivating our capacity to live off balance and dwell with the unknown, he invites us to open ourselves to the unborn dimensions of our existence. He has pointed to a passage in Kabbalah where God contracts in order to make room for others. Perhaps we, too, are being called on to contract, to make room for the unknown in both ourselves and in those we encounter in our personal and professional lives, meeting the catastrophic with Faith, and sustaining contact with those uncanny intimations that remain wordless.

References

Bion, W. R. (1965). *Transformations.* London: Karnac

Bion, W. R. (1992). *Cogitations.* London: Karnac.

Freud, S. (1911c). *Psycho-analytic Notes on an Autobiographical Account of a Case of Paranoia. S. E., 12*: 3–82. London: Hogarth..

Freud, S. (1920g). *Beyond the Pleasure Principle. S. E., 18*: 7–64. London: Hogarth.

Kafka, F. (1915). The Metamorphosis. In: *The Complete Short Stories* (pp. 114–164). New York: Schocken Books.

Winnicott, D. W. (1958). Primitive emotional development. In: *Collected Papers: Through Paediatrics to Psycho-analysis* (pp. 145–156). London: Tavistock.

PART III

REVERIES

CHAPTER FOURTEEN

Michael Eigen's *Ecstasy* as/and poetry

Peter Anderson

"Everywhere I go, I find that a poet has been there before me"
(Caption attributed to Freud on a wall in the Freud Museum in Vienna)

"What does a poem want?" I like to ask my classes in poetry writing. The answer, which the students soon get to know well, is both simple and unforgettable: "Another poem."

In this chapter, I focus on Michael Eigen's *Ecstasy* (the first and perhaps the most brilliant work in his trilogy, *Ecstasy*, *Rage*, and *Lust*), aiming to respond to *Ecstasy*'s call for what it wants: more writing of its own kind, "a kind of psychoanalytic poetry" (2001, p. viii). With one proviso: I am not a psychologist; I am a writer. I write fiction, non-fiction, and poetry. I teach postcolonial literary studies and creative writing at a small liberal arts college in North Texas. Although located in America by force of circumstance, I am South African, not American, and my article will inevitably reflect the South African experience, including poetry that sprang from that experience, particularly under apartheid.

I take Eigen as the prime living poet of psychoanalysis. In this article, I hope to mirror the form of *Ecstasy* itself, using, like his own, an "'argument' [that] is less rationalistic and linear, more a moment to moment showing of creative and destructive forces at work" (p. vii). In short, I intend to reply in lyrical–dramatic–narrative–confessional form, poetry to poetry. The aim is to show an understanding of *Ecstasy* through responding to it, insofar as I can, on its own terms. I shall, too, to some extent, analyze Eigen in relation to the poet with whom he appears to have most affinity: William Blake.

In many ways, I believe Eigen in *Ecstasy*, as in other of his works, is attempting to restore to psychology a dimension suppressed by the scientistic ambitions of the academicized discipline, where the drastic attempt to reduce language to a vehicle for hard data makes of language itself nothing but an empty shell, good only to serve as a frame for the apparent objectivity of statistics. Where Freud could only grudgingly wonder at poetry as a form of psychological gnosis, Eigen understands that poetry—and, very possibly, therapy, too—has the function of revealing who we are. "Poetry is dusting off the true self," he suggests to a patient, a young poet, who responds, "Therapy, too?" (p. 34).

In *An Unknown Destiny: Terror, Psychotherapy, and Modern Initiation: Readings in Nietzsche, Heidegger, Steiner* (2008), Michael Gruber writes of "a linguistic experience where words are less data of information than containers of transformative energy that facilitate a concentration and expansion of consciousness to the point of an awakening of the sacred" (p. 47). Gruber wasn't—but could well have been—speaking of *Ecstasy*.

* * *

Two books: *The Psychotic Core* (1993), which first appeared in 1986, and *Ecstasy*, 2001. In the first, the argument outlined in the opening statement hinges on the possibility of "a psychotic kernel in every person" (p. 3). In the second, the opening sentence declares, "Ecstasy is the heart's center." The heart, the core. The ecstatic, the psychotic—are these then one and the same? Appalachian snake handlers wrapping rattlesnakes around their wrists, snatching mouthfuls of strychnine from Mason jars ranged beside the pulpit, and hollering, Jesus, Jesus, I love you, Jesus. Indonesian trance dancers piercing their cheeks, their tongues, their eyelids, with spikes, with daggers, and dancing in the grip of the god, dancing, spinning, but not bleeding. The young man, explosives packed, strapped all around his torso, who turns his face up to the sky, and makes his final, shattering cry that God is great.

* * *

"I'm OK," mutters Rowanne, "I'm OK. Just let me cut off my head." She rocks backward, eyes wide, pleading with terrible force: "Give me a knife. Please. If you are my friend—" I have hold of her hands, which, to my surprise, are limp to the point of total passivity, almost a sweet gentleness. I expected more of a struggle. A tall woman, strong (she likes to boast that she is a Valkyrie), she could, if she so chose, throw me off with a flick of her wrist. Helen, my wife, kneeling beside us on the floor, is distraught, perplexed. She does not know what to say or do. But suddenly, shaken by anger, she very nearly slaps her. "Stop it, Row. Stop it! Now. Right now. OK? You're not a crazy person, do you hear? You're not, and you know it. OK? You're not going to hurt yourself, not now, not ever. Too bad, but you're not. We won't let you, you hear?" (Strange how cruel and biting such words can sound when you are pinning someone down in the middle of the night, even though all you are doing is attempting to prevent her from hurting herself. The erotic element cannot be denied, either, only ignored.) Rowanne shakes her head, rolls it round, stares at us in turn. "Bad. I'm a bad girl. Evil. My head is full of the wrong ideas. They twist around inside, hurt me. Like thorns. They hurt Dieter, too. You see? It's wrong. I can't . . . Please, just let me cut myself. Here, I can start here, just above the eyebrows. Please. I have to. Give me a knife."

I tell her we don't have a knife. I tell her she doesn't really need one. Listen, I say, me, I have bad thoughts, too. And, you know what? Helen has, too, I say.

"Plenty," Helen puts in. "Plenty of bad thoughts. The worst."

"Please," moans Rowanne. "Please. Just let me cut off my head."

Two days before, Dieter, Rowanne's husband, asked us to help take care of her while he, exhausted after keeping virtually sleepless watch for weeks on end, escaped to a motel to rest. Out of respect for our friends' religious pacifism, Helen and I do little more than hold Rowanne down when the bizarre but life-threatening fixation that gets into her late at night (and only late at night) makes her beg for a knife. To our relief, our custody is over before long. Dieter returns one morning, and he and Rowanne decide to try what Helen cynically calls the "geographic solution." They will move, they say, and go to live in Cape Town, a thousand miles away. Helen tells them it is futile. After all, she points out, you can't leave yourself behind. True, agrees Dieter. Nevertheless, within a month, they leave for that most beautiful of cities; gradually but inevitably, we lose touch.

Years later, I meet Rowanne again. She and Dieter have divorced, she tells me. Also, she has left the religious community (the "cult," she calls it now) to which they used to belong. She is on medication, she says. On and off. More on than off, as things go. Hard core stuff, she says. It blows your mind. But, she adds, there are times when she just opts out.

"You mean . . .?" I say.

"I stop. Step over the edge."

"But why? What for?"

Her face goes tight, wary. For a moment, I fear she will not speak. Her hair, I see as she bends her head, is streaked with grey. It seems we are both growing old.

"You can't just go on and on like that," she remarks. "The drugs do nothing. All they do is set up a wall, a floor, between you and what you feel. Between you and yourself, in the end. Meanwhile, you know it's still there, deep down inside you, the blackness, the terror. You know it, but you can't get to it. It's the thing you fear most, but it's the thing you want most, too."

"But why?"

She narrows her eyes. Concentrates.

"It gives . . . everything . . . meaning." She smiles. "OK?"

I smile, too.

"OK." Then, perhaps because I once held her hands, I say, "I think of you as the woman with the crown of thorns inside your head."

She swirls the coffee round in her cup, tosses it back.

"If I were you," she says, "I wouldn't think."

* * *

Raw ecstasy of psychosis. Is God, too, then, mad? To William Blake, he is. The God of Creation—Urizen (Your Reason/Horizon) in the first of Blake's Prophetic books—himself precipitates the catastrophe of Creation by splitting away from the state of unity-in-multiplicity characteristic of the Eternals, and willfully plunging through the fires of his dark desire to emerge isolated, if self-aggrandizing, in a void of his own making:

> First I fought with the fire, consum'd
> Inwards, into a deep world within:
> A void immense, wild, dark, & deep,

> Where nothing was, Nature's wide womb,
> And self-balanc'd, stretch'd over the void,
> I alone, even I!
>
> (Blake, 1997, II: 5: 14–19)

Poised over his own emptiness, which he sees as external to himself, and objectifies as "Nature's wide womb," Urizen is about to impregnate himself and, thus, to ensure that all he brings forth, from the illimitable reaches of the astronomical universe to poor, gender-split humankind, will be as flawed as he is. In the beginning, therefore, is the Fall. Of God, not man.

As above, so below.

* * *

In *Ecstasy,* Eigen the psychoanalytic psalmist gives way to a burst of splendid optimism as he traces, following in the footsteps of Federn and Freud, evidence for an ideal, indeed a god-like ego, in ontogeny:

> The ego is the id's first love object, and the ego is its own ideal. What an amazing ego or I. Pumped up from the beginning. No wonder Paul Federn picked up on these Freudian threads and saw the early ego as a cosmic I, boundless. Streams of erotic energy feeding I-feeling, I-feeling feeling ideal. Is everything a comedown after this? The radiant I, pulsating, sun-like, ecstatic in its own existence. Freud tells us that the early I's boundaries are coextensive with all that is. One = All. (p. 7)

But, for Blake, "all that is" is already Urizenic. This does not mean a simple negation: One ≠ All. The point is, rather, that the One is a usurper, displacing the ineffable completeness of being, the confluence with eternity for which it is no substitute.

Everything is a comedown after this.

In the Urizenic world, the One is nothing but a mode of consolidation of power. So much is evident when Urizen wields "with strong hand the Book / Of eternal brass" he has written, decreeing

> Laws of peace, of love, of unity,
> Of pity, compassion, forgiveness.
> Let each chuse one habitation,
> His ancient infinite mansion.
> One command, one joy, one desire,

> One curse, one weight, one measure,
> One King, one God, one Law.
>
> (Blake, 1997, II: 5: 34–40)

"One", here, is pounded in damning repetitiveness. Also, the "Book," capitalized, can refer only to one book, while its "brass" could imply a brazen act, the act of a tyrant, an upstart, demonstrably bent upon reigning without end. While "Laws of peace, of love, of unity," and so on, may at a glance seem wonderful, a moment's reflection reveals them to be oppressive in the extreme. No one can love, pity, or forgive on the basis of heavy-handed authoritarian fiat; besides, there would be no need for any such good, kindly qualities if the world were not inevitably already a site of negativity, suffering, and cruelty.

Archetypally identical both with Yahweh and Enlightenment Reason (in fact, his name is derived from the latter), Urizen hurtles on, trapped in the whirlwind of his own (un)doing, the stupendous enormity of his vain attempt upon breaking from the Eternals to create a world in his own image without at the same time wreaking universal death and destruction. The epic of Urizen is mythic—that is to say, a poetic account of something that never actually did happen, but that always is happening. Historically, the case in point is the European Enlightenment. With its claim that the world can be explained without reference to God, the Enlightenment mythically replicates the schizoid split of the Beginning. Isolating itself in the interests of achieving dominance as the One Truth, Reason broke away, and succeeded in its aim, so that today, not only in the West but increasingly throughout the globe, scientific rationalism rules. Post-Enlightenment Reason, and the bounds formed by a strictly rational–materialist understanding of things, have thus become "your horizon." Meanwhile, as "your reason," the governing power of ego, Urizen arises within us, too.

> The Eternals said: "What is this? Death.
> Urizen is a clod of clay."
>
> (Blake, 1997, III: 11: 59–60)

We are all made of the same clay.

* * *

Immanuel Kant, the philosopher who proceeded to write *The Critique of Pure Reason* after waking, as he memorably put it, from his dogmatic slumbers, and gave to the Enlightenment its driving imperative, "Dare to think," once observed that great art

> induce[s] much thought, yet without the possibility of any definite thought whatever, that is *concept* being adequate to it, and which language, consequently, can never get quite on level terms with, or render completely intelligible. (quoted in Young, 2001, p. 44, original italics)

Urizen cannot comprehend poetry, but poetry can comprehend Urizen.

* * *

How to reconcile Blake and Eigen?

Where Eigen writes, as he does in *Ecstasy*, of the "divine-demonic," Blake, in *The First Book of Urizen*, writes, we could say, of the "demonic-divine."

Mirror images.

But for Blake, Urizen = Yahweh. While for Eigen, Yahweh ≠ Urizen.

Even so, Blake's Gothic Gnosticism, opposed as it is to Eigen's psychoanalytic Judaism, might be paralleled with Eigen's Kabbalistic postmodernism. Perhaps at a point beyond God and before the Beginning—A in Soph for Eigen, the Eternals for Blake—the two could connect. Or (and this may amount to the same thing) at a point both here and now, where theological superstructures are not yet an obstacle:

Eigen: I avow that the core of our existence is ecstasy. (2001, p. 92)

Blake: For every thing that lives is Holy. (Blake, 1975, p. 27)

Blake's strength of emphasis falls upon "lives": "For every thing that *lives* . . ." For Eigen, strength lies in the stance: "I avow . . ." where he iterates his central assertion. Yet both statements are themselves ecstatic.

The holy, said Heidegger, the holy is prior to the gods. And it is the task of poets in a destitute time (our own) to reveal, if not call into being, the holy.

Blake and Eigen: their task.

* * *

It is no great secret that during work on his masterpiece, *Being and Time* (1996), Martin Heidegger was in love with a young Jewish student of his, Hannah Arendt. At that time, too, he wrote some very beautiful love poems to her, which he enclosed in his letters. Under strain, not least because Heidegger was married, the relationship proved stormy, if intensely passionate: There can be little doubt that Hannah Arendt was his muse. Then came the cataclysm of Hitler's rise to power. Arendt, like so many others, was forced to flee, while Heidegger, for a brief period in the early 1930s, became infatuated with Nazism. He seemed to see in it the possibility of a truly revolutionary conservatism; his sense of destiny was fired, his intense nationalism reinforced. With the audacity to imagine a triumvirate of Hölderlin, Heidegger, and Hitler, he wished no less than to mediate between poetic genius and the will to power, intending to awaken in the messianic dictator so profound an insight into Being that political transformation would be assured of an intuitive rightness, and Germany attain a splendor of supremacy like that of ancient Greece, becoming an inspiration to the Western world across the millennia. At the height of his fervor, Heidegger had photographs taken of himself sitting around in a brown shirt. Moreover, as rector of the University of Freiburg from 1933 to 1934, he occasionally made speeches containing claims like: "The führer alone *is* the present and future German reality and its law ... Heil Hitler!" (www.searchquotes.com/quotation/112375/)

Of course, the Nazis themselves had no use for him. To their eyes he was no more than a posturing professor, a political clown. (Chaplin had not yet revealed who the real political clown was, but even Chaplin, as late as 1940, had no idea of the abyss of horror which was the Third Reich.) More importantly, however, by his own account, Heidegger's inner allegiance to the Nazi party was soon over. He resigned his rectorship in April 1934, taking care to let his more discerning students know the extent of his disaffection, while maintaining sufficient ambiguity in his lectures not to rouse the suspicion of the Nazis present. By 1935, however, in his *Introduction to Metaphysics* (2000), he was far more open in his criticism of Nazi militarism, totalitarianism, and racism, not to mention the crude populism of the Nuremberg rallies.

Those who have ears, let them hear.

* * *

In the first paragraph of his preface to *Ecstasy*, Eigen tells how once, years before, he heard Hannah Arendt speak of "the secret ecstasy in intellectual work." He further recalls: "She said she felt a little embarrassed using a term usually reserved for mystics, lovers, or poets. But above all, she confessed, it is ecstasy that drives the love of thinking" (p. vii).

If there is a secret ecstasy here, its name is Heidegger. As for his disastrously naïve attempt to ride the Nazi tiger, it is difficult to see that as tainting this philosopher's entire corpus. Heidegger remains today a leading thinker, his influence extending beyond philosophy to numerous other intellectual fields: theology, ecology, literary theory (particularly, perhaps, deconstructionism), and architecture, to name only a few. He was, however, also a mystic, a lover, and a poet. To Hannah Arendt, at a level of the deepest intimacy, Heidegger was, I think, *the* mystic, lover, and poet. I mean her own. In the ecstatic union of thinking, these two high intellectuals seem to have been able to withstand all the forces of destruction and alienation that the most violent and conflicted century in history could hurl at them.

After the war, Arendt and Heidegger made contact again. She seems even to have helped protect him from de-Nazification by declaring, ironically enough, that he was such a nonentity he could in no way pose a threat.

Heidegger did not cancel his membership of the Nazi party until 1945. Neither did he ever publicly recant his Nazism, although in private he spoke of it as the biggest "stupidity" in his life. And he never once mentioned the Holocaust, or expressed regret or remorse for it.

* * *

The opening of Vassily Grossman's epic novel of the Second World War, *Life and Fate* (2006), is set in a Nazi death camp. Two inmates are talking in a hut by night. Beyond them is the "crimson-black glow" of the crematoria. Innikov, the "holy fool" (or, rather, as Grossman is at pains to explain, a man so battered and broken by repeated horrific experience that he has become crazed, a simpleton, but one who—at, so to speak, if not over, the brink—is able to ask ultimate questions), says, "in his sing-song voice: 'Good? But what is good?'" Mostovskoy, the communist, laughs at him, tells him, "'The Red Army is finding an answer right now'"—for which read: the Russians are busy breaking the spine of the German invasion. He then continues to taunt the "fool" roughly, irritably.

> "Don't make fun of me." Innikov was standing to attention and his mournful voice now sounded tragic. "I didn't come over here just to make you laugh. On the fifteenth of September last year I saw twenty thousand Jews being executed—women, children, and old men. That day I understood that God could not allow such a thing and therefore he did not exist. In the darkness of the present day I can see your power and the terrible evil it is fighting. (Grossman, 2006, pp. 27–28)

Grossman had been one of the Red Army's leading war correspondents. His book, which is based on first-hand knowledge of total war, focuses ultimately upon the pivotal Battle of Stalingrad. It may be worthwhile to note, too, that Grossman's mother, together with all the other Jews of his home town of Berdichev, numbering some thirty thousand, was put to death by the Nazis in September 1941. *Life and Fate* is dedicated to his mother.

* * *

"Why is evil part of the sea of beauty, the mysterious?" asks Eigen. "Why is evil part of ecstasy?" And, a little earlier,

> Can cruelty glow? Poison glow?
>
> Blake's tiger burning bright, tiger's fearful symmetry: "Did he who made the lamb make thee?"
>
> Tiger glows, lamb glows—cruel radiance, joy radiance.
>
> We are attracted to what glows.
>
> We like watching light. (2001, p. 87)

The cadence of Eigen's words, the almost magical touch of "radiance," "glows," and "light" very nearly dispels, makes enchanting, the lurid attraction of evil.

But can we make light of evil?

* * *

I set my students a test.

Is Eigen's "ecstasy" possible in the absence, the possible non-existence, of God? Why/Why not? Refer closely to the text of *Ecstasy* in developing your answer. (*Note*: You are not being asked whether you personally believe or do not believe in God. Your personal opinions on the sacred are not at stake in this essay—Eigen's are. Although you are free to use "I" in the essay, the focus has to fall squarely upon Eigen's multi-layered argument for the centrality of ecstasy in human experience. Could Eigen's argument be just as, if not even more effective without reference to "God"? How do you know? Quote, and analyze what you have quoted, in support of your thesis.)

Template:

While some would say that God is . . . to Michael Eigen's vision of human reality in *Ecstasy*, because . . ., I see Eigen's position differently. Let me be clear: I understand those who would argue against me, saying . . ., and no doubt pointing to Eigen's own words, like . . . Nevertheless, as I will show below, I hold the position that . . .

* * *

It is all in Eigen.

Ecstasy is not to be achieved by cutting away from the body in pursuit of ever-higher planes of the intellect, as if it were possible to consummate identity with the godhead only in the realm of absolute purity of thought, as Plotinus once advocated. In any case, no such neo-Platonic sublime would appear to be operative today, although a parallel practice, relatively mindless as well as inverted, exists among those who perform acts of cutting upon their body—"cutters" Eigen calls them. (Sylvia Plath in *The Bell Jar*, I remember—or rather, her alter ego, Esther Greenwood—at first feels "nothing," but then "a small, deep thrill" when she experimentally cuts her lower leg with a razor blade.) *Contra* Plotinus, Eigen sees ecstasy as arising primarily in the body, not the mind. Like Plotinus, he believes that ecstasy at its highest issues in "union with God," but ecstasy for Eigen is always already connected to our living, physical being, indivisible from "the body's movements, muscles, mucous membranes, flow of breath and blood. In the Bible," he adds, "Israel is told not to eat the blood of animals because the soul is in the blood. Ecstasy is in the blood. Blood ecstasies can be terrible" (2001, p. 3).

* * *

It is all in Nietzsche.

Little in the whole of Western literature can match the ecstatic brilliance of Nietzsche's *Thus Spoke Zarathustra*. The founders of psychology as a clinical practice—Freud, Jung, Adler, et al.—are all, to my eyes, Nietzsche's children. Eigen's *Ecstasy*, in structure a series of relatively brief but highly stimulating sections that culminate at times in epigram, is, too, not unlike a typical Nietzsche text.

A myriad-minded philosopher who liked (not without justice) to see himself as a psychologist, Nietzsche took great pride in smelling out, particularly in the most elevated, rational, and impersonal texts, like Kant's *Critiques*, those suspect points that might betray the abstract thinker as all too human in the end. He would no doubt, therefore, have been beyond delight envious of Eigen's aphorism: "Psychology sniffs the ass of the higher philosophies."

In the parable of the death of God, effectively the prelude to *Thus Spoke Zarathustra* (Nietzsche, 2001), a madman (Nietzsche's alter ego) ventures into the marketplace, and announces, brandishing a lantern: "I'm looking for God." But, Nietzsche tells us, "since many of those who did not believe in God were standing around together just then," he is greeted with hoots of laughter and derision. Hurling his lantern to the ground, the madman turns at bay, gazes with piercing intensity into the jeering crowd, and cries:

> God is dead! God remains dead! And we have killed him! How can we console ourselves, the murderers of all murderers! The holiest and the mightiest thing the world has ever possessed has bled to death beneath our knives: who will wipe this blood from us? (pp. 119–120)

It is parodic, a travesty to think of Nietzsche as an impudent atheist. He is not. If any thinker has dared to think, it is he. Dared to think, and then to leap. Light years though it may be beyond the ability of the marketplace to comprehend the death of God, Nietzsche himself presents it as both a terrible irony and a world-historic catastrophe. The heading to an early draft of the opening passage on Zarathustra reads: *Incipit tragoedia*: the tragedy begins. And for this particular philosopher, let us not forget, tragedy meant not catharsis, but ecstasy.

Unsurpassed, perhaps unsurpassable, *Thus Spoke Zarathustra* is a climactic affirmation of the invincibility of the spirit in the face of the perilous, disorienting openness, the cold and limitless space suddenly revealed in and to a world now and forever bereft of the ruling grandeur of God. As a philosophical text, however, it remains an embarrassment to scholarly gravitas, an affront to all logic, a piece, some fear, of incipient madness. Its vertiginous insights, being identical with its poetic power (cf. "Night is also a sun"), are all too often discounted. Needless to add, *Thus Spoke Zarathustra* is resistant to any attempt to reduce it to systematic exposition.

"Of all that is written," says Nietzsche/Zarathustra, "I love only that which one writes with his blood. Write with blood, and you will experience that blood is spirit" (p. 27).

Write with blood. Write what you know.

* * *

It is all in Blake.

In *Ecstasy*, Eigen offers "a little Blakefest" containing, among others, the following:

> He who sees the Infinite in all things sees God. He who sees the Ratio only, sees himself only.
>
> Exuberance is Beauty.
>
> Energy is the only life and is from the body and Reason is the bound or outward circumference of Energy.
>
> Energy is Eternal Delight.
>
> Excess of sorrow laughs. Excess of joy weeps.
>
> Joys impregnate. Sorrows bring forth.
>
> If the doors of perception were cleansed everything would appear as it is: infinite. (p. 85)

* * *

"Poetry," writes Sarah, a gifted young poet, "is a primal force of creation *and* destruction."

Elated, I note her comment down in my journal. In class, I ask her permission to quote her.

"Cool," she agrees.

On my way home that afternoon, I stop off at a coffee shop. In the queue, giving way to impulse, I buy a new Dylan CD: *Tempest* (2012).

"Sounds a bit like Tom Waits," I remark aloud as I listen to the opening tracks on the cheap stereo that I keep in the carport. Leaning against the sheet metal wall, I stand looking out into the yard. It is raining and I like to watch the rain.

Then Dylan sings two lines of an otherwise mild and comforting ditty that seem to flicker like lightning:

> Tiger, tiger, burning bright
> I pray the Lord my soul to keep

I play the track again. Dylan, I suspect, would never be so slack as to string or strum together any two old lines simply in order to keep things flowing. It seems to me these particular lines have been dropped into place with a purpose. What comes to mind is Blake's dictum: "Without contraries is no progression." Although the child's prayer, "Here I lay me down to sleep," could, I feel, almost be one of the *Songs of Innocence*—comparable, say, to "Little Lamb, who made thee?"—Blake's tiger is sprung from hell. "Tyger, Tyger" (to use his own spelling) is a key poem in *Songs of Experience* (1984), as is "Little Lamb" to *Innocence* (1971). Obviously, innocence and experience are contraries. But I can't help but feel that the tiger could also stand in contradistinction to something else. In *Paradise Lost*, Blake's great predecessor, Milton, intensifies the suffocating darkness of hell by suggesting that its flames burn without casting light. Blake's tiger, however, is both "burning" and "bright." A Gnostic image, at once contrary to and a progression upon Milton's Puritan vision, Blake's tiger is not merely a savage beast born of an impenetrable darkness, the Fall, which, as Milton tells us in the very first line of his epic poem, was precipitated by "man's first disobedience." For the tiger here, as superbly beautiful as it is magnificently violent, blazes with the signs of fallen divinity. As such, it brings into sharp focus the questionable relation to morality, not simply of humankind, but, above all, of the Creator himself. At the same time, its allure is, as the rhythm of the poem suggests, spellbinding:

> Tyger, tyger, burning bright
> In the forests of the night,
> What immortal hand or eye
> Could frame thy fearful symmetry?

Challenge taken. Yet, we do actually know what "hand or eye" has forged this creature. The tiger is Urizen's masterpiece.

Dylan, by reversing Blake's order, and placing, as it were, a song of innocence after a song of experience, constructs a contrary of his own. If we were to lie abed (or to hang around anywhere, for that matter—in a podunk town in North Texas in the rain, say), awake to the threat, the terror brought home by the tiger, and if we were then to repeat with Dylan the words of the prayer, we might know why. In the face of an encounter with so overpowering, menacing, and destructive a force, we might be capable of nothing but to submit to a transcendent safety we can only supplicate.

In *Ecstasy,* employing a postmodern playfulness, Eigen writes, more or less autobiographically, "Some babies turn into tigers. When a tiger reaches old age, soul claps its hands and sings" (p. 4).

A mix of metaphors, allusions, poets (Blake, Yeats).

Making light.

* * *

The town where I grew up, a hard and distrustful white suburb, was built upon the reef, the gold reef to the west of Johannesburg. A couple of sway-backed mine dumps dominated the horizon, their white dust rising in long wisps on windy days, the dust itself coating the floor and furniture in our cold lounge and entrance hall. I remember as a small child running my finger through the dust dulling the cut-glass vase, the most magisterial piece, almost always empty, that stood in the middle of the polished hall table.

It seems to me now like a fairytale, but the queen of England once visited our town. Young and beautiful, the queen. Dark-eyed, quick-minded, willful. (Not that I actually saw her; I was not yet born. But perhaps my mother's womb was like a goldfish bowl, and I could press my nose up against the side, and view the passing scene with wide-eyed wonder.) In elbow-length gloves, in the luxury of an open-roofed Rolls-Royce, the young queen sat raising her scepter, regally blessing the bleak streets as her motorcade proceeded in stately fashion, all sleek, black and shiny, down past the OK Bazaars and the Obelisk Cinema, turned left at the post office, drove by the imposing new police station and the squat brick jail, and descended the hill to the artificial lake that was our town's centerpiece. The desolation of the vista, the seemingly endless flat stretch of waters that reflected only empty sky and the two distant desert-white mine dumps, gave the young queen a taste of utter remoteness, anxiety, futility. How could beauty ever grace this place? Turning to her retinue, she decreed that a pair of swans be bequeathed to the lake in perpetuity. Then, as she lingered for a moment on the bank, trailing the meager wands of an iron-collared willow between her fingers, a sudden tremor ran through the earth. She looked round, startled. Of course, her retinue did all they could to soothe her, smother her fears. *It is really only a very minor earthquake, your majesty. A perfectly natural phenomenon in these parts.* Natural, however, the tremor was not. Far down below the bottom of the lake, not to mention the soles of the royal shoes, through a mile or more of solid rock, work-gangs she would never see, made up of men who themselves saw little of daylight, were toiling in the stifling heat of the mine's cramped tunnels and galleries, dynamiting the rock face for gold—the very gold from which her own elegant circlet was made, the gold upon which her empire battened for its world-girdling power.

Years later, I sketched the following opening to a poem:

> Cyanide dust of the golden void
> Bright metal mirror of the mind
> Muddied swan's feather I once held poised
> Balance of all I have yet to find,
> Yet to seek.

And there I stopped, blocked. Evocative poetry, it seemed, was out of the question. It had no right to exist. Not under apartheid. What was needed was a poetry of direct statement. If any.

Beside the lake stood the Magnolia Hotel. Crenellated like a castle, its walls chalk-white, the whole pile looked like a stale wedding cake. One afternoon (I was in my twenties now), my younger brother Stevie and I dropped in to the Magnolia for a beer. The bar was packed and rowdy. This was a time of war to the north of us. In Rhodesia, the tiny population of English settlers, enormously outnumbered though they were, were attempting by sheer force of arms to hold power "for a thousand years." Of course, they hadn't a snowball's hope: freedom fighters sprang up all around them, as if from the rich red earth underfoot; Rhodesia was destined soon enough to become Zimbabwe, and then to remain for decades under the strongman rule of Robert Mugabe. But these were early days yet, and there was plenty of bravado to go round—particularly in a bar in South Africa. Some young white men wanted nothing so much as to go and "*moer* the terros" (fuck up the terrorists) in Rhodesia. And some actually did.

In the middle of a small gang of listening men stood a squat, muscular young guy by the name of Barry Rider, also called Rocko. A few years ahead of me at high school, Rocko had been a first-team rugby player, and once briefly the object of popular commiseration when he got his front teeth kicked out in a scrum. Now, lit up by alcohol, his face shone. His cheeks were flushed, and spit flew as he talked, holding the floor.

Stevie and I pushed our way through to the counter. On his own, to one side, stood Kurt Kohler, an elderly man from, we had heard, the former German colony of South-West Africa. With his back to the crowd, his head raised, Kurt stood listening. I remember his small neat ears, his stone-white hair. He had only two fingers to the hand with which he gripped his glass. Neither Stevie nor I spoke to him. Old Kurt never spoke to anyone, a fact we knew and respected.

A burst of uproarious laughter erupted from the gang, together with shouts for Rocko to continue. Waving one arm, he finished off another mug of beer to a chant of, "Down, down, down!" Then he wiped his mouth on the back of his hand.

"Fuck you, *ous*," he said in high-spirited abuse, a form of banter. Fuck you, guys. "First thing next morning, we hit this kraal. I'm telling you, you should have seen. We go in, take a few pot shots into the huts—bing, bang, thank you, ma'am—and the *munts* run round and shit themselves, jabber, scream, evaporate. Now you see them, now you don't. Afterwards, we count. We only knocked out three. You got to know, though, this is a hot spot. Terros come down here for a break. They stock up—*mieliepap*, kaffir beer, ammo too maybe, grab a piece of fat black pussy for the night—then they are gone, back to their dirty bloody mud-holes in the bush. We decide to do a search, me and Danie. Go from hut to hut. Look—look—look. Nothing. *Niks*. Forget it. Then, under a pile of bags and rags in the back of one of their stinking *kaias*, what do we find but this little black whore, curled up, hiding. Danie pulls her out. Bare tits, young, maybe sixteen, seventeen. This for a terro can only be, 'Happiness is . . .' Big bouncy fat black arse. We lead her out into the sunshine. Nicely, nicely, at first, we ask, 'Okay, so where are your fucking terro friends? How can we find them?' She plays dumb. Screams a lot. 'Shut up,' says Danie. 'Talk.' But she won't. She gags. She screams. She cries. We haven't got time to waste. In the middle of it all, lance-jack Morgan gives a shout. Out he comes from this hut, in one hand an AK, in the other a box of live ammo, and stands waving them in the air: 'Look what I found!' 'Talk, bitch,' says Danie. 'Talk, or I'll slit you open, nose to tail, true as bob.' She still won't talk. 'Okay,' he says. 'That's it.' We pull down her pants, and he splits her open with his bayonet, cunt to tits. She screams like fuck, there's blood and guts everywhere, blue guts, buckets of blood. But still she won't tell. She coughs, she snorts, she dies. So, next thing, we—"

Before the young drunk can say what they did next, Kurt slams down his glass. He turns to face him.

"A dirty little war," he says, speaking slowly, distinctly, every word weighted with contempt.

"What?" Rocko tenses up, stares, clenching his fists. "What's that you say?"

Even more slowly, derisively, Kurt repeats:

"A dirty *little* war."

"Who . . .?" Rocko sways, staggers, takes a step or two towards Kurt. "Who the fuck do you think you are, old man? Who the fuck, the *fuck*, are you to talk?"

"I?" says Kurt. He stands with his head thrown back, looking down as if from a great height. "I have seen the lights of Moscow."

"You . . .!" Rocko makes a blundering rush, swinging his fists, but a couple of his bar buddies intercept him, grab him by the arms, and push him, struggling, into a corner.

"You," he howls. "You, you fucking old Nazi!"

Kurt turns back to the counter. Unperturbed, he lifts the tumbler with his eagle claw, and tips it back.

How many men in the bar, I wonder, are aware that not one in ten of the Wehrmacht men returned alive from Stalin's Russia?

But Stevie has already drained his beer. He glances around nervously, and says, "Let's go."

I raise my tankard. Smile, nod to Kurt.

"Lachaim!" The Jewish toast—a test if not a taunt.

Kurt nods. His gaze is very sharp and clear. He says nothing. Nor does he smile. I notice how very lean he is, almost ascetic.

"Do you know he has one glass eye?" says Stevie under his breath.

"Which one?"

"I don't know. Come on, let's go."

A few months later, Rocko Rider was dead—killed, according to one account, in a mortar blast. According to another, cut down by a burst of automatic rifle fire while on night patrol. Yet another account claimed that the "heroic" tales were all wrong, a pack of lies: Rocko had simply choked to death on his own vomit after a drunken orgy.

As for old Kurt, we would sometimes see him in the Magnolia bar again, standing to one side, alone as ever. Stevie and I used to lay bets as to which eye was real, which of glass. But we never did find out.

Whenever he looked our way, we felt forced to look down. To look down, and talk about something innocuous, as if nothing could possibly be wrong.

* * *

From inside the South African liberation struggle, a statement poem.

On October 18, 1985, a young ANC guerrilla, Benjamin Moloise, convicted of "terrorism" against the apartheid state, was hanged in Pretoria Maximum Security Prison. On the same day, a small liberal-left newspaper, *The Weekly Mail*, printed an untitled poem by Moloise, written on death row:

> All the armies that ever marched
> All the parliaments that ever sat have not
> affected the life of man on earth as
> that one
> solitary life . . .
> I am proud of what I am . . .
> The storm of oppression will be followed by the rain of my blood.
> I am proud to give my life, my one solitary life.
>
> (Moloise, 1985)

What does a poem want?

* * *

As for me, I come from the wrong side of history.

On the ship from the Netherlands, over two hundred years ago, my forebears changed from the plain Dutch name of van der Riet to Niemand, No One. A bitter and alienated move that has always fascinated me. Negative ecstasy, self-erasure.

I toy with the idea of doing the same. Here, in America, I could drop my diasporic Scots last name, adopt the legacy of my father's mother's side of the family, and say, I, too, am No One, Niemand.

After all, what did I have to say to a hanged man?

What did I know? What right had I even to exist?

How far could (or should) I take my reply? Blood for blood, mine for his?

In the end I could only write what I knew of the blunt facts.

Trigger-Point

I hear that
After the funerals
Of those already killed
In the townships,
Youths taunt the cops.

Cops
In their Casspirs armored cars
Sit back and wait,
Cradling their rifles
And cracking the odd joke.

Kids run across the empty
Dirt streets,
Holding up sheets
Of corrugated iron
Thin as water
Between themselves
And the guns, crying:
"Me! Shoot me, cops!"
And the cops,
As if it clinched something,
Do.

(Anderson, 2000, p. 18)

* * *

I play Dylan's *Tempest* album, flip through my scored and underlined copy of Eigen's *Ecstasy* in search of the point where he remarks that failure is not ecstatic. Not too surprisingly, I fail to find it.

What I do find, time and again, is the word, "light." In what way, if any, is an evocation of light sufficient to dispel the terrible darkness in which we live? Yet, the simplicity, the sincerity, the unassuming plainness of statement, together with Eigen's unmistakable reverence, is first disarming, then uplifting:

> There is a Light of lights, and when one sees it, no questions remain. There is nothing more beautiful. One feels secure, trust. One is satisfied in the Light's presence, whatever death is. Whether one lives on in some form or other, goes through hell, purgatory, heaven or nothing, or never lives again – one lives forever now. One asks nothing of the Light, no more than just to be. (Eigen, 2001, p. 35)

And over sixty pages later:

> The Light opens everything up to radiance. The Light makes everythin seem worthwhile, whole, beautiful, astonishing. Is it a bonus, or the meat? "In Your light do I see light." Thrills, shivers when I think this, feel this. Indescribably beyond thrills and shivers. (p. 98)

I think of the menorah candles that entranced the man as a child, and that led to this way of light. *Ecstasy*, in the end, is a rhapsody to the Light of lights. What Eigen urges, it would seem, is very nearly identical to the imperative at the heart of "The Heart Sutra":

OM GATE GATE PARAGATE PARASAMGATE BODHI SVAHA

a Sanskrit mantra which may be translated as: Go, go, go beyond, go thoroughly beyond, and establish yourself in Enlightenment.

The Urizenic Enlightenment of Europe has led to the disappearance of the self into nothing but a chain of chemical reactions, an immense field of exploitation for the pharmaceutical industry. Unapologetically aggressive, this industry seems only too pleased to fund, and thus to drive, the current imperialist "mapping" of the brain. As we have seen, however, the balance imposed by pharmaceutical control of the brain is a far cry from the holy, the ecstatic.

What then is to be done?

Write what you know. Write with blood.

* * *

It is all in *Buddha in Redface* (Duran, 2000).

For instance, at the point where Tarrence, the native American shaman, broken in body but lucid in mind, tells the young psychologist, Eduardo Duran, "In the blood is the map, the blueprint of the original dream. God is the spiritual essence of blood, and therefore blood is not tied to space and time. I don't mean just physical blood; I'm talking about the original and absolute awareness" (p. 63).

* * *

This took place years ago, and I do not often speak of it, but—

Boston. Two a.m. A full and lovely Midsummer's night. Walking home, climbing the last steep hill to the Victorian subdivide where I have been living, I count the street lights. I know there are twelve from the foot of the hill to the top. The night beyond is deeply still, a well of comfort to me. I am very tired, a good tiredness. I have been with her I love all evening, and I am, for the moment, at peace.

Passing streetlight number four, I become aware of a fragrance in the air. I look up. Just beyond the circle of light, between a darkened mansion and the denser darkness of an apartment block, stands a flowering tree. I go up to the stone wall that divides the sidewalk from the properties beyond, place my hands on the stones, and breathe the heady fragrance. I could reach out and touch the blossoms of the closest, heavily laden branch. The petals gleam softly, white in the dark. Towering above me, the tree spreads its rich canopy, its limbs black against the dim violet upglow of the city; here and there a tiny star pierces through.

Too tired to stay very long, I resolve to come back and see the tree in daylight.

I sleep late. It is nearly nine o'clock before I go back down the hill. I walk quickly, eager for the sight. At the apartment block, I look round. For a moment, I don't understand. Is this the right place? But it is, I know it is. What makes no sense is that there is nothing to be seen save a wide expanse of lawn between the mansion and the blind brick wall of the apartment. There is no tree.

Fearing I might somehow have made a mistake, I go all the way to the bottom of the hill, then all the way up again to the top. But I have made no mistake. There is no tree.

("You were walking in your sleep," she will say with a smile, kissing me on the cheek. "You dreamt that tree.")

So vivid was the presence of the flowering tree that I could draw it in detail, down to the last blossom on a branch tip: the delicate cup of white petals, the protruding pistil, stamens. But I do not wish to meddle with pencil and paper. Nor do I wish to explain, or explain away, what I saw. I wish rather to stay with the wonder of it.

It seems to me the blossoming tree was both there and not-there at the same time. It is as if I can still almost touch the blossoms, the cool, still petals.

An ecstatic gift of love and night.

* * *

I'd like to ask Eigen:
Why is it that "light" should rhyme with "night"?
Is it simply a coincidence, meaningless? Or does it mean that,
Yes, in the end,
Night is also a sun?

References

Anderson, P. (2000). *Vanishing Ground.* Johannesburg: Quartz

Blake, W. (1971). *Songs of Innocence.* Toronto: Dover.

Blake, W. (1975). *The Marriage of Heaven and Hell.* Oxford: Oxford University Press.

Blake, W. (1984). *Songs of Experience.* Toronto: Dover.

Blake, W. (1997). *The Book of Urizen.* Toronto: Dover.

Duran, E. (2000). *Buddha in Redface.* Lincoln, NE: Writers Club.

Dylan, B. (2012). *Tempest.* New York: Columbia Records.

Eigen, M. (1993). *The Psychotic Core.* London: Karnac.

Eigen, M. (2001). *Ecstasy.* Middletown, CT: Wesleyan University Press.

Eigen, M. (2002). *Rage.* Middletown, CT: Wesleyan University Press.

Eigen, M. (2006). *Lust.* Middletown, CT: Wesleyan University Press.

Grossman, V. (2006). *Life and Fate.* New York: New York Review of Books.

Gruber, M. (2008). *An Unknown Destiny: Terror, Psychotherapy, and Modern Initiation: Readings in Nietzsche, Heidegger, Steiner.* Great Barrington, MA: Lindisfarne.

Heidegger, M. (1996). (Originally published 1927). *Being and Time.* Albany: State University of New York Press.

Heidegger, M. (2000). *Introduction to Metaphysics.* New Haven, CT: Yale University Press.

Kant, I. (1999). *The Critique of Pure Reason.* Cambridge: Cambridge University Press.

Milton, J. (2000). *Paradise Lost.* London: Penguin Classics.

Moloise, B. (1985). All the armies that ever marched. Johannesburg, *Weekly Mail*, October 18–24, front page.

Nietzsche, F. (2001). *The Gay Science*, B. Williams (Ed.), J. Nauckhoff & A. del Caro (Trans.). Cambridge: Cambridge University Press.

Young, J. (2001). *Heidegger's Philosophy of Art.* Cambridge: Cambridge University Press.

CHAPTER FIFTEEN

Two poems

Rachel Berghash

Heaven Moment

I asked if they would do an event for me,
I said I wasn't famous, my book not sensational,
my publisher small,
I hoped they would find a niche for my book
so that this life would be a little heaven,
a little heaven of fame,
but they said, no,
not because I'm not famous,
or because my publisher is not big,
or my book not replete with sensations,
but because of a technical reason. I then sat
on one of their chairs and skimmed through a couple
of beautiful books, and felt good that I had asked,
and felt good I wasn't hurt,
and felt good about bearing frustration,
and felt good about my life that felt real,
and felt good for being on the front line,
and went home and ate a hearty lunch and read
the Tanya about the different categories of the soul,

and realized my soul fits the "in-between,"
good and bad, and praised God
for helping me face what needs to be faced—
a heaven that is not about what I thought,
but about this other thing sometimes called life.

Like the Salt of the Earth

For Michael Eigen

There was a leper who lived
in my city on a steeped hill,
and when we happened in the neighborhood
we pointed to the direction of his house
and whispered "leper, leper."
We thought the walls of his house
were pitted with green
and the stones in his garden had shiny spots,
and we thought that at night he held his head,
whitening hair,
and cried.

But in that house someone
stroked the leper's head,
and washed him every morning,
and every evening he anointed him with oil.
And the leper was not afraid of his body.
He knew he was worth more than
his leprous body. He walked in his lush garden
among the carob trees and the climbing vines,
and by the cactus, the lonely stem.

The stones in the garden to him
were an altar, and his house
was the desert's holy tent, and when
he entered his house he shook the dust off his shoes
and within his sacred walls he sang.

Though we shunned him,
the leper felt like the salt of the earth.
Though we shunned his garden,
the vine and carob trees flourished,
and the cactus grew to a giant size.

CHAPTER SIXTEEN

Tangled up in Mike

Anthony Molino

Ring the bells that still can ring.
Forget your perfect offering.
There is a crack, a crack, in everything.
That's where the light comes in.

(Leonard Cohen, "Anthem", 2009)

For some reason, ever since I was asked to contribute to this volume and write about Michael Eigen, music and musicians have come to mind. Art and artists, too, in a broader sense. But more about them, about one artist in particular, later. Just now that I have finally sat down to make some sense of all the intuitions and intimations that I have haphazardly scribbled on loose scraps of paper over the past year, a title for this directionless and as-yet unformed exercise imposes itself. There's a song by Dylan, from his album *Blood on the Tracks* (1974), called "Tangled Up in Blue." It just came to me, now, no sooner had I penned the epigraph to this free-wheelin' essay and finished listening to Leonard Cohen's song, "Anthem". Two modern-day bards, two mystics of a sort, poets pretty much of the same age as Eigen, oddball postwar prophets with a sensitivity that for decades has captured the light, sometimes searing, often filtered, that seeps deep through the common cracks of our pained humanity. Same thing that Michael Eigen's done, forever. In every page he has ever written, in a voice as unmistakably stripped and honest and lyrical as those of his Biblical forefathers: from Jeremiah (*Age of Psychopathy* anyone?) to Job, to the all-too-human and remarkably imperfect man that was King David (another poet, by the way). "Nowadays, I think of psychoanalysis as an aesthetic, as a form of poetry ... You have all these psychoanalytic singers and poets trying to express their aesthetic experience" (Eigen, in Molino, 1997, p. 104) No doubt Eigen was also, if not primarily, referring to himself when he spoke these words to me back in 1994, almost twenty years ago, when he agreed to meet with me for my book *Freely Associated*.

* * *

Another title I had played with for some time, before ever writing a line of this essay, was "Being Mike Eigen." You know, echoing the film *Being John Malkovich* and trying to transpose the experience from the screen to the page. There is something so distinctly ... Eigenish in the man's writing that he gives his readers, or at least he has always given this reader, the profound and peculiar sense of somehow being in his head, at the same time that he provides the kind of absorption and dissolution of self that consummate writers achieve *and* provide. So, for a while, I thought that I would write about Michael Eigen ("Mike" from here on, as I have always called him) from the fantasized position of being inside his mind. (Molino, a novel Athena, transsexualized, waiting to be reborn from the head of Eigen/Zeus after crumpling up, miniaturized, to assume a most awkward and unlikely fetal position.) Going even further, another idea I had was to take on the guise and voice of the man's very mind: a voice disembodied yet incarnate in the fertile illusion that I might know the man much, much better than I do. But such literary strategies are, happily, behind and beyond me. Still, I figure I would let you in on my thinking, so you know just how tangled up in Mike I have been for the past year.

But anyway. Another reason I did not go ahead with such fanciful strategies is that I kept remembering a passage from my conversation with Eigen in *Freely Associated*, a vision and personal memory of his that is so Eigenesque (not -ish!) that by itself it does and says more than I, or perhaps anyone else, can to suggest what it must be like to be Mike Eigen. It is so telling a passage that I'd like to quote it here, in its entirety:

> When I was in the Nevada desert, a guide told me that a cactus would grow straight forever, would grow forever straight if it didn't get wounded, and that the branches of the cactus grow out at the place where it's traumatized, at the place where it's wounded. Freud depicts the personality in the same way, displacing itself, or deforming itself, around the point of impact, of wounding impact. Hit the psyche, and it displaces the self like ripples or waves, it deforms itself around the points of wounding. (Eigen, in Molino, 1997, pp. 94–95)

There is a crack, a crack, in everything. That's where the light comes in. A crack out of which life grows, branches out. In all its gore and glory. With all its contortions and prickly defenses. I have long had the impression that *all* of Mike Eigen is in this passage; indeed, that he inhabits and has grown out of those very wounds: his own, never denied, and those, even the most festering, of others. Wounds, deforming points of impact, out of which every page he has ever written still grows and glows. Places, spaces he inhabits, literally, every day, with his every patient, whose songs of sorrow, misery, and anguish he registers, amplifies, and helps transform. The words of another singer–songwriter come to mind, of an Italian contemporary and kindred spirit of Dylan and Cohen, who sadly did not get to live as long as his more celebrated Anglophone siblings. Fabrizio De Andrè closes one of his more famous songs, "Via del campo" (1967), a parable of sorts about the love, otherwise condemned and misjudged, that even a streetside prostitute can give, with these lines: "Nothing is born of diamonds / but flowers are born of manure." God knows how many tons of emotional shit Eigen the analyst has survived, shovelled, and helped transform into flowers for people over the course of his professional lifetime. And he has done so, I like to imagine, out of a relentless commitment to Cohen's commandment: "The perfect offering? Forget it." Know what? Just thought of another title: "Eigen: Celebrations of the Imperfect." But, like I said, I have no idea where all this is going . . .

And as long as we are talking music, do indulge me. I have been listening to De Andrè for years, but it is only now, at this very moment, in the midst of my serendipitous association of him with

Dylan and Cohen, that I learn that he actually translated and adapted into Italian, back in 1974, Dylan's "Desolation Row" (1965) and Cohen's "Suzanne" (1967) and "Joan of Arc" (1971). The power of free association. Freeing power of the unconscious.

* * *

Mike and I share an ancestor. Met him, actually, through Marie Coleman Nelson, a supervisor of his long before she became mine. Iconoclast. Witty. Sharp-tongued. Brilliant lady. New York transplant to Africa. Kenya. Where she planted a psychoanalytic tree. Must have cracked. The tree. Because she did come back. Wounded, somehow. There was heartthrob to her loneliness when I met her. Somehow homeless. Worked with Mike before leaving, called him a son, with me after she returned. Generations. Ironclad irony, she was. Worldwise, but never weary. Wandering Jew of a woman, if not that she wasn't Jewish. Called Kenya and its non-human surround "the belly-button of the world". And loved to talk of slits, her take on Lacan and lack. Cuts. Slits. Slots. She, too, shone, obliquely. Though not in female company. "I enjoy being with men, in sex, in edifying discourse—and a happy combination is best of all!" (Nelson, in Molino, 1996, p. 99). Thus spoke Marie Nelson. In a long conversation with me, printed in my first book, *Elaborate Selves* where, come to think of it, my talk with Mike first appeared. She loved us both. Mothered us, in a way. Where Mike would talk of a "friendship of self," making friends with and across one's multiple self states, Marie spoke of a "peaceful federation of selves." Had a metaphor for her federation: "I think of these selves as a harp, which is a vertical concept somewhat like Lacan's" (Nelson, in Molino, 1996, p. 87). Space between the chords. Slotted. Crack of another kind. Courbet, *The Origin of the World*. Belonged to Lacan, that painting, though he kept it hidden. He had to die for the thing to be seen. Music for the eyes.

* * *

I spent two days with Mike back in 1994, in his Brooklyn home, for our work together. I'll never forget the welcome I received. It was early December, Hannukah, the Jewish Season of Lights. I must have arrived on a Saturday afternoon, late in the afternoon, in the middle of a family prayer around the menorah. Ushered graciously into the Eigen dining room, I was in another world. Disoriented. Embarrassed.

I remember respectfully carving a niche for myself in the corner of the room closest to the doorway, feeling like an intruder who had somehow, unwittingly, crossed the line of a domestic *temenos*. My memory here fails me, but I guess the prayers recited were in Hebrew. Had to be. Around the sacred candelabrum that captivated my attention.

Light. More light. Flickers of light. Symbol of the burning bush in which the Un-nameable appeared to Moses. From which YHWH is said to have spoken. Candlesticks, seven of them, one for each day of the week of Creation. The central one, a fulcrum, evoking the original Day of Rest. Or the Day of Original Rest, remembrance and primeval celebration of a timeless time before the original utterance: "Let there be light." Words, breath, that gave birth to the cosmos. When All was rest. When Nothing was All. Many years after visiting with Mike I purchased a splendid Murano paperweight, with a golden menorah englobed in the pearl royal blues of the master Venetian glassblowers. Branches of light, bursting, like six groping arms issuing from a single, sturdy, centered tree trunk. Spinal column of light. Root of all time. First ever, ever, ever point of impact. Primeval crack. In a nameless, otherwhere dimension where trauma and creation, rupture and birth, are One. All.

> The age-old folklore that we're children of God before we're children of our parents probably hasn't been tapped as well as it might in psychoanalytic thinking, where we're always children of our parents first . . . It may actually take some time for an infant to de-infinitize . . . It can't be taken for granted that the sense of infinity or of the emotionally infinite doesn't somehow antedate the experience of the mother or even the infant. (Eigen, in Molino, 1997, p. 106)

These words of Mike's from that weekend together have stuck with me for years. Kerouac's elsetime. Served as the foundation for a family myth of sorts. When my son was still a child, before the birds and the bees started buzzing and flitting and pressing for attention, I told him that before being born unto his mother and me he had been a baby star, scuttling across the universe in search of a womb, a home, a family, into which to settle and become incarnate. I told him that he had honored us with his choice, that in a way unknown to all of us it was he who had decided just who his parents would be. That his mother and I, together, were the blessed recipients of his grace. Things have not worked out ideally, as his mother and I have separated, and

I sometimes wonder to what extent the story has stuck with him, and if he thinks that he somehow made a bad choice in his stellar life. Personally, I like to think he didn't. Now a teenager, he is still that star, my source of light. But he is also a branch reborn of a wound, an impacted psyche who will by necessity father in turn other shoots, other branches, and other imperfections. Other cracks. And, in turn, more light.

* * *

In a lot of ways, I am a late bloomer. Never went to a museum, for instance, until well into my undergraduate years at Temple University, when a theologian with a passion for art, Sam Laeuchli, who, twenty years later, became my son's godfather, took our class to the Philadelphia Museum of Art. It was the first time for me, after spending fifteen of my first twenty years living in Philadelphia, with the museum practically around the corner from my home. Still today I often come to things late. Not too late—it's never *too* late—but late enough to have routinely generated within me a mixed sense of regret, for the time and treasures lost, and of gratitude for whatever gift life may yet bestow upon me. Something of the sort happened at Mike's twenty years ago, when, after dinner at a Chinese restaurant and a premium Scotch sipped in the course of a bedazzling and far-reaching conversation, we called it a night and I got ready for bed.

In the room where I was hosted there was a small pile of books. Turns out that my bedtime reading that night introduced me to Francis Bacon, a painter I didn't know. It was all so strange: displaced, adrenalized, sleepless in anticipation of part two of our interview, I end up reading another, with one of the most famous, or infamous, artists of the twentieth century. I can't recall if Mike had already talked about the cactus, about its wounds and branches and how its apparent deformity was a response to environmental impacts. He probably had, since that story of his trip to Nevada is early in the published version of our conversation. So, just a few hours after hearing the story, I find myself looking, gaping, with the kind of quasi-perverse fascination that Bacon's work inspires, at some of the most deformed, writhing representations of the human figure ever to appear in the history of Western art. Corporeal, fleshy, dis/figured, sometimes bloodied branches or mutilated trunks that would scream out, laughing, haughtily, defiantly, from the page. Dark.

And yet, if you look at Bacon's paintings, you will see that even he lets in the light. Eerie, for sure. But still it is something he does often enough. Differently. The blunted, quasi-cosmic, draping light of paintings like *Landscape* (1978), or *A Piece of Wasteland* (1982), which evoke no human form. Apocalypse now. "Light that never was on sea or land" (Satori in Paris, 1966, Jack Kerouac quoting Matthew Arnold). The blinding light in which a contorted, truncated creature basks—albeit under a smothering black beach umbrella, in two of the panels of a work like *Triptych* (1981), or think of his famed painting, *Blood on the Floor* (1986). Even there is a light-bulb hanging (something of a fixture, actually, in Bacon's work), and a light switch on the wall. A switch, mandated by the macabre, essential to the grotesque. Like an umbrella, meant for the rain, sprung open under a vicious midday sun. A slight.

Funny thing, Bacon's lights. This one, the light-bulb, illuminating the space of an empty interrogation. Where blood marks the spot. Of the absent. The wounded. Bleeding. Of one, or two? Who cracked? Gone. Bludgeoned? Negative space, nightmarish rendition of the consulting room. Emptied of all soul. The floor itself a slab, cold couch for a Christ deposed. Deposed, then dragged off. But no holy sepulcher here, no Jerusalem. No resurrection. Something else. Enigma of the unconscious, truer, deeper than any Dalì. Depths, all the same, lit. As an aside: How many of Mike's patients, of whom he's written in such all-encompassing and unembellished detail over the years, could take up and inhabit the space of that painting? Or, otherwise, serve as models, psychic simulacra, for Bacon's gross but beautiful, holy but—dare I say—ungodly bodies? And there, might Bacon have learned there from Courbet? (By the way, they found the head of the woman who started it All. The painted fragment showed up. Still looking, though, for the upper appendages of Bacon's headless life forms. Androids. Guillotined.)

* * *

> Ooh, baby don't you know I suffer?
> Oh baby can you hear me moan? . . .
> Glaciers melting in the dead of night
> And the superstar sucked into the supermassive
> (Ooh ooh ahh, you set my soul alight) . . .
>
> (Muse, "Supermassive Black Hole", 2006).

Thanks to my teenage son, I recently discovered Muse. This time not too late, albeit in the pockets of a generational gap, and amid the rightful aesthetic disparities and dissonance that such gaps engender. At about the same time that I became acquainted with the band and the song "Supermassive Black Hole" (though, like a lot of people my age, before I even knew who Muse were, their radio-popping, top-of-the-charts hit aptly titled "Madness" had drilled its way into my head), I had read an article by a woman named Elena Dusi, in the cultural pages of *La Repubblica*, one of Italy's foremost daily newspapers. Here's the headline: "The scream of the dying star, gobbled up by a black hole" (2012). Turns out that when an errant star gets captured by the monstrous gravitational field of a black hole, not only does it get dismembered and torn to astral shreds, but, as it spirals to its death and dissolution, it screams. An agonizing cry, Munch multiplied to the zillionth power, that astronomers measure via the star's intensified emission of X-rays at the edge of the luciferous abyss. Here are the closing lines of the article: "At the sound of the star's cry for help the universe remained completely indifferent. If not for a handful of curious, earthbound astronomers" (2012).

Upon reading the article, and every time that I reread it, I am overtaken by a sense of unease, if not of dread. It is as if even the stars can sing, "Baby, don't you know I suffer? Can't you hear me moan?" Even stars cry, agonize, moan. I knew that they "died", but I never imagined they "suffered". I was already tangled up in Mike when I read the article, caught in the early exercise of "being Michael Eigen" and trying to figure how he would resonate with the news. But I couldn't go that far. I thought of Mike's patients, tried to imagine him at work with them. The lyrics of "Supermassive Black Hole" echoed through every fiber and filament of my brain. I thought of the mystic who could envision the birth of the human infant as a step in the process of de-infinitization. For some reason, I found I was more attuned to a suffering star than I am at times to my own patients. Earthly, passionate, an avid reader of Camus as a youth, in the mind-and-flesh-and-blood of being me I felt more akin to another Dylan, Thomas, and his invitation to rage, to "rage against the dying of the light." I had hit a wall, crashed into my own limits. Of thought. Of feeling and imagination. At one and the same time I had found and caused a crack of my own. Yet another. "That's where the light comes in," I remembered. Enter Michael Eigen. To set my soul. Alight.

* * *

I thought I had finished writing when memory, or the unconscious, did what it's supposed to do, and set me back to work. I remembered that the book I had flipped through at Mike's house contained what I now learn was a famous, striking interview with Bacon by David Sylvester, which I easily found on the web. I am sure that the author of books like *Rage* (2002) and *Lust* (2006) would have a field day with a character like Bacon, and that I, too, could have plenty of nasty fun with such an impenitent nihilist, who surely doesn't come across as too nice a guy. But without getting into anything like a psychobiography, or a psychopathography, of our painter friend, there is one exchange between him and Sylvester that is absolutely germane to what I have written thus far. At one point, Bacon is asked: "The open mouths—are they always meant to be a scream?" He replies:

> Most of them, but not all. You know how the mouth changes shape. I've always been very moved by the movements of the mouth and the shape of the mouth and the teeth. People say that these have all sorts of sexual implications, and I was always very obsessed by the actual appearance of the mouth and teeth, and perhaps I have lost that obsession now, but it was a very strong thing at one time. I like, you may say, the glitter and colour that comes from the mouth, and I've always hoped in a sense to be able to paint the mouth like Monet painted a sunset. (Sylvester, 2007)

Amazing, isn't it? Through our mouths we suck and feed and bite our way into the world, know our mothers before there is any Other. And while Mike speaks extensively, and lovingly, in *Elaborate Selves* (1996) and *Freely Associated* (1997) about the infant's experience of the mother's eyes—suggesting, even, that not only is her face a source of light, but a matrix of faith—here the faithless Bacon would have light issue from the mouth and its weaponry, and in so doing claims Monet as an ancestor! It is as if Bacon tastes the world through his eyes, sees it through his mouth. In *Ecstasy* (2001), Eigen asks at one point: "And what of creative horror?" Monet–Bacon–Munch. Now there's a trilogy, or a triptych for you . . . There is a crack, a crack, in everything. Courbet *docet*. Amen.

Postscript

There are sessions I have experienced in the thirty years I have been an analyst, rare ones, I admit, that have left me bewildered by the beauty they encircle. By a circular motif or movement, by the perfect symmetry of a patient's unconscious communications whereby the session's end is in its beginning, the beginning in the end, and I am left with a sense of bliss, as if captured in the brushstroke of a Japanese calligrapher scripting ecstasy on a canvass of Time. The wondrous sense that everything fits, and all is well with the world, maybe even with the patient. Bion's "O" approximated. Why these words? Perfection is surely not of this world, but Eigen would be the first to maintain that eternity, potentially, is. Well, let the trumpets sound, for I have been blessed. I shared these entanglements of mine with Mike shortly after wrapping up the piece. Again, now, for the second time, the sense that I had finally finished comes undone. Happily. Turns out that "Tangled Up in Blue" is the name of a group of folksingers to which Eigen's son belonged in college. The same son, I'd bet, whose room I used back in 1994. But no matter . . . No matter. The writing has come full circle, synchronicity holds sway, and the title that chose me connects in song with Mike's own seed, with the man's very bloodline. Sends me back to the deep dreamy blue of a Murano paperweight, mound, breast, I need, I crave, to pin this thing down, to stop.

References

Cohen, L. (1967). Suzanne. *Songs of Leonard Cohen*. Columbia Records.

Cohen, L. (1971). Joan of Arc. *Songs of Love and Hate*. Columbia Records.

Cohen, L. (2009). Anthem. *Leonard Cohen Live in London*. Sony Music.

De Andrè, F. (1967). Via del Campo. *Volume 1*. Bluebell Records.

Dusi, E. (2012). L'urlo della stella che muore. Article in *La Repubblica*, 9 August.

Dylan, B. (1965). Desolation Row. *Highway 61 Revisited*. Columbia Records.

Dylan, B. (1974). Tangled Up in Blue. *Blood on the Tracks*. Columbia Records.

Eigen, M. (2001). *Ecstasy*. Middletown, CT: Wesleyan University Press.

Eigen, M. (2002). *Rage*. Middletown, CT: Wesleyan University Press.

Eigen, M. (2006). *Lust*. Middletown, CT: Wesleyan University Press.

Kerouac, J. (1966). *Satori in Paris*. London: Penguin Classics, 2012.

Molino, A. (1996). *Elaborate Selves: Reflections and Reveries of C. Bollas, M. Eigen, P. Young-Eisendrath, Samuel & Evelyn Laeuchli, and M.C. Nelson*. Binghamton, NY: Haworth Press.

Molino, A. (1997). *Freely Associated: Encounters in Psychoanalysis with C. Bollas, N. Coltart, M. Eigen, J. McDougall and A. Phillips*. London: Free Association Books.

Muse (2006). Supermassive Black Hole. *Black Holes and Revelations*. Warner Bros.

Sylvester, D. (2007). One continuous accident mounting on top of another: an edited extract from Interviews with Francis Bacon in 1963, 1966 and 1979. *Guardian*, 13 September 2007. Accessed at: www.theguardian.com/theguardian/2007sep/13/greatinterviews

CHAPTER SEVENTEEN

On fragmentation, expansion, pieces of more

Merle Molofsky

Introduction

Dr. Michael Eigen's playground is vast and unboundaried. In his explorations of psychoanalysis, Kaballah, psychosis, and emotions that sometimes dare not speak their names, such as rage, lust, and ecstasy, Eigen opens up vistas of possibility, inviting us to explore the richness of experience and thought that comprises the interiority and relationality of the analyst. To read Eigen's work, to participate in his seminars, and to experience him as a human being, is to become aware of all that psychoanalysis can be for each of us—the possibility of a psychoanalysis as big as the world. His level of comfort with fragmentation, whether the fragmentation of Lurianic Kaballah, psychotic states, or the everyday expansions and contractions of self, invites an openness to experience, creative thought, and to the inclusion of what has previously been omitted. His work has inspired me to be truer to myself in the I–Thou as human being, psychoanalyst, poet, thinker, writer, and all the pieces of more that fragmentation and expansion encompass.

Am I crazy?

In his more than twenty books, Eigen invites us to fully experience all aspects of our psychic life. That experience may well be madness. The first of Eigen's books I ever read was *The Psychotic Core,* which I came across shortly after it was published in 1986. I was well along in my psychoanalytic training, which was inspired by my own experiences in analysis. My sense of myself, and my understanding of what I could expect from psychoanalytic training, did not encompass psychosis. Reading *The Psychotic Core* was akin to playing "hot potato"; I inwardly yelped and shuddered and tried to toss Eigen's insights somewhere, anywhere I could, rather than hold on to them myself and blister my hands—or scar my sense of self. I did believe I was crazy and I didn't believe I was crazy. Both self-perceptions existed within me, braided together, yet unrecognizable as subject matter. Crazy? As in, *psychotic* crazy?

I knew what the medical term "psychosis" meant—a mental condition in which someone loses touch with reality—and I knew what the colloquial term "crazy" meant. Colloquially, crazy could mean psychotic, but it could have myriad other connotations. It did not have to indicate a severe mental illness; rather, it could indicate an unrecognizable intensity, a quality of experience not ordinarily accounted for. Unmirrored states, creative ecstasies, feelings, and perceptions no one else seems to be talking about, for instance, can all be *experienced* as "crazy". I knew I was not psychotic.

After a few years had passed, I discovered in my own analysis a core experience for which I had no words. I had been desultorily reading *The New York Times,* happily adrift in the arts section, when I came across an image—a small, black and white newsprint smear, a photograph of a painting. It electrified me, preparing me to eventually walk the "electrified tightrope" that Eigen later writes about. The image was of a creature resembling a dog, in a desolate wilderness landscape. The creature's body faced left, but its head was turned to face the viewer; its face was a human face—a stunned, dazed human face. The landscape it inhabited was beyond bleak—with nothing growing, nothing green, it could have been a moonscape. The only thing sprouting in the wilderness was rock.

The creature was me. As soon I could, I rushed uptown, to the Upper East Side of Manhattan—relatively unknown territory for me then—to the gallery where the image hung. In the gallery was the most amazing painting, large and looming. I was no longer seeing through a glass darkly, no longer looking at a minuscule newspaper photograph. I confronted myself face to face. In my memory of this moment, the paint is still wet and the gallery smells of paint; it is as if the painting were a portrait of me, commissioned as I traveled by subway to get there.

Later, when I lay on the couch in my analyst's office and began to describe the experience, I fell silent. I could not talk at all; I could not begin to describe the feeling, the state of being, the "me" that I saw in the painting: a creature locked into an empty world, a world without anything or anyone, an objectless world, a world without language, a world without the possibility of response, a world within me I did not remember until I saw "my portrait", first in the newspaper and then in the gallery. The psychotic core. Eigen's book makes psychosis viable, viable because I am not psychotic, except for the me that is isolated in a landscape of rock, looking toward a potential other—if such an other is even possible—with desperation and despair, a self-state that is so primitive that it predates/precedes/foreshadows the dark night of the soul.

In a 2006 interview conducted by Regina Monti for Dharma Café, Eigen points out how in *The Psychotic Core* (1986) he describes Sigmund Freud's tripartite structure of the mind as "heavily steeped in a phenomenology of psychosis." He explains how Freud presents the id as a "seething cauldron of emotions," the superego as "persecution gone haywire," and the ego as both "hallucinatory organ and an adaptive agent with anti-hallucinatory properties." These structures of the mind are universal, and Eigen describes them as having psychotic-like qualities. It is in this sense that I use the words "psychotic" and "crazy"—ordinary, everyday sort of psychotic potential; psychotic moments.

I had the benefit of working with an analyst who was able to hold and contain my silence, my emptiness. And the benefit of what we so quaintly call strong ego functions, positively cathected internal objects, healthy relationships, and—a rarity, I'm told, among psychoanalysts—a happy childhood. One of my warmest memories of childhood is my father singing the song "Nature Boy", made famous in 1948 by Nat King Cole, and written by Eden Ahbez. The song ends with the lyrics: "The greatest thing you'll ever learn / is just to love and be loved in return." I was secure in a childhood that I loved, and I was loved. Yet, I wondered, if someone with a happy childhood, filled with love, could experience such bleakness and despair in an inner psychotic reality embedded in a non-psychotic self, then what else did I need to learn about the psychotic core of others?

Eigen's writings have a boomerang effect. The reader reads, the reader learns, the reader takes the teachings in, and the reader goes out into the world emboldened by the teachings. But the teachings arc outwards and come back suddenly and violently, leading to another moment of awakening. Fortunately, the boomerang is soft, padded, and gentle, and the violence of return is tempered by the joy of renewed discovery. The synergy of what I have learned from Eigen, my analyst, and my self-experience, is that I do not have to be clinically psychotic to experience my own psychotic states. Receiving this gift of understanding has allowed me to stay open to what otherwise might shut me down in an encounter with another's psychotic state, a state embedded perhaps in a highly functioning self, perhaps in a fragmenting, chaotic self.

Does feeling matter?

Another lesson that all psychoanalysts must learn, experientially—from within, not by rote, and not as an intellectual construct—is the necessity of *feeling* feelings. The "countertransference revolution" of the 1970s and onward taught us to pay attention to our feelings in session: feelings that we are conscious of, and feelings that we are avoiding, but which manifest in disguise and which we have to *learn* to recognize. This became the foundation of the psychoanalytic enterprise, drawing on the 1950s and 1960s work of Sandor Ferenczi, Paula Heimann, Enid Balint, and Heinrich Racker, and, later on, the pioneering countertransference supervision groups of Arthur Robbins. Winnicott's play space takes place in a two-person field.

I remember my excitement at recognizing that my feelings were indeed useful. I discovered that feelings are information, and emotions became as important to me as sensory input. Tip of the iceberg. I could now dedicate my feelings, in the transference–countertransference matrix, to the psychoanalytic undertaking of resonating with, recognizing, and even understanding the feelings of the other.

Still the tip of the iceberg. During the Second World War, the British poet Henry Reed published his brilliant anti-war poem "Lessons of the War". In the first part of the poem, "Naming of Parts", Reed begins by naming the parts of a rifle, among which is the safety-catch. The "naming of parts" takes place in a garden in springtime, among japonica and almond blossoms, with bees buzzing backwards and forwards. For me, naming the parts is like naming the emotions. And, in naming the emotions, I had kept the safety-catch closed. Love, hate, anger, envy, resentment, loneliness, joy, sorrow, fear, disgust, and disdain, are all bravely situated in the bedrock of the drives libido and aggression. We encounter and embrace the full range of our emotions, and the power of the drives.

In 2007, Karnac published Eigen's necessary and aptly titled book, *Feeling Matters.* Just as Eigen shares with us the profound explosions, implosions, and fragmentations within the psychotic core, so he shares with us the essence of psychoanalytic work, the healing core—where feeling matters. His book delves into the richness of feeling uncovered and explored during the psychoanalytic encounter. He emphasizes the point that *every feeling, every nuance of feeling, matters.* I also remember the "happy shock" of encountering those of Eigen's books that have one-word titles, feeling-words: *Ecstasy* (2001), *Rage* (2002), *Lust* (2006). With titles like these, more of the submerged iceberg breaks the surface of the water, the depths of the unconscious.

Rage

My immediate association of the word "rage" is the first three lines of the poem "Do not Go Gentle into that Good Night" by Dylan Thomas: "Do not go gentle into that good night, / Old age should burn and rave at close of day; / Rage, rage against the dying of the light" (Thomas, 1951, p. 207). The image conjured by those three lines is an image of a mad lust for life, a rejection of anything peaceful or reasonable. The rage against death is a burning and raving, an uncontrollable demand for life. Eigen's gloss, his Midrash on the poem, is that "[t]he poet rages against the coming of the night. He does not expect to stop death" (Eigen, 2002, p. 163). Rage is passionate enough to confront the impossible and not be daunted.

Rage, the book, and rage, the death-grip emotion, are both infiltrated by a serpent, swallowed by a serpent, crushed by a serpent, and personified as a serpent—a serpent slithers through the book like a metaphor. Metaphors slither because they cannot be the thing itself, the *ding an sich*, they can only signify. Here, Eigen seizes the metaphor by the tail, twirls it like a lasso, and forms it into a uroboros, and the snake greedily, lustfully, feeds on its own tail. If the Tao that can be said is not the Tao, and if the thing itself cannot be spoken, then language turns upon itself and, donning a disguise, dreams in metaphor.

In his chapter "Snake bite," Eigen explores a powerful dream image. Jack dreams he is being bitten by a poisonous snake, "bringing back childhood terrors" (Eigen, 2002, p. 111). In his discussion of the dream, Eigen offers us a split, a "reversal of affect," "a snake in the garden of one's soul" as well as the "[L]aw of the Dream: No amount of goodness will silence or end the work of the biting, poisonous snake" (Eigen, 2002, p. 111). Two-thirds of the way through *Rage*, we are bitten by terror. Eigen uses the intensity of the metaphor, the intensity of the terror of snakes, to take us back to the Garden of Eden, where paradise is destroyed by a snake, so that humankind will forever remember paradise lost, and fear further loss. In the final tercet of his poem, "Not Ideas About the Thing, But the Thing Itself", Wallace Stevens tells us, "It was like / A new knowledge of reality" (Stevens, 1972, p. 388). What is so telling in this last "thought" are the three words, "It was like." It was not the Thing Itself; it was like something, like a new knowledge of reality. We have no way to speak of the Thing Itself, the Tao, the Ineffable, without resorting to all our magnificent tricks of language—imagery, metaphor, simile, symbols, tripping merrily, and tip-toeing through the tropes. Eigen gives us the snake, an ancient image from an ancient story to capture our imagination and guide us safely through the terrors at the heart of rage.

In his 2003 essay, "The Dead Poets Society ventures into a radioactive analytic space", Patrick Kavanaugh explores the idea of the "Mind Poet". He writes,

> Through the ages, various cultures have recognized the poet's sacred obligation to be The One Who Remembers . . . In our more contemporary Westernized cultures, is the analyst not the One Who Remembers in *words* in the analytic space? Is he or she not a poet of the mind? (Kavanaugh, 2003, p. 342)

Kavanaugh compares the psychoanalyst to a shaman. His understanding of the poetic element in psychoanalysis is a perfect description of Eigen's role as a Mind Poet. Eigen is a master of metaphor, and translates the fantasy and dream imagery of his analysands into meaning. Not only does he understand the metaphors and imagery that his analysands bring to him in their free associations, memories, and dreams, but he also uses vivid poetic language to communicate to them the deepest hidden processes of their minds. He reveals themselves to themselves by being exquisitely attuned to their language, and by the elegance, playfulness, and poetry of his own language. In his willingness to meditate on the snake imagery in Jack's dream, and, indeed, on the dream productions and language play of all his analysands, Eigen is a consummate Mind Poet.

"Snake bite" ends with an allusion to the return of the repressed, with "Return of the snake as a momentary terror in the night" (Eigen, 2002, p. 115). Jack becomes willing to contemplate the snake within: "A good life does not dissolve the rage of the snake. Snake rage. Meanings do not slake its thirst" (Eigen, 2002, p.115). By studying Jack's dream, mediated through Eigen's interpretation, we are given the opportunity to consider the fear that belies our own rage.

Lust

Often, people experience lust as a "crazy" feeling. Desire is a much tamer word, and a tamer experience, than lust. Even libido sounds tame next to lust. Similarly, aggression sounds almost benign next to rage, and assertiveness, an aspect of aggression, has gentler connotations. Aggression is what we must have, what we need, in order to get what we want. Aggression is in the service of libido—we assertively look for love (or sex, if you want to be a bit more down to earth). But lust? Lust has an added kick. Lust for life. Lust for power. Lust for sex. No other word evokes the same intensity as lust; it even sounds aggressive. Sex is a biological given—we are animals, *ergo* we are sexual. Desire has a yearning aspect. Libido announces itself as a quality, something we possess, something that motivates us or, if we get closer to the source, something that drives us. A fancy name for sex. But lust demands, it has the special status of being a deadly sin; lust is uncontrollable.

In my practice, I have encountered men who voiced shame in describing experiences of lust. One young man said he knew that women needed romance, and that he had to court women during the sexual act. He felt that if he gave way to his lustful feelings in a consensual sexual encounter there would be no difference between his behavior and that of a rapist. Similarly, I have worked with women who fear their own lust, and project their lustful feelings on to the men who desire them. A number of women have expressed variations of the old saying, "Men are only interested in sex." As they explored their fear of male sexual desire, they found themselves acknowledging that they thought their own lustful feelings were "disgusting." One woman said that if she allowed herself to truly give in to the demands of lust, she would be a slut, a whore. "That kind of sex is only for men. It's not 'pretty' for a girl to act that way," she told me. Once these thoughts are articulated in the psychoanalytic encounter, the depths of the unconscious begin to yield memories, fantasies, and more. Eigen's *Lust* (2006) is a roadmap to guide the analyst in this work.

Eigen tells us that each of these feelings is worth a full book of our attention. And, in so doing, he offers us freedom. The freedom he offers us is the freedom he takes. He dances with possibility, with the infinity of what he might think and feel next. In any and every next moment, in any and every now, the reality of intensity exists. Are we free to experience our own experiences, to recognize and revel in intensity? When Eigen free associates poetically, with vision and discipline, he finds every nook and cranny, every corner of human experience, just as he discovers the vast expanses, the ever-increasing universe of just plain old being.

How many emotions can dance on the head of a pin? And how many analysts feeling those emotions can dance on the head of a pin? And which of those emotions are the analyst's, which the analysand's, which are both at once, and which are someone else's entirely? When Eigen explores intensity, offering vignettes of what happened between and within two people in his consulting room, he invites us to consider what really occurs if at least one person in that room respects the reality of fantasy, the reality of intensity, the reality of memory, and the reality of self and other.

In *Lust*, Eigen describes how he once answered an analysand's threat to commit suicide off a bridge by saying that he would join him in the jump, that they could hit the water together. How many analysts would have the imagination or courage to match this instance of Eigen's intensity and freedom? In this daring and poignant example, Eigen enters into the reality of the despondent analysand, holds the projective identification, and gives it back to him, so that the analysand feels the intensity not only of his own despairing suicidal wishes, but of the impact of a suicidal gesture on the other. Because Eigen gave substance to his analysand's suicidal fantasy, his analysand felt the intensity of the potential that Eigen, too, might die, and suicide was no longer an option for the patient (2006, p. 58).

Eigen's poetic imagination allows him to imagine the drama of the analysand's image. In taking this image seriously, and using it dramatically, he offers the analysand a reflected image of his mind. In joining the analysand and sharing the dramatic action of the image of jumping off a bridge, he opens a doorway to the potential of two minds willing to share and consider an idea together. By joining the fantasy, he creates intimacy without the dangers of merger. He does so by using the word "together", so that they are not a merged oneness, but, rather, two differentiated people. He showed the analysand that he was not afraid of the analysand's mind; he was not afraid of whatever the analysand could imagine and, therefore, the analysand did not have to be afraid of overwhelming Eigen. They could co-exist in the analysand's fantasy without psychic danger.

Ecstasy

Ecstasy can be seen as a completely involving altered state of consciousness; a full body and soul demand of the self toward the self; to give oneself over, to lose control; to be wholly, unutterably engaged. Ecstasy, too, may be imbued with terror. In *Ecstasy* (2001), Eigen offers us splits and integration, the extremes of experience of terror and joy, the intensity of transcending the self and integrating and grounding the self.

The word "ecstasy" is derived from the ancient Greek *ekstasis*, meaning standing outside the self, or, more literally, a state of being that is outside of where one stands—an elsewhere. In *Ecstasy*, the book, and perhaps in ecstasy, the state of being, as Eigen roams through his own life experience, his clinical experience, his meeting with Wilfred Bion and the impact of that encounter on his entire sense of self and how he works, his immersion in the works of the poets, of Shakespeare, of David the Psalmist, of the Torah as a whole, he offers us an elsewhere that becomes here and now, the ecstasy of being alive.

"But I avow the ecstasy of being alive is the core of our existence . . ." (Eigen, 2001, p. vii). In his introduction to *Ecstasy*, Eigen tells us that his intent with the book is to write "psychoanalytic poetry"—and he does. The poetry of *Ecstasy*—and the poetry of ecstasy—is the discovery of extremes, the polarizations and sameness of feeling. Poetry is a special use of language that conveys intensity of feeling, an intensity that involves extremes of experience and emotion. As ecstasy itself can be thought of as the utmost intense, extreme experience, to bring psychoanalytic insight to understanding and exploring ecstasy is to acknowledge the underlying poetic aspects of ecstasy. Eigen's language is itself poetic, both elevated in its condensation and expressiveness, and down to earth and accessible in its connection to lived experience.

Core truth

In becoming analysts, we encounter the perils and cruelties of splits within the psychoanalytic community. These are not merely the splits of competing theories, of prescriptions and proscriptions of clinical practice, but of something much worse: the ecstasy of searching for an authentic self, the ecstasy of freedom within the psychoanalytic journey, contrasting and conflicting with the personae we begin to believe we should assume as members of a psychoanalytic community, and the need to present ourselves as "well-analyzed."

If we attain the ecstasy of authenticity and integration, of personal vision, of contact with the inner depths and core of self and being, can we maintain that freedom within our community? Can we assert, "Here am I, here I stand, outside of where once I stood, ecstatic in just being me?" Or do we deny what we have attained, regress to an earlier conflicted, inhibited self, and show up neatly packaged at psychoanalytic gatherings, participating in scholarly discourse with appropriate aplomb? In essence, by accepting the freedom Eigen offers in his writings, we have the ability to choose freedom for ourselves, in the face of whatever anxieties and regressive pulls we feel. If we are drawn to freedom, we can find the courage to ignore the limitations we otherwise may have accepted as "officially approved revealed truth."

The concept of analytic neutrality, when misunderstood or misused, can become toxic, both clinically and within the psychoanalytic community. Because psychoanalytic work can, at times, be so emotionally intense and challenging for the practitioner, the concept of neutrality needs to be addressed in order to help the analyst remain true to emotional experience instead of avoiding experience. Eigen's work offers an antidote to this kind of misunderstanding and misuse of neutrality. To fully appreciate what Eigen offers, it may be useful to revisit the problems associated with neutrality. Neutrality masks withholding in the clinical setting; it masks a fear in the analyst of feeling too much. It can become so much a part of an analyst's ego ideal that the analyst creates a bland, neutralized, neutered personality, both while working and while interacting with colleagues.

Eigen's willingness to explore ecstasy, in terms that allow the reader to share in the joy of doing so, can be seen as a fulcrum between the constrictions of misused analytic neutrality and the invitation to ecstasy exemplified by "oceanic feeling." "Oceanic feeling," a term coined by Romaine Rolland, is a sense of oneness with everything, without boundaries. In Freudian institutes, we learn that Freud considered "oceanic feeling" a primitive, regressive ego state, that religious ecstasy is infantile. In *Ecstasy*, Eigen offers us ecstasy as an outcome of psychoanalysis, integration, a healing of splits. He considers the symbolism of "Hillel's sandwich," created and eaten during the Passover Seder. Hillel's sandwich is made of *matzoth* (unleavened bread), *maror* (bitter herbs), and *charoset* (a concoction of wine, chopped fruit, and chopped nuts). The bitter herbs represent all that is bitter in life and, in the Passover story, the bitterness of slavery when the Israelites were slaves in Egypt. The *charoset* represents the mortar that the Hebrew slaves used to build the pyramids. Thus, Eigen points out, what is bitter and what is sweet are brought together. The sweetness of mortar, of cement, binds to the bitterness; experience is one (Eigen, 2001, p. 68).

Experiencing that experience in one is the healing of splits. Eigen tells us that the work of psychoanalysis consists of *restoring the capacity to feel*, becoming a feeling self (Eigen, 2001, p. 70). And, if this is true, and we become feeling selves, and we feel oceanic feeling, then Eigen, by example, evokes in us the freedom to be true to ourselves.

If we are indeed ecstatic, visionary, drunk with the divine (and, therefore, on the road to becoming the best psychoanalysts we can be because we are becoming the best people we can be), it is because we are true to ourselves. Following Eigen, I discovered that I could be true to myself in writing about psychoanalysis. I wrote from my core, what is sacred within me. I was true to myself; I had to be.

When I was a psychoanalytic candidate and I first began writing psychoanalytic articles in the hope of publishing, I tortured myself into writing how I thought I was supposed to write, how I was told to write. I gritted my teeth and began with a "review of the literature." I had taught college English and creative writing, and I knew that a good essay could either begin with a thesis statement, followed by an outline of the three main ideas to be developed, or with an anecdote or even a joke. How to write an essay? Thesis statement, first idea, second idea, third idea? Or an anecdote that would bring to life the thesis and the three main ideas, that would introduce the concepts in a vivid, engaging way? Either/Or. But does there have to be a split? Or can writing an essay be a fresh experience; can the essay find its own way? Similarly, I wondered how Winnicott was able to pen fascinating article after fascinating article without resorting to merely citing the literature. He does cite the literature, but only after his own contribution. I loved reading his articles because he is not strictly "logical." He does not lead us to obvious and evident conclusions—he leaves us hanging, trying to figure out for ourselves what comes next, after we have finished reading and closed the covers of the book. He does not offer answers, he offers mystery. I knew that I could never write like him, that he was a one and only. And I knew that if I wrote authentically, as Winnicott did, I would never get published.

Therefore, I felt fortunate when I discovered Eigen's writings. He wrote the way I felt, and he wrote what I wanted to read; his writings resonated with me. He wrote like a poet. He wrote the way psychoanalysis is. Eigen had blazed a path, ventured into the wilderness and left guideposts for those who were similarly drawn to the wilderness. I also experienced this in direct contact with Eigen in his seminars.

In these seminars, which are not psychoanalytic sessions, but profound learning experiences, Eigen's presence is important. In 1927, the Greek-Armenian mystic G. I. Gurdjieff published a book in Russian that was translated into English as *Meeting with Remarkable Men* in 1963. The English title conveys somewhat the pleasure of being in Eigen's presence when he reads out loud, comments, digresses, and engages his audience. I think many who attend his seminars feel something similar to what I do—the sense of meeting anew a remarkable man. His presence is quietly charismatic. He is not a "showman"; he is genuine and his authenticity communicates directly. Sometimes we are fortunate enough to meet someone who just *is*—is true to him/herself, not flashy, and not unduly humble. Eigen is simply himself. He is generous with his knowledge and insight, and open to, and accepting of, those with whom he engages.

In his writings and his seminars on Kabbalah and psychoanalysis, Eigen emphasizes that what psychoanalysts have to tolerate in contacting the depths is fragmentation. For only by sustaining ourselves in the presence of someone who might be shattering, fragmenting, can we create our presence for that other, a presence that will stay whole even when shattering. But how do we remain one as we shatter?

Sometimes, when people encounter the catastrophe of trauma that Eigen often speaks about in his Bion seminars, they search for true contact with themselves. Eigen explores how the effect of truth-seeking affects the "sensitive self", the self we all have. He asks, "[W]hat is truth, how does one use it, how does one relate to fanatic use of 'truth,' hallucinated truth, the omnipresence of truth, and so on?" (2001, p. 7). He further describes catastrophic annihilation: "It may happen that emotional fields are so annihilating that ability to 'process' annihilation remains stunted" (2001, p. 170). And he offers the remarkable view that the binding of fragmenting, annihilating emotion does not necessarily arise only from secondary process, but from primary process as well—once primary process is not used defensively by schizophrenics—in "spinning," rather than processing.

I found this concept illuminating in understanding my experience several years ago of working with someone who lived in a "fragmented" state, but somehow found a way to use her primary process to move toward achieving wholeness.

"Candy" tried to efface her personality. She wore baggy, casual clothing; she had a low voice and usually an expressionless face. She was the sole employee of a small business, her employer was often not on the premises, and she maintained only two friendships, both with severely emotionally disturbed young women. She put a great deal of effort into staying bland, affectless, and quiet. I tried to listen for affect, but I heard only fear of affect.

Candy and one of her friends began to experiment with using a Ouija board. She told me that when she held the planchette, she received messages on the Ouija board from a demon, an evil spirit, telling her to kill herself.

I said to her, "I don't think these messages are coming from an evil demon, from anything outside of you. I think the message is coming from within you, from a part of yourself we need to find out more about."

She was startled, and for the first time I saw signs of life in her dead eyes and frozen facial expression. She answered that yes, she knew that there were many parts of herself. And then, for months on end, for significantly over a year, she told me about the various personalities who lived within her. None of them ever took over to "run the show"—she was always her own main personality, her own "self" with her own name—but they sometimes advised her; sometimes one suggested what to buy for dinner, for instance. They did not emerge or relate to the outside world on their own, but they had very intense relationships among themselves.

They were male and female, of various ages and various ethnicities. Candy told me that there were hundreds of them and that she knew them all by name. They quarreled; they formed deep friendships, passionate love affairs, and furious rivalries among themselves; they attacked one another, raped one another, defended one another, and sheltered one another. She began to hold "town meetings" with them, where they came together to discuss grievances and make plans for the future. She taped the meetings and brought me a tape or two to listen to, to help me understand how important and intense the meetings were. Eventually the rapes and killings stopped. The attackers were told that they had to learn to control themselves or they would be banished. Banished, that most unsettling word. To be banished is to be forced into isolation, abandoned; it is terrifying. They learned to control themselves.

The older selves began to cherish the younger selves, particularly a very young self who had the same name as the main personality, Candy. We watched her develop from a newborn baby self, and on to a toddler, then a little girl. This very young self told the main personality that she would help her remember what the main self could not remember, could not allow herself to remember. This young self had a lot to say about her experience in the world. And every other self mobilized to protect her, reassuring her that they would take care of her, and would stop fighting because it bothered her.

While working with Candy, I was learning what I would later learn in more depth, and with more theoretical structure, from Eigen. I learned that a fragmenting self, caught in a vortex of extreme catastrophe, which Eigen describes so well and so often in his work, could find a way to organize itself, even if that way might seem like "madness" to others. In this vortex, Candy found a way to organize her fragmenting self in her own primary process, like those Eigen describes so movingly, and in such rich detail, in *Coming Through the Whirlwind* (1991).

In *Kabbalah and Psychoanalysis* (2012), Eigen alerts us to the explosive nature of fragmentation: "I am a catastrophe in process. My personality is catastrophic. Something awful has happened. I am undergoing a state of disintegration, flying off into space. I am happening to me; I am a constant disturbance to myself" (Eigen, 2012, p. 20). But he also offers hope:

> The intensity of pouring oneself into an insoluble problem perforates the psyche and you find yourself in another place, a place you might not have imagined before it happened. The unsolvable can promote growth of experience in unsuspected ways . . . The seminar as an incomplete moment, a sense of beginning. (Eigen, 2012, p. 78)

In his seminars, Eigen emphasizes Lurianic Kabbalah—the teachings of the sixteenth-century Jewish mystic, Isaac Luria, focusing on the concept of *tzimtzum*, God's contraction and withdrawal in the act of creating the universe. If God is everything, how can he create anything? In order to create, God had to make room for more, for the Otherness of his Creation; he had to contract, withdraw, and shatter. The created world—matter—consists of fragments of divinity that, in shattering, became creation.

In *Freud's Moses* (1991), the great scholar and historian Yosef Hayim Yerushalmi cites the Menahot exegesis from Deuteronomy 10 in the Talmud, which claims that both the intact tablet of the Ten Commandments, and the broken pieces of the original tablet, which Moses dashed to the ground in wrath, were preserved in the Ark. Both the intact and the fragmented are therefore revered as holy.

What did I learn from contemplating Eigen's description of Lurianic Kabbalah? Because I felt I was in the presence of an inordinately gifted person who integrates psychoanalysis and mysticism, I translated the Kabbalistic vision into the psychoanalytic encounter. We, as psychoanalysts, have to make room for the other. We have to shatter without losing our center. As Eigen points out, we can stay true to ourselves while following Bion's injunction to encounter the other without memory, desire, or knowledge. We have to let our sense of ourselves as "knowledgeable psychoanalysts" shatter, to make room for the here and now. Whatever assaults we encounter in someone else's emotional experience, even if we feel that we are coming to pieces, we do not have to lose our center. The experience of shattering is our emotional resonance with the other. It is the foundation of empathy.

Is this what Eigen meant? I don't know. But it is what I learned. I learned it in his presence, from his presence. He endures, and without a "they", then "I", and "we", endure, and learn, and grow.

References

Eigen, M. (1986). *The Psychotic Core.* London: Karnac, 2004.

Eigen, M. (1991). *Coming Through the Whirlwind: Case Studies in Psychotherapy.* Brooklyn, NY: Chiron.

Eigen, M. (2001). *Ecstasy.* Middletown, CT.: Wesleyan University Press.

Eigen, M. (2002). *Rage.* Middletown, CT.: Wesleyan University Press.

Eigen, M. (2006). *Lust.* Middletown, CT.: Wesleyan University Press.

Eigen, M. (2007). *Feeling Matters.* London: Karnac.

Eigen, M. (2012). *Kabbalah and Psychoanalysis.* London: Karnac.

Gurdjieff, G. I. (1963). *Meetings with Remarkable Men.* New York: E. P. Dutton.

Kavanaugh, P. B. (2003). The Dead Poets Society ventures into a radioactive psychoanalytic space. *Psychoanalytic Review, 90*: 341–360.

Monti, R. (2006). Faith and disillusionment: an interview with Dr. Michael Eigen. Dharma Café. Accessed at: http://www.dharmacafe.com/lifecycles/faith-and-disillusionment-an-interview-with-dr-michael-eigen.

Reed, H. (1942). Lessons of the War. *New Statesman and Nation*, 4(598): 92.

Stevens, W. (1954). Not Ideas About the Thing, But the Thing Itself. In: H. Stevens (Ed.), *The Palm at the End of the Mind: Selected Poems and a Play* (pp. 387–388). New York: Vintage, 1972.

Thomas, D. (1951). Do not Go Gentle into that Good Night. *The Poems of Dylan Thomas*, D. Jones (Ed.). New York: A New Directions Book.

Yerushalmi, Y. H. (1991). *Freud's Moses: Judaism Terminable and Interminable*. New Haven, CT: Yale University Press.

CHAPTER EIGHTEEN

Sensing the mustard seed: defense, awakening, and fragmentation

Louis Rothschild

Introduction

Imagine a lunch counter as a stage set circa 1956. This time of nuclear anxiety affords a satisfaction in regard to my present aim as it occurs after world wars but before cultural revolutions boiled over in 1968. There a beatnik speaks with another traveler while sitting at a café counter. "The weather calls for Z and more Z through the weekend," says the beatnik. The fellow traveler, a businessperson, not a bohemian, replies, "Heard that report before. Didn't like it then, and, though I've come to respect it, I really don't like it any more now. Hard to avoid Z though." The beatnik looks to the other with curiosity. Lights fade.

The "hard to avoid" Z, as most who are familiar with Michael Eigen's work will know, is Winnicott's (1971) idea of a dimension consisting of the dire, if not irreparable, aspects of traumatic history. In an original manner, Eigen (2009, 2012) eloquently works and reworks Winnicott's portrayal of a mother who is gone for a period of time beyond which a baby can bear, and subsequently, even upon the mother's return, the baby remains forever changed. This change, a Z dimension, arises due to not being held, and lost in space long enough so that one may become afraid of being held in the future (Shabad, 2004), or afraid of being creative (Eigen, 2011). Here, I wish to bring attention to the manner in which Winnicott's mother may also be changed (we hope in a loving direction) upon recognizing that Z is part of her child. Each member of the dyad may come to know each side of this relational matrix. To that end, mother is used as a gender-neutral verb applicable to acts of conscious holding (Rothschild, 2009a). Not only may a mother be traumatized, but, through development and maturity, the baby may one day be capable of self-soothing. As one's soothing becomes conscious, we may refer to a Self-mother, or Self-compassion. Such recognition, or mindful holding, constitutes the witnessing capacities necessary to be mindful with Z. This is a sort of mindfulness that stands as a witness outside of recurring tragedies in a manner that allows traumatic repetition to be contained. It is in the contexts of trauma and traumatic witnessing that I approach Eigen's particular influence on my work in accordance with his affirmative preference for frames of mindful engagement ranging from Buddhism to Judaism that are anchored in psychoanalysis (see Eigen, 1998).

Central to Eigen's preference for multiple frames is the suggestion that one embodies an attitude appropriate for an encounter with poetry. He (Eigen, 2009) writes of poetry lust as a particular addiction that gives birth to experience. Eigen (2009) recommends a mindfully poetic attitude for clinical work, and also as a way to read psychoanalytic meta-theory. I take this to be an articulation that emphasizes play and simultaneously entails a radical respect for engagement with the coercive qualities of defensive structures that may undermine play. Eigen's (2009) conceptualization that toxicity and nourishment travel together places coercion and play in a uniquely audible register where tragic and lyric poetry do not so much co-exist alongside each other as intermingle. I became assured that his poetic preference is a genuine attitude of hearing and being in email correspondence with him following one of my reviews of his work (Rothschild, 2009b). In addition to Rainer Maria Rilke, Eigen surprised me as he wondered if I was familiar with Lawrence Ferlinghetti. This line of questioning led to a memory and reverie of my time as an undergraduate student in San Francisco, studying the Kabbalah with a professor known to Ferlinghetti for his Kabbalistic beat-era poetry (Meltzer, 2011). Prior to that brief exchange via email, I had not explicitly linked my psychoanalytic psychologist self to this part of my history, even though I had read psychoanalytic texts with that same professor during my undergraduate studies. Eigen's question illuminated a space that, while not quite lost, had been neglected.

I also became aware of this neglect and hunger for rapprochement when I first heard him speak (Eigen, 1995). Two decades ago, I had less space to look back and rework, yet I had room to marvel at Eigen's capacity to move from individual psychology to social or critical theory with artistic grace. Then and now, such illuminating contact is a most important influence. In many ways, I think Eigen's work stands as an achievement, reconstituting not only *mysticism* but also *art* within psychoanalysis. An overarching rubric is that his work is a reconstitution of joy. To return to my aforementioned stage set from this perspective is to encounter my own desire for temporal connection and pleasure in a vertical transmission of art, culture, and other fare fit for psychic taste buds. The desire for connection and continuity stands in bold relief against a postmodern *zeitgeist* of relentless a-historical "no brow" culture in which depth and distinction are diminished, if not repudiated outright (Strenger, 2005). *Pace* Eigen's language, historically embodied cultural connectivity marks movement from absence in a time before teeth to a time in which teeth mark relational embodiment in a rich living history affording a good feed where we can learn to nourish what is vital and not destroy it (Eigen, 2007). In such a world, my own Z-ness is not only encountered, but also, quite often, contained. Lights flicker on.

Flickering lights may signal the past, but they do so in the present. The poet May Sarton writes of the soul being unencumbered in the pristine moment as a definition of poetry (Sarton, 1997). Within psychoanalysis, some (e.g., Bion, 1970; Symington, 2012) have suggested that such conscious presence is a common factor of phenomenological encounters across psychoanalysis, Buddhism, poetry—across any mindfulness or mystical practice. Such an explicit argument is an important correction to observations that Western psychologists are tantalized by the flavor of immediate experience due to being dislocated from such experience as a result of being stuck within theories and conceptions of psychology as opposed to being with the psychological in the present (Trungpa, 2005). Like Chögyam Trungpa Rinpoche (Trungpa, 2005), Eigen does not seem to take a position that Buddhists and psychoanalysts are conducting the same work, yet Eigen suggests that psychoanalysis adopt big Buddha ears for its logo

(Eigen, 2010). His suggestion, I think, points to several observations shared by Trungpa in the 1970s: To emphasize the present moment, that a basic sanity exists before sickness (of the Z dimension), and the idea that situating dependency through testimony and support is a difference between mediation and psychotherapy. Of course like Eigen, Trungpa challenges such tidy distinctions. Chögyam Trungpa writes, "The work you do doesn't have to have a title or a name particularly. It is just being ultimately decent. Take the example of Buddha himself—he wasn't a Buddhist!" (Trungpa, 2005, p. 138).

As I contemplate this spacious lack of particularity applied to decency and to Buddha himself, I wonder about intrapsychic life, self-analysis, or, as James framed it, how I relate to me (James, 2003). Perhaps Eigen is Eigen and Buddha, if not Buddhist, is a Buddha. Through Eigen we see that the road to decency is no simple journey. He finds in Tillich the idea that greatness is obtained through a journey into the dissociated darkness of one's self (Eigen, 1993). Additionally, Eigen writes of Bion as helpful when "barbed wire surrounds the soul and cuts into it" (Eigen, 2010, p. 40) in order to develop a capacity to sing "in the center of our gnarled selves" (Eigen, 2007, p. 92). Eigen writes of the impossibility to be consistently decent as an enacting of Z that is a shattering within the therapeutic hour (Eigen, 2012). Eigen considers that this journey into darkness is a dangerous one, and finds in the example of Jack Kerouac's tragic death evidence that great care is required (Eigen, 2001). Caring, or being ultimately decent, sets the bar high, into the heavens. It is to be hoped that lights are found on at the end of, if not during, a session and a life. In order to be basically decent or good enough, the overwhelming quality of Z needs to be negotiated so as to embody what Eigen (1999, 2012) refers to as a *spontaneous recovery rhythm*. Encounters with decency, then, are encounters with grace, a fantastic moment occurring after one storm and before another. Previously, I have written (Rothschild, 2009b) that Eigen's writing led me to dwell on some of the most challenging aspects of my clinical work, and here I focus on how his work additionally aided me during a challenging time in my *personal life*.

Winter's scream

I began to know of Z in a different manner when my son underwent emergency surgery. That separation and subsequent reunion permanently changed me. The week that he spent as an inpatient led to difficult associations ranging from my identification with Demeter's rage in Persephone's absence as an explanation for the origin of winter to Odysseus's desire not only to return home, but to have remained at home in the first place (Hamilton, 1969). In such stress and vulnerability, my own desire to deny fragility and separation was strong. If only the lights would stay on. How I wanted to undo what has been done, to attack all links while simultaneously reaching out. Here, I found a need to make space for the part of me that does not want to acknowledge space. Such work may be considered an effort to find compassion in regard to our wish to dissociate and not embody compassion as a place to begin making contact or associating (Bromberg, 1998).

A few months after we left the hospital, these thoughts were rekindled while watching members of the UK's National Health Service dance bedside with children who played pediatric patients while Harry Potter author J. K. Rowling (1997) read from *Peter Pan* (Barrie, 2000) during the opening ceremony of the 2012 Summer Olympics. There, Greek mythology, object relations, and the warrior stance of sport exploded across my television screen in a celebration of life. While Rowling reads of Pan, her own literary creation of perverse omnipotence is defeated before our eyes by none other than Mary Poppins in alliance with the bedside medical staff on the grounds of the Olympic stadium. Due in no small part to the very real communal influence found in the British psyche to protect all children during the Blitz as a stimulant and marker of the maternal turn in object relations (Zaretsky, 2010), Mary Poppins represents a sort of healer providing care in the aftermath of Z.

One could consider Mary Poppins meeting Harry Potter through Peter Pan simply an escapist flight to the Imaginary. Yet, with a little bit of fairy dust, we might alter this frame and find that it is not so much an invitation to escape as it is an invitation to be *creatively present*. Such a presence considers that art has afforded a Symbolic space, opening a lane from which to approach O, or the Real. That these stories may be further linked in a connection of the literary to the clinical is artistic genius on the part of Danny Boyle and various British authors in general who seem to know a thing or two about situating Z within everyday life. Blogging for the *Guardian*, chief arts writer Charlotte Higgins (2012) suggests that only a British citizen could make such art, and that viewers abroad would most probably not understand. Literacy, however, may be understood through knowledge that central roots of North American psychoanalysis originated in Great Britain (e.g., Izod, 2008). From North American shores, a National Health Service with Mary Poppins aboard looks sweet. Part of Eigen's contribution is that ideal experiencing such as this may not simply be reduced to the pathological (Eigen, 1981). That observation helps make legitimate such a lively space within psychoanalysis itself. In my opinion, Eigen's ability to situate joy within psychoanalysis allows our consulting rooms to grow warmer.

Such warmth is vital as multiplicity and, by extension, thinking itself seems to depend on traumatic separation. Eigen considers that many carry such knowledge of separation and he recently refers to this as knowledge of having been skinned (Eigen, 2012). Does separation always truck with trauma (Ferenczi, 1949), leaving a confused or confusing mark of Z, or is it simply hard to avoid? Avoiding Z certainly has a fantastic feel to it. Yet, if against such fantastic thought, one finds that Z has not been avoided, we may hope to embody, if not to simply *accompany* (Eigen, 2007), such separation in our praxis so as not to be confused or disembodied in the wake of trauma (Stolorow et al., 2002). There, a wish for union is also a wish for reunion, a wish to be whole. Eigen writes that we are partial beings who ache for total states (Eigen, 2009).

. . . Staggering ascent

Before the Olympics, I emailed with Eigen a second time. I had planned to attend one of his talks on Kabbalah and psychoanalysis in New York during the spring of 2012, but my plans were interrupted until I was able to hear him speak in the fall of that year. My email was sent following a scream cry—not just crying, not simply screaming, in which I found myself in Hades. My son was in the hospital and each day felt like a crossing of the river Styx. Where the hell was Mary Poppins when I needed her? My wish that Mary would be on the shore of the River Styx might have been facilitated by the Percy Jackson series (Riordan, 2005) that I had been reading with my son prior to his hospitalization. In those pages, the Greek myths are real and take place in New York. Children's stories provided a touchstone for my son and me. In the holding environment of contemporary media, my son and I have also most recently finished reading *The Hobbit* (Tolkien, 2012). In those pages, I am reminded of having also thought of Bilbo Baggins while in the hospital. Unlike Kerouac, Bilbo knew journeys to be dangerous and did not want to leave home. Ulysses, Demeter, and countless others not all born of British authors embody Bilbo's resistance to separation. Bob Dylan captures this in his contemporary Midrash about the potential sacrifice of Isaac:

> Oh God said to Abraham, "Kill me a son."
> Abe said, "Man, you must be puttin' me on."
>
> (Bob Dylan, 2004, p. 178)

Abraham's suggestion that God must be joking is natural. To imagine such separation is painful beyond comprehension. A mark of Z left as if made by Zorro's hand is resisted. Scar is the translation of Odysseus, and, true to his namesake, Ulysses spends his adult life reworking disturbances reminiscent of the boar-inflicted injury that he encountered as a child (Shay, 2002). That Ulysses, like Bilbo and others, rises to the occasion of facing painful loss may be read as illustrations of a capacity to work with Z. *Z marks an adventure most would not choose*. In response to my email sent from hospital lodging, Eigen's heartfelt concern came across with his words that life is fragile. He wrote then of sitting across from a playground, watching children play and weeping. Almost a year later, there is joy in watching my son play. Cries in the dark work to light candles. Such light may be linked to homecoming or, by extension, a Sabbath.

Eigen (1981) writes of an irony of radical sincerity in Bion's work, and this stance is maintained in Eigen's (2012) working with Bion's comment that Kabbalah is a frame for psychoanalysis. Kabbalah may be considered a container of trauma. This capacity to contain is illustrated by the timely popularization of Kabbalah as one response to the traumatic dislocation of the Inquisition (Patai, 1967). Simply, Jewish mysticism may be considered another practice of working with Z. To work with Z through the ironic apprehension of dislocation also embodies something of what Trungpa Rinpoche aims at in his advocating of decency as compassionate containment. In that regard, these divergent traditions overlap on love. Eigen (2012) speaks of a reading of the Jewish commandment that one love God with all one's heart as a commandment that one bring a loving attitude to all relational spaces. Decency, then, is recognition of life and the darkness found in life in a manner that fully expresses the joy of living through wisdom (Trungpa, 2009). From this perspective, words such as decency, compassion, and containment have much in common.

That cultivating decency is hard work is illustrated in many traditions. Following recovery from the intoxicating effect of lotus eating, Odysseus is keenly aware of danger so as to be able to order his men bound to their rowing benches just as he will bind himself to the mast in order to maintain a mediated relation to pain and desire in order to escape the tantalizing intoxicant offered anew by the Sirens (Homer, 1997). Eigen (2010) writes of the pea becoming part of the princess's warp much as Odysseus's scar defines his identity. Decency, compassion, and containment are all loving responses that bear witness to the warping that is Z.

Buddhist thought begins with the observation that pain is found in life, and the Shambhala tradition (Trungpa, 2009) considers the warrior one who occupies a raw space without skin. That ancient Greeks stamped nipples into their breastplates used as armor moves in this direction. Armor may also be a product of mind that does not facilitate, but interferes with, nakedness. In Shambhala, as in psychoanalysis, special attention is given to the hard, internal edges that inhibit one's relating with a big heart. Fearlessness, then, is being ordinary and simpleminded—naked in encounters with obstacles.

Containers of mustard seed

Ironically, it is often through breaking that we become, as sometimes "it" moves faster than we would like. A traumatized woman carries her dead son through the streets. Eventually, she is told to go to see the Buddha for help with Z (one extended version of this story may be found in Conover, 2005). Buddha sees that she is carrying a corpse, and tells her that in order for him to help her she must return with a single seed of mustard obtained from a home in which no one has died. As this story is set in India, everyone has mustard seed in their homes. However, the woman soon learns that every home has also known death. This knowledge changes her grief. She readies her son for a funeral, and she subsequently joins Buddha in a monastic life.

A search for a mustard seed that does not exist creates an opening where self-compassion may be found. Self-compassion, in its own right, may require time, and is no simple matter. Bi-directional compassion—that is, compassion toward self and toward another—can be trickier. The night before my son had surgery, I went to the bathroom in the pediatric intensive care unit while a boy in the next room was dying. There was a bustle of hopeful doctors and nurses with large implements moving around his body. In the hallway, his parents sat near the nurses' station. As I slowed near them on the way back to my room, I felt as though the boy's father was vibrating out of his own skin. Such vibrations might well be what the mother felt before searching for mustard seed. Although this catastrophe was occurring just outside of our room, I could not speak of it to my wife or son. Hope is not quite the same as faith, and we simply were not available. The next morning, the other room was no longer occupied. I remember the room, stark in its emptiness as seen through some curtains and I also remember my focusing on an unopened Monopoly game with the thought that it had not been left due to an oversight, but was intentionally left because it would never be used. A nurse kindly told me not to confuse that family's outcome with my own. A few hours later, we discussed what was to be a long day with our surgical team. It is easy to be confused in regard to what is inside and outside.

The rotation structure for nurses in the ICU made clear that the nursing staff knew how real and potentially dangerous such confusion can be. Rotating among a patient group aims to prevent getting close in a manner that could interfere with technical work. Big Buddha ears, psychoanalytic taste buds, may be seen as a hazard. Unique instruments used for particular work. Eigen recommends that a therapist not only needs big ears, but needs to be prepared to sit with a terrifying and terrified scream, providing a background, possibly for decades, so that something may grow over time (Eigen, 2010, 2012). Such work has a different pace and subject matter. Simply situating a recovery space in which to seek spontaneous rhythm may require time. Bion (1970) proposes the use of the term *intuit* to illustrate this different subject matter in order to move alongside the sensations that exist readily for the physician. Intuit is not readily seen, and Bion (1970) recommends becoming artificially blind in order to work with what is dark. I am pleased to do this in session, and ever so happy that the ICU nurses did not.

Eigen has developed a character, Dr. Z (2009). That a doctor of Z may also embody Z is to find a wounded nourisher (Eigen, 2010). This is a more complicated than Kohut's Mr. Z (1979), as that different treatment style might instill what Eigen has called a "tyranny of goodness" (Eigen, 1981). Dr. Z is not so good in regard to tyrannical neatness. Favored here is an uncertainty that affirms shifting qualities over a tidy but pathological foreclosure (Eigen, 1993). The doctor's humanness is writ large. Dr. Z speaks of the manner in which we twist ourselves out of shape in order to stay alive. A hardening of parts of the self is an aspect of individuation (Eigen, 2009), and therein is Z and a need for self-compassion. Eigen's Dr. Z (2009, p. 114) asks, "Are poets suicide bombers? Are comedians?" These questions ask that we notice that what may be constructive may also be destructive. Dr. Z accompanies a patient named Grace in a chapter entitled "Something wrong" (Eigen, 2009), and they speak of focusing on what is wrong in order to find what is right. Eigen's focus extends beyond the consulting room to our culture in general. His character Grace speaks of dreams as being like a respirator in an intensive care ward. Soon, Grace refers to the USA as a dream-eating monster. Curtain falls. Is this intermission? Pass the mustard, please.

Was this not Buddha's original observation, that pain does not feel right, and that making space to breathe requires great care. Grace articulates the danger of destroying platforms that are life sustaining. Following Buddha, little seeds of mustard come to be viewed as signifiers of a testimony that we can work with what is wrong. A mother of an older boy who had surgery some years ago and is now doing well tells me, "Its just PTSD" in regard to our upcoming surgical anniversary. Through social media, I learn that a childhood acquaintance from summer camp has lost her son, and that another from high school discusses transplant surgery with his son who thinks that he will die. To bear hearing requires faith. Is such faith possible? Eigen (2011) recommends an attitude of beginning that allows for bearing witness to Z in order to see if faith is possible.

A client says, "I want to be able to hide—to not disappoint."

Another, "The transition lasts forever."

In a case of severe trauma, "Someone has to die."

My patient who speaks of being stuck in a time says, crying, "To think it's a problem of labeling is helpful." From this patient's perspective, Z is understood as an index of badness becoming a marker and generator of excessive guilt and shame. Here, a label actively stands in the way of joy, and ironically becomes an entrance to care—a psycho-spiritual wormhole (Eigen, 2009). To enter such a wormhole requires faith, and Eigen has made this explicit.

Considering where it has been republished, Eigen's writing (1981) on an area of faith is regarded as foundational (e.g., Eigen, 1999). A recent visit (March 2013) to the Psychoanalytic Electronic Archive finds this article oft cited, ninety-eight citations and growing. One of those who cite it is Jessica Benjamin (1988). With thinking close to Eigen's, Benjamin suggests working rapprochement around Winnicott's awareness that destruction provides a chance to distinguish inside and outside (cf. Winnicott, 1963, cited in Eigen, 1981). Eigen (1981) focuses on the manner in which Winnicott highlights the creative aspects of destruction and, therefore, moves from guilt to joy. However, with trauma, destruction is not found to be creative, and the inside–outside distinction is confused. This sort of confusion may bind, and create what Eigen (2007) calls trauma clots. As with all pathology, trauma illustrates the importance of health or a non-intrusive presence of an optimal disengagement so that a home for curiosity may be found (Benjamin, 1988). When the other survives, and is recognized as one who can survive or be grieved, joy is possible. The story of the mustard seed illustrates what a profound challenge traumatic grief can be. Eigen places Bion and Winnicott (1981, 2009) in concert with each other, and Winnicott's lack of intrusion is Bion's restraint that allows one to look with an "intense beam of darkness" so that healing may occur when the decency of compassion is needed (Bion, 1970).

A dark vision for dark times. Death is both a psychological and biological reality. Gary Wills (2012) writes about child sacrifice as the worst case of coercion in which a parent does not value a child on behalf of the child. Wills calls attention to the idea that the sacrifice of a child to a God is considered archaic, as it is marked as a crime in both ancient Greek and Biblical systems. Simply, civilizations' ability to render such an act murder is an achievement of child welfare. Sadly, a history of and prohibition against child sacrifice is no guarantee that authority will afford non-intrusive safety. Akin to a dream-eating monster, Wills (2012) writes of child sacrifice as a failure to contain writ large following the massacre at Sandy Hook Elementary School in Newtown, Connecticut. Being compassionately present in response to screaming matters. The ability to respond compassionately or embody a decent presence in response to Z may create a containment that fosters stability, thereby averting further disaster. Interestingly, the fragile vulnerability found in the containment of trauma also seems to have applicability to recent thinking in physics;

"The universe is seemingly teetering on the cusp of eternal stability and total ruin" (Gian Giudice speaking about the implications of the Higgs particle in Chalmers, 2012).

Living as a near death experience

Abraham knows that his covenant will be realized through Isaac. God has told him this before he is asked to take Isaac to Moriah in order to make a burnt offering of him (Plaut, 1981). The details matter, and we may hope that Abraham is aware that the name Isaac, translated as "to laugh" is indeed a covenant in laughter, not tears, and, one hopes, not maniacal laughter but a laughter that is joyful. Abraham tells his servants that he will return. It is Isaac who does not know, and is the one who asks—where is the sheep for the sacrifice? Abraham tells him that God will provide one. Does Abraham hope or have faith? He does bind his son and hold a knife to him. At the last moment, a ram is provided and Isaac lives. Elohim, a generic form of God, issues the demand for Isaac's sacrifice, and it is Adonai, a particular form of God that stops the sacrifice. One interpretation is that this story of different Gods marks movement from a vengefully detached conceptualization to a compassionate and particular conceptualization of the Godhead (Plaut, 1981).

Waking to an intubation tube is to wake to protracted dislocation. After long moments of pushing hands, distressed eyes, and overheard talk of lung function, my son was able to speak. The tube was out. He said, "I'm not going to make it." I wanted Mary Poppins. He needed a ram. Both would be helpful. Holding hands, too many tubes, my chest dropped. I managed to try speaking in faith. It may have been then or a few moments later that I found aid in a metaphor and said, "Your scar is bigger than Harry's, Voldemort is dead, and you are the boy who lived." Metaphors help, and I was grateful to Ms. Rowling (1997) in Ms. Poppins' absence. If we are fortunate, metaphors grow tired and their limits are breached. Soon enough I saw in his face, "No, you dope, I'm not Harry, I'm your son." We were making progress, and destructiveness has never felt so good.

I called to Dr. Z while walking up and down Moriah with my son. Every Yom Kippur, Jews mediate on life and death. Pointing to the journey of Abraham and Isaac and a compassionate God, a ram's horn (Shofar) is sounded. Similar to mustard seed working to contain grief, the Shofar reminds us to have faith and choose life. On a day where we feel a need for idealized mustard seed, we are shocked to find that we need not search, as the sun is already shining on the mountain. It could be different. Big Buddha ears may be used to hear clots and recovery, the Shofar, and each other, so that we find faith while listening to loss. The song of the Shofar is one of shock and difference in which we may come to appreciate each other. In trauma, survival is a fantasy. Yet, creativity may make it a reality. Survival in reality allows destruction to become a fantasy or something that may be contained, and in this "joyous shock of difference," the encounter is sustaining in its own right (Eigen, 1981, p. 416). This is a place ". . . where destructiveness makes love real, and love makes destructiveness creative" (Eigen, 1981, p. 416).

Through Eigen's use of Z, Odysseus (scar) may play with Isaac (laughter). In accord with such a creative matrix: "Real fearlessness is like mixing sweet and sour together. The tone of joyful sadness is like the sound of a flute, which is so melodic and beautiful" (Trungpa, 2009, p. 79).

References

Barrie, J. M. (2000). *Peter Pan*. San Francisco, CA: Chronicle Books.

Benjamin, J. (1988). *The Bonds of Love: Psychoanalysis, Feminism, and the Problem of Domination*. New York: Pantheon Books.

Bion, W. R. (1970). *Attention and Interpretation: A Scientific Approach to Insight in Psycho-Analysis and Groups*. London: Tavistock.

Bromberg, P. M. (1998). *Standing in the Spaces: Essays on Clinical Process, Trauma, and Dissociation*. Hillsdale, NJ: Analytic Press.

Chalmers, M. (2012). The Higgs? Damn. *New Scientist, 216*(2890): 34–37.

Conover, S. (2005). *Kindness: A Treasury of Buddhist Wisdom for Children and Parents*. Spokane, WA: Eastern Washington University Press.

Dylan, B. (2004). Highway 61 revisited. *Lyrics, 1962–2001*. New York: Simon and Schuster.

Eigen, M. (1981). The area of faith in Winnicott, Lacan and Bion. *International Journal of Psychoanalysis, 62*: 413–433.

Eigen, M. (1993). Psychopathy and individuation. In: A. Phillips (Ed.), *The Electrified Tightrope* (pp. 9–20). Northvale, NJ: Jason Aronson.

Eigen, M. (1995). Discussion of the film *Nell*. Annual Convention of the American Psychological Association, August 12, New York.

Eigen, M. (1998). *The Psychoanalytic Mystic*. London: Free Association Books.

Eigen, M. (1999). The area of faith in Winnicott, Lacan and Bion. In: S. A. Mitchell & L. Aron (Eds.), *Relational Psychoanalysis: The Emergence of a Tradition* (pp. 1–37). Hillsdale, NJ: Analytic Press.

Eigen, M. (2001). Mysticism and psychoanalysis. *Psychoanalytic Review, 88*: 455–481.

Eigen, M. (2007). *Feeling Matters*. London: Karnac.

Eigen, M. (2009). *Flames from the Unconscious: Trauma, Madness, and Faith*. London: Karnac.

Eigen, M. (2010). *Eigen in Seoul: Volume One, Madness and Murder*. London: Karnac.

Eigen, M. (2011). *Contact with the Depths*. London: Karnac.

Eigen, M. (2012). *Kabbalah and Psychoanalysis*. London: Karnac.

Ferenczi, S. (1949). Confusion of tongues between the adult and child. *International Journal of Psychoanalysis, 30*: 225–230.

Hamilton, E. (1969). *Mythology: Timeless Tales of Gods and Heroes*. New York: A Mentor Book.

Higgins, C. (2012). What Danny Boyle's Olympics opening ceremony said about Britain's cultural landscape. *Guardian*. Posted online 28 July 2012. Accessed at: www.guardian.co.uk/culture/charlottehiggins-blog/2012/jul/28/olympics-2012-danny-boyle.

Homer (1997). *The Odyssey*, R. Fagles (Trans.). New York: Penguin Classics.

Izod, K. (2008). How does a turn towards relational thinking influence consulting practice in organizations and groups? In: S. Clarke, H. Hahn, and P. Hoggett (Eds.), *Object Relations and Social Relations: The Implications of the Relational Turn in Psychoanalysis* (pp. 163–184). London: Karnac.

James, W. (2003). *Essays in Radical Empiricism*. Mineola, NY: Dover.

Kohut, H. (1979). The two analyses of Mr Z. *International Journal of Psychoanalysis, 60*: 3–27.

Meltzer, D. (2011). *When I Was a Poet*. San Francisco, CA: City Lights Books.

Patai, R. (1967). *The Hebrew Goddess*. Jersey City, NJ: K'tav.

Plaut, G. (1981). *The Torah: A Modern Commentary*. New York: Union of American Hebrew Congregations.

Riordan, R. (2005). *Percy Jackson and the Olympians, Book 1: The Lighting Thief*. New York: Hyperion Books.

Rothschild, L. (2009a). Finding a father: repetition difference and fantasy in *Finding Nemo*. In B. Reis & R. Grossmark (Eds.), *Heterosexual Masculinities: Contemporary Perspectives from Psychoanalytic Gender Theory* (pp. 217–230). New York: Taylor and Francis.

Rothschild, L. (2009b). Review of the book M. Eigen, *Feeling Matters*. *Newsletter of Division 39 of the American Psychological Association*. Winter 2009 issue.

Rowling, J. K. (1997). *Harry Potter and the Sorcerer's Stone*. New York: Scholastic.

Sarton, M. (1997). *Coming into 80*. New York: W. W. Norton.

Shabad, P. (2004). Through the mind's eye: the problem of self-consciousness and the need for reality. In: J. Reppen, J. Tucker, & M. A. Schulman (Eds.), *Way beyond Freud: Postmodern Psychoanalysis Observed* (pp. 156–172). London: Open Gate Press.

Shay, J. (2002). *Odysseus in America: Combat Trauma and the Trials of Homecoming*. New York: Scribner.

Stolorow, R. D., Atwood, G. E., & Orange, D. M. (2002). *Worlds of Experience: Interweaving Philosophical and Clinical Dimensions in Psychoanalysis*. New York: Basic Books.

Strenger, C. (2005). *The Designed Self: Psychoanalysis and Contemporary Identities*. Hillsdale, NJ: Analytic Press.

Symington, N. (2012). The essence of psycho-analysis as opposed to what is secondary. *Psychoanalytic Dialogues*, *22*: 395–409.

Tolkien, J. R. R. (2012). *The Hobbit or There and Back Again*. New York: Houghton Mifflin Harcourt.

Trungpa, C. (2005). *The Sanity We Are Born with: A Buddhist Approach to Psychology*, C. R. Gimian (Ed.). Boston, MA: Shambhala.

Trungpa, C. (2009). *Smile at Fear: Awakening the True Heart of Bravery*, C. R. Gimian (Ed.). Boston, MA: Shambhala.

Wills, G. (2012). Our Moloch. *The New York Review of Books NYR Blog*, 12/15/2012. Accessed at: http://www.nybooks.com/blogs/nyrblog/2012/dec/15/our-moloch/?utm_medium=email&utm_campaign=December+18+2012&utm_content=December+18+2012+CID_2a376c0d1d593739082addeff7aadfdc&utm_source=Email%20marketing%20software&utm_term=Our%20Moloch.

Winnicott, D. W. (1963). The development of the capacity for concern. *Bulletin of the Menninger Clinic*, *27*: 167–176.

Winnicott, D. W. (1971). *Playing and Reality*. London: Tavistock.

Zaretsky, E. (2010). Psychoanalysis, vulnerability, and war. In: A. Harris & S. Botticelli (Eds.), *First Do no Harm: The Paradoxical Encounters of Psychoanalysis, Warmaking, and Resistance* (pp. 177–200). New York: Taylor and Francis.

APPENDIX

Michael Eigen: bibliography of main works

Compiled by Loray Daws

Articles

Eigen, M. (1973). The recoil on having another person. *Review of Existential Psychology & Psychiatry, 12*: 52–55.

Eigen, M. (1973). Abstinence and the schizoid ego. *International Journal of Psychoanalysis, 54*: 493–498.

Eigen, M. (1973). The call and the lure. *Psychotherapy: Theory, Research & Practice, 10*(3): 194–197.

Eigen, M. (1974). On pre-oedipal castration anxiety. *International Review of Psycho-Analysis, 1*: 489–498.

Eigen, M. (1975). Psychopathy and individuation. *Psychotherapy: Theory, Research & Practice,* 12(3): 286–294.

Eigen, M. (1975–1976). The differentiation of an androgynous imago. *Psychoanalytic Review, 62*: 601–613.

Eigen, M. (1977). On breathing and identity. *Journal of Humanistic Psychology, 17*(3): 35.

Eigen, M. (1977). On working with 'unwanted' patients. *International Journal of Psychoanalysis, 58*: 109–121.

Eigen, M. (1979). Common failings in analysis and therapy. *Psychotherapy: Theory, Research & Practice, 16*(3): 246–251.

Eigen, M. (1979). Ideal images, creativity and the Freudian drama. *Psychocultural Review, 3*: 287–298.

Eigen, M. (1979). Female sexual responsiveness and the therapist's feelings. *Psychoanalytic Review, 66*: 3–8.

Eigen, M. (1979). On the defensive use of mastery. *American Journal of Psychoanalysis, 39*: 279–282.

Eigen, M. (1980). A note on soft and hard qualities. *American Journal of Psychoanalysis, 40*: 267–271.

Eigen, M. (1980). A shift of focus. *American Journal of Psychoanalysis, 40*: 347–348.

Eigen, M. (1980). Instinctual fantasy and ideal images. *Contemporary Psychoanalysis, 16*: 119–137.

Eigen, M. (1980). The resolution of a countertransference . . .: Letter to the Editor. *Psychoanalytic Review, 67*: 155.

Eigen, M. (1980). An apprenticeship. *Voices, 15*: 18–21.

Eigen, M. (1980–1981). On the significance of the face. *Psychoanalytic Review, 67*: 425–439.

Eigen, M. (1981). Breaking the frame: stopping the world. *Modern Psychoanalysis*, 6: 89–100.

Eigen, M. (1981). Comments and criticisms. *Contemporary Psychoanalysis, 17*: 152–154.

Eigen, M. (1981). Comments on snakes, symbolism and mind–body relations. *American Journal of Psychoanalysis, 41*: 73–79.

Eigen, M. (1981). Guntrip's analysis with Winnicott—a critique of Glatzer and Evans. *Contemporary Psychoanalysis, 17*: 103–111.

Eigen, M. (1981). Maternal abandonment threats, mind–body relations and suicidal wishes. *Journal of the American Academy of Psychoanalysis, 9*: 561–582.

Eigen, M. (1981). Reflections on eating and breathing as models of mental functions: food breath "minds". *American Journal of Psychoanalysis, 41*: 177–180.

Eigen, M. (1981). The area of faith in Winnicott, Lacan and Bion. *International Journal of Psychoanalysis, 62*: 413–433.

Eigen, M. (1981). A note on soft and hard qualities. *American Journal of Psychoanalysis, 40*: 267–271.

Eigen, M. (1981–1982). On the psychoanalysis of developmental arrest. *Psychoanalytic Review, 68*: 593–593.

Eigen, M. (1982). Aspects of a psychoanalyst's journey: the ideal and the mundane. *Voices, 18*: 17–19.

Eigen, M. (1982). Creativity, instinctual fantasy and ideal images. *Psychoanalytic Review, 69*: 317–339.

Eigen, M. (1983). A note on the structure of Freud's theory of creativity. *Psychoanalytic Review, 70*: 41–45.

Eigen, M. (1983). Depression as pseudo self-repair in a case of blocked mourning. *American Journal of Psychoanalysis, 43*: 81–83.

Eigen, M. (1983). Dual union or undifferentiation? A critique of Marion Milner's View of the Sense of Psychic Creativeness. *International Review of Psycho-Analysis, 10*: 415–428.

Eigen, M. (1983). On time and dreams. *Psychoanalytic Review, 70*: 211–220.

Eigen, M. (1984). An unexpected greeting. *The Psychotherapy Patient, 1*(2): 13–15.

Eigen, M. (1985). Aspects of omnipotence. *Psychoanalytic Review, 72*: 149–159.

Eigen, M. (1985). Discussion of "Recovering Bion's Contributions to Group Analysis". *American Journal of Psychoanalysis, 45*: 341–347.

Eigen, M. (1985). The sword of grace: Flannery O'Connor, Wilfred R. Bion, D. W. Winnicott. *Psychoanalytic Review, 72*: 335–346.

Eigen, M. (1985). Toward Bion's Starting Point: Between Catastrophe and Faith. *International Journal of Psychoanalysis, 66*: 321–330.

Eigen, M. (1986). Aspects of mindlessness–selflessness. *The Psychotherapy Patient, 2*(2): 75–81.

Eigen, M. (1986). Dependency and truth. *The Psychotherapy Patient, 3*(1): 71–80.

Eigen, M. (1991). Boa and flowers. *Psychoanalytic Dialogues, 1*: 106–119.

Eigen, M. (1991). The immoral conscience. *The Psychotherapy Patient, 7*(3–4): 33–44.

Eigen, M. (1992). Counterparts in a couple. *Contemporary Psychotherapy Review, 7*: 42–55.

Eigen, M. (1992). The fire that never goes out. *Psychoanalytic Review, 79*: 271–287.

Eigen, M. (1992). The fire that never goes out: erratum. *Psychoanalytic Review, 79*(4): 609.

Eigen, M. (1994). From attraction to meditation. *Contemporary Psychotherapy Review, 9*: 28–41.

Eigen, M. (1994). Response: the psychoanalytic writer. *Contemporary Psychotherapy Review, 9*: 49–54.

Eigen, M. (1995). On Bion's no-thing. *Melanie Klein and Object Relations, 13*: 31–36.

Eigen, M. (1995). Goodness and deadness. *Melanie Klein and Object Relations, 13*: 43–53.

Eigen, M. (1995). Moral violence. *Melanie Klein and Object Relations, 13*: 37–45.

Eigen, M. (1995). Two kinds of no-thing. *Melanie Klein and Object Relations, 13*: 46–64.

Eigen, M. (1995). Primary process and shock. *C.R.E.A.T.E., 5*: 64–68.

Eigen, M. (1995). Disaster anxiety. *The Psychotherapy Patient, 9*(1–2): 59–76.

Eigen, M. (1995). Psychic deadness: Freud. *Contemporary Psychoanalysis, 31*: 277.

Eigen, M. (1995). Stones in a stream. *Psychoanalytic Review, 82*: 371–390.

Eigen, M. (1995). The destructive force within. *Contemporary Psychoanalysis, 31*: 603.

Eigen, M. (1996). Nell. *Psychoanalytic Review, 83*: 948–952.

Eigen, M. (1997). Musings on O. *Melanie Klein and Object Relations, 15*: 213–226.

Eigen, M. (1997). A bug-free universe. *Contemporary Psychoanalysis, 33*: 19–41.

Eigen, M. (1998). Inner objects and catastrophic change. *Journal of the American Psychoanalytic Association, 46*(3): 925–932.

Eigen, M. (1998). Empty and violent nourishment. *Melanie Klein and Object Relations, 16*: 349–365.

Eigen, M. (1998). Soundproof sanity and fear of madness. *Melanie Klein and Object Relations, 16*: 411–423.

Eigen, M. (1999). Tinkering. *Fort Da, 5*: 64–83.

Eigen, M. (2001). Mysticism and psychoanalysis. *Psychoanalytic Review, 88*: 455–481.

Eigen, M. (2002). A basic rhythm. *Psychoanalytic Review, 89*: 721–740.

Eigen, M. (2002). Half and half. *Fort Da, 8A*: 7–17.

Eigen, M. (2004). A little psyche-music. *Psychoanalytic Dialogues, 14*: 119–130.

Eigen, M. (2004). Alone with God. *Journal of Religion & Health, 43*(3): 185–200.

Eigen, M. (2004). Trauma clots. *POIESIS: A Journal of the Arts and Communication, VI*(May).

Eigen, M. (2004). Dream images. *Journal of Religion & Health, 43*(2): 115–122.

Eigen, M. (2005). Healing longing in the midst of damage. *Psychoanalytic Dialogues, 15*: 169–183.

Eigen, M. (2005). Notes on the history of The Psychoanalytic Review. *Psychoanalytic Review, 92*: 805–806.

Eigen, M. (2006). Age of psychopathy. Available at: www.psychoanalysis-and-therapy.com/human_nature/eigen/pref.html

Eigen, M. (2006). Editor's note. *Psychoanalytic Review, 93*: 845.
Eigen, M. (2006). Homage to Jan Stensson. *International Forum of Psychoanalysis, 15*: 17–18.
Eigen, M. (2006). Introduction to the Special Issue: Fundamentalism and Terrorism. *Psychoanalytic Review, 93*: 141–143.
Eigen, M. (2006). *The Annihilated Self*. *Psychoanalytic Review, 93*: 25–38.
Eigen, M. (2006). Tiny quivers. *Contemporary Psychoanalysis, 42*: 1–12.
Eigen, M. (2006). Introduction to the Special Issue: Fundamentalism And Terrorism. *Psychoanalytic Review*(April): 141–143.
Eigen, M. (2007). Guilt in an age of psychopathy. *Psychoanalytic Review, 94*: 727–749.
Eigen, M. (2007). Incommunicado core and boundless supporting unknown. *European Journal of Psychotherapy & Counselling, 9*(4): 415–422. doi:10.1080/13642530701725940.
Eigen, M. (2007). Preface. *Psychoanalytic Review, 94*: 1.
Eigen, M. (2008). Feeling matters: from the Yosemite God to the annihilated self. *Psychoanalytic Review, 95*(1): 157–159.
Eigen, M. (2008). Hallucination and psychopathy. *International Forum of Psychoanalysis, 17*: 4–15.
Eigen, M. (2008). Primary aloneness. *Psychoanalytic Perspectives, 5*: 63–68.
Eigen, M. (2009). Out of the spiritual closet. *Tikkun, 24*(4): 28.
Eigen, M. (2012). Distinction–union structure. *Psychoanalytic Inquiry, 32*: 246–256.
Eigen, M. (2012). On Winnicott's clinical innovations in the analysis of adults. *International Journal of Psychoanalysis, 93*: 1449–1459.
Eigen, M. (2013). Psychoanalytic taste buds. *Psychoanalytic Review, 100*: 665–667.
Eigen, M. (2013). Response by Michael Eigen. *International Journal of Psychoanalysis, 94*: 118–121.
Eigen, M. (2014). There is no no. *Psiche, 2*: 307–318.
Robertson, L. R., & Eigen, M. (1991). Letter to the Editor. *Psychoanalytic Dialogues, 1*: 391–395.

Reviews

Eigen, M. (1974). Review of public and private lives of psychotherapists. *Psychotherapy: Theory, Research & Practice, 11*(4): 390–391.
Eigen, M. (1975). The Privacy of the Self. M. Masud R. Khan. London: Hogarth Press, 1974. 339 pp. *Psychoanalytic Review, 62*: 349–350.

Eigen, M. (1977). On not Being able to Paint. Marion Milner. New York: International Universities Press, 1973 (paperback). 184 pp., 49 illustrations. *Psychoanalytic Review, 64*: 312–315.

Eigen, M. (1979). Illusion in Loving: A Psychoanalytic Approach to the Evolution of Intimacy and Autonomy. Joel Shor and Jean Sanville. Los Angeles: Double Helix Press, 1978; New York, International Universities Press, 1979. *Psychoanalytic Review, 66*: 453–456.

Eigen, M. (1983). Plea For a Measure of Abnormality. Joyce McDougall. New York: International Universities Press, 1980. *Psychoanalytic Review, 70*: 281–283.

Eigen, M. (1984). Do I Dare Disturb the Universe? A Memorial to Wilfred R. Bion. James S. Grotstein (Ed.). Beverly Hills: Caesura Press, 1981. *Psychoanalytic Review, 71*: 346–348.

Eigen, M. (1984). Freud and the Culture of Psychoanalysis. *Cithara, 24*: 76–77.

Eigen, M. (1987). Narcissism and Character Transformation: The Psychology of Narcissistic Character Disorders. Nathan Schwartz-Salant. Toronto: Inner City Books, 1982. *Psychoanalytic Review, 74*: 436–438.

Eigen, M. (1987). The Broken Connection: On Death and the Continuity of Life. Robert Jay Lifton. New York: Basic Books, 1983. *Psychoanalytic Review, 74*: 579–580.

Eigen, M. (1991). Impasse and Interpretation: Therapeutic and Anti-Therapeutic Factors in the Psychoanalytic Treatment of Psychotic, Borderline, and Neurotic Patients. Herbert Rosenfeld. London: Tavistock, 1987. *Psychoanalytic Review, 78*: 468–469.

Eigen, M. (1993). The Primitive Edge of Experience. Thomas Ogden. Northvale, NJ: Jason Aronson, 1989. *Psychoanalytic Review, 80*: 657–659.

Eigen, M. (1998). Before We Were Young: An Exploration of Primordial States of Mind. By Michael Ian Paul. Binghamton, NY: Esf, 1997. *Psychoanalytic Review, 85*: 459–463.

Eigen, M. (1998). Inner Objects and Catastrophic Change: Sincerity and Other Works: Collected Papers of Donald Meltzer. Edited by Alberto Hahn. London: Karnac, 1994.

Eigen. M. (1998). Psychotic Metaphysics. By Eric Rhode (foreword by Donald Meltzer). London: The Clunie Press/Karnac, 1994. *Journal of the American Psychoanalytic Association, 46*: 925–932.

Eigen, M. (2001). The Dove That Returns, the Dove That Vanishes: Paradox and Creativity in Psychoanalysis by Michael Parsons. Published by Routledge, London, 2000. *British Journal of Psychotherapy, 17*: 408–410.

Eigen, M. (2014). Bothered by Alligators. By Marion Milner. London: Routledge, 2012. *Psychoanalytic Review*, *101*: 129–131.

Eigen, M. (2014). Non c'é nessun no [There is no no]. *Psiche. Revista di cultura psicoanalitica*, 307–319.

Chapters in books

Eigen, M. (1980). Expression and meaning. In: A. Robbins (Ed.), *Expressive Therapy*. New York: Human Sciences Press.

Eigen, M. (1982). Between fear and joy. In: E. M. Stern (Ed.), *On this Side of the Couch*. New York: Pilgrim's Press.

Eigen, M. (1987). The personal and anonymous I. In: K. Gibson, D. Lathrop, & E. M. Stern (Eds.), *Carl Jung and Soul Psychology*. New York: Haworth Press.

Eigen, M. (1989). Aspects of omniscience. In: M. G. Fromm & B. L. Smith (Eds.), *The Facilitating Environment* (pp. 604–628). Madison, CT: International Universities Press.

Eigen, M. (1991). A flying phobia: Mind-body splits and individuation. In: E. Thorne & S. H. Schaye (Eds.), *Psychoanalysis Today* (pp. 133–154). Springfield, IL: Charles C. Thomas.

Eigen, M. (1991). Winnicott's area of freedom: the uncompromiseable. In: N. Schwartz-Salant & M. Stein (Eds.), *Liminality and Transitional Phenomena* (pp. 67–88). Wilmette, Il: Chiron Publications.

Eigen, M. (1993). The counterpart. In: M. Stein (Ed.), *Mad Parts of Sane People* (pp. 37–51). Wilmette, IL: Chiron.

Eigen, M. (1995). Mystical precocity and psychic short-circuits. In: E. G. Corrigan & P. E. Gordon (Eds.), *The Mind Object: Precocity and the Pathology of Self-Sufficiency* (pp. 37–51). Northvale, NJ: Jason Aronson.

Eigen, M. (1996). Foreword. *Being and not Being: Clinical Applications of the Death Instinct*. O. Weininger. Madison, CT: International Universities Press.

Eigen, M. (1997). Miscarriages. *Mind–body problems: Psychotherapy with Psychosomatic Disorders* (pp. 333–351) Lanham, MD: Jason Aronson.

Eigen, M. (1997). Being too good. In: M. H. Rock (Ed.), *Psychodynamic Supervision* (pp. 57–76). Northvale, NJ: Jason Aronson.

Eigen, M. (1998). One reality. In: *The Couch and the Tree: Dialogues in Psychoanalysis and Buddhism* (pp. 217–230) New York: North Point Press.

Eigen, M. (1998). Wilfred R. Bion: infinite surfaces, explosiveness, faith. In: P. Marcus & A. Rosenberg (Eds.), *Psychoanalytic Versions of the Human Condition* (pp. 183–205). New York: New York University Press.

Eigen, M. (2005). Foreword. In: M. Bakur & P. C. Weiner (Eds.), *Psychotherapy and Religion*. Lanham, MD: Jason Aronson.

Eigen, M. (2006). Destruction and madness. In: J. Mills (Ed.), *Other Banalities: Melanie Klein Revisited.* London: Routledge.

Eigen, M. (2014). Variants of mystical participation. In: M. Winborn (Ed.), *Shared Realities: Participation Mystique and Beyond*. Skaitook, OK: Fisher King Press.

Molino, A. (Ed.) (1997). *Elaborate Selves: Reflections and Reveries of Christopher Bollas, Michael Eigen, Polly Young-Eisendrath, Samuel and Evelyn Laeuchli and Marie Coleman Nelson* (pp. 105–142). New York: Haworth Press.

Molino, A. (Ed.) (1997). *Freely Associated: Encounters in Psychoanalysis,* with Christopher Bollas, Joyce McDougall, Michael Eigen, Adam Phillips, and Nina Coltart. London: Free Association Books.

Books

Coleman-Nelson, M., & Eigen, M. (Eds) (1983). *Evil, Self and Culture.* New York: Human Sciences Press.

Eigen, M. (1986). *The Psychotic Core.* Lanham, MD: Jason Aronson.

Eigen, M. (1992). *Coming through the Whirlwind: Case Studies in Psychotherapy.* Wilmette, IL: Chiron.

Eigen, M. (1993). *The Electrified Tightrope,* A. Phillips (Ed.). Lanham, MD: Jason Aronson.

Eigen, M. (1995). *Reshaping the Self: Reflections on Renewal through Therapy.* Madison, CT: Psychosocial Press.

Eigen, M. (1996). *Psychic Deadness.* Northvale, NJ: Jason Aronson.

Eigen, M. (1998). *The Psychoanalytic Mystic.* Binghamton, NY: Esf.

Eigen, M. (1999). *Toxic Nourishment.* London: Karnac.

Eigen, M. (2001). *Damaged Bonds.* London: Karnac.

Eigen, M. (2001). *Ecstasy.* Middletown, CT: Wesleyan University Press.

Eigen, M. (2002). *Rage.* Middletown, CT: Wesleyan University Press.

Eigen, M. (2004). *The Sensitive Self.* Middletown, CT: Wesleyan University Press.

Eigen, M. (2005). *Emotional Storm.* Middletown, CT: Wesleyan University Press.

Eigen, M. (2006). *Lust.* Middletown, CT: Wesleyan University Press.

Eigen, M. (2007). *Feeling Matters.* London: Karnac.
Eigen, M. (2009). *Flames from the Unconscious: Trauma, Madness, and Faith.* London: Karnac.
Eigen, M. (2010). *Eigen in Seoul:* (Volume one) *Madness and Murder.* London: Karnac.
Eigen, M. (2011). *Contact with the Depths.* London: Karnac.
Eigen, M. (2011). *Eigen in Seoul:* (Volume two) *Faith and Transformation.* London: Karnac.
Eigen, M. (2012). *Kabbalah and Psychoanalysis.* London: Karnac.
Eigen, M. (2014). *The Birth of Experience.* London: Karnac.
Eigen, M. (2014). *A Felt Sense: More Explorations of Psychoanalysis and Kabbalah.* London: Karnac.
Eigen, M. (2014). *Faith.* London: Karnac.
Eigen, M. (2015/2016). *Image, Sense, Infinities, and Everyday Life.* London: Karnac, forthcoming.
Eigen, M., & Govrin, A. (2007). *Conversations with Michael Eigen.* London: Karnac.

INDEX